A GLORIOUS FATE

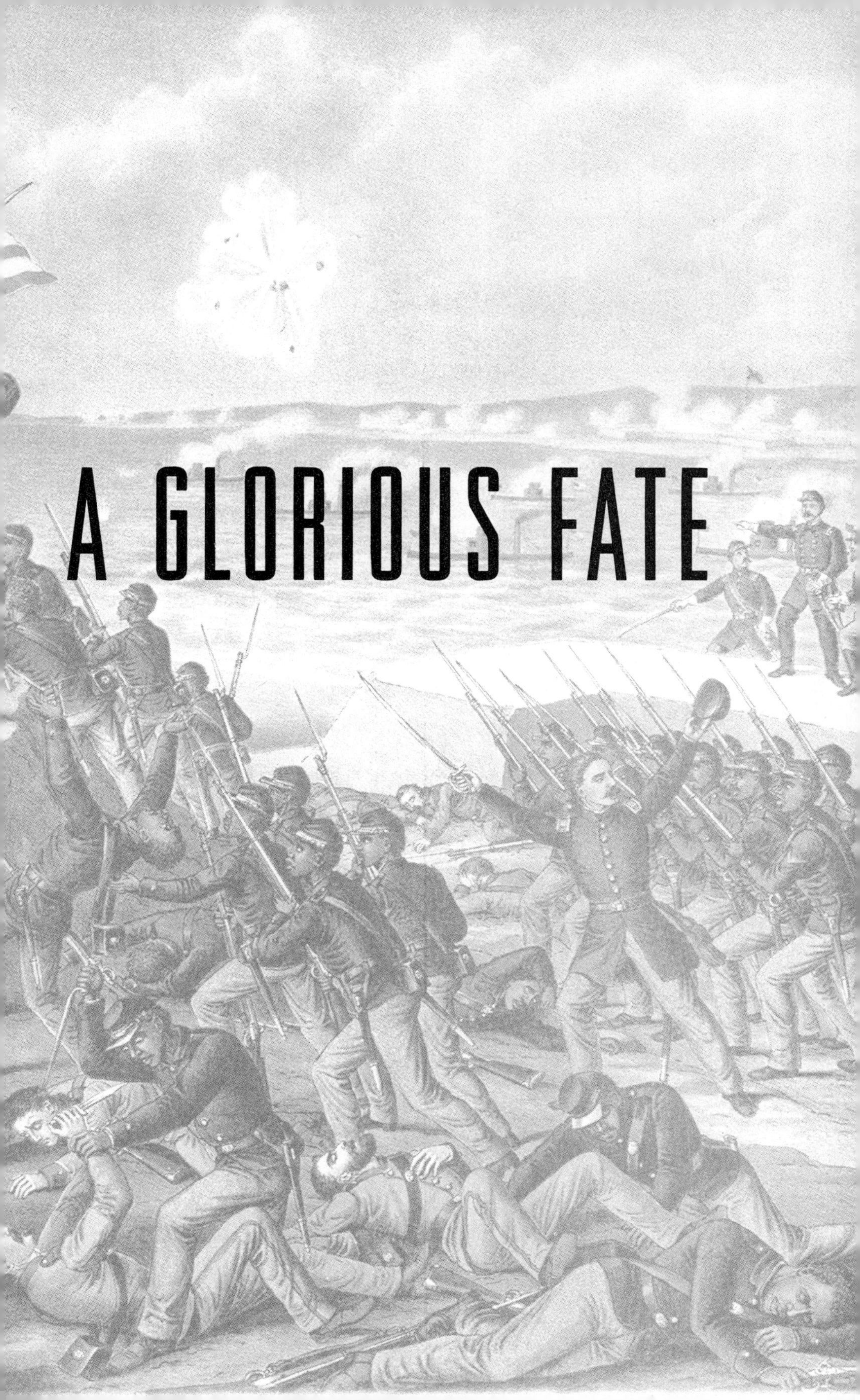

CIVIL WAR AMERICA

Caroline E. Janney and Aaron Sheehan-Dean, editors

This landmark series interprets broadly the history and culture of the Civil War era through the long nineteenth century and beyond. Drawing on diverse approaches and methods, the series publishes historical works that explore all aspects of the war, biographies of leading commanders, and tactical and campaign studies, along with select editions of primary sources. Together, these books shed new light on an era that remains central to our understanding of American and world history.

A complete list of books published in Civil War America is available at https://uncpress.org/series/civil-war-america.

A GLORIOUS FATE

The Life and Legacy of Colonel Robert Gould Shaw

KEVIN M. LEVIN

THE UNIVERSITY OF NORTH CAROLINA PRESS

Chapel Hill

This book was published with the assistance of the American History Fund of the University of North Carolina Press.

Designed by Jamison Cockerham
Set in Arno, Cutright, and Iva
by codeMantra

Cover art: Shaw, ca. 1861–1863, photograph by John Adams Whipple; *background: Storming Fort Wagner* by Kurtz & Allison, 1890. Courtesy Library of Congress.

Manufactured in the United States of America

LIBRARY OF CONGRESS CATALOGING-IN-PUBLICATION DATA
Names: Levin, Kevin M., 1969– author
Title: A glorious fate : the life and legacy of Colonel Robert Gould Shaw / Kevin M. Levin.
Other titles: Civil War America (Series) (bcp47)
Description: Chapel Hill : The University of North Carolina Press, [2026] | Series: Civil War America | Includes bibliographical references and index.
Identifiers: LCCN 2026015080 | ISBN 9781469697178 cloth | ISBN 9781469686905 epub | ISBN 9781469697185 pdf
Subjects: LCSH: Shaw, Robert Gould, 1837–1863 | United States. Army. Massachusetts Infantry Regiment, 54th (1863–1865)—History | Soldiers—Massachusetts | African American soldiers—History—19th century | United States—History—Civil War, 1861–1865 | United States—History—Civil War, 1861–1865—Participation, African American | LCGFT: Biographies
Classification: LCC E513.5 54th .L48 2026 | DDC 973.7092 [B]—dc23/eng/20260409
LC record available at https://lccn.loc.gov/2026015080

For product safety concerns under the European Union's General Product Safety Regulation (EU GPSR), please contact gpsr@mare-nostrum.co.uk or write to the University of North Carolina Press and Mare Nostrum Group B.V., Doelen 72, 4831 GR Breda, The Netherlands.

FOR PETE

CONTENTS

ACKNOWLEDGMENTS

This is my third book and, like its predecessors, owes its existence to the assistance and generosity of many others. I am grateful to a number of people who shared their expertise and who took the time to listen to some of my ideas; I am thankful, too, that they shared with me documents that I had overlooked. These individuals include Bryan Cheeseboro, Rich Condon, Mark Dunkelman, Benjamin Edwards, Douglas R. Egerton, Lorien Foote, Hilary Green, Todd Mildfelt, Holly Pinheiro, Marcy Sacks, Ellen M. Shear, Kelly Boyer Sagert, David D. Schafer, Shawn P. Quigley, Gordon Rhea, and Jonathan White. Much of this book's content first appeared on my blog and newsletter Civil War Memory, which I have maintained for over twenty years. I am deeply grateful to readers who have engaged with my writing online by sharing their insights and suggestions, all of which has enriched my understanding of this history. The community we have built together has become one of the most rewarding aspects of my work as a historian, and I look forward to continuing these conversations for years to come.

John Hennessy provided invaluable insights through our numerous conversations about the 2nd Massachusetts Infantry and the regiment's evolving attitudes toward slavery and race in 1862. John also shared his collection of newspaper accounts about the regiment and an unpublished essay examining how the 1862 Virginia campaign challenged Union soldiers' racial assumptions. Thanks to Lydia Moland, who shared with me correspondence between Lydia Maria Child and Sarah Blake Shaw, which greatly enriched this book's final chapter. My neighbor and fellow historian Kanisorn "Kid"

Wongsrichanalai, chief historian at the Massachusetts Historical Society, has been an exceptional resource throughout this project. As the foremost authority on college-educated New Englanders who served in the Civil War, Kid supported my research from its inception by identifying overlooked sources and engaging in thoughtful discussions about how these young men experienced the war.

Christopher Barr at Reconstruction National Historical Park generously carved out time from his busy schedule to give me a personal tour of Beaufort, South Carolina, in 2022. Standing on Robert Smalls's porch, overlooking his meticulously maintained garden while discussing the intertwined histories of Robert Gould Shaw, the 54th Massachusetts Infantry Regiment, and the Port Royal Experiment remains one of the most memorable experiences of my research in the region.

W. Todd Groce, President and CEO of the Georgia Historical Society, has been an extraordinary supporter of this project from the very beginning. Early on in my research, Todd sent me a reproduction of a carte de visite photograph of Shaw that, from that day on, remained on my desk throughout the writing process, serving as a constant reminder of my subject. Beyond benefiting from his extensive knowledge of Georgia and Civil War history, I am deeply grateful for his hospitality during a 2022 research trip. Though the archive room was closed to the public during my visit, Todd graciously made an exception—an act of generosity I will not soon forget. He also provided a scan of his carte de visite of Shaw in civilian clothing for inclusion in this book. I also want to thank fellow historian Zachery Fry, who took time from a cross-country move to scan his carte de visite of Shaw for this project.

I am deeply grateful for the wisdom and friendship of my Book Squad colleagues: Liz Covart, Sara Georgini, Megan Kate Nelson, Nina Silber, Caitlin G. DeAngelis, Joseph Adelman, and Karin Wulf. Their thoughtful critiques of my book proposal and early chapters opened new interpretive possibilities, highlighting questions and themes I had not previously considered. During moments when I contemplated abandoning this project, their encouragement and intellectual support provided the motivation necessary to see it through to completion. I also appreciate the opportunities to speak on the life of Robert Gould Shaw at the Civil War Institute at Gettysburg College, David Woodbury's Central Coast Conference, the Virginia Museum of History and Culture, the Rhode Island Civil War Round Table, the Olde Colony Civil War Round Table, and the New Bedford Civil War Round Table.

Thanks to the staffs at the Massachusetts Historical Society, the Commonwealth of Massachusetts Archives, the George Eastman Library, the

Houghton Library at Harvard University, the Lenox Library Association, the New York Public Library, and the library at West Virginia University for their assistance in their respective manuscript rooms and for their help in providing images for this book.

Once again, I thank Mark Simpson-Vos at the University of North Carolina Press for his unwavering support and patience. Thanks, as well, to Valerie Burton and Steph Attia for their assistance with copyediting and for preparing the manuscript for publication.

This project could not have been completed without my family's unwavering support, particularly following my father's unexpected passing in December 2024. In the months since, my mother and brother have provided the emotional foundation that made it possible to continue this work. Their resilience in the face of loss, their steadfast encouragement, and their love have sustained me through the most difficult period of my life while keeping me focused on the future. As with every project I have undertaken, my wife, Michaela, has been my constant companion and collaborator, offering both intellectual insight and personal strength when I needed them most. It is impossible for me to imagine being able to complete a project like this without her by my side.

This book is dedicated to my friend, mentor, and fellow historian Peter S. Carmichael, whom we lost tragically in July 2024. I cannot recall when our paths first crossed, but from our earliest encounters, Pete championed my work with characteristic generosity. He pushed me to submit manuscripts for publication, encouraged me to present at academic conferences, and solicited the proposal that became my first book with the University Press of Kentucky. Year after year, he invited me to join the Civil War Institute's summer conference faculty, creating opportunities that shaped my career. I will treasure my memories of walking battlefields with Pete as well as our countless conversations about Civil War history. He possessed a relentless curiosity and intellectual energy that transformed every discussion into an adventure of discovery. Pete challenged me, as he did all his students and colleagues, to step outside comfortable assumptions and consider new perspectives and questions. His enthusiasm was infectious. He made everyone in the room want to work harder and think more carefully about our obligations as historians. Pete embodied what it means to be a faithful caretaker of the past. He understood that history belongs not to scholars but to all who seek to understand how we became who we are. I would like to think that a small spark of Pete's passion for history lives on in these pages.

54TH MASS.

A GLORIOUS FATE

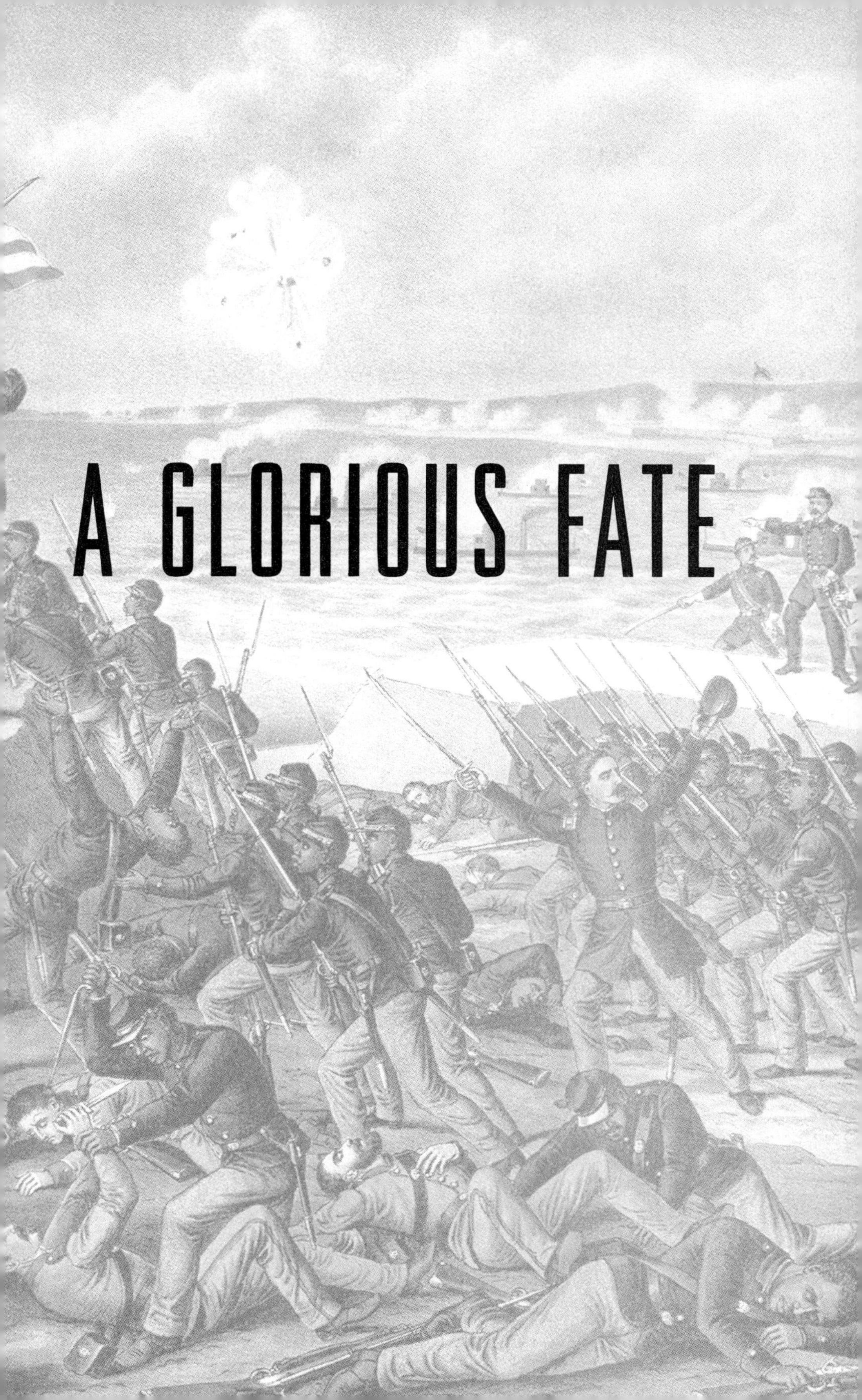

54TH MASS.

INTRODUCTION

On July 18, 1863, Col. Robert Gould Shaw died leading the 54th Massachusetts Infantry Regiment against Confederate defenses at Fort Wagner, which guarded the southern approaches to the harbor at Charleston, South Carolina. The assault led by the North's first Black regiment ended in failure; Shaw's regiment suffered heavy casualties, and Union reinforcements failed to break the battery's defensive wall, defeated by a hail of rifle and cannon fire. But the assault would transform Shaw into a martyr for racial equality, a transformation that began almost immediately following his death with the memorializing efforts of those who had known him. Famed abolitionist, literary writer, and Shaw family friend Lydia Maria Child crafted one of the earliest tributes in the *National Anti-Slavery Standard,* establishing a pattern that would define Shaw's legacy for generations. Like other memorial writers, Child attributed Shaw's courage and sacrifice to his parents' influence. "With moral courage beyond all praise," she wrote, Frank and Sarah Shaw had "stood side by side with a despised band of reformers" for "the cause of Freedom."

In Child's story, the young Shaw, along with one of his many cousins, sits with his grandfather and namesake shortly before the latter's death in 1853. "My children," the elder Robert Gould Shaw informed his two grandchildren, "I am leaving this stage of action, and you are entering upon it. . . . I exhort you to use your example and influence against intemperance and slavery."[1] Child's message was clear. The young man's embrace of abolitionism and his willingness to fight for it on battlefields far from home and ultimately sacrifice his life in the process was no accident; rather, it was a belief nurtured and encouraged at a young age.

Child's source for this family story remains unclear, though her close relationship with Shaw's mother, Sarah, suggests the grieving mother likely shared it with Child through their correspondence. The anecdote served multiple purposes. It aligned Shaw with his family's decades-long abolitionist crusade while reinforcing slavery as the war's fundamental cause, exactly the narrative that Child and other memorial writers sought to establish. The story was undeniably compelling and politically useful; but chronological evidence suggests it was fictional. Given the timing of Shaw's grandfather's death and young Robert's residence in Europe during that period, the intimate grandfather-grandson conversation Child describes almost certainly never occurred.[2]

But if the story is mere legend, it does shine a light on the divide between history and memory. Shaw emerged from the war as one of three especially prominent martyrs to the Union cause. The most significant, of course, was President Abraham Lincoln, felled in one of the final acts of the war by assassin John Wilkes Booth. His martyrdom was secured almost immediately by mourners who were convinced that his death was part of God's plan to firmly secure for future generations the outcome of the four-year conflict, namely, the preservation of the Union. For Black and white abolitionists and many others, Lincoln's assassination transformed him fully into the "Great Emancipator" who had brought the slaveholding South to its knees and helped to destroy slavery once and for all.

The first martyr of the war was Col. Elmer Ellsworth, a friend to the president as he launched his campaign for the White House from Springfield, Illinois. The legendarily tall Lincoln called Ellsworth, who stood merely five-foot-six, the "greatest little man I ever met." After Confederates forced the Union's surrender of Fort Sumter, Ellsworth responded to Lincoln's call for volunteers by organizing the 11th New York Volunteer Infantry Regiment, outfitting his men in the colorful uniforms of the French army's Zouaves. The day after Virginia formalized its secession from the Union on May 23, 1861, Ellsworth's troops set out across the Potomac to raid Alexandria, Virginia. Their first target was a large Confederate flag defiantly flown by the rebel proprietor of a hotel within a field glass's sight of the capital's high ground. After Ellsworth stormed into the building, climbed to the roof, and cut down the flag, the hotel owner met him in the stair and shot him dead, rendering him the Union's first officer killed in action.

Shaw's death differed fundamentally from those of Ellsworth and Lincoln in both timing and impact. His sacrifice came at the war's midpoint, just two weeks after the Union's decisive victories at Gettysburg and Vicksburg, when Union triumph remained uncertain despite these strategic gains. While his death failed to rally national sentiment as powerfully as Ellsworth's early martyrdom or Lincoln's assassination at war's end, Shaw was swiftly transformed into a symbol of emancipation, abolition, and racial equality. Memorial efforts began within days of his death. Advocates quickly proposed erecting a monument on Morris Island following the Shaw family's refusal to retrieve their son's remains from a mass grave at Fort Wagner. Even before the war's conclusion, both Black and white Americans commemorated Shaw through poetry, music, portrait busts, and mass-produced illustrations that spread his image throughout the United States.

The public response to Shaw's death—like the reactions to Ellsworth's and Lincoln's deaths—provided Americans opportunities for collective mourning that reinforced an evolving national identity. These acts of public grief allowed citizens to process loss while affirming their understanding of the war's meaning and purpose, transforming individual tragedy into shared commitment to the causes for which these men had died.[3]

This intense focus on Shaw continued after the war ended in the spring of 1865. Indeed, for decades following his death, Robert Gould Shaw was celebrated and mourned by a wide range of people, including his family, friends, former abolitionists, and veterans of the 54th Massachusetts. These efforts culminated in 1897 with the dedication of Augustus Saint-Gaudens's Shaw Memorial, located across from the Massachusetts State House on Boston's Beacon Hill. Saint-Gaudens's detailed and beautiful bas-relief placed Shaw on horseback leading his men, thus commemorating the regiment's triumphant parade through the streets of Boston on May 30, 1863, before embarking for Beaufort, South Carolina, and its date with destiny. More than any other commemorative moment installed during the postwar period, the memorial highlighted a memory of Shaw united with his Black soldiers in a war to abolish slavery and make men free.

Close to one hundred years later, the Hollywood movie *Glory* (1989), directed by Ed Zwick, helped to rekindle interest in Shaw, the 54th Massachusetts, and the broader story of Black military service during the Civil War—a history that had been largely forgotten for much of the twentieth century, especially among white Americans. The movie benefited from the news surrounding the discovery of the remains of Black soldiers from the

55th Massachusetts Infantry Regiment on Folly Island, located just south of Morris Island, South Carolina, close to where the 54th Massachusetts had fought. The remains of nineteen soldiers who had died of disease in a hospital were eventually reinterred at Beaufort National Cemetery in a ceremony attended by Massachusetts Governor Michael Dukakis shortly before the release of the movie.[4]

Glory remains one of the most popular Civil War movies, both for its willing portrayal of the racial discrimination Black soldiers faced and for its celebrity cast, starring Matthew Broderick as Shaw, and featuring Morgan Freeman, Denzel Washington, and Andre Braugher among the African American actors depicting the US Colored Troops. The film centers on the story of Shaw's six months with the 54th Massachusetts Infantry Regiment, beginning with its organization and training in February 1863 and concluding with the regiment's fateful assault on Fort Wagner in July 1863. Like most Hollywood movies set in the past, *Glory* gets a number of things wrong. Most significantly, the regiment is depicted as made up mainly of freedom seekers from the slaveholding South when, in fact, the majority were free-born African Americans from the North. That decision, however, highlights the movie's thematic arc from enslavement to freedom and Shaw's own evolution in coming to identify with, and eventually embrace, the cause of the men in his regiment.

In the movie, a prominent scene depicting a regimental pay crisis emphasizes this storyline. When the men of the 54th learn they will receive less pay than white soldiers, Trip—a former slave played by Denzel Washington—leads his comrades in tearing up their pay vouchers. The filmmakers depict Shaw joining the protest by tearing up his own voucher, symbolizing his growing identification with his men and their cause. In another scene, an Irish drill sergeant publicly flogs Trip in front of the regiment after he leaves camp without permission. Though the film suggests Shaw remains powerless to stop the army's prescribed punishment for a soldier absent without leave, the camera focuses on Trip's silent tears and on Shaw's horror in seeing a formerly enslaved man beaten by his white superior.[5]

In the movie's climactic scene, Shaw leads his regiment in the assault on Fort Wagner, marking their final triumph over adversity and their collective sacrifice for their freedom. The regiment's "glory" is revealed not only through the regiment's sacrifice and death, but also by the movie director's decision about where and when to end the story. The historically accurate final scene of Shaw being buried with his men in a mass grave, juxtaposed against contemporary images of the Saint-Gaudens memorial, aims to leave the audience with feelings of national pride and a clear sense that the white officers and Black enlisted men triumphed over their racial differences and willingly gave their lives in a war for freedom and equality.

The film was nominated for five Academy Awards and won three, including Best Supporting Actor for Washington. Though some criticized Zwick for making a "white savior movie," the film received positive reviews in the *Boston Globe*, the *Washington Post*, the *New York Times*, and other major newspapers. A reviewer in Charleston, South Carolina, praised the film's realism and pointed out that it ambitiously tries to portray "several complicated issues." He described *Glory* as a "must-see film for the Charleston audience." But some critics such as Manning Marable, professor of African American studies at Columbia University, suggested the film failed to emphasize the full history of how African Americans struggled to free themselves during the war. "Freedom handed down from above to the oppressed, is no freedom at all," Marable wrote.[6]

Most people today who know anything about the life of Robert Gould Shaw have likely learned about the young colonel through *Glory*. Despite its popularity and accessibility on most streaming services, however, anyone wanting to know more about Shaw's life has been confined to two biographies.

In 1965, Peter Burchard published *One Gallant Rush: Robert Gould Shaw and His Brave Black Regiment*. Burchard is the author and illustrator of numerous nonfiction books for young adults on topics that include Frederick Douglass, Lincoln, and the Underground Railroad; his work on Shaw appeared at the height of the Civil Rights Movement and at the tail end of the Civil War centennial, whose celebrations had largely steered clear of references to slavery, emancipation, and Black military service. According to Burchard, it was left to Shaw "to write a story of Negro bravery for all the world to see, to pave the way for widespread participation of the American Negro in what, with the signing of the Emancipation Proclamation, had become his own crusade."[7] This embrace of Shaw as committed to racial justice at a time of deep division over civil rights during the 1960s made the book an obvious choice to use as the basis for the screenplay for *Glory*.

Burchard's *One Gallant Rush* offers a highly readable but largely uncritical account of Shaw and his military service with the 54th Massachusetts and depicts Shaw's death as solidifying his family's deep abolitionist convictions. "To New Englanders of his own time, Shaw, in his youthful Victorian innocence," the author writes, "seemed a kind of saint. . . . In the last few months of his life, in his latter days and final hours, he had drawn on his forefathers' deep convictions and sense of duty and his own devotion to the cause which had rekindled the imaginations of New England's poets and scholars, preachers and teachers and practical men." According to Burchard, "In his last hours, Shaw had indeed caught fire, and to those who had devoted their lives to the breaking of the back of the American shame, his death was an evening and a dawn."[8] His death signaled the inevitable end of slavery and pointed to a "new birth of freedom."

In 1992, historian Russell Duncan published Shaw's wartime letters in *Blue-Eyed Child of Fortune*. Duncan's extensive endnotes provide relevant context, and his introduction offers a brief but thorough overview of Shaw's life, making this volume an indispensable source both on the young colonel's life and on the broader social and cultural world in which he lived. Seven years later, Duncan expanded his introduction from *Blue-Eyed Child* into what became *Where Death and Glory Meet: Colonel Robert Gould Shaw and the 54th Massachusetts*.

Compared to Burchard, Duncan offers a much more sober assessment of Shaw's life. In his view, Shaw volunteered in 1861, motivated primarily by a sense of duty, not by a particular passion for the Union cause, and because the sectional crisis had grown pervasive in its impact on his daily life. Shaw, Duncan opines, "craved a nation freed from this disorderly opprobrium so that he could get on with the pleasures of living."[9] When it appeared, *Where Death and Glory Meet* challenged the mythology surrounding Shaw as an abolitionist warrior that had taken shape almost immediately following his death in 1863. But Duncan's focus on Shaw's command of the 54th Massachusetts limits its insight into Shaw's trajectory of personal development before and during the war.

This biography sets out to offer the fullest possible portrait of Shaw as he truly was, recognizing the still-powerful memories and myths about the meanings of his life and death. It should come as no surprise that much of what has been written about Shaw has focused on his command of the 54th Massachusetts. In addition to the continued popularity of *Glory*, this narrow focus has been fueled in recent decades by a growing public interest in the history of slavery, emancipation, and US Colored Troops amid ongoing contests over contemporary memory of the Civil War, as evidenced by the removal of hundreds of monuments from public spaces over the past decade. Shaw's service with the 54th Massachusetts and his leadership at Fort Wagner fall neatly into a comforting narrative, embraced by many people today, that celebrates racial progress. Shaw's death at such an early age and at a point midway through the war removed any possibility of his achievement being overshadowed by his own actions or views concerning the end of slavery in

1865, Reconstruction, and the broader question of equal rights. The result, however, is a skewed understanding of Shaw and his place within the broader history of the Civil War.

Shaw spent roughly six months with the 54th Massachusetts in the first half of 1863, but before that, he had served for two years, first briefly in the 7th Regiment of the New York Militia and then, from May 1861 to February 1863, with the 2nd Massachusetts Infantry Regiment. Though Burchard and Duncan address this early period of Shaw's military career, they tend to frame it in anticipation of his acceptance of command of the 54th Massachusetts. And apart from an opening scene set at the battle of Antietam, where Shaw was slightly wounded, *Glory* completely ignores this earlier stage of Shaw's military career.

During his time with the 2nd Massachusetts, Shaw first experienced the horrors of battle and the pain of losing close friends. At the same time, thousands of African Americans took to the roads and narrow paths throughout Virginia and elsewhere, forcing officers like Shaw to reflect on their own racial assumptions, emancipation, and the question of whether freed slaves should be enlisted in the army. During those first two years, Shaw confronted not just Confederates in the field but enraged civilians, who thought little of shooting at Yankee soldiers, whom they viewed as invaders. In short, Shaw was a seasoned and experienced junior officer by the time he accepted Massachusetts Governor John Andrew's offer to command Black soldiers of the 54th.

Closely considering Shaw's earlier military service allows us to more clearly discern his evolving understanding of the war and the changing nature of the war itself. In addition, overlooking or minimizing the early portion of his career has had the unintended (and sometimes intended) result of framing Shaw's acceptance of command of the 54th as inevitable. Nothing could be further from the truth. In fact, it is very likely that if the war had ended before January 1, 1863, without emancipation, Shaw would have celebrated its end and looked forward to the opportunity to return to his private pursuits. Unlike his parents, Shaw never fully embraced emancipation and the end of slavery as a wartime goal. This led to sharp disagreements with his abolitionist parents on more than one occasion over the first two years of the war, especially following President Lincoln's release of the Preliminary Emancipation Proclamation (issued on September 22, 1862), after the battle of Antietam. The proclamation presented an ultimatum to the Confederacy: rejoin the Union by January 1, 1863, or face the freeing of all enslaved people in rebellious territories. Enslaved people living in loyal Union states, however, would not be freed. In addition, Shaw and his parents clashed over Lincoln's leadership, over controversial generals such as George B. McClellan, and on the personal front, over his decision to get engaged to and marry Annie Kneeland Haggerty just weeks before shipping out with the 54th at the end of May 1863. As will be shown in the pages of this book, the gulf between Shaw and his family was much wider than has previously been shown.

While Shaw insisted that he had a duty to serve his country in its hour of need, he never expressed a deep commitment to any ideological principles. He never identified himself as an abolitionist, a source of frustration for his mother long before the war began. More than anything else, Shaw sought advancement in rank and honor on the battlefield. Ultimately, his acceptance of the colonelcy of the 54th Massachusetts had more to do with realizing these goals than with the embrace of an abolitionist agenda. Appreciating this insight opens up new interpretive space through which to understand Shaw's brief but notable military career.

Fifty years ago, historian David Potter cautioned against reducing Northern attitudes toward slavery to simple proslavery or antislavery categories; Potter argued that such binary thinking obscures the complex ways slavery intersected with competing priorities and moral frameworks. Before the war, Northern opinion encompassed multiple positions that resisted easy categorization: some opposed slavery morally but rejected racial equality; others opposed slavery's expansion while accepting its existence in current slave states; still others prioritized Union preservation over taking any position on slavery at all. These competing priorities became even more entangled once the fighting began, particularly for soldiers like Shaw who faced the gap between abstract political and moral principles and battlefield realities. Men who had never seriously considered slavery's moral dimensions suddenly encountered freedom seekers fleeing to Union lines, forcing immediate decisions about federal policy and personal responsibility that peacetime politics had not prepared them to make.[10]

Shaw's own journey illustrates Potter's insight about the inadequacy of stark alternatives. Shaw's views evolved through military experience, family pressure, career ambition, and direct contact with enslaved people seeking freedom. His support for Black military service emerged as much from strategic calculation and personal ambition as from moral conviction, while his racial prejudices persisted even as he commanded Black troops. Potter's framework helps explain why Shaw's transformation was so gradual and incomplete. Rather than experiencing a sudden moral conversion, Shaw navigated competing priorities—military advancement, family expectations, racial assumptions—that pulled him in different directions simultaneously. His story demonstrates how individual attitudes toward slavery and race could be internally contradictory and contextually dependent rather than ideologically consistent.[11]

More than twenty-five years have passed since Duncan's biography of Shaw was published. That book, along with much of the scholarship published at the time, reflected a post–civil rights interpretation that drew a sharp distinction between Northerners, who fought in defense of the Union before eventually embracing emancipation, and Southerners, who fought to create a new nation committed to preserving and expanding the institution of slavery and white supremacy. The four years of fighting left roughly 750,000 Americans dead, but the freedom of four million African Americans and the end of slavery rendered the outcome worth the price.[12]

The standard story of Shaw and the 54th Massachusetts fits neatly into that interpretive framework. Throughout the commemoration of the 150th anniversary of the Civil War, between 2011 and 2015, public programming emphasized the story of emancipation and celebrated the end of slavery as the war's greatest achievement. The history of US Colored Troops was front and center at historic sites and in a wide range of public programs across the nation. It would not be an exaggeration to suggest that the Black Union soldier was the face of the Civil War sesquicentennial and the National Park Service's theme: "From Civil War to Civil Rights."[13]

Yet some scholars pushed back against this interpretation with what historian Yael Sternhell describes as "an emphatic antiwar stance on the Civil War" that highlights, among other subjects, Northern atrocities, the violence and disease experienced by enslaved families in contraband camps, and desertion among African American soldiers. Emphasizing the war's brutality has enriched and complicated our understanding of the era and its costs, but it has also made it more difficult to maintain any primarily celebratory narrative of the conflict and its consequences.[14] The recent reckoning over American history that began in the wake of the mass shooting of nine African American churchgoers at the Mother Emmanuel AME Church in Charleston in 2015 and continued after the police murder of George Floyd in Minneapolis in 2020—much of it centered on the legacy of the Civil War and Reconstruction—has only complicated the challenge of finding a place for Robert Gould Shaw in the nation's collective memory, as have more recent efforts to replace difficult and troubling narratives of the past with paeans to American greatness. The overt and intentional politicization of American history today leaves little room for complexity and nuance.

The nation's fascination with the Civil War has long encouraged and rewarded mythmaking. Robert Gould Shaw has been an actor in this drama since his death in 1863. The postwar martyrdom of Shaw transformed him into a symbol of freedom and abolitionism—a position he neither sought nor desired. Such a transformation, however, was never necessary to appreciate Shaw's importance to the broader story of the Civil War and American history. More than anything else, Shaw sought honor on the battlefield, but he did not set out to take part in a social revolution that would fundamentally transform the nation within a few short years. His short life and even shorter military career offer a narrow, but revealing, window into this defining moment of American history. Like many people, Shaw struggled to make sense of the dramatic shifts that took place around him during the first half of the Civil War. Each step forward raised new questions that Shaw struggled to answer. With hindsight, we can now more clearly discern the myriad and complex ways in which the very movement of freedom seekers across the South, the movement of armies, the escalating violence, the continued advocacy of the abolitionist community back home, and his own ambition helped place Shaw among a coalition of loosely connected actors that led to emancipation and the eventual abolition of slavery in 1865. A new biographical treatment of Shaw's life allows us to more clearly discern these key historical elements of place and time and appreciate how they impacted his priorities and his understanding of his role in the war.

Shaw left us no inspiring words about the immorality of slavery, emancipation, and racial equality. It was the contingency of war that led Shaw and the men of the 54th Massachusetts to that sandy beach on Morris Island; and in the moment where his own life and that of the future of the nation hung in the balance, Shaw stepped forward and answered the call of duty. Shaw did not live to see the results of his labors, nor could he have anticipated the many challenges that the nation would confront long after the guns fell silent. That responsibility has been left to us.

AUTHORS NOTE ON LANGUAGE USE

In this book, I have chosen not to spell out certain historical racial epithets or similar terms in full. One common pejorative will appear as either "n——" or "n——s." This decision is meant to acknowledge the historical and emotional weight these words carry without gratuitously compounding the harm they continue to cause. The choice reflects a respect for readers, a recognition of the ongoing impact of language, and a commitment to fostering critical engagement without normalizing slurs or their echoes.

ONE

There Is No Use Doing Disagreeable Things for Nothing

Robert Gould Shaw entered the world on October 10, 1837, in Dartmouth, Massachusetts, as the first son of Francis "Frank" George Shaw and Sarah Blake Sturgis Shaw. Named for his grandfather and known affectionately as Rob, he was born into expectations of wealth, privilege, and social responsibility that characterized Boston's emerging elite families. Naming their newborn son after the elder Shaw symbolized continuity in a clan whose men had long been expected to expand its family's business interests and contribute to improving society.

From their family home atop Boston's Beacon Hill, just a few blocks from the Massachusetts State House, with its gleaming copper dome, the Shaw family could glimpse the source of their fortune, spread across Boston Harbor. Ship masts crowded the waterfront just blocks from their home at 44 Beacon Street—vessels that had made the Shaws one of Boston's wealthiest families through generations of global trade. Generations of Shaw men had amassed fortunes in overseas trade, helping to turn Boston into one of the wealthiest and most cosmopolitan cities among the original thirteen colonies and eventually the new United States. No doubt, many family members and close acquaintances fully expected this newest addition to the Shaw family to take his place alongside his father and grandfather and carry on the family's legacy. Within three years of his birth, however, Rob's parents would choose a very different path for their family's future.

Though the Shaws could trace their family's lineage back to the earliest years of the colony's history, the family fortune began with Francis Shaw Sr., born in 1721. Described as a man of "medium height with light complexion, reddish brown hair, well-cut features, and keen, penetrating eyes," by age forty-two, Francis had built a substantial fortune through his partnership with Boston financier Robert Gould, timing his success perfectly with Boston's expanding global trade networks after the Seven Years' War ended in 1763.[1] This impressive accumulation of wealth took place as trade ties between Boston and other parts of the world expanded dramatically.

Unlike most of Boston's wealthy Puritan families, Francis Shaw Sr. and his wife, Sarah (Burt) Shaw, embraced the Episcopal Church. This religious difference did not hurt their social standing or their ability to advance their financial interests through strategic marriages and business partnerships with the Cabots, Sturgises, Lowells, Appletons, and Hutchinsons—relationships that cemented their place among Boston's elite. Francis and Robert Gould built their fortune through lumber, real estate, and West Indies trade. Like most Boston merchant families, their wealth was built directly or indirectly on the Caribbean slave economy. By the mid-eighteenth century, despite occasional European wars, these profitable trade routes had become the backbone of Boston commerce.

Francis Shaw Sr. may not have directly traded slaves, but his family's wealth depended entirely on their forced labor. The system was brutally efficient. Boston merchants like the Shaws exported grain, timber, livestock, and fish to Jamaica in exchange for molasses and sugar. Boston distilleries converted that sugar into rum, which ships carried to West Africa and then used as currency with which to purchase enslaved people. Those people were sold in the Caribbean, except for the "refuse," deemed unsellable, who were crammed into ship holds bound for North American ports. Between 1700 and 1774, roughly 200 ships sailed annually from Boston to the Caribbean. By 1750, Boston's 1,500 residents of African descent—10 percent of the population—lived as enslaved people whose sale had been advertised in local newspapers and conducted openly on wharves and streets.[2]

Shaw's and Gould's biggest gamble proved their worst mistake. Scouting Maine's (then still part of the colony of Massachusetts) dense forests in the 1770s, the partners saw opportunity in cheap land, endless timber, and potential profits from a large-scale lumber operation. They secured a township grant from the crown, established a coastal trading hub at Gouldsborough, and sent Shaw's eldest son, Francis Jr., just 21, to oversee its clearing and construction. The timing could not have been worse. Rising tensions with Britain soon exploded into the American Revolution, destroying any chance of success. The war ruined both men financially. Shaw was forced to mortgage his own home to cover the venture's massive losses. Francis Shaw's financial ruin devastated the family. With their fortune gone and their reputation in tatters, his nine children faced the monumental task of rebuilding from nothing.

Francis Jr. stayed in Maine with his wife and infant son, Robert Gould Shaw, born June 4, 1776, just a month before American independence. Commissioned as a militia colonel despite his inexperience, Francis Jr. tried a desperate gambit to negotiate neutrality with the British to protect coastal towns like Gouldsborough from naval raids. The strategy backfired spectacularly. Critics accused him of protecting family business interests over patriotic duty, or worse, of outright disloyalty to the American cause.[3]

Back in Boston, Francis's younger brother Samuel Shaw burned with rage at the British occupation. The Boston Massacre in 1770 and Tea Party in 1773 had already stoked his fury, but Maj. John Pitcairn's arrival in 1774 with six hundred marines pushed Samuel over the edge, especially when Pitcairn and Lt. John Wragg took up residence in the Shaw family home.[4] One particular story of Samuel's bravery tells of an event that took place in the Shaw home sometime during the British occupation of Boston in the early 1770s. As the story goes, Samuel challenged Wragg to a duel after the lieutenant described Americans as "cowards and rebels." Samuel reportedly threw a glass of wine in Wragg's face. Only the efforts of Pitcairn, who in April 1775 would lead British soldiers in a disastrous expedition to secure powder and arms in Concord, managed to secure an apology from Wragg, thus preventing the two parties from coming to blows.[5] Decades later, this story of defiance would become family legend, likely thrilling the younger Robert Gould Shaw with tales of his ancestor's courage against British tyranny.

This family legend perfectly positioned the Shaws as Revolutionary War heroes and may have helped erase the stain of Francis Jr.'s questionable loyalty in Maine. But the story was almost certainly apocryphal. The British Army did not force elite Boston families to house officers. Rather, they paid for lodging. The Shaws were likely renting rooms to Pitcairn and Wragg for profit, a business decision that probably infuriated the patriotic Samuel. The wine-throwing confrontation, if it happened at all, likely stemmed from his rage at his father's collaboration with the enemy under their own roof.[6] It would not be the last time war divided the Shaw family.

Samuel Shaw left home at the age of twenty-one to join the Continental Army in 1775, rising to major and serving as aide-de-camp to Gen. Henry Knox. He fought at Trenton, Princeton, Brandywine, and Monmouth—all bloody battles where raw American recruits faced seasoned British professional soldiers. For Samuel, the Revolution served dual purposes. Military service could restore the Shaw name and secure the family's place, once again, among Boston's elite. He cultivated relationships with nationalist leaders who envisioned a strong federal government that hoped to stabilize the economy and open foreign trade routes, which was exactly what the Shaw family needed to reclaim their merchant empire.

Victory brought opportunity. In 1784, thirty-one-year-old Samuel sailed to China a merchant agent aboard the first American ship to attempt the voyage. When the *Empress of China* returned a year later, Samuel brought back silk, tea, and most importantly, the intelligence about untapped markets that could rebuild his family's fortune. His timing was perfect. Appointed America's first consul at Canton, Samuel made a second voyage in February 1786, urging fellow Boston merchants to follow his lead into Chinese trade. By 1790, confident enough to risk everything, he commissioned his own frigate, the *Massachusetts,* and sailed for Canton once more. The gamble paid off, and Samuel sold the ship to the Danish East India Company for $65,000; but his luck ran out on his fourth voyage. On May 30, 1794, Samuel died at sea, his body committed to the waves that had made his fortune.

Robert Gould Shaw likely heard his first condemnation of slavery from family stories about his great-great-uncle Samuel's voyages. Witnessing the institution's brutality firsthand had transformed Samuel into a fierce critic. "Can it be a man," Samuel wrote, "who this trampling upon the principles of universal benevolence . . . can become a fiend to torment his fellow creatures?"[7] Yet even as Samuel raged against the evils of slavery, the new US Constitution was cementing it into American law through the Three-Fifths Compromise and the twenty-year extension of the slave trade.

The Shaw family endured relentless heartbreak. When Samuel died in 1794, it had been only nine years since his brother Francis Jr.'s death—a tragedy that had left young Robert Shaw without a father at just nine years of age. Samuel had pleaded with the boy's mother for the chance to raise his nephew, but fate intervened before he could fulfill that promise. Robert now found himself apprenticed to yet another uncle, William, whose iron discipline knew no family favoritism. The harsh physical punishments were commonplace for apprentices of that era, accepted as necessary regardless of blood ties. Yet this severe conditioning achieved its aim. As the Shaw fortunes began their recovery in the 1790s, Robert mastered every aspect of the business—overseeing the troublesome Gouldsborough properties that had once destroyed his father, learning the intricacies of commerce in the Dock Square countinghouse, and building crucial relationships among Boston's merchant class at the busy wharves. When William's death came in 1803, Robert stood prepared to take on responsibility for advancing the family's financial interests.[8]

The elder Robert Gould Shaw was later remembered by his son Frank as a responsible businessman, "always careful not to enter into operations which might carry him beyond the depth, and to meet all just demands upon him as promptly as possible."[9] The family's financial troubles in Maine did not prevent Shaw from investing further in land in the Kennebec Valley, a decision that brought him into direct conflict with scores of squatters who had claimed the backcountry land for themselves. These yeoman farmers embraced a Revolutionary War rhetoric couched in the language of natural rights, that hard work and improvement to the land justified their claims of ownership. That many of these men had served in the American Revolution made little impression on Shaw and other speculators, who believed that their ownership of property outweighed the yeoman farmers' claims to the land.[10]

Robert Shaw rebuilt the family empire methodically. He launched an auction and commission business in 1803, then dissolved his partnership with Shaw, Tuckerman and Rogers seven years later to join forces with William Perkins. Building on his uncle Samuel's overseas connections, Robert Shaw's ships soon crowded harbors worldwide. The American consul in Genoa marveled that "more than half the vessels entering this port have been owned by Rob Gould Shaw."[11] Shaw diversified aggressively, investing in real estate, manufacturing, railroads, and Boston waterfront wharves, all of which greatly expanded the city's trading capacity. By the 1840s, his net worth had reached $1.5 million—making him one of America's wealthiest men. But with financial success came responsibility.

Adding to his good fortune, Robert Shaw married Elizabeth "Eliza" Willard Parkman. Born in 1785, the two first met when she was four and he was thirteen. Their eventual union proved both loving and strategic. The couple lived well but not ostentatiously, filling their home with fine furnishings and Gilbert Stuart portraits that announced their arrival among Boston's elite. Soon eleven children filled the house with noise and laughter, starting with Francis "Frank" George Shaw in 1809. Each child became a link in Boston's social chain, marrying into the Sturgis, Russell, Parkman, Lyman, and Agassiz families, resulting in a family tree that grew so tangled with elite Boston bloodlines that even genealogists struggle to trace its branches.[12]

Robert Shaw's fortune elevated his family into Boston's "Brahmin" class, a term Oliver Wendell Holmes Sr. would coin in 1860 for families who believed wealth carried moral obligations. These merchant princes funded Harvard University, Massachusetts General Hospital, libraries, and orphanages, transforming Boston through calculated philanthropy. By positioning themselves as society's natural problem-solvers, the Brahmins reinforced the very class hierarchy that kept them on top. Their good works became proof of their right to rule—a self-perpetuating system in which helping the poor justified their keeping them powerless.[13] This moral and paternalistic world view was transmitted to all the Shaw children; but it arguably had the greatest influence on Frank.

Unlike his father and grandfather, Frank Shaw grew up surrounded by luxury from birth. Frank remembered his father as a strict disciplinarian, who nevertheless encouraged his children to think for themselves and arrive at their own conclusions on subjects such as religion and other moral questions—a position that perhaps explains the unconventional beliefs and trajectory that Frank would eventually embrace. That freedom, however, came with the expectation that the children would always look out for the well-being of the entire family. This liberal approach to parenting was clearly evident in Frank's brother, Joseph Shaw, who first attended Harvard University, and who, after spending time in Europe, chose to convert to Catholicism. Shortly thereafter Joseph was ordained a priest. Later in life he recalled that his father was "unwilling to make an opposition to the wishes of his children, so long as they are in the path of virtue & hence of happiness."[14]

Frank attended Boston Latin School and Harvard, but in 1828 he left without graduating to join his father's mercantile firm. There Frank learned how the family business worked by observing it in action, traveling to the West Indies and to Europe as well as to Southern ports, where he witnessed the violence of slavery firsthand. Frank struggled to reconcile the tension between a life surrounded by greed-driven businessmen and the poverty and social problems that plagued so many in growing urban areas such as Boston. He also observed his own father, who gradually became disillusioned and

Francis "Frank" George Shaw retired from business pursuits at a young age and devoted the rest of his life to various reform causes, including the abolition of slavery. *Collection of the Massachusetts Historical Society.*

frustrated with his chosen career. Robert Shaw amassed great quantities of wealth but spent little time with his wife and family and in the pursuit of his own personal interests. For Frank, it was a life that left little to desire.[15]

Frank found salvation in Sarah Blake Sturgis, his half first cousin who shared both his reformist passion and his love of arts and literature. Six years younger, Sarah came from equally deep Boston roots. The Sturgises had arrived in 1646, and her mother could trace her lineage to Puritan leader John Cotton. Like the Shaws, her family had built their fortune on shipping and commerce after surviving eighteenth-century economic storms. But Sarah offered Frank something his family could not. Together, they questioned wealth's purpose rather than simply accumulating it. They married on June 9, 1835. These two young idealists quickly set out to reshape their inherited privilege.[16]

Frank and Sarah's children arrived in quick succession at 44 Beacon Street: Anna "Nan" in 1836, Robert "Rob" in 1837, Susanna "Susie" in 1839, and Josephine "Effie" in 1843. Rob's world centered on the Shaws' elegant Beacon Hill home overlooking Boston Common, with excursions to visit his eighty-five cousins scattered throughout the city's elite neighborhoods. The family's location was perfect for a curious boy. Just steps from the state capitol's gleaming dome, the Boston Common had been transformed from a muddy cow pasture into an urban paradise of "lofty elms," rolling knolls, and an artificial lake. For young Rob Shaw, it became an endless playground where Boston's aristocratic children learned to see the city as their personal kingdom.[17]

The Shaw home offered sanctuary from Boston's urban chaos. Though landfill projects were slowly connecting the city to the mainland, Boston still felt like an island jutting out into the harbor. Stately mansions and elegant squares coexisted with teeming slums, brothels, and gambling dens. Seven railroad lines terminated downtown, filling the streets with smoke, noise, and grime. Boston's population exploded from 58,000 to 137,000 between 1825 and 1850. Most residents crammed into boardinghouses and worked as dockworkers, stable boys, or factory hands for subsistence wages, while open sewers reeked and garbage rotted in the streets. The mid-1840s brought tens of thousands of Irish refugees fleeing the potato famine, overwhelming the city's infrastructure and creating the perfect conditions for disease.[18]

In 1840, Frank Shaw shocked Boston society by walking away from the family business at age thirty-one. Commerce had become America's false god, he declared: "Mammon, the great god of our incomplete civilization."[19]

Sarah Blake Shaw, ca. 1835. Sarah encouraged her son to embrace reform causes, especially abolitionism, from an early age. Later, the two would disagree sharply over the purpose and ultimate goal of the Civil War.
Collection of the Massachusetts Historical Society.

His decision to retire at such an early age may have been exacerbated by the recent Panic of 1837 and the financial devastation it wrought on families throughout the country. His retirement was not just an escape from commerce, it was a moral reckoning. He and Sarah had watched their family fortune feed the very social problems now consuming Boston's streets, and they refused to be complicit any longer.[20]

Frank and Sarah's Unitarian upbringing had planted the seeds of social conscience, but Ralph Waldo Emerson's transcendentalism ignited them into action. The philosopher—himself a Unitarian minister's son—rejected organized religion's claim that divine truth required biblical revelation. Instead, he proclaimed each individual's capacity for direct spiritual discovery.

Emerson's message resonated powerfully with the disillusioned Shaws. In an age of crude party politics, he argued, Americans had become mere statistics, "reckoned in the gross, in the hundred or the thousand." His defiant response became the Shaws' rallying cry: "We will walk on our own feet; we will work with our own hands; we will speak our own minds." True wisdom, Emerson taught, came not from Harvard lecture halls but from studying "the literature of the poor," "the philosophy of the street," and "household life." For Frank and Sarah, this philosophy offered liberation from Calvinist predestination, from family business obligations, and from the passive acceptance of social problems. Transcendentalism promised that individuals could choose their moral path and perhaps even perfect society itself.[21]

While young Rob took his first tentative steps around the house, his parents plunged into Boston's thriving reform movement. The city teemed with idealistic crusaders. Julia Ward Howe and Ednah Littlehale Cheney fought for women's suffrage just blocks from the Shaw home, while Dorothea Dix championed the mentally ill and Dr. Samuel Gridley Howe advocated for the disabled. Prison reformers, education activists, and religious liberals all competed for attention in drawing rooms across Beacon Hill.[22]

No cause ignited Frank and Sarah's passion like abolition. Boston pulsed with antislavery fervor. Theodore Lyman, William Ellery Channing, Henry I. Bowditch, and Lydia Maria Child all lived within a few miles of Beacon Street. Just across the Common, at Park Street Church, William Lloyd Garrison called for slavery's immediate end and full Black citizenship through his radical newspaper, *The Liberator*. Young Rob played innocently in the Garrison's garden with Willie and George, while inside, their parents discussed how best to challenge America's "Peculiar Institution." At nearby Faneuil Hall, both Black and white abolitionists like Garrison and Charles Lenox Remond delivered speeches that drew furious crowds. Violence often spilled into the streets as proslavery mobs threatened speakers with death.[23]

The beating heart of Black abolitionism lay just blocks from the Shaw home on Beacon Hill's north slope. There, in 1829, David Walker had published his incendiary *Appeal to the Colored Citizens of the World*, a work so radical it depicted slavery in biblical terms and openly urged violent rebellion. Walker's warning to slaveholders burned with prophetic fury. "You may do your best to keep us in wretchedness and misery, to enrich you and your children, but God will deliver us from under you. And wo, wo, will be to you if we have to obtain our freedom by fighting."[24]

Although Massachusetts had virtually eliminated slavery after the American Revolution, racial segregation defined city life in the decades leading up to the Civil War. During this time, prominent Black leaders, including William Cooper Nell, Lewis and Harriet Hayden, Benjamin Roberts, Robert Morris, and Maria Stewart campaigned tirelessly to end segregation in public schools and transportation.[25]

When Rob was just one year old, Frank and Sarah joined both the American Anti-Slavery Society and later the New England Anti-Slavery Society. Frank threw himself into the cause by supporting legislative efforts in Washington, DC, to end the slave trade both internationally and between states. He also provided financial help to free fugitive slaves and signed petitions calling for recognition of the Republic of Haiti, which had gained independence through a slave rebellion against French colonial rule in 1804. Years later, Frank and Sarah's daughter Josephine remembered that, "My mother and father were among the earliest abolitionists in Massachusetts."[26] While this claim was likely an exaggeration, it is clear that the Shaw children, including Rob, grew up in a household where conversations about the suffering of enslaved people and the moral duty to end slavery were constant fixtures of daily life.

In 1842, Rob experienced the first of many family moves when his parents relocated to a new home with expansive grounds in West Roxbury, a rural suburb of Boston. This move allowed Frank and Sarah to further distance themselves from their parents' political and financial circles in Boston, and it brought them close to Brook Farm, an experimental communal community founded by George Ripley just one year earlier. Ripley hoped "to prepare a society of liberal, intelligent, and cultivated persons, whose relations with each other would permit a more simple and wholesome life, than can be led amidst the pressure of our competing institutions."[27] The community's living arrangements were based on the ideas of French philosopher and early socialist Charles Fourier, who believed society should be reorganized into self-sufficient cooperatives called phalanxes.

Frank Shaw was optimistic about the experimental community's potential to "supplant existing evils, until all our laws, in principle and practice, represent justice under the invariable direction of love."[28] However, this enthusiasm did not lead the family to actually move to Brook Farm. Frank provided financial support to Ripley's venture, but like Ralph Waldo Emerson, the Shaws were unwilling to give up certain personal comforts.

Despite not living there, the family remained closely connected to the community. The Shaw children enjoyed Brook Farm's costume parties and concerts, while Frank and Sarah attended lectures by notable figures like Emerson, Margaret Fuller, and Theodore Parker. They also participated in discussions with prominent intellectuals, including Amos Bronson Alcott, James Russell Lowell, Harriet Beecher Stowe, and William Lloyd Garrison. Brook Farm provided the Shaws with an opportunity to deepen their reform commitments and Christian activism. In this stimulating environment, their dedication to ending slavery was just one of many social causes that captured their attention. Passionate conversations ranged across numerous topics, from unjust social relations to overcrowded penitentiaries and poorhouses.[29]

Frank actively contributed to the Brook Farm community's intellectual life by translating several books into English, including a biography of Charles Fourier. He also wrote essays for *The Harbinger*, Brook Farm's official magazine, covering a wide range of reform topics from gender equality to the threats that technology and greed posed to working people. Frank's vision extended beyond these specific issues to a broader transformation of society. "The time is not far off when the world will wonder," he wrote, "that it ever allowed such a swarm of blood-suckers to fatten on its vitals and gorge themselves with the life-blood of its most useful members." Frank looked forward not only to ending racial slavery in the American South, but to "the annihilation of all kinds of slavery."[30]

Meanwhile, Sarah formed a close friendship with writer and fellow reformer Lydia Maria Child and took part in Margaret Fuller's popular "Conversations," which were designed to encourage self-expression and independent thinking among women. Both Frank and Sarah were drawn to Fuller's company and embraced her philosophy about the unity of masculine and feminine qualities in human nature. Fuller challenged conventional gender roles with her belief that "there is no wholly masculine man, no purely feminine woman." She argued that every person should be allowed to achieve "fullness of being" by expressing their unique combination of both masculine and feminine traits. If society permitted this natural balance to flourish freely, Fuller believed, it would finally end what she called the "discordant collision" that inevitably resulted from rigidly separating the sexes into opposing categories.[31]

Rob and his sisters were probably too young to retain clear memories of their Brook Farm years. As a former resident later recalled, "Mr. Shaw, on his horse, with his young son, a tiny little fellow, on a pony by his side, often galloped over to the Farm to call."[32] Despite his youth, Rob's lifelong love of music likely began during this period at Brook Farm. While his sisters attended school at the Farm, Rob was enrolled at Miss Mary Peabody's grade school in Boston. There he would have learned to read using the accordion-style alphabet books popular at the time, before progressing to illustrated Bible stories and childhood classics like *Mother Goose*, Hans Christian Andersen's tales, and *The Arabian Nights*. On Sundays, the Shaw children attended Sunday school and joined their parents for sermons by Rev. Theodore Parker. Parker's progressive teachings reinforced the family's antislavery convictions and their belief in equality between men and women.[33]

Frank and Sarah were, by all accounts, devoted and loving parents. They encouraged their children to think independently and form their own opinions, though they clearly hoped that Rob and his siblings would eventually embrace the family's reform causes as their own. Frank's retirement from business affairs provided him with more time to spend with his family compared with most nineteenth-century fathers, including his own. The Shaw children witnessed a deep, mutual respect between their parents, a marriage of equals that was certainly unusual in mid-nineteenth-century America. Despite this partnership, Sarah took on the primary responsibility for raising the children. She was tasked with nurturing both their intellectual curiosity and their moral development, shaping the next generation of what the family hoped would be committed reformers.[34]

The Brook Farm experiment collapsed in 1846 due to a combination of factors, including a smallpox outbreak, mounting debts, and growing disillusionment among its members. The end of this community left the Shaws without their close social network just as Sarah began experiencing serious health problems. She suffered from failing eyesight and periodic mental breakdowns. These circumstances prompted another family move, this time to the West New Brighton neighborhood on Staten Island. There, Sarah could receive treatment from Dr. Samuel MacKenzie Elliott, a thirty-six-year-old Scottish physician who specialized in eye care. Dr. Elliott had built a reputation among reform-minded intellectuals and treated many of the Shaw family's acquaintances. Boston reformers occasionally made the journey to consult with him, including Sydney Howard Gay (editor of the *National Anti-Slavery Standard*), James Russell Lowell, Henry David Longfellow, Charles Dana, and Brook Farm's founder, George Ripley.[35]

Staten Island offered the Shaw family a dramatically different landscape, with large estates and sweeping vistas overlooking the tidal strait Kill Van

Kull. Rob and his sisters took full advantage of the island's natural beauty, exploring thick forests, tidal creeks, and coastal wetlands. On clear days, Rob could gaze toward the Robbins Reef Lighthouse and, beyond it, the distant outline of Manhattan. Their new home provided endless adventure for the children, including horseback riding in spring and swimming at the Staples boathouse in summer.[36] Initially, Rob attended a private school nearby. However, in 1850, despite the family's Unitarian beliefs, he was enrolled at St. John's College Roman Catholic School at Fordham. This unusual choice was made because his uncle Joseph was studying there to become a Jesuit priest.[37]

Boarding school life proved extremely challenging for the adolescent Rob. While he found some joy in his violin lessons and creating sketches based on book illustrations to send to his mother, he was overwhelmed by homesickness and feelings of abandonment. After one brief visit home, he wrote, "I wish I didn't feel this way every time I go home." Even more painful was his sense of isolation from his classmates. He felt ashamed that "the boys who were homesick when they first came here are not so now, even that little one who used to be crying all the time."[38] Rob's distress eventually drove him to run away from the school. Somehow, he managed to find his way back to Staten Island. His escape, however, proved short-lived as his father simply escorted him back to Fordham.

Once back at St. John's College, Rob wrote a letter calculated to pull the heartstrings of his mother and to remind her of just how close he came to running away again:

> If they had whipped me then I am almost certain I should have run away again, I should have been so mad. As it was I came near going the second time I was sent out of the study room. One of the boys ran away from here during vacation, and they thought he was up here; but he went aboard a sloop on the Hudson river and worked there for a month. After I came up from New York with Father, this boy asked me to run away with him again, and do the same as he did before; and I would have done it then if it wasn't getting cold, but I wouldn't do it now.[39]

Rob likely knew that the mention of whipping would evoke images of both slavery and corporal punishment for his reform-minded mother. He was essentially casting himself as an enslaved person resisting a cruel overseer's treatment while also making a veiled threat to run away and find work on a sloop. However, Sarah remained unmoved by her son's dramatic comparison and implied threats. Despite his emotional appeals, both parents insisted that Rob stay at Fordham.

Rob's earliest letters reveal a young man coming of age, one who was unusually open to sharing his deepest feelings and frustrations with his family, but who also possessed a strong rebellious streak. This defiant side emerged clearly when he was eleven years old and his mother insisted on regular correspondence from boarding school. Rob's response was blunt and defiant: "I don't want to write every week. It's too much trouble, and I shall only write when I want something."[40]

Frank and Sarah struggled to find the right balance in raising their son. In doing so, Frank drew from his own upbringing. His father had encouraged all his children, including his daughters, to form their own convictions and make independent choices, even if those choices led to unconventional lifestyles that challenged social norms. Following this example, Frank and Sarah wanted to give Rob a similar experience of freedom while also instilling in him a strong social conscience. They hoped he would learn to balance his personal desires with his obligations to address society's larger problems. As one historian noted, the couple "took particular care to make an explicit link between private morality and public activism in the service of the community."[41] However, at this stage of his life, Rob showed little ability or interest in seeing himself as part of this larger world. He remained focused primarily on his own immediate needs and frustrations.

In January 1851, thirteen-year-old Rob prepared for an extended European tour with his parents and sisters, a trip suggested by fellow reformer Margaret Fuller. Rob was undoubtedly thrilled to escape the confines of St. John's College and reunite with his family for this grand adventure. Such European tours were accessible only to America's wealthiest families and could last several years. The typical itinerary included culturally and historically significant destinations across France, Italy, and Germany. As their ship departed New York City, Rob may have paced the deck imagining the wonders awaiting him such as ancient Roman ruins, masterpiece paintings and sculptures in Europe's finest museums, and architectural marvels that Americans eagerly imitated back home. However, this was not simply a pleasure trip. Along with traveling and sightseeing, Rob would be expected to continue his formal education by attending European schools.[42]

The family's departure came at a critical moment in America's deepening crisis over slavery. The United States' victory in the Mexican-American War (1846–48) had added vast new western territories and threatened to upset the delicate balance in the Senate between free states and slave states, an arrangement that had been established by the Missouri Compromise of 1820. Congress attempted to address this crisis through what became known as the Compromise of 1850. Under this agreement, California entered the Union as a free state, while the two new territories of Utah and New Mexico would decide the slavery question through "popular sovereignty"—allowing residents to vote on the issue themselves. The compromise also banned the slave trade in Washington, DC, but simultaneously enacted the Fugitive Slave Act. This final provision particularly outraged the Shaw family. The new law empowered federal authorities to hunt down freedom seekers even in Northern states, directly contradicting the family's abolitionist principles. The Shaws had long supported vigilance committees in cities like Boston and New York that protected these same runaway slaves. While many Americans hoped the Compromise of 1850 would permanently resolve the slavery question, it became increasingly clear as the Shaw family began their European journey that this crisis was far from over.

Although Rob's earliest letters to his friends and relatives in the United States do not mention slavery, he undoubtedly overheard his parents discussing the issue with friends and associates. Frank and Sarah most likely included the children in these conversations as well. The five years Rob would spend abroad proved to be a crucial period in American history. The national debate over slavery intensified dramatically, erupting by 1855 into open violence in the Kansas Territory. For many young American men coming of age during this turbulent time, these events shaped their political and moral development in profound ways. Rob, however, would experience this pivotal moment in his country's history only through distant news reports and letters from home.

Rob traveled with his family throughout the summer of 1851 before enrolling at the school of Monsieur and Madame Roulet in the Swiss town of Neuchâtel. The new school was a vast improvement over his experience at Fordham. His room boasted a magnificent view of Mont Blanc and the surrounding peaks along the French-Italian border. Rob quickly developed a good relationship with the headmaster and appreciated his generally even temperament. Roulet apparently became angry only when students broke the rules or displayed rudeness; and when the headmaster did lose his temper, the transformation was dramatic. As Rob wrote to his mother, "But when he does get angry, he's just like a wolf and calls the boys all kinds of names."[43]

Despite the improvements, Rob still chafed against the strict supervision of students. He complained of being "rather tired of having to ask Mr. Roulet, every-time I want to go any-where, not getting permission sometimes, and when I'm doing any-thing a little out of the way, always being afraid he'll come along and catch me at it." Rob also bristled at Roulet's suggestion that he attend religion classes, writing to his mother that whether he was "good or bad" was none of the headmaster's business.[44] This resistance to religious instruction reflected a broader pattern in Rob's life. While he occasionally attended Protestant services, he never formally committed to a church or adopted the religious faith that anchored his parents' reform activism.

Rob still experienced occasional bouts of loneliness and homesickness, sometimes losing himself in thoughts about what his family was doing without him or feeling disappointed when a planned visit from his mother was canceled. However, these difficult moments were offset by exciting class trips to Switzerland's stunning mountains, lakes, and forests. In the classroom, Rob's curriculum included novels and plays in both English and French, Byron's poetry, and continued violin instruction. He also studied German, though he confessed to his family, "I've not worked very hard at it."[45] This casual attitude toward his language studies, unfortunately, extended to most of his other classes as well.

Sarah tried her best to guide Rob's moral development from a distance. She encouraged him to share his beliefs with fellow students, particularly the family's Unitarian faith—a suggestion he flatly rejected as having little practical value. From Rob's perspective, such conversations "would be very stupid and tiresome; and as I don't want to become a reformer, apostle, or anything of that kind, there is no use doing disagreeable things for nothing."[46] This blunt rejection of his family's core mission must have been painful for his parents to read. However, Frank and Sarah likely interpreted it as the words of a frustrated and immature young man rather than a permanent rejection of their values. At this stage of his life, Rob was simultaneously testing the boundaries of his parents' long-distance authority while trying to establish his own independent intellectual identity.

Despite Rob's attempts to distance himself from his parents' political causes, Sarah continued updating him on news from the United States, including the 1852 publication of Harriet Beecher Stowe's bestselling *Uncle Tom's Cabin*. Through her novel, the Connecticut-born author had exposed the violence of slavery to a broad reading public, energizing the abolitionist movement while enraging white Southerners. Like many abolitionists, Sarah was convinced that the book's vivid portrayal of slavery "will do much good, for when we become fairly ashamed of our slavery, we shall soon abolish it—it is the only blot on our fair country." Her optimism stemmed from several aspects of Stowe's approach, particularly her attempt to present a balanced view with "good masters and happy slaves, as well as bad masters and wretched slaves. Sometimes it makes you cry, and sometimes laugh." Sarah urged Rob to read the book in English rather than in the French translation to preserve the slave dialect she felt was essential to its impact. She was "sure" her son would "feel how dreadful a thing slavery is" after reading it. Whether Sarah sent the book to Rob remains unknown, but he did eventually read it. In fact, he read it multiple times and later wrote that he "always like[d] it better than before and [saw] more things in it."[47] Rob's response suggests that despite his proclaimed disinterest in reform causes, the book made a deeper impression on him than he might have expected.

Rob also read Stowe's follow-up work, *A Key to Uncle Tom's Cabin*, which she published the following year (in 1853) to respond to critics and to document the sources that had informed her portrayal of slavery. His engagement with both books clearly demonstrated that Rob was beginning to pay attention to the slavery crisis back home. He also stayed current with political developments, including a harsh new Illinois law passed in 1853 that prohibited both free and enslaved African Americans from entering the state. Any African Americans who remained in Illinois longer than ten days faced prosecution for a high misdemeanor and a fifty-dollar fine. Rob condemned this legislation as "worse than that of 1850"—likely referring to the Fugitive Slave Act of 1850.[48]

Despite enjoying some aspects of life at Neuchâtel, Rob longed to reunite with his family. His parents, particularly Sarah, were equally eager for this reunion, in part, because they hoped to rein in Rob's growing independence and rebellious tendencies. These family gatherings also provided them with crucial opportunities to continue to shape Rob's moral character and encourage his commitment to abolitionism. In late summer 1853, Rob traveled to Sorrento, Italy, to join his family. He may also have known in advance about a planned visit from Fanny Kemble, the British stage star who had achieved tremendous fame in America during the 1830s. Her celebrity had been so widespread that young women copied her hairstyle in "Fanny Kemble curls," and a tulip variety was even named in her honor. However, her private life had become the subject of considerable scandal.

In 1834, Kemble married Pierce Butler, a Philadelphia native who would inherit a massive Georgia plantation fortune. Two years later, Butler became heir to Georgia's second-largest slave-owning empire, and the marriage began to crumble as the former actress grew increasingly horrified by slavery. The couple's relationship deteriorated rapidly. Kemble attempted to flee to their Philadelphia home after only four months of marriage and mockingly called her husband "my lord and master." In 1835, she published *Journal of a Residence in America,* a satirical critique of American society that included her controversial antislavery views. Kemble also kept detailed records during her time on Butler's Georgia plantation, records that were eventually published in 1863 as *Journal of a Residence on a Georgian Plantation.* The experience left a lasting impact on her conscience. Writing to a friend in 1839, one year after leaving Georgia, Kemble reflected, "I have sometimes been haunted with the idea that it was an imperative duty, knowing what I know, and having seen what I have seen, to do all that lies in my power to show the dangers and the evils of the frightful institution."[49]

While the exact amount of time Rob spent with Kemble in Italy remains unclear, the sixteen-year-old would likely have been eager to meet such a celebrated public figure. Sarah almost certainly encouraged these interactions, seeing them as valuable opportunities to expose her son to someone with firsthand knowledge of slavery's horrors. Such encounters were rare and precious, especially as Rob continued his European education in the German city of Hanover, far removed from the American debates that were shaping his generation.

Hanover proved to be the ideal city in which Rob could complete his classical education in preparation for Harvard admission. Rather than enrolling in a formal school, his parents hired private tutors to instruct him in various subjects. His studies included Spanish and reading the works of Goethe and Schiller in their original German. The city itself captivated Rob. Located on the Leine River, Hanover featured narrow cobblestone streets, charming gingerbread houses, and a bustling market square. Most exciting for Rob were the city's theater and opera house, where he delighted in performances of *A Midsummer Night's Dream* and *Hamlet.* His time there also coincided with celebrations marking the centennial of Mozart's birth, highlighted by a performance of *Don Juan.*[50] These cultural experiences and newfound

Tivoli Beer Garden, Hanover, Germany, 1893. During the family's European sojourn, Shaw spent time in Hanover, where he engaged the assistance of a private tutor to further his education. He enjoyed the city's many attractions, including its concert hall and many beer gardens, where he discussed the latest news from the United States with friends and acquaintances. *Photograph by Bert Underwood. Courtesy Library of Congress.*

independence had a profound effect on Rob. "You can't conceive how big inside I've got since I've been here," he wrote proudly to his mother. "I'm at least five years older than when I came; but it is a natural consequence of being left alone and at my own disposition. I begin to find you treat me too *little* in your letters." Rob was clearly beginning to see himself as an adult rather than a child.[51]

With minimal oversight, Rob was now free to indulge his taste for pleasure and his tendency to overspend. His late nights in taverns and theaters quickly depleted his allowance. Desperate for funds, he even tried to convince his mother to buy "engravings of two hounds" from him as Christmas presents for his sisters.[52] When Sarah didn't respond to this scheme, Rob complained of living in the "greatest poverty," unable to "buy a dressing gown" and "obliged to sell two coats, two waistcoats and two pairs of trowserloons which is rather disturbing." His financial troubles persisted throughout his time in Germany as he immersed himself in the city's bohemian social circles, attending balls, gambling freely, and participating in regular drinking "sprees."[53] This behavior alarmed his parents, who had always encouraged their children to live modestly and avoid extravagance. When Sarah attempted to rein in his spending, Rob cleverly enlisted his father's support, arguing that his mother was unfairly treating him as though he had "committed some awful crime."[54]

Rob was likely sorely disappointed if he expected to gain his father as an ally against his mother. Both parents were united in offering stern guidance to their children, hoping to steer them toward responsible, moral lives and meaningful careers. However, Rob's emotional maturity lagged far behind his physical development. He remained stubbornly self-centered, as evidenced by his blunt confession to his mother in November 1854, writing, "I have no taste for anything excepting amusing myself!" On another occasion, he wrote with remarkable candor about his expectations for returning home. "I hope that when I come home I shall be as much at liberty as I am now for after having had my own way as much as if I were of age for two years it would be nasty to be a child again. It's very unwillingly that I ask you to let me do anything because that's submission, but I haven't enough money to do it otherwise."[55] This letter revealed Rob's casual disregard for his parents' feelings and his transactional view of their relationship. He would submit to their authority only when financial necessity demanded it. Frank and Sarah must have wondered whether their son had actually regressed during his years away from their direct supervision.[56]

Rob also found himself distracted by romantic interests during his time in Hanover. His mother's reaction to her son's confession is unknown, but he openly admitted to using his opera glasses to spy on "two young ladies . . . who are always sitting at the window" across the street from his room. Perhaps Rob was trying to reassure Sarah that while he was looking at women, he wasn't pursuing anything more serious.[57] He also confessed to falling "in love with a 'princess' who lives opposite our lodgings" and expressed uncertainty about returning home, wondering whether he could follow his mother's "principle of not marrying a cousin."[58]

Alongside his commitment to entertainment and his travels to Paris, Bremen, Berlin, and even Norway with student friends, Rob managed to stay informed about events back home. He regularly read the *New York Daily*

Tribune, likely sent by his mother, which kept him updated on America's deepening divisions over slavery. Though Hanover was far from the heated congressional debates and growing threats of disunion, the city provided ample opportunity for Rob to discuss contemporary issues, particularly slavery. Many of Hanover's residents had emigrated to the United States following the failed Revolution of 1848, and they wrote letters back to loved ones, keeping them informed of the latest news across the Atlantic. These so-called Forty-Eighters attempted to create a new Germany based on liberty, democracy, and national unity, only to become exiles in a new country, where they would soon have the opportunity to demonstrate their loyalty to their new adopted country.[59]

Rob frequently engaged these German acquaintances in political discussions during tavern visits and walks through town. However, he complained that the German press exaggerated America's problems. Despite his defensive patriotism, Rob found it increasingly difficult to deny that the situation back home had deteriorated significantly.

In 1854, Congress passed the Kansas-Nebraska Act, which overturned the long-standing Missouri Compromise and opened both Kansas and Nebraska territories to "popular sovereignty," allowing residents to vote on whether to permit slavery. While Southern slaveholders celebrated, many Northerners were outraged that a vast section of the American West might become additional slave states rather than free states. The legislation shattered the nation's two-party system of Democrats and Whigs. The Whig Party soon collapsed, giving way to a new, regional Republican Party that was committed to preventing slavery's expansion into western territories and that the Shaws quickly embraced.

Meanwhile, Kansas became a violent battleground. Proslavery "Border Ruffians" from Missouri clashed with antislavery "Jayhawkers" led by figures like John Brown and James Montgomery, each side fighting for control of the territory's future. By late 1855, Americans were killing one another in Kansas over the slavery question. It was a grim preview of the larger conflict to come.

During his time abroad, Rob likely also followed the increasingly violent news from his former home of Boston, where the 1850 Fugitive Slave Act was being aggressively enforced to return freedom seekers to slavery. On May 24, 1854, Anthony Burns, a fugitive slave from Alexandria, Virginia, was arrested by federal authorities and scheduled to be returned to his owner. Local abolitionists—many of them Shaw family acquaintances—rallied to Burns's defense.

This was not Boston's first confrontation with the Fugitive Slave Act. In 1850, city residents had successfully foiled attempts to recapture freedom seekers Ellen and William Craft from Georgia. That same year, in an even more dramatic case, Bostonians had stormed the courthouse and rescued Shadrach Minkins, who was about to be transported back to Norfolk, Virginia. However, the unrest and violence from these earlier rescues had prompted federal authorities to implement stricter security measures that would ultimately doom Burns's chances for freedom. Abolitionists led by Thomas Wentworth Higginson made a desperate final attempt to rescue Burns, using a battering ram to break into the courthouse where he was being held. In the violent confrontation that followed, a deputy was killed. Burns was convicted under the Fugitive Slave Act and escorted to Boston's waterfront for his return to Virginia. The event was watched by a crowd estimated in the tens of thousands. The entire affair proved to be another stark reminder of how deeply the slavery crisis had penetrated even into the heart of abolitionist Boston.[60]

The failed rescue of Anthony Burns and similar cases likely came up in correspondence between Rob and his parents, given their long-standing support for fugitive slaves. However, it was a horrific account published in the *New York Tribune* in 1855 that truly captured Rob's attention and stirred his emotions deeply. The newspaper reported on an enslaved man in Sumter, Alabama, who had been accused of murdering a young girl and who was subsequently lynched by a mob. An eyewitness described the victim's "fearful cries resounded through the air, while the surrounding Negroes who witnessed his dreadful agony and horrible condition sent up an involuntary howl of horror." The *Tribune* spared readers few of the horrific details, including how the mob broke into the prison where the man was being held and dragged him to the "stake on the very spot where the murder was committed." Reading this brutal account in the pages of a major newspaper must have felt vastly different from Rob's experience with the fictional *Uncle Tom's Cabin*. This may not have been his first exposure to lynching stories, as he had written to his mother, "I didn't think the last would ever happen again."[61]

Despite such jarring moments, Rob's fundamental outlook on slavery and abolition changed very little during his time in Europe. He had spent most of this period away from his parent's gaze—a testament to their commitment to allow their son to pursue his education and perhaps discover some sense of purpose and direction on his own. Any chance of guiding their son more directly was cut short by the demands of his schooling. While in surviving letters to his mother he never explicitly stated his position, Rob likely believed slavery was immoral and probably sympathized with the suffering of enslaved people. However, this intellectual understanding never translated into personal action. Most importantly, Rob never accepted that he bore any moral responsibility to work toward ending slavery. His correspondence from this period reveals a young man largely insulated from the world's pressing problems, content to pursue the pleasures and distractions of youth. The outside world—no matter how violent or urgent—seemed rarely to interfere with his ability to enjoy himself. Perhaps Sarah and Frank comforted themselves with the fact that Rob was young. There was still time.

As Rob prepared to sail for home in spring 1856, his future remained completely uncertain. While he had relished his independence in Hanover, the lack of supervision had also meant that no one pushed him toward serious consideration of a career path. At one point, he had mentioned to his parents the possibility of attending West Point. "I think I should like it, and what else can I do? I can't think of any thing else, for I don't want to be a Merchant, or Doctor, or Minister, or anything like that."[62]

Whatever thoughts Rob had about his future, he understood that his education was far from complete. As the eighteen-year-old prepared to rejoin his family, he asked his mother to hire "crammers" (tutors) to prepare him for admission to Harvard. Rob optimistically believed he was "pretty well up in the Rudiments" of Greek and that his math skills were "alright I think." His confidence extended to his expectations about class placement as well. He hoped to enter as a junior but was willing to accept sophomore status if necessary. However, reality proved more humbling, and Rob eventually entered Harvard as a freshman, suggesting his academic preparation had been less thorough than he had imagined.[63]

This placement was a realistic assessment of Rob's academic development during his years abroad, an assessment his parents likely endorsed. Frank and Sarah probably looked forward to seeing their son apply himself more seriously to his studies in Cambridge while finally settling on a career path as he approached adulthood. Despite the deepening sectional crisis over slavery that cast doubt on the nation's future, Rob's personal prospects appeared promising. The question remained whether he would rise to meet his family's expectations and the challenges of his times.

TWO

I Can't Help Hoping That There Will Be a Disunion Some Time

In May 1856, Rob Shaw arrived at his family's new home in Staten Island, where his mother, Sarah, had resumed treatments for her failing eyesight. While Sarah and Frank were likely struck by their son's physical growth, Rob's recent correspondence with this mother had made it all too clear that he had made very little progress in his personal development. His reckless spending habits and penchant for amusement had continued throughout his time in Germany.[1] Now he was about to enter Harvard—as was expected of a young man from his social class—even though he had demonstrated very little talent for or interest in serious scholarly study. More importantly, he would still have little direction. Harvard would simply offer a new environment for four more years of self-indulgent behavior, while the question of what career he would ultimately choose would continue to linger.

Desperate for help, Rob's parents enlisted Francis Channing Barlow, a Harvard valedictorian three years Rob's senior, who had already launched his legal career. Francis and his mother, Almira, were fellow transcendentalists who had briefly lived at Brook Farm before Almira's scandalous "fondness for the society of men" got them expelled. The contrast between tutor and pupil could hardly have been starker. Barlow possessed everything Rob lacked, including academic excellence, clear purpose, and iron discipline. Frank and Sarah may have hoped that this future "boy general" could inspire their wayward son to find direction.[2]

After breezing through the entrance exams he dismissed as "very easy," Rob crossed the Charles River to Cambridge and Harvard Yard. The campus in 1856 looked much like it had when it was founded in 1636 to train enlightened clergymen, before gradually secularizing in the eighteenth and early nineteenth centuries. Red brick Georgian buildings were clustered around the Yard, their windows reflecting the river's calm waters. A new granite library housed thousands of volumes that Rob would largely ignore. Harvard remained a rich man's club despite reformers like Horace Mann's efforts to expand public education. At $400 annually (in 1856)—nearly three times the 1810 cost—only Boston's wealthiest families could afford the privilege of attendance. For Rob, this meant four more years surrounded by his own class of privileged young men whose fathers' money shielded them from any real consequence.[3]

Rob entered Harvard during a bitter battle over the purpose of an elite education. The state-appointed Board of Overseers wanted to democratize the curriculum—they wanted, essentially, to turn Harvard into "a giant lyceum where anyone might study anything."[4] But the Corporation, controlled by Boston's merchant-industrialist families, had a different vision, preferring to support scientific training to produce the next generation of business and industrial leaders. The Corporation's deep pockets won. Their donations funded new courses in geology, chemistry, physics, and applied mathematics—subjects that would fuel America's industrial expansion while keeping power in familiar hands. Rob's friend Wilder Dwight captured the prevailing philosophy. According to Dwight, a college education should encourage the development of a "healthy, active" mind that is "ready both to acquire and use knowledge." Dwight maintained that "a complete education should qualify one for the discharge of all his duties and should strengthen and develop all the faculties to their utmost capacity so as to give vigor, comprehensiveness and liberality of mind."[5] In short, a Harvard education would polish young Brahmins for the leadership roles they had been born to inherit.

Rob's Harvard freshman year erupted with the chaos of the 1856 presidential election. Slavery dominated national politics as the brand-new Republican

Harvard College as it looked when Shaw was a student during the late 1850s. The campus proved to be a hotbed of activity and debate surrounding the growing sectional rift over slavery; but Shaw took little interest in this issue, preferring instead to focus on his social life. *Courtesy Library of Congress.*

Party—founded explicitly to stop slavery's westward expansion—offered the first serious challenge to the nation's political structure. The campaign split Boston's reform community. William Lloyd Garrison's abolitionists scorned electoral politics entirely, working instead for change outside the system. But Frank Shaw chose a different path. After the Whig Party's collapse in the wake of the Kansas-Nebraska Act, he grudgingly embraced the Republicans despite their celebration of the capitalism he had rejected years earlier. The Republicans' antislavery stance mattered more than their economic philosophy.[6]

Frank Shaw threw himself into the Republican cause, helping nominate explorer John C. Frémont—the famous "Pathfinder"—at the party's first national convention. He campaigned tirelessly for Frémont, only to watch Pennsylvania Democrat James Buchanan crush Republican hopes in November. But the loss masked a terrifying reality for slaveholders. Republicans had nearly won on Northern votes alone. The South now faced the real possibility that in four years a major political party could seize the presidency without a single Southern electoral vote. That fall, the defeated candidate John Frémont and his wife, Jessie, attended Anna Shaw's wedding to George William Curtis, the popular writer and editor of *Putnam's Monthly*.

Harvard's antislavery advocates remained a tiny, barely tolerated minority on campus. The Board of Overseers preferred that students remain focused on their studies rather than on "radical" politics—an attitude that perfectly suited Rob Shaw, who stayed studiously aloof from the slavery debates throughout his college years. The institution's silence served powerful interests. Harvard's major donors included men like textile magnate Abbott Lawrence, whose nearby factories transformed slave-grown cotton into finished goods sold worldwide. The university's financial survival depended on slavery's continuation, creating an unspoken conspiracy of complicity that extended from the Southern plantations to Cambridge's lecture halls.[7]

Harvard's racial hypocrisy exploded into view just before Rob's arrival. In 1850, the Harvard Medical School admitted three Black students—and then promptly expelled them after white students and alumni protested. Dean Oliver Wendell Holmes Sr. personally orchestrated the dismissals, bowing to racist pressure. The racism exhibited on campus was buttressed by professors like Jeffries Wyman and Louis Agassiz, whose "scientific" theories reinforced the widely held belief that Black people possessed inferior intelligence and moral character. "It is impossible for me to repress the feeling," Agassiz revealed, "that they are not the same blood as us."[8]

Harvard's growing Southern contingent added explosive tension to campus life. Between 1850 and 1854, the percentage of undergraduates from slaveholding states doubled from 6 percent to 12 percent, with an even sharper increase reflected in the law school student body. Boston's elite welcomed these Southern students with open arms. As Thomas Wentworth Higginson observed, Southerners impressed Yankees with their "charming manners, social aptitudes, imperious ways, abundant leisure, and plenty of money; they were graceful dancers, often musical, and sometimes well taught."[9] But these same students also earned a reputation for violence and other disruptive acts such as interrupting public lectures and taunting prominent public speakers like Ralph Waldo Emerson, who spoke out against slavery.

The deep divisions within Harvard regarding slavery's future reached a crisis point during the trial of fugitive slave Anthony Burns in Boston in late May 1854. Harvard students were present at the proceedings, and several Southern students, including law student Charles C. Jones from Savannah, Georgia, offered their services to guard the prosecuting attorney as a demonstration of their proslavery stance. Writing to his father just days after the trial began, Jones described the volatile atmosphere in Boston: "Mob law, perjury, free-soilism, and abolitionism are running riot. Never before in all my life have my feelings been so severely tried as they have been during these past and present occurrences."[10]

While Burns's forced return to Virginia probably pleased Jones and other Southern students, those who viewed the Fugitive Slave Act as unjust—even without fully embracing abolitionism—focused their outrage on Judge Edward G. Loring, who not only presided over the case but also taught at Harvard. The sharply divided reaction to Loring's ruling mirrored the growing sectional tensions between North and South that were now generating calls for disunion. Jones reported that Southern law students welcomed the judge's return to the classroom, but they were met with "a storm of hisses, and other marks of disapprobation" that clearly expressed Northern students' anger over how the case had been resolved.[11]

Shaw encountered many chances to engage in slavery debates with both professors and classmates. His parents certainly hoped that his Harvard education—situated near one of the country's most vibrant abolitionist communities across the Charles River in Boston—would shift his perspective toward reform. Instead, they found themselves disappointed.

Shaw rapidly grew disenchanted with Harvard. Within two months, he declared, "I hate Cambridge just as much as I used to dislike school." He contemplated leaving to "go into a store" and acknowledged that his dissatisfaction stemmed from having "had such a good time (so much better than any body else of my age!) for the last five years."[12] Shaw frequently arrived late to class or skipped classes entirely. Harvard faculty repeatedly issued "private admonishments" to Shaw for his "neglect" of mathematics and Greek as well as for his "absence" and "tardiness from recitations."[13]

By contrast, Shaw made ample time for his social activities, maintaining the same enthusiasm for entertainment and socializing as he had shown in Hanover. His letters brimmed with detailed descriptions and blow-by-blow accounts of the most recent football matches between freshmen and sophomores. Whether his mother welcomed his vivid portrayals of "black eyes, bloody noses & broken teeth" or the "good many blows" her son himself received remains unclear.[14] Shaw also pursued membership in various clubs during 1858, including the Pierian Sodality—a musical society that allowed him to perform on his violin publicly twice weekly—and Harvard's most elite organizations like the Hasty Pudding Club. Starting in April of that year, Shaw wore a blue shirt with red trim and a straw hat adorned with blue ribbons stamped in gold as he rowed the Charles River alongside his classmates aboard the shell *Sabrina*.

During the winter, Rob enjoyed joining classmates like Casper Crowninshield, Charles Mudge, Edward G. Abbott, Thomas Bayley Fox Jr., and Thomas Rodman Robeson at skating parties on nearby Fresh Pond, and he participated in the gambling and drinking gatherings that characterized college life, though never to excess. Occasionally, Rob took a horse-drawn omnibus into Boston or boarded the steamer *Empire State* for quick trips along the New England coast and through Long Island Sound to experience New York City's appealing attractions. The social bonds Shaw forged at Harvard would later prove crucial during the war.[15]

Despite all the diversions college life provided, Rob treasured every chance he had to spend time with family, including with his younger sister Susie, who was also attending school in Cambridge. The siblings enjoyed taking long walks together and going sleighing in winter.[16] As for Cambridge's other young women, however, Rob remained unimpressed. He instead fondly recalled the daughter of a German acquaintance who, according to a letter from Hanover, had only "increased in loveliness, sweetness." Shaw promised to write to her but never did, likely because he met an unnamed young woman during one of his New York trips. Rob confided to his mother about his "M.L." (Much Loved) after one visit, writing, "I was more smitten than before . . . and I hope they will ask me again."[17]

Shaw's social activities, however, could never completely overshadow his awareness of the nation's deepening slavery crisis. He occasionally made short trips to attend services at Theodore Parker's church in West Roxbury—near his family's former home and Brook Farm—where slavery's moral implications frequently appeared in sermons; yet he rarely attempted to express his views in student debates or other campus forums. For his inaugural speech as a new debate society member in 1857, Shaw selected Norway as his topic, confessing to his mother that it "would be easiest to write" about. It was an admission that likely struck her as entirely predictable.[18]

Overall, Rob grew weary of the constant slavery discussions he encountered in and around Boston among family and friends. "For the last month," he wrote his mother in April 1857, "I have heard of nothing but Mrs. Kemble and am so tired of her that I wouldn't go to hear her again for anything." This reference to Sarah's friend and fellow reformer must have stung. These were no longer the words of a rebellious child but those of a young man preparing to enter the world. On another occasion, Shaw resisted the persistent slavery talk while trying to reassure his parents: "Because I don't talk and think Slavery all the time, and because I get tired . . . of hearing nothing else, you say I don't feel with you, when I do."[19]

Rob may have shared his mother's moral revulsion toward slavery, but there is no evidence that her pleas for him to adopt abolitionism as his own cause influenced him. The conservative political atmosphere among Harvard students undoubtedly shaped Shaw's perspective. His class of 1860 included seventy-five Republicans and nine Democrats among just over one hundred students, yet despite the Republican majority, these students remained devoted to moderation and worried about extremist positions that might endanger the nation's peace and prosperity.[20]

Shaw certainly shared his parents' firm belief that slavery was immoral and hoped for its eventual abolition, but he worried about how the widening sectional rift might affect the nation. Slavery, he argued, "is the only fault in America."[21] Like many Americans of his era, Shaw embraced "Manifest Destiny," a concept introduced by newspaper editor John O'Sullivan in 1845 to characterize the nation's "exceptional" global role. Shaw was probably also acquainted with George Bancroft's influential US history and his conviction that the Union represented progress and that Americans possessed an inherent and inevitable right to expand westward, extending their political, economic, and social institutions.[22]

The ongoing slavery conflict in the late 1850s, however, jeopardized the nation's progress and its unique position among world powers. Shaw followed these political discussions and anticipated a Republican victory in the upcoming presidential election, yet he also expressed hope "that there will be a disunion sometime"—a sentiment that may have reflected his frustrations and desire to eliminate the slavery controversy permanently.[23] In addition to the violence in Kansas Territory, Republican Senator Charles Sumner—a Shaw family friend—was brutally assaulted on the Senate floor on May 22, 1856, following his speech condemning slaveholders. The next year, the US Supreme Court under Chief Justice Roger Taney ruled in the infamous Dred Scott case that slaveholders could not be barred from taking their property into the territories, effectively nullifying the Kansas-Nebraska Act and raising questions about whether slaveholders might even bring their enslaved people into free states. Additionally, the court declared unequivocally that the US Constitution did not grant the rights and privileges of American citizenship to Black people of African descent. That same year, the United States plunged into another destabilizing economic crisis.[24]

Few people articulated the mounting anxiety and uncertainty felt by Shaw and many others better than Abraham Lincoln. After serving one congressional term from 1846 to 1848, Lincoln had returned to his Springfield, Illinois law practice; but the Kansas-Nebraska Act drew him back into active politics. At the Illinois Republican Party's June 1858 senatorial nominating convention, Lincoln cautioned, "A house divided against itself cannot stand. I believe this government cannot endure, permanently half slave and half free. I do not expect the Union to be dissolved—I do not expect the house to fall—but I do expect it will cease to be divided. It will become all one thing, or all the other." Lincoln secured the Illinois Republican senatorial nomination and campaigned throughout the state in a series of highly publicized debates with Democratic Senator Stephen Douglas. Although Lincoln lost that November's election, the public and media attention benefited him considerably and helped secure his Republican presidential nomination in 1860.[25]

Rob's hope for disunion expressed as much anxiety about the nation's condition as it reflected his personal circumstances and mounting dissatisfaction with Harvard life. His grades were decent, but except for in one botany course his father had recommended, Shaw never showed himself to be a dedicated student.[26] He complained to his mother that the "faculty are very much displeased with the whole class"; and he perhaps revealed more about his own mindset when he confessed, "They say we are the laziest class they have had for a long while." His Cambridge social life remained his priority. By October 1857, Shaw had already considered leaving Harvard to pursue business, but he now recognized that remaining in school had been the smarter decision given the economic downturn.[27]

Rob returned to Cambridge for his junior year in 1858, but his future remained uncertain. He felt restless and even contemplated western farming after exchanging letters with a Hanover acquaintance who was studying agriculture in Philadelphia. "I don't suppose that a man can make much money [at farming]," he conceded.[28]

A position in his uncle Henry P. Sturgis's New York City mercantile firm remained a possibility, but it held little attraction for him. As Shaw had written earlier from Europe, "I had rather be a chimney sweep."[29] Making matters worse, the economy had not yet recovered, and Rob speculated that even if he were to accept a position with Sturgis's firm, "There will be nothing for me to do . . . for the first 5 or 6 months as there will be . . . very little business."[30] Family members urged Rob to "not let this opportunity go," and in December

This portrait of Shaw likely dates to when he was a student at Harvard in the late 1850s. His restlessness during this period led him to consider moving out west to become a farmer and even enlisting in the US Army. *Courtesy of W. Todd Groce, private collection.*

1858 he petitioned Harvard's president for a leave of absence, which was approved on the condition that he first complete his junior year. Shaw had wanted to depart before term's end but summoned a final surge of effort to finish on strong academic ground.[31]

New York City in 1859 was both bustling and violent. When William Howard Russell arrived around the same time to serve as a correspondent for the *London Times,* he entered New York harbor to see "a forest of masts close by a low shore of brick houses and blue roofs, above the level of which again spires of churches and domes and cupolas announced a great city."[32] The ships and frigates crowding the docks above West and South Streets, along with his uncle's mercantile offices, became Rob's new classroom. New

York City provided many diversions for a twenty-three-year-old, particularly its numerous theaters and concert halls. Shaw enjoyed his urban experience but also eagerly anticipated the brief ferry ride to Staten Island and the drive along the shore road to the family home in West New Brighton.

A return to his parents' home and the enjoyment of big city life, however, could not compensate for the fact that he was unsuited for business. Rob's honeymoon period at his uncle's firm ended quickly, perhaps mirroring his father's own reservations about the business world and Francis's decision to retire at an early age years before.

Rob's sole comfort was that business life offered potential overseas travel opportunities. "I am in the East India business," he wrote to his German friend Heinrich, "and I may go to China some time within two or three years in which case I want first to go to England, Germany, or Norway in summer, and from there through Siberia, in winter to China." When Heinrich traveled through the United States in 1859 and hoped to persuade Shaw to join him on a hunting expedition, Shaw replied with disappointment, "How I would like to go on that deer-hunt. But I am a slave now and, even if I were invited, I could not go."[33] Only the gathering storm of disunion and an approaching presidential election could divert Shaw from his despondent mood.

The political atmosphere in New York City's business community differed dramatically from Shaw's Cambridge experience. The city was a stronghold of Democratic Party support, particularly among the merchants and financiers in Shaw's new circle. The party's popularity stemmed largely from its willingness to appease Southern slaveholding interests to preserve the profitable cotton trade that flowed through New York City to the rest of the nation and beyond. Although New York State had abolished slavery in 1827, the city maintained strong ties to the slaveholding South. Mercantile trade, insurance companies, and banks all financed the cotton industry.[34]

Meanwhile, the city's free Black community lived in constant fear of kidnapping and of the "slaver" ships that regularly arrived in the harbor to unload cargo, occasionally concealing African slaves aboard for sale as part of a lucrative, though illegal, enterprise. Many New York shipbuilders and merchants participated in the illegal transatlantic slave trade during the 1850s. Throughout Shaw's brief time at his uncle's mercantile house, from 1859 to 1861, approximately 100 slaver ships departed New York City for destinations along Africa's western coast, and an estimated 53,000 people may have been transported from West Africa to Cuba on American vessels.[35] The extent to which Shaw understood this dimension of New York's business world remains unclear, but he likely exercised caution when discussing his views on slavery or his family's political allegiances.

Still, in New York City in 1860, Rob likely intended to support Republican candidate Abraham Lincoln for president. He did not attend Lincoln's February 27, 1860, speech at the Cooper Union Institute, which helped the Illinois lawyer secure his party's nomination. On that occasion, Lincoln sought to leverage the national media attention from his unsuccessful 1858 Senate campaign against Stephen Douglas by charting a moderate path between the radical abolitionists demanding slavery's immediate end and the Democratic Party's opposition to the restriction of slavery's expansion. Lincoln told the packed, attentive audience that the Republican Party was honoring the Founding Fathers' intentions by limiting slavery's spread and that the Southern states lacked constitutional authority to secede from the Union. Lincoln articulated what he viewed as slavery's fundamental problem: "If it is right, we cannot justly object to its nationality—its universality; if it is wrong, they cannot justly insist upon its extension—its enlargement." He also deliberately distanced himself from John Brown's failed raid at Harpers Ferry, Virginia, in October 1859, when the veteran of the fighting in "Bleeding Kansas" had tried to spark a slave uprising by seizing a federal arsenal and arming the enslaved. "John Brown was no Republican," Lincoln declared, reminding his audience, "you have failed to implicate a single Republican in the Harper's Ferry enterprise."[36] Brown was captured, tried, and ultimately executed; but slaveholders now possessed all the proof they needed of Northerners' malicious intentions to incite Southerners' "loyal" slaves to murder their masters.

A few weeks later, Rob voted for Lincoln. Though the Illinois "railsplitter" ultimately carried New York State, he lost Manhattan decisively by 24,000 votes, a result that reflected the city's economic connections to the South and fears that a Republican victory would disrupt commerce.[37] Lincoln's support had come overwhelmingly from the free Northern states, while a regional Democratic Party split over slavery had produced two nominees. Stephen Douglas represented the party's Northern wing while John Breckenridge advocated for the interests of Southern Democrats. John Bell's Constitutional Union Party provided a lukewarm third-party option, which had attempted to steer a middle path. News of Lincoln's victory sent shockwaves throughout the South. In South Carolina, calls immediately arose for a special convention to consider secession.

As the country debated the significance and likely impact of Lincoln's election, Shaw embarked on a trip that took him from New York City through

Boston to Niagara Falls and Toronto, Canada. Shaw's brother-in-law, George Curtis, who was conducting a lecture tour, accompanied him for part of the journey. Rob attended George's lecture in Buffalo on Charles Dickens and enjoyed the "beer and oysters" afterward.[38] The trip's highlight, however, was Niagara Falls, which he called "the greatest sight I ever saw." "Isn't it wonderful to think," he mused, "that it was roaring as it is now in the time of Abraham & thousands of years before." On his return journey Shaw stopped in Boston and attended a Hasty Pudding Club meeting, where he enjoyed reuniting with former Harvard classmates.[39]

Rob likely followed the news from the South, along with the rest of the nation, in the weeks after Lincoln's election. There seemed little doubt that South Carolina would secede, fearing that the new Republican administration posed a direct threat to slavery. Indeed, in the early morning hours of December 20, 1860, state delegates assembled in Charleston's St. Andrew's Hall and unanimously passed a secession ordinance. "And then a mighty shout arose," recalled Rev. A. Toomer Porter, an Episcopal clergyman and former South Carolina planter. "It rose higher and higher until it was the roar of a tempest. It spread from end to end of the city, for all were of one mind. No man living could have stood that excitement."[40] Soon cannon fire echoed across the city, marking the momentous occasion. A special edition of the *Charleston Mercury* quickly appeared with a bold headline declaring, "THE UNION IS DISSOLVED." South Carolina's departure prompted six other Deep South states to follow, including Florida, Georgia, Alabama, Mississippi, Louisiana, and Texas. On February 4, 1861, their representatives convened in Montgomery, Alabama, to establish the Confederate States of America and elected Jefferson Davis as president and Alexander Stephens as vice president. Slavery, Stephens proudly proclaimed publicly, would be their new nation's "cornerstone."

An atmosphere of uncertainty gripped the nation during the so-called secession winter of 1860–61. Rather than risk losing additional Southern states, Lincoln chose to remain largely silent publicly, while a number of attempts at compromise failed. Shaw's correspondence is unfortunately quiet during this period. He probably spent Christmas with his family on Staten Island, but we can also picture him contemplating both his future and the nation's future while working at a job that brought him little satisfaction or sense of purpose.

Shaw began the new year by enlisting in the 7th New York Militia Regiment, commanded by Col. Marshall Lefferts, a former electrical engineer.

The 7th, also called the "Silk Stocking Regiment" due to its many socially elite New Yorkers, traced its origins to the early Republic. Shaw may have chosen the 7th New York as an appropriate place for his service, given its prestigious status and his previous consideration of a military career. Local militia units were authorized by the Militia Act of 1792 and embodied the "citizen soldier" ideal and a military service ethos in which men sacrificed for their local communities and the nation. State militias were originally designed to replace a regular standing army, but by the 1850s, enlistments had dropped dramatically nationwide following the surge in recruitment during the Mexican-American War.[41]

This trend began to change during the late 1850s through the efforts of a young man named Elmer Ellsworth, who believed that a revitalized volunteer militia might advance his own social and economic prospects. Ellsworth sought guidance from West Point graduates. His units would consist of citizen volunteers who, like himself, aspired to middle-class respectability. "Ellsworth envisioned a voluntary militia," according to one historian, "composed of disciplined white male citizens who were physically fit and followed a strict moral code."[42] Shaw may have followed the extensive news coverage of Ellsworth's Chicago Zouaves during their twenty-city tour, including New York City in summer 1860. Their colorful uniforms, mastery of light infantry tactics, and discipline captivated audiences. The *New York Herald* praised the cadets for "astonishing our military men and citizens by their excellent and unsurpassed discipline, gentlemanly deportment and modest bearing."[43]

The 7th New York that Rob joined in 1861 distinguished itself among antebellum militia units. Ellsworth acknowledged that the unit served as a "model" for his own recruitment efforts and credited it as the "secret of our success." In the decades before the war, the regiment had helped suppress popular uprisings such as the 1849 Astor Place riots, during which the men maintained the discipline necessary to endure multiple volleys of stones from unruly crowds. The regiment's reputation also earned them invitations to participate in ceremonial functions such as escorting former president James Monroe's remains from New York to Richmond's Hollywood Cemetery in 1858, and attending the dedication of an equestrian monument to George Washington in the nation's capital in 1860.[44] By the time Rob enlisted in early 1861, the regiment had an active strength of 895 men. Rob may have observed the regiment's training while it was encamped on Staten Island during summer 1860, but when he enlisted, the unit was using the Armory at Tompkins Square in Manhattan as its headquarters and training facility. While serving

Annie Kneeland Haggerty, ca. 1860–1870, before her marriage to Shaw. Shaw's sister Susie introduced him to Annie while he was working in New York City. The two began a correspondence before becoming engaged in late 1862. Their marriage would take place a few weeks before Shaw's departure with the 54th Massachusetts in May 1863. *Courtesy of the Lenox Library Association.*

in the 7th New York, Shaw learned military fundamentals through regular inspections, reviews, and company and battalion drills.

During this same period, Rob's sister Susie introduced her brother to Annie Kneeland Haggerty during an opera outing. Born two years before Rob, Annie shared his eye and hair color. Following the fashion of her era, Annie wore her hair tightly arranged under a knitted hairpiece. Annie's father, Otis Ogden Haggerty, had inherited his wealth and established an auction and commission house in New York City. Rob probably saw her several more times before departing for war in April 1861, after which they exchanged portraits and maintained occasional correspondence.[45]

While talk of war intensified, Rob's parents departed on the steamer *Karnak* for a vacation in Nassau and Havana. During their absence, Rob supervised the Staten Island property but found time to attend a Winter Garden performance of *Macbeth* featuring renowned actors Edwin Booth (brother of John Wilkes Booth) and Charlotte Cushman. "It was really splendid. The house was jammed from top to bottom," he recalled of the performance.[46]

Shaw also took responsibility for renting out one of his uncle's homes. On the assumption that his uncle would not "want any secessionists about," Rob declined one potential renter's offer after discovering that a relative who would also be staying at the property was from New Orleans.[47] The weather stayed miserable throughout March 1861. Heavy snow blanketed Manhattan, followed by soaking rain. Gray skies intensified the gloomy atmosphere that was worsened by constant war talk. Amid all this uncertainty, Shaw again questioned his career choice. A supervisor tried to convince him that with "more confidence in [himself he] should get along a good deal better."[48] The advice likely did little to effect a change in Shaw's attitude.

After taking the oath of office on March 4, 1861, Lincoln was informed of the deteriorating situation at Fort Sumter, a federal fort in Charleston Harbor. Just days after South Carolina seceded, US Army Maj. Robert Anderson had abandoned Fort Moultrie and moved his force to the more defensible, though still unfinished, Fort Sumter, where he prepared for an assault. South Carolina repeatedly demanded the fort's abandonment, and an attempt by the steamer *Star of the West* to reinforce the garrison was repelled on January 9, 1861, by cadets from Charleston's military academy, the Citadel. The situation became more desperate when Lincoln learned the garrison had only enough food to last until April 15. Anderson would be forced to surrender unless he were resupplied. Lincoln faced a difficult decision. Resupplying the fort might trigger open hostilities, while abandoning it would demonstrate federal inability to enforce the law, potentially prompting additional states to leave the Union.[49]

Rob and his father discussed the best course of action for the federal government. Frank Shaw favored abandoning Fort Sumter but holding Fort Pickens along the Florida coast, since it could be more easily resupplied. Rob appreciated the significance of the moment. "From the many conflicting reports," he wrote his father, "I infer that Mr. Lincoln is sharp enough to keep his plans to himself, and leave the papers to guess what is going on."[50]

Shaw's positive impression of Lincoln was reinforced through conversations with friends and acquaintances. He was pleased to overhear at a social gathering that the new secretary of state, William Seward—who had run against Lincoln for the Republican presidential nomination in 1860—believed the new president to be a "pure, honest-minded, patriotic man, and that whatever he did would be for the good of the country."[51] By early April 1861 Rob shared with his sister Susie, who was still attending school in Cambridge, "It is now almost certain that Mr. Lincoln is going to re-enforce the United States forts and in that case the Southerners will almost surely resist. All the vessels of the Navy are being got ready for sea, and several sail from here to-day." Shaw was confident that "something decisive is to be done."[52]

Lincoln chose to notify Charleston authorities that he intended only to resupply the Fort Sumter garrison with provisions. In doing so he placed the decision to initiate open hostilities into their hands. Regardless of the outcome, Shaw hoped Lincoln and the federal government would take a decisive stand against the secessionists and refuse to make "concessions." Doing otherwise would only postpone the inevitable: "We should have the same row over again at every Presidential election," he wrote, "and if we give them an inch they would be sure to want thousands of ells, as is proven by their history and our[s] for the last 50 years." For Shaw, the crisis presented an opportunity to take "a long step forward" and "turn out the pro-slavery government which has been disgracing us for so long."[53]

The opening salvos from Confederate guns surrounding Fort Sumter in the early morning hours of April 12, 1861, and Anderson's eventual surrender the following day marked the first "step forward." Having already enlisted in the 7th New York, Shaw was positioned to play a role in defeating the secessionists and defending the Constitution and the Union.

Whether his role would be small or large, only time would tell.

THREE

Goodbye, the Drum Is Beating

By midday on April 19, 1861, New Yorkers packed the streets to witness history. Word had spread that the elite 7th New York Militia Regiment was marching to war, and no one wanted to miss bidding farewell to husbands, sons, and brothers heading into the unknown. Their destination was Washington, DC, where a beleaguered new president desperately needed rescue. Fort Sumter's bombardment and Lincoln's call for 75,000 volunteers resulted in four more states joining the rebellion and the Confederacy, including Virginia, North Carolina, Tennessee, and Arkansas. The decision was quickly made to relocate the Confederacy's capital from Montgomery, Alabama, to Richmond, Virginia, in anticipation of the fighting to come. Lincoln's government now faced a nightmare scenario. Virginia controlled the southern approaches to Washington, while Maryland teetered on the brink of secession to the north. If Maryland fell, the federal capital would be trapped behind enemy lines—a prize ripe for Confederate capture.

A thousand men of the 7th New York assembled at Tompkins Market as the city erupted around them. Businesses were shuttered and offices emptied for the day. All New York seemed determined to witness this historic send-off. Broadway overflowed with the rich and poor, old and young, men and women from every neighborhood, plus entire militia units in full dress uniform. "Never before were the people roused to such a pitch of patriotic enthusiasm," the *New York Times* marveled. The Stars and Stripes blazed everywhere, "on housetops, on flagstaffs, on horses attached to all kinds of vehicles, on ropes stretched across the streets, on the masts of shipping in the harbors, on breastpins, on the lappets of coats [and] on the fronts of men's hats."[1]

The 7th New York marched behind a colorful Zouave escort whose exotic French North African uniforms and unconventional drill steps drew cheers from the crowd. The regiment itself cut a more traditional figure in gray uniforms and sky-blue overcoats. Confederate units would soon adopt similar gray uniforms across the South, causing confusion in some of the earliest battles. Each soldier carried a knapsack, a rolled blanket, extra boots, a mess-kit, and rations. Their weapons were 1856 rifle muskets fresh from the Harpers Ferry arsenal, the same armory John Brown had tried to seize just eighteen months earlier.[2]

Tears streamed down faces as loved ones marched past in perfect formation. "Was there ever such an ovation?" marveled playwright Fitz-James O'Brien, marching with the regiment. Another soldier would never forget how "the marble walls of Broadway were never before rent with such cheers as greeted us."[3] The *New York Times* declared the day a "triumphant vindication of the loyalty of our citizens' thus promptly volunteering to the hardships of a soldier's life."[4]

Within the regiment's ranks marched Robert Gould Shaw, just another privileged son whose merchant family had granted him leave from business duties to answer the country's call for volunteers. Around him stepped dozens of similar young men, heirs to shipping fortunes and banking empires, who had traded counting houses for rifles. Shaw marveled at the mob's intensity. "The crowd and enthusiasm were tremendous. The people would hardly let us pass, actually catching hold of our hands and slapping us on the back, yelling and screaming like wild men."[5] Shaw savored the crowd's wild enthusiasm as they surged up Broadway, but darker thoughts may have crept in. Would those shots fired in Charleston Harbor lead to full-scale war? Was this triumphant parade the beginning of something far bloodier than anyone could imagine?

At the Hudson River ferry to Jersey City, Shaw witnessed heartbreaking scenes of "tender farewells." Tears flowed as fathers clasped sons' hands perhaps for the last time, while mothers, sweethearts, and sisters planted desperate kisses on beloved cheeks. Shaw watched alone. His family remained in Cuba, and for the first time since enlisting, he may have regretted leaving before their return. While other young men savored final embraces, Shaw would be heading toward his first taste of war—and possibly death—with no loved ones to send him off.

The night before his departure, Shaw had wrestled with guilt in his family's Staten Island home, trying to explain his sudden decision in a letter to his mother. "It is very hard to go off without bidding you goodbye," he confessed, "and the only thing that upsets me, in the least, is the thought of how you will feel when you find me so unexpectedly gone." He may have pinned his hopes on Sarah's abolitionist principles. Surely her sense of honor and duty would help alleviate some of her anxiety and concern.[6]

Shaw tried to ease his mother's fears with his own optimistic military analysis. The loyalty of Virginia and Maryland remained uncertain, but "if we can get into Washington, before Virginia makes trouble, we shall not have much fighting." Finally, he appealed to Sarah's own sense of patriotism. "Won't it be grand to meet the men from all the States, East and West, down there, ready to fight for the country, as the old fellows did in the Revolution?" Before closing his letter, Shaw assured his family that he would "come back safe."[7]

Though Shaw wished he could bid farewell to his family in person, once he stepped out the door, he never looked back. In a family filled with passionate reformers dedicated to social and racial justice, Shaw embraced military service as a calling that might finally bring meaning and purpose to his life, even if he did not yet understand the war's deeper meaning or what his role in the Union victory might be. But for the first time in his life, marching with the 7th New York through cheering crowds, Robert Gould Shaw knew exactly where he belonged. He may have been desperate to escape his gilded cage. But now, surrounded by comrades and purpose, he was finally free.

Colonel Lefferts had planned to march the 7th New York straight through Baltimore to Washington, but mob violence changed everything. That very morning, pro-Confederate rioters had attacked the 6th Massachusetts Infantry Regiment, leaving four soldiers and dozens of civilians dead in the streets. Northern newspapers noted the bitter irony of Massachusetts blood being spilled again on April 19—eighty-six years to the day after the opening battles of the American Revolution at Lexington and Concord. Rather than risk another massacre, the 7th New York was diverted to Annapolis via an overcrowded steamer. Shaw found himself "piled together like pigs" with his comrades on deck, grateful only for pleasant weather as they sailed toward an uncertain reception in Maryland.[8] The honeymoon phase of the war was already over.

The regiment arrived in Annapolis on the evening of April 22 without incident, apart from having to assist a steamer transporting the 8th Massachusetts Infantry Regiment, which had run aground in Chesapeake Bay.

Shaw found Annapolis a "lovely place." Its capitol dome overlooking the harbor appeared to be a smaller version of Boston's State House dome. The city carried revolutionary symbolism. George Washington had surrendered his commission in the Maryland State House in 1783, choosing republic over empire. The 7th New York encamped in an old War of 1812 fort near the Naval Academy, where Southern secession had already carved deep wounds. Shaw estimated that only 120 midshipmen remained after the mass resignations of young Southerners, who had abandoned their oaths by joining the rebellion, just as Southerners had done at West Point. Those who remained impressed Shaw with their "dark navy-cloth, well-fitting jackets and trousers" and crisp drill precision. "I have seen some very handsome and fine faces," Shaw noted, studying these young men who had chosen Union over their native states.[9]

Annapolis fell without a shot being fired, and the enemy remained invisible, fueling dangerous optimism among the Union troops. "I am determined to stand by the stars and stripes to the bitter end," one soldier wrote home with confidence that would soon prove tragically naive. "We will show these traitors, before we are through with them, that we are as brave as they; I believe God and the right are on our side, and we must succeed."[10] Shaw shared that confidence completely, but sixty miles of hostile Maryland territory still separated them from Washington. Though the state had not officially seceded, Baltimore's bloody streets and reports of guerrilla attacks made every mile dangerous.

With three days' rations in hand, the regiment marched out on April 24 into hostile territory. Shaw's company drew the dangerous assignment of securing a railroad depot halfway to Washington, while Confederate saboteurs prowled the countryside. The march became a nightmare of vigilance and exhaustion. Damaged tracks forced them to proceed on foot with rifles loaded, ready for ambush "at any moment." Many in the 7th New York caught their first sight of enslaved people as they emerged to observe the uniformed men march by. Twenty-four hours of continuous marching, combined with the sleepless nights since leaving New York, pushed the men beyond endurance.

"We actually fell asleep standing up," Shaw recalled, "and scores of the men would drop their pieces and just catch themselves as they were toppling over."[11] Their vigilance paid off. The regiment reached the railroad junction without encountering the guerrillas who had terrorized other units, and within hours they had secured transportation for the final twenty miles to Washington.

The train's arrival from Washington was the first sign that the capital still stood. Until that moment, as one soldier admitted, "we did not know whether our Uncle Sam was still a resident of the capital." Everyone cheered when the train finally entered the city and the Stars and Stripes were seen flying atop the Capitol dome.[12]

Pierre L'Enfant's vision for the capital city of Washington, DC, was agonizingly slow to take shape. Charles Dickens captured the disappointment of many travelers when he visited in 1842. It is "sometimes called the city of Magnificent Distances," he wrote mockingly, "but it might with greater propriety be termed the City of Magnificent Intentions." The city had "spacious avenues, that began in nothing, and lead nowhere; streets, mile-long, that only want houses, roads, and inhabitants; public buildings that need but a public to be complete; and ornaments of great thoroughfares, which only lack great thoroughfares to ornament."[13] By 1861, Washington's residents had gradually filled the city's outer reaches, but its beating heart remained the narrow strip of Pennsylvania Avenue connecting the White House to Capitol Hill. Respectable hotels—Willard's, the National, the St. Charles, and Kirkwood House—lined this unpaved thoroughfare alongside shops and businesses. The capital's raw frontier character showed on windy days when dust clouds forced pedestrians to cover their faces with handkerchiefs.[14]

Wealthy mansions stood within sight of Washington's underbelly, most notoriously "Murder Bay," a maze of alleyways where prostitutes, pickpockets, and pimps conducted business from clapboard shanties. Juvenile delinquents and other lowlifes crowded the saloons, creating a dangerous netherworld just blocks from the halls of power.

Progress and decay battled for Washington's identity. The new Smithsonian Institution graced the Mall's northern edge near the unfinished Washington Monument, a symbol of American ambition reaching skyward. But their promise was compromised by the Washington City Canal's overwhelming stench. What canal boosters had envisioned in 1815 as a commercial artery connecting the White House to the Capitol had become an open sewer by the 1850s. A US Army engineer described it as a "receptacle not only of the excrement and sediment of the sewers, but also of the surface drainage." One horrified observer counted "70 distinct stinks" rising from its fetid waters. With no garbage collection, residents dumped trash and dead animals directly into the canal. Disease flourished in this toxic environment, and newspapers routinely reported cholera, typhoid, and smallpox outbreaks while fires periodically swept through neighborhoods.[15]

Each December, Washington transformed from sleepy backwater to bustling political theater when Congress reconvened. Young bachelors rented rooms in boarding houses while established politicians brought their families to the social whirlwind that would determine the capital's hierarchy for months. The real power brokers were the senators' and congressmen's wives, whose invitation lists made front-page news—inclusion meant influence, exclusion meant political death. Meanwhile, in hotel bars and restaurants throughout the city, politicians cut deals with lobbyists seeking legislative favors and ambitious men hunting for federal appointments.[16]

The Capitol Building loomed over Washington's skyline as democracy's grandest symbol and its most fragile promise. Throughout the 1850s, as Congress fought over slavery, the building itself remained unfinished, its massive dome still under construction in a project overseen by Mississippi Senator Jefferson Davis. Lincoln's election had paralyzed even this symbolic work. With the spread of secession, the formation of the Confederacy, and the firing on Fort Sumter, construction crews abandoned their scaffolding. No one knew whether the construction of the dome would ever be completed or whether the nation itself would survive.

After disembarking from the train, the men of the 7th New York marched directly to the White House for an audience with President Lincoln and his family. That night they bedded down in the House chamber itself, now converted into barracks. Shaw marveled at the surreal scene. Each man had "a desk and easy-chair," though many ignored the furniture for blankets on the marble floor.[17] Architect Thomas Walter watched in horror as four thousand soldiers transformed his "magnificent building" into a fortress. Despite Shaw's reverence for the Capitol's grandeur, such a large number of young men with rifles inevitably wreaked havoc on democracy's temple. Elmer Ellsworth's New York Zouaves were the worst offenders, using their bayonets to carve up a Democratic senator's desk and rigging ropes from the unfinished dome as swings. Basement kitchens filled the building with smoke that "invaded the Library and spread soot through the stacks," while trash, lice, and vermin contaminated both chambers.[18]

The Capitol's physical damage paled beside its symbolic power. For most volunteers, including Shaw, this marked their first glimpse of the nation's capital. Many had never traveled beyond their home states. The sight of flags throughout the city, the unfinished dome and monuments, and the White House itself stirred powerful emotions in the young men who had otherwise only read about these landmarks in newspapers. More profound still was the human connection. Soldiers from Massachusetts, New York, and Pennsylvania shared stories and meals, discovering their common cause despite their regional differences. In the House and Senate chambers, they staged mock debates and reenacted the famous speeches that had driven the nation to war.

On April 26, 1861, the 7th New York was mustered into the service of the United States for thirty days. "We raised our right hands," recalled one private "and repeated the solemn obligation in the name of God to be faithful soldiers to our country."[19] The ceremony was attended by Lincoln as well as by the secretary of state and the secretary of war. The president's attendance offered Shaw another opportunity to size up the new leader. "A boy came by with a pail of water for us, and the President took a great swig from it as it passed." Rather than be shocked by such behavior, Shaw "couldn't help thinking of the immense responsibility he has on his shoulders, as he stood there laughing and talking." Shaw also noted that he had "seen many uglier men"—an observation likely made in response to the many unflattering physical reports of the president that filled the newspapers.[20]

A few days later, Shaw and Pvt. Rufus King—the son of Columbia College's president—received the honor of a private audience with Lincoln. They found the president drowning in correspondence, "perfectly covered with letters & papers of every description." Despite the chaos, Lincoln received them warmly. Shaw studied the president's face with fascination, finding it "very striking" and "pleasanter or more kind-hearted looking" than expected. Most surprisingly for a young Bostonian aristocrat, he detected no trace of "anything like the Western twang or slang" in Lincoln's speech.[21] Shaw's fascination with Lincoln's speech reflected the president's carefully cultivated campaign image as a rough-hewn rail-splitter more comfortable with an axe than with a law book. Meeting the real Lincoln—articulate, refined, unmistakably presidential—shattered those frontier stereotypes.[22]

Shaw's thirty days in Washington passed peacefully. Camp life revolved around endless drills and routine military duties, but the 7th New York's privileged background required unique adjustments from the men who had largely taken their pampered lives for granted. By May 4, the regiment had moved two miles north to Meridian Hill on the road toward Harpers Ferry. Shaw shared a tent with five comrades and quickly learned that food packages from home became "common property," a jarring lesson in military equality for one of Boston's elite sons. The transformation was both comic and profound. As one private observed, "Fellows who would at Delmonico's have sent back a turban de volaille aux truffles because the truffles were rough, here cheerfully took their place in file between decks, plates and tin cups in hand, in order to get an insufficient piece of beef and a vision of coffee."[23] All in all, Shaw took these challenges in stride.

Washington forced Shaw to confront what this war truly meant. Before enlisting, he had viewed the slavery crisis primarily through a narrow selfish lens. Would sectional conflict disrupt his personal plans? Like many privileged Northerners, he had denounced the slaveocracy's power and corruption while secretly hoping for any settlement that would restore his comfortable routine. Shaw had even been willing to accept Southern independence if it meant peace. But something fundamental shifted for him during those thirty days in the capital. Surrounded by soldiers from across the North, sleeping in democracy's halls, meeting Lincoln himself, Shaw was becoming committed to seeing the fight through to its conclusion and "enlisting for the war."[24] "Was there ever so much enthusiasm seen in the country?" he asked his sister Josephine. "Of course it will die out somewhere in time but still it will do a great deal of good. It is a pleasant feeling to be here bullying the Southerners."[25]

Shaw never penned deep reflections on liberty or the importance of union, but the "enthusiasm" and "pleasant feelings" that he experienced in Washington revealed something profound. Like most of the volunteers who would enlist before conscription began in 1863, Shaw now believed the American experiment was worth fighting for. Everything in the capital had contributed to this transformation, including the sight of men from distant states answering Lincoln's call and the deep sense of purpose that pervaded the streets of the capital. Shaw could not yet articulate this new sense of duty, but he certainly could feel it. For many young men, including Shaw, the rebellion struck at everything their grandfathers' military service during the American Revolution had secured. Confederate slaveholding aristocrats threatened not just the Union but democracy itself in America and around the world.[26]

As Shaw's thirty-day enlistment expired, he faced a crucial decision about his military future. Rather than re-enlist as a private, he sought an officer's

Men from the 7th New York pose outside their tent at Camp Cameron in Washington, DC, May 1861. Shaw spent one month in Washington, DC, as a private in the 7th New York Militia Regiment, following the firing on Fort Sumter. During his brief stay, he had an interview with President Lincoln and the opportunity to meet fellow recruits from around the country. *Courtesy Library of Congress.*

commission, a rank he believed befitted his social station. The question was whether to pursue this through one of the many volunteer regiments being raised or via the regular army. Volunteer units troubled him with their "want of discipline," yet he recognized that they "will see more service & be the most prominent in the war." However, the regular army offered better training and the option to "resign or keep his commission" after peace returned, a calculation that suggests Shaw was considering a military career.[27]

Shaw accepted a commission as a second lieutenant in the 2nd Massachusetts Infantry Regiment. The unit was one of the first three-year regiments raised and was organized and led by Col. George H. Gordon and Lieut. Col. George L. Andrews, both West Point graduates and strict disciplinarians. Gordon brought combat experience from the Mexican-American War, where he had been breveted for gallantry at Cerro Gordo. Like many peacetime officers, Gordon resigned after Mexico to study law at Harvard and to practice in Boston. Now that the crisis had called him back to uniform, he traded legal briefs for military command.[28]

The 2nd Massachusetts resembled a Harvard reunion more than a typical regiment. Shaw served alongside former classmates Francis "Crownie" Crowninshield, Wilder Dwight, Samuel Miller Quincy, Robert Morris Copeland, Henry Lee Higginson, Charles J. Mills, James Savage, and his close friend Charles "Charley" Morse. These young Brahmins would forge unbreakable bonds over the coming eighteen months of shared hardship and danger. Their elite education fostered both confidence and arrogance. Based on their perceived superiority of breeding, character, and social position, they expected unquestioning obedience from enlisted men. War, they believed, would only enhance their status, proving their fitness to lead both in military ranks and postwar society.[29]

The first recruits arrived at Camp Andrew (named in honor of Massachusetts Governor John Andrew) located in West Roxbury, just outside Boston on May 11.[30] Shaw arrived a few days later and joined the regiment on the familiar grounds of Brook Farm to begin learning the duties of an officer as well as to begin the training of new recruits for life in the military. While he found it "odd to be back at Brook Farm" his memory of the community likely extended little beyond the recognition of the physical landscape and the few buildings that remained.[31] Perhaps Shaw acknowledged the strange tension between a site that was once used to model a utopian community and the possibilities of social reform and its current occupants, now training to kill their fellow Americans. Memories of the sounds of men and women sharing in the labor of farming or gathering for a concert and lecture were now replaced by the sights and sounds of officers barking orders, the formation of men engaged in their daily drills, and the crack of rifles during target practice.

The military camp imposed martial order on Brook Farm's once-boundless idealism. Tents stretched in perfect rows across the slope, bisected by a regulation street that would have appalled the community's free-spirited founders. Shaw and his fellow officers claimed the high ground "behind where the Pilgrim house stood," the building that had once housed the community's laundry, tailor shop, and newspaper.[32] Cookhouses provided meals for the men, and the regimental band was housed in separate quarters. The drill field was located adjacent to the tents, while a short walk led to a peaceful hollow where the chaplain, Alonzo H. Quint, conducted Sunday worship. It would have very likely been the only activity familiar to Brook Farm's original residents.[33]

Shaw may not have remembered much of his time at Brook Farm as a child, but his return as an officer instilled in him a level of confidence and sense of purpose that thus far had eluded him. Shaw's optimism stemmed from the "great difference between the life of a private and that of an officer." He now enjoyed the comfort of a cot to sleep on and "servants in abundance from among the men." As the regiment continued to fill up, Shaw enjoyed the "great many acquaintances of mine at the camp" as well as a steady stream of visitors.[34] Visits with members of his extended family, who lived nearby, punctuated the few moments when duty did not call. "I dreamt last night," Shaw shared with his father with some enthusiasm, "that this regiment was sworn into service for forty-seven years!"[35]

Whether Shaw would succeed as an officer remained an open question. Being a Boston Brahmin guaranteed nothing on the drill field, where competence mattered more than bloodline. Shaw first needed to learn the responsibilities of an officer, much of which centered around the organization of roughly one hundred men under the command of a captain. His duties as a second lieutenant were extensive. Shaw was required to take daily roll calls, conduct inspections of the troops, assist with record-keeping, oversee the posting of guards in camp and pickets when in the field as well as the command patrols and fatigue parties. Most importantly, he assisted with the drilling of the company. For this, Shaw could have consulted any number of military manuals such as the *Revised United States Army Regulations of 1861* or *The Ordnance Manual for the Use of the Officers of the United States Army*. But mastering a manual constituted only a tiny part of the challenges associated with military command.

Camp Andrew imposed military clockwork on young men accustomed to leisure. Reveille shattered the dawn at 4:45 a.m., followed by roll call and inspection thirty-five minutes later. Surgeon's call and breakfast came by 7:00 a.m., then drilling from 8:30 to 10:30. Dinner sounded at 1:00 p.m., followed by camp cleaning and equipment maintenance before another drill session until 6:00 p.m. The evening included a roll call and parade ground formation, followed by supper. After that, and at the end of an exhausting day, soldiers could read letters from home, socialize, and tend to personal needs before

Shaw in 1861, after being commissioned as a second lieutenant in the 2nd Massachusetts Infantry Regiment, where he served until he assumed command of the 54th Massachusetts in early 1863. During his time with the 2nd Massachusetts, he experienced three major battles, confronted the loss of close friends, and sought out every opportunity to advance in rank and responsibility. *Courtesy Library of Congress.*

tattoo at 9:00 p.m. and taps at 9:30 p.m., having only to repeat the same cycle over again the next day.[36]

The volunteers flooding the military camps in 1861 were quintessentially American. They were individualistic, highly suspicious of authority, and protective of their democratic rights. These citizen-soldiers faced an unnatural, but necessary, transformation into soldiers. Military discipline demanded, as one historian has noted, that they "forgo their survival instincts, their democratic prerogatives, and even their sense of individuality."[37] Shaw faced an impossible timeline for turning civilians into soldiers with war looming. His family's pedigree meant nothing to the men who judged officers by their competence, not their bloodline. Trial and error became his teacher as he juggled his competing roles as motivator, instructor, and disciplinarian. Every day brought new challenges, including resolving conflicts, managing bruised egos, and building unit cohesion. Shaw's success hinged on attaining a delicate balance. On the one hand he needed to demonstrate genuine concern for his men's welfare while demanding absolute obedience to orders on the other.[38]

Recruits needed to learn how to march and follow a list of orders with the utmost precision, but Shaw was also responsible for the appearance of the men under his care. Clothes must always be clean; hats should be properly fitted and "worn squarely with some style," while coat buttons "must be tight and in place." Beards and mustaches were to be properly groomed, while the "hair must be neatly brushed and neatly trimmed." Shaw was expected to instill in his men a "personal pride in their personal appearances" and to "present at all times a bold, clear cut, well set up military experience."[39]

Shaw's prejudices showed most clearly in his treatment of Irish recruits. "We have a good many Irishmen in our company," he wrote his mother, "who were very hard to manage at first, but they are getting toned down by degrees." Worse still, he claimed, "The Irishmen seem sometimes utterly unable to learn or understand anything." These ugly observations reflected Boston's virulent anti-Irish sentiment. Famine refugees flooding American cities had triggered a nativist hysteria about Catholic "leeches" overwhelming hospitals and poorhouses. Many Bostonians, including Shaw's social circle, supported outright deportation to stem what they saw as diseased, dependent masses. Shaw never advocated such extremes, but his casual distinction between Irish recruits and "Americans" reveals a similar mindset.[40] These attitudes reflect Shaw's unquestioned belief in natural hierarchy. Providence had ordained some men to command and others to obey, with young Boston elite men like himself clearly destined for leadership roles.[41]

By mid-June, Camp Andrew buzzed with preparation for war. Wagons, horses, equipment, and supplies streamed in daily, all clear signs that the regiment's peaceful training days were numbered.[42] On July 1, 1861, the regiment received its Massachusetts state flag bearing the inscription, "We bear the flag and keep step to the music of the Union."[43] Shaw took pride in his company's rapid transformation. After just weeks of training, he found the recruits "remarkably well disciplined for the short time we have been here." The harsh reality of life in the military had shocked most recruits. "Most of them find soldiering very different work from what they expected," he informed his mother, "but having been sworn in, they seem resigned to the hard work & army rations."[44]

As the regiment's departure date grew nearer, the recruits embraced opportunities to visit with family who were able to travel to Camp Andrew. Shaw's parents remained on Staten Island. As he had done before departing with the 7th New York, Shaw tried to reassure them that he would be safe. "After all when you look at it coolly," he opined, "there is not much more danger in war than in peace at least for officers."[45] Shaw predicted that disease would kill more soldiers than bullets, which would prove grimly accurate, though in July 1861 he had little evidence to support this claim. No major battle had yet tested either army's mettle, and Shaw surely understood that Confederate volunteers were drilling just as intensively as his Massachusetts recruits. The war had remained remarkably bloodless apart from two ominous exceptions that hinted at the carnage to come.

On May 24, 1861, Col. Elmer Ellsworth was killed while trying to remove a Confederate flag atop a hotel in Alexandria, Virginia, that could be seen from the White House. Ellsworth's death shocked the nation and Lincoln, whom Ellsworth had briefly clerked under in his Springfield law office. More personally devastating for Shaw was the death of his close friend Theodore Winthrop during a skirmish at Big Bethel on June 10. Winthrop's loss forced Shaw to confront his own mortality with a characteristic bravado that captures how many volunteers viewed the war at this early stage. "I find that thinking continually of the possibility of getting hit accustoms one so to the idea, that it doesn't seem so bad, after all." It was an observation that he would soon be forced to reassess.[46]

As Frank and Sarah Shaw watched their son prepare for war again, they fought their own battle for the conflict's moral meaning. Like fellow abolitionists, they saw the struggle as a conflict of good versus evil, of freedom against bondage. Restoring the Union was not enough; slavery itself had to die if America was to be redeemed. Most loyal Americans disagreed. They would fight the Confederacy to preserve the Union, but they resisted waging war against slavery itself. Lincoln shared this cautious approach; he was committed to saving what he called the "last best hope of earth" without alienating the slaveholding Border States, which remained tenuously in the Union. Any premature move toward emancipation might drive Maryland, Delaware, Kentucky, and Missouri into Confederate arms. Lincoln himself maintained, "I hope to have God on my side, but I must have Kentucky." But abolitionists like the Shaws saw opportunity in this uncertainty. They believed they could "nudge the nation onto higher ground from inside the war effort, transforming a war for Union into a crusade for human freedom."[47]

For the Shaws, the war became a coordinated family campaign. While Rob trained for combat, Frank wielded political influence to shape military policy toward escaped slaves. By 1862, he had joined the National Freedman's Relief Association that helped African Americans navigate the treacherous transition from bondage to freedom.[48] Sarah and her daughters transformed their home into a war production center, joining the Women's Association of Relief and the US Sanitary Commission. Days blurred together rolling bandages, cutting shirts, and organizing supply shipments to soldiers desperate for basic necessities. The Shaw home became a neighborhood headquarters for the war effort. Josephine recalled "giving out work" to as many as twelve women daily, their elegant parlors now buzzing with purposeful activity. The war was teaching even privileged families about sacrifice and service. As Josephine wrote in her diary, "This war will purify the country of some of its extravagance and selfishness."[49]

The Shaws were not alone in their military commitment. The war had mobilized their entire extended family. Henry Sturgis Russell and George Russell served alongside Shaw in the 2nd Massachusetts, while cousins Theodore Lyman, Charles Russell Lowell, James Jackson Lowell, and William Forbes filled the ranks of other regiments.

The men of the 2nd Massachusetts enjoyed an extra forty-five minutes of sleep on July 8. This was to be an extra busy and demanding day as the regiment was scheduled to leave camp. The men packed their belongings, broke down their tents, loaded them into wagons, and assembled into formation by 10:00 a.m. "The regiment was drawn up in line of battle," reported the *Boston Daily Advertiser,* "and presented a fine and soldierly appearance. Their movements all indicated a high state of efficiency and drill."[50]

Families crowded the parade ground for final farewells as the regiment began its slow march to West Roxbury Station. The weight of responsibility must have pressed heavily on Colonel Gordon when one family member pleaded with him to "return again in safety all these young men to their homes."[51] In Boston, the regiment marched down Tremont and Beacon Streets in a procession thick with memory. Shaw passed his own boyhood home before reaching the Common, where local citizens had prepared a farewell feast. Families claimed their final moments with sons, husbands, and brothers in scenes of barely controlled emotion. Henry Newton Comey captured the day's painful goodbye with his family: "I tried hard to assume the role of a brave soldier, but I knew my eyes were wet with tears."[52]

The regiment arrived in New York City early the following morning and marched to City Hall Park, where the Astor Hotel had prepared a feast fit for heroes. After weeks on army rations, the soldiers marveled at the abundance. One soldier recalled, "There seemed to be no limit to the eggs, bacon, ham, steaks and coffee for this hungry army."[53] The breakfast offered Shaw time for a brief reunion with his family before boarding the side-wheeler *Flora* for their brief journey across the upper harbor to a waiting railcar at Elizabethport, New Jersey. As the steamer passed the Staten Island ferry that was carrying his parents and sisters homeward, Shaw climbed atop the paddle box and waved his handkerchief in a final farewell.[54]

The painful separation carried one consolation. Shaw left home knowing that his family fully supported his decision to fight for the Union and that he carried with him their hopes for a redeemed nation through the destruction of slavery. Whether he would live up to those expectations, however, was not yet determined. Yet, Frank and Sarah harbored quiet hope that war's crucible might finally forge their son into the moral leader they had always believed he could become. The question hovering over the family farewell was whether their son would merely serve the Union or help transform it.

FOUR

We Shall Have Much More Soldiering to Do Than We Expected When We Started

As the train rumbled south through New Jersey farmland and Pennsylvania's rolling Lehigh and Cumberland Valleys, Shaw watched the picturesque landscapes scroll past his window. The journey carried his regiment over the Susquehanna River, past Harrisburg, and finally toward Hagerstown, Maryland. For many of the men in the 2nd Massachusetts this was already the farthest distance from home they had ever traveled.

Shaw's second passage through Maryland revealed how fragile Union loyalty remained. Though Lincoln's crackdown on civil unrest had kept the state from seceding, Confederate sympathies simmered beneath the surface. "The people of Hagerstown seem very loyal now," Shaw observed warily, "because a Connecticut regiment is quartered there, but we were told that a little while ago there were a good many secessionists among them."[1] From

Hagerstown, the regiment marched to Williamsport and waded across the Potomac River into enemy territory. Virginia soil felt different beneath their boots. By July 12, 1861, they had reached Martinsburg, poised at the entrance to the Shenandoah Valley.

The Shenandoah Valley's 140 miles of picturesque farmland stretched from Rockbridge County to the Potomac River, cradled between the Allegheny and Blue Ridge Mountains. The Massanutten Ridge split the valley for forty miles, dividing the North and South forks of the Shenandoah River until they reunited at Front Royal and joined the Potomac at Harpers Ferry. The Valley's peculiar geography created confusing directions—travelers moved "down the Valley" heading north and "up the Valley" heading south as elevation increased. Thomas Jefferson once stood transfixed at Harpers Ferry, declaring the region "worth a voyage across the Atlantic." The Potomac's passage through the Blue Ridge, he wrote in his *Notes on the State of Virginia,* offered "one of the most stupendous scenes in Nature."[2]

Generations of inhabitants, beginning with Native Americans, took advantage of the Shenandoah Valley's beauty, rich soil, abundant water, and mild climate. In the eighteenth century, German and Scotch Irish families from Pennsylvania joined eastern Virginia planters, creating an unstable frontier buffer against French and Indian raids from the western mountains. By 1860, slavery had woven itself into the Valley's economy. Though large plantations were rare, enslaved labor powered railroads, farms, industries, and businesses throughout the region. Valley residents initially sought a middle ground by voting for Constitutional Union Party candidate John Bell in the presidential election of 1860. Lincoln's call for volunteers after Fort Sumter shattered that neutrality. Virginia's secession vote transformed the moderate Valley population into a Confederate stronghold almost overnight, its residents now committed to defending the very institution many had hoped to avoid confronting.[3]

Military officials on both sides quickly recognized the Shenandoah Valley's strategic importance, especially as an avenue for Confederate offensives into Maryland and possibly even Pennsylvania—offensives that could potentially be shielded by the Blue Ridge Mountains. The region witnessed a great deal of violence and destruction throughout the war, with towns like Winchester and Harpers Ferry changing hands repeatedly as armies swept back and forth through the Valley.

Shaw's eleven months in the Shenandoah Valley transformed him from a naive volunteer into a hardened veteran. Like so many others, the experience shattered his comfortable assumptions on numerous fronts. Runaway slaves fleeing to Union lines forced him to confront emancipation as both a moral imperative and a military necessity. Hostile Confederate civilians challenged his notions about the rules of war, including the question of whether armies should target those who aided the enemy. Most brutally, the regiment's baptism by fire in 1862 taught him that courage meant watching friends die while continuing to fight. Shaw processed these revelations through letters to his family and in late-night conversations with fellow officers who had become his closest confidants during long months of boredom punctuated by moments of sheer terror on the battlefield.

The regiment was assigned to Gen. Robert Patterson's command, which numbered roughly 18,000 men. Patterson, who hailed from Pennsylvania, had served in both the War of 1812 and Mexican-American War. Patterson's men had already experienced combat in early July 1861, by chasing Confederate Gen. Joseph E. Johnston through the Shenandoah Valley, culminating in a small but encouraging victory at Falling Waters in Berkeley County. Shaw eagerly anticipated his first taste of combat. After months of drills and theory, he was finally ready to test himself against a real enemy.[4]

A few weeks later, another skirmish gave General Johnston the opportunity he needed to slip away from Patterson's army to join Gen. P. G. T. Beauregard near the Manassas railroad junction. Their combined Confederate armies smashed Brig. Gen. Irvin McDowell's federal assault on July 21, sending Union troops fleeing back to Washington's defenses in the war's first major battle at Bull Run. Shaw watched the disaster unfold from a distance, recognizing Patterson's catastrophic failure. "The linking of the two forces probably was the means of their gaining the day," he concluded with bitter accuracy.[5]

The 2nd Massachusetts settled around Harpers Ferry as the nation absorbed Bull Run's shocking lesson that the war would likely last longer than first anticipated. The lull in fighting gave Shaw his first education in hostile occupation, where every civilian interaction crackled with mistrust and hatred. Virginia's residents made their feelings abundantly clear. In Middleway, locals "scowled at our flag and gave us disgusting looks," Henry Comey recalled. In Charlestown, Virginia, where John Brown had met his fate in December 1859, "the women scowled and sp[a]t as we marched into town," their contempt as visceral as their loyalty to the Confederate cause.[6]

Harpers Ferry offered a warmer reception. Colonel Gordon ordered the regiment to enter "with all the pomp and circumstance" they could muster, and his instincts proved correct. A small group of Unionist women had sewn an American flag specifically for the first federal regiment to liberate their town. Gordon accepted their gift with ceremony, attempting to heal sectional wounds through shared history. "Our fathers and your fathers fought together to establish the government which the old Star-Spangled Banner represents," he declared to the assembled crowd.[7]

Shaw admired the beauty surrounding his new camp site and described it as "the prettiest encampment we have had."[8] Many of the men were overwhelmed by the sounds of the confluence of the Potomac and Shenandoah Rivers as well as by the sheer size of Maryland and Bolivar Heights, which enclosed Harpers Ferry and rendered it difficult, if not impossible, to defend. The beauty of the surroundings stood in sharp contrast with the destruction that greeted the regiment. Only a few of the buildings that had once housed the federal arsenal remained after the Confederates torched the facility and carried off any machinery that could still be used to manufacture small arms and other weapons. The covered bridge that spanned the Potomac from the Maryland side had also been destroyed, along with some of the tracks.

Even after close to two years, the ghost of John Brown continued to cast a shadow over the town and the surrounding area. One local resident admitted, "We have not dared to command our slaves since John Brown came." Maj. Wilder Dwight observed, "The man's name is a terror and a bitterness to them."[9] The arrival of the Union army likely stoked fear among slaveowners and non-slaveowners alike that another slave rebellion was on the horizon. Reminders of Brown's failed attempt to incite slaves to rebellion were all around, including at the engine house near the tip of the peninsula—now being used as a guardhouse—where Brown made his final stand.[10]

Shaw's parents and many of their abolitionist friends revered John Brown as a martyr and considered the engine house where he made his last stand sacred ground.[11] They must have been disappointed by their son's coldly tactical assessment of Brown's final refuge. Shaw noted the "loop-holes" for firing and the "marks of musket-balls on the walls," before delivering a damning military critique: "It seems to be the worst place he [Brown] could have chosen to defend against an attack," Shaw insisted, "for when the doors are shut, it is like a brick box, as all the windows are high up, and his loop-holes are so small that they give no range at all to the men firing through them."[12] Shaw's visit to the engine house failed to inspire any thoughts about the righteousness of Brown's cause and sacrifice or the morality of slavery. Instead, he offered his parents little more than an assessment of the building's poor defensive assets.

Rather than focus on Brown, the freedom fighter, Shaw chose to highlight his own commitment to his new role as a military officer. Shaw took his responsibilities seriously, beginning with the regiment's earliest days at Brook Farm. In the wake of McDowell's defeat at Bull Run, the organization and training of the army under the new command of Gen. George B. McClellan took on a new urgency. Shaw maintained that "a great change in the army" was needed.[13] Support for McClellan stemmed from his West Point training and experience in the Mexican-American War as well as from a series of small victories against a relatively unknown Confederate general by the name of Robert E. Lee in western Virginia. Despite McClellan's Democratic leanings and his parents' objections, Shaw remained confident that the newly christened Army of the Potomac could be quickly molded into a tough fighting machine.[14]

Shaw blamed undisciplined volunteers for hampering both the Army of the Shenandoah and the Army of the Potomac. He took pride that his 2nd Massachusetts was "well trained and disciplined" compared to other units whose men "seem to do just as they please & go about wherever they want to."[15] While guarding a Potomac ferry crossing, Shaw witnessed military discipline collapse before his eyes. The 5th Connecticut Infantry Regiment's river crossing turned into a drunken disaster as "a great many of the men wandered off and got drunk." Their officers proved utterly helpless, eventually begging Shaw to "send their own men to their quarters, and to lock the unruly ones up in our guard-house!" The humiliating spectacle confirmed Shaw's rigid views on military hierarchy. Without absolute officer authority, he concluded, armies became armed mobs. "If officers are to have no more command over their men than these gentlemen did, we might as well be without them."[16]

Shaw and his fellow elite officers saw punishment as essential to controlling the army's immigrants and "roughs" who, it was believed, lacked the self-discipline and moral fiber necessary for victory. In their view, harsh military justice could force manly virtues onto men who had not been born with them.[17] Military punishment in Shaw's army was deliberately brutal. Officers employed a range of punishments, including confinement in guardhouses, extra duties, suspension by thumbs with feet off the ground, tying soldiers to barrels, and gagging. Shaw documented these punishments in shocking detail for his family, describing one soldier tied to a tree branch "by the thumbs about 15 feet from the earth" as "fearful torture."[18] His casual tone when describing such cruelty revealed how quickly he had absorbed the military's dehumanizing culture.

Shaw erupted when a Boston newspaper criticized the 2nd Massachusetts for treating soldiers "much too severely." In an angry letter to his sister written on September 17, 1861, he defended strict military discipline as essential to reinforcing wayward soldiers' "sense of duty." Worse, he worried that such "imaginary wrongs" reported in newspapers might incite already "discontented ones" to "rebellious points."[19] Shaw desperately wanted his family and others back home to acknowledge that victory would come about only if the volunteers could be shaped into a fighting force that was prepared for all the challenges of military life, especially battle.

The other issue that occupied Shaw's attention was the War Department's directive that allowed the men of each company to elect all officers up to the rank of captain in the event of a vacancy. Shaw and his fellow officers feared the implications of this order as it raised the very real possibility that men would be elected for reasons that had little or nothing to do with their qualifications for a command position. The attempt to instill some sense of democratic values through the election of officers threatened Shaw's sense of entitlement and social standing within the army. Wilder Dwight captured the concerns of many of his fellow officers: "To-day our army is crippled by the ideas of equality and independence which have colored the whole life of our people. Men elect their officers, and then expect them to behave themselves! Obedience is permissive, not compelled, and the radical basis is wrong."[20] For Shaw, democracy in the ranks was not progress. It was chaos that undermined the natural order that he had been raised to defend. The possibility that Irish immigrants or working-class "roughs" might choose their own leaders struck at the core of everything Shaw and his fellow officers believed about their fitness to command. Finally, the new policy forced elite officers like Shaw and Dwight to pander to the men in the regiment for their votes, a step that both Shaw and Dwight were loath to take and that they maintained threatened unit cohesion. According to Shaw, "The volunteer system is a perfectly rotten one."[21]

A growing dissatisfaction with General Patterson led to him being replaced by Maj. Gen. Nathaniel Prentice Banks during the last week of July 1861. Banks was one of the many political generals appointed at the beginning of the war. His humble origins made him a compelling choice. Forced into a Waltham, Massachusetts, textile mill at the age of fourteen after his family's financial collapse, he earned the nickname "Bobbin Boy Banks," a name that followed him through his rise to governor and congressman. Though Banks had no prior military experience, Lincoln hoped that he would be able to attract recruits and raise money for the Union cause.[22] Shaw took little notice of the new commander.

Overall, Shaw took to military life with relative ease. He was pleased with the progress of the men under his command, but he also looked for "a chance to do something."[23] Apart from minor cavalry skirmishes, the 2nd Massachusetts languished in frustrating inactivity through September. Shaw chafed at his irrelevance. Weeks of drilling and discipline seemed pointless if his men never engaged the enemy. But while Union soldiers grew restless in camp, enslaved people throughout Virginia were seizing the initiative. They viewed the approaching federal armies as liberators. In growing numbers, they forced reluctant commanders to confront for the first time slavery's role in the conflict.

Three enslaved men—Frank Baker, James Townsend, and Shepard Mallory—owned by Confederate Col. Charles K. Mallory changed the war's trajectory on May 23, 1861, when they rowed across Hampton Roads seeking sanctuary at Fortress Monroe, which guarded the mouth of the York and James Rivers. The following morning, Mallory's representative arrived at Fortress Monroe demanding the three men's return under federal fugitive slave laws. Maj. Gen. Benjamin Butler, who commanded the federal installation, refused with lawyerly precision. Learning that the men had been forced to build Confederate fortifications, he declared them "contraband of war," essentially enemy property subject to seizure. Butler argued that he was "under no constitutional obligation," to return fugitive slaves "to a foreign country, which Virginia now claims to be."[24] Congress eventually brought order to the legal chaos with the First Confiscation Act, passed in August 1861. The law allowed Union forces to seize enslaved people as "contraband" only if it could be proved that they were being used for military purposes, such as building fortifications and hauling supplies.

The enslaved population of the Shenandoah Valley numbered just shy of 25,000 and made up roughly 20 percent of the total population in 1860. John Brown's failed 1859 raid had left slavery intact, yet Union armies arriving in 1861 exposed the system's vulnerabilities. Some enslaved people acted boldly. On May 26, 1861, before Union soldiers had arrived in the region, a small group of enslaved people near Winchester attempted an uprising with help from an unidentified Massachusetts man; but the uprising was quickly crushed by local authorities. Shortly after the 2nd Massachusetts arrived in Virginia, thirteen freedom seekers from farms in the area followed the regiment to Harpers Ferry, hoping that by doing so they might gain their freedom. They were wrong. Patterson ordered them returned to their masters "with all due haste"; he coldly explained, "The law considered them as 'property,' and we had no choice but to obey the law."[25] Shaw may have witnessed these desperate people dragged back to bondage as his army enforced the very system his parents fought to destroy. The moral contradiction was stark, but there is no evidence that this troubled his conscience.

The Confiscation Act's legal technicalities could not ease the moral anguish Union soldiers felt when confronting desperate families seeking freedom. Under the restrictive new rules, most freedom seekers were turned away or were returned to masters who would likely inflict brutal retribution through whippings or sale to Deep South plantations. Soldiers, like Henry Comey, wrestled with enforcing policies that violated their deepest convictions. "No human being should be owned by another," Comey declared, yet federal law forced him to participate in slavery's enforcement.[26] These soldiers had enlisted to fight rebels, not to drag children back into bondage.

Most officers and soldiers in the 2nd Massachusetts had never encountered enslaved people. Their understanding of slavery came from *Uncle Tom's Cabin,* abolitionist newspapers, and sentimental illustrations that sanitized slavery's brutality. Nothing prepared them for the raw testimony of Black families who reached Union lines. Scarred backs told the stories that no novel could capture. Accounts of children sold away from parents and families deliberately shattered every romantic notion about the "peculiar institution." Charley Morse watched in horror as "a man almost white" was surrendered to "a miserable slave owner who got him by merely saying he was a Union man." The casual cruelty shattered Morse's faith in military protocol. He vowed never again to "take a black man to the guard tent," even if it meant breaking direct orders.[27] The regimental chaplain described slavery as a "shameful business."[28]

Shaw's silence about slavery's horrors revealed his moral detachment more clearly than any commentary could. While his comrades wrote home about scarred backs and shattered families, Shaw offered his abolitionist parents a sanitized assessment. The "slaves here seem well cared for," he informed his family and "they are evidently glad to see us."[29] A few days later, while describing the confiscation of the property of known secessionists Shaw also mentioned "the delighted darkies," who "treated all our 25 men to pork

& hoe cake."[30] Shaw had witnessed the same scenes that had begun to turn other soldiers to the antislavery cause, yet he chose to minimize what he had seen rather than confront its implications. Perhaps he feared confirming his parents' radical views, or maybe acknowledging slavery's full horror would have demanded a moral response he was not ready to make.

Shaw tended to view enslaved people through a cold military calculus—as strategic assets rather than as human beings seeking freedom. Escaped slaves possessed invaluable intelligence about local terrain and Confederate troop movements, making them potentially useful to the military. Some regiment members had already hired escaped slaves as camp servants, whom Shaw dismissed as an "unscrupulous set of rascals."[31] His contemptuous language suggests that even when enslaved people served the Union's military interests, Shaw saw them as inherently dishonest and morally deficient.

This did not, however, prevent Shaw from considering one of the most radical uses of enslaved people: arming them as soldiers to fight. Writing to family friend Sidney Howard Gay of the *New York Daily Tribune*, Shaw inquired, "Isn't it extraordinary that the Government won't make use of the instrument that would finish the war sooner than anything else,—viz, the slaves?" Considering the subject in the form of a question allowed him to use Gay as a sounding board. "I have no doubt they could give more information about the enemy [more] than any one else," Shaw continued, "and that there would be nothing easier than to have a line of spies right into their camp." Enlisting slaves to fight against the Confederacy would undercut the enemy's morale, and Shaw was convinced that the enslaved people "would probably make a fine army after a little drill, and could certainly be kept under better discipline than our independent Yankees."[32]

The young lieutenant sought validation from Gay, asking whether similar proposals had surfaced through his newspaper connections. Shaw's inquiry revealed how isolated such thinking remained. Few people, especially in the army, were contemplating Black military service in late 1861. The most vocal proponent was the famed Black abolitionist Frederick Douglass, who urged Lincoln and his administration to "*let the slaves and free colored people be called into service, and formed into a liberating army*, to march into the South and raise the banner of Emancipation among the slaves."[33] Lincoln rejected Douglass's call, fearing that any move toward emancipation or Black enlistment would drive the crucial Border States—Missouri, Kentucky, Maryland, and Delaware—into the Confederate fold. In addition, Northern racism ran too deep to support such radical measures in 1861, and Shaw's privileged social circle likely blinded him to this political reality. The vast majority of loyal Americans were fighting to preserve the Union, not to abolish slavery or challenge the nation's racial hierarchy. General McClellan and most military commanders agreed that their mission was crushing the rebellion, not transforming Southern society.[34]

Shaw's support of Black military enlistment was influenced by fellow officers in the 2nd Massachusetts, most notably by Maj. Robert Morris Copeland, who had served as regimental quartermaster before joining the staff of General Banks as an aide-de-camp.[35] At the outbreak of the war, Copeland had called on the federal government to enlist Black men. It is possible that Shaw and Copeland discussed this issue while in training at Camp Andrew. "Besides their value as soldiers," Copeland believed, "the history of past times seemed to teach, that men in no way are better fitted for freedom than by fighting for it." If properly trained under the guidance of white officers, Copeland confidently anticipated that these Black men "would become a people whom we could gladly call Americans."[36]

Shaw never considered what military service might mean for Black people themselves, only what it could accomplish for the Union war effort and his own promotion through the ranks. Unlike Copeland, who was "always fuming and raging about it," Shaw treated Black enlistment as just another military option rather than a moral crusade. He believed that advocating for the policy was a "waste of breath," given the military leadership's resistance, though he was encouraged by Copeland's appointment to Banks's staff, which he saw as a suggestion the general might be receptive to the idea. In the end, Shaw's embrace of Black enlistment at this early stage was a pragmatic or practical decision. Shaw viewed Black enlistment as a means to end the war as quickly as possible and to avoid a "war of extermination."[37] This issue would surface again in May 1862.

Shaw's interest in emancipation remained secondary to his immediate military ambitions and prospects for promotion. But he shared his family's outrage when Lincoln forced Maj. Gen. John C. Frémont—family friend and former Republican presidential candidate—to rescind his August proclamation freeing all Missouri slaves belonging to secessionists. Frémont's bold order had exceeded even the First Confiscation Act's limited scope, prompting wild celebration on Staten Island. Josephine captured the family's euphoria in her diary: "Oh! If Frémont only has freed the slaves, what a step it will be. Joy! Joy! Joy! Hurrah! Hurrah! Hurrah!"[38]

Promotion and advancement in the army was constantly on Shaw's mind, even in connection to Frémont and the question of emancipation. In a letter to his sister Susie, Shaw agreed that it would be "disgusting if Frémont is superseded," but he admitted, "The only thing I have thought about lately, as *very* desirable . . . is a place on General Frémont's staff."[39] Overall, Shaw remained preoccupied with the training of the men under his command and the broader state of military affairs. He continued to respond to criticisms that the officers in the 2nd Massachusetts were too tough on their men in maintaining discipline and instilling what were viewed as necessary punishments in response to various violations.

McClellan's continued inaction fueled growing criticism from Republicans who questioned both his Democratic loyalties and his hostility toward emancipation—views shared by Shaw's parents. Josephine captured the family's mounting frustration: "Nothing seems to be done by us and everything is done by the Rebels. Discontent with the Administration is growing fast, and if they don't do something, there are many people who will be disgusted with war and ask for peace."[40] In contrast, Shaw praised McClellan for his efforts to improve the Army of the Potomac's combat readiness and maintained that his influence had filtered down, "for all the regiments have improved very much in respect of discipline."[41] Shaw was far from alone in his praise for McClellan. Charley Morse acknowledged the gulf between the army and the home front when he asserted that the "people of the North" have little "idea what a fine army ours is becoming under McClellan's influence."[42]

Despite Shaw's frustrations with the challenge of instilling and maintaining discipline in the army, the election of officers, and disagreements with his family over the conduct of the war, military life suited him. He slipped seamlessly into his role and easily adjusted to the regularity and routine of camp life, including the drudgery of paperwork that needed to be completed along with the constant drilling and parades. Shaw was struck by the beauty of the countryside. While encamped on Maryland Heights, overlooking Harpers Ferry, Shaw acknowledged "the very magnificent view across the river into Virginia . . . and the sunsets which we have here" that "are really finer than ours."[43] Though not affiliated with any denomination, Shaw joined others for Sunday services and reflected on the sermons delivered by Alonzo Quint. During those infrequent moments when he found himself alone in his tent, Shaw enjoyed reading Shakespeare, poetry, and the essays of Francis Bacon and Thomas Babington Macaulay.[44] Mostly, he enjoyed the company of his fellow officers, who he described as "real nice fellows & some of them very superior men."[45]

During a brief convalescence following a "slight attack of dysentery," Shaw stayed in the modest home of a Mrs. Buckles for a few weeks that first summer in Virginia.[46] The log home had two rooms, which Shaw shared with four children, "a fat black woman" and another man. Both "Mrs. B" and a woman identified as Aunt Betty washed his clothes and prepared his food for which he was "very grateful."[47] On one occasion Shaw was joined by fellow officers for dinner at the home; they were served "nice boiled chickens, apple sauce, bread and molasses" all "set out in tempting array on a clean white cloth, and altogether we had the most christianlike meal I think since we left home."[48]

Shaw and his fellow officers may have appreciated Southern hospitality, but they viewed Virginia society with barely concealed contempt. Coming from a region that celebrated roads, canals, churches, and schools as marks of progress, these New Englanders saw firsthand how slavery had corrupted white Southern culture, breeding laziness and stifling initiative. Shaw's observations dripped with regional superiority. Virginia boasted "many fine places," he admitted, "but the houses generally seem shabby inside." Only the "many fine horses" bred by wealthy families impressed him, perhaps because horses, unlike humans, could not be enslaved and thus retained their natural vigor. Shaw showed no respect for property rights or privacy when families fled the advancing Union forces. He recalled with smug satisfaction "stamping round" inside abandoned homes and "eating & smoking pipes on the front piazza."[49]

On August 20, 1861, the 2nd Massachusetts crossed back into Maryland and marched to Darnestown to rejoin Banks's command, twenty-five miles northwest of Washington. The new location changed very little. Military routine continued its relentless cycle of reveille, drill, dinner, dress parade, and 9 p.m. tattoo. Days blurred together in mind-numbing repetition. Only guard duty broke the monotony, though Shaw found it "not a very pleasant variety."[50] The move did, however, bring the regiment within close proximity to the 20th Massachusetts Infantry Regiment, commonly known as the Harvard Regiment because of its large number of alumni among its officer corp. Shaw made it a point to visit whenever possible and to reconnect with a "good many friends and acquaintances," including Harry Sturgis, Oliver Wendell Holmes Jr., James Jackson Lowell, and Caspar Crowninshield.[51] More than an opportunity to rekindle old friendships from his days in Cambridge, Shaw bonded with fellow officers outside his own regiment who held similar views about the war, who were committed to instilling discipline in the volunteers, and who were convinced of the crucial leadership role that their education and training afforded them and that they believed would help to restore the Union.

Shaw likely confided to his Harvard friends his hunger for combat before the war ended, sharing the naive optimism that still infected many officers in late 1861. Despite Bull Run's sobering lesson, many people clung to hopes for a short war, a delusion that looks absurd in retrospect but that felt reasonable to men who had never witnessed sustained warfare. "I sincerely hope the war will not finish without a good, fair battle," Shaw wrote, "as we should never hear the end of Bull Run."[52] More remained at stake than the future of the nation for young and ambitious men like Shaw, who hoped to make his mark by proving his manhood and merit as a leader, thereby accessing opportunities for advancement.

Lincoln declared September 26, 1861, a day of national thanksgiving and fasting, but Shaw's regiment found no rest. They marched three miles in the heat to join other units for a marathon religious service featuring eleven chaplains, including their own. Shaw endured the ceremony with barely concealed irritation, viewing it as military theater rather than spiritual renewal. His one satisfaction came from observing that Massachusetts regiments "were the best-equipped, best-behaved, and most soldierly-looking men on the ground." The forced piety accomplished nothing except exhausting already restless soldiers. The regiment trudged back to camp "dusty, thirsty, and hungry," having wasted a day on public prayer when they needed rest or training.[53]

While the religious service failed to inspire reflection, six months of military life and thoughts of autumn back home stirred deeper contemplation in Shaw. "What a difference between October 1860 and Oct 1861 in America—and where will we all be the next year at this time?" His speculation ranged from catastrophic to triumphant. Perhaps "Jefferson Davis will be in New York" as Confederate president of a conquered nation, Shaw speculated. Yet Shaw maintained a stubborn optimism about ultimate Union victory, predicting even "if England, France & all the world should declare war against us, we should still come out right in the end."[54]

Shaw had thus far observed death from comfortable distance. Casualties were still largely statistics in dispatches, not faces he recognized. That insulation shattered when the 20th Massachusetts marched toward Ball's Bluff on October 21, 1861, carrying his Harvard friends into their first real battle.

McClellan had ordered Gen. Charles Stone to probe Confederate positions near Leesburg, perhaps hoping to force their withdrawal. In darkness, Capt. Chase Philbrick's scouting party reported discovering an unguarded enemy camp. At dawn, Col. Charles Devens led the 15th Massachusetts Infantry Regiment across the Potomac to attack what proved to be shadows—little more than a line of trees mistaken for Confederate tents. The phantom camp quickly turned into real combat when Devens's men encountered Mississippi infantry. Col. William R. Lee's 20th Massachusetts received orders to cross the Potomac and reinforce the 15th, but too few boats delayed their arrival along the river's steep bluffs. Confederate resistance stiffened throughout the day, pinning the federal forces against the cliff edge with their backs to the river. As dusk approached, Confederate attacks finally broke Union lines. Soldiers tumbled over the bluff into the Potomac, some drowning, others surrendering rather than risking the desperate swim to Maryland. The casualty toll was staggering. More than half the 1,700 Union forces engaged became casualties, including 223 killed, 226 wounded, 553 captured.[55]

At dawn on October 22, the 2nd Massachusetts rushed through pouring rain toward Conrad's Ferry, directly across from the Ball's Bluff disaster. Along the muddy roads, they encountered survivors, many "in their shirts, having thrown off their clothes to swim" the Potomac under Confederate fire. At first Shaw thought these men "exaggerated the story," but his opinion soon changed once he arrived on the scene. Wounded and dead soldiers lay in rows on the wet ground of a temporary hospital on a small island in the middle of the Potomac. One soldier from Shaw's regiment attempted a desperate rescue mission, piloting a small skiff across to retrieve thirteen stranded men from the 15th Massachusetts. He managed to save twelve before Confederate fire forced him back, leaving one comrade to capture or death.[56]

James Lowell lay unconscious, refusing surgery because he believed his wounds were mortal. John Putnam lost an arm, while Henry Higginson seemed unlikely to survive his injuries. Colonel Lee and Maj. Paul Joseph Revere—grandson of the colonial patriot—were missing, their fates unknown. The casualty list Shaw sent his mother read like a Harvard class roster. "Poor [Oliver] Wendell Holmes has a ball through one leg, and one through the lungs," he reported home, his clinical language barely concealing his anguish.[57] These weren't anonymous soldiers anymore. They were college friends who had shared dreams of military glory and who now lay bloodied in the Virginia mud.

Shaw wrote his mother immediately, reassuring her of his safety while grappling with war's new reality. Though he acknowledged that battle and death "is a terrible thing and we must get used to it," accepting the suffering of his close friends proved impossible. Ball's Bluff had personalized the war's cost in ways no amount of training could have prepared him for. Shaw found himself serving as battlefield correspondent for Boston's grieving elite families, sharing updates about Holmes's and Lowell's conditions with their anxious relatives. Despite the disaster, Shaw insisted the men and officers "behaved splendidly," directing blame instead toward Washington's leadership rather than battlefield performance. His friend Wilder Dwight offered cold comfort, dismissing Ball's Bluff as "an insignificant blunder on the outskirts of the main enterprise" that was now "part of the past, without any grave consequences to follow."[58]

November brought the campaign season's inevitable end as temperatures dropped and snow began falling, but Shaw and his regiment were "still in the dark" about where they would spend the winter. Their current position near Darnestown offered none of Harpers Ferry's scenic beauty—Darnestown was a location that Shaw characterized as "the worst camp ever." Constant rain transformed their location along the Muddy River into a "perfect bog" that sent a steady stream of sick soldiers to field hospitals. The miserable conditions affected everyone regardless of rank, making each supply shipment a cause for celebration. Officers and enlisted men alike eagerly awaited new stockings and dry clothing to combat their sodden, unhealthy surroundings.[59] Shaw found refuge from the November misery beside a small stone fireplace that kept his tent "warm and dry." He passed the dreary hours in comfortable companionship with fellow officers Stephen Perkins, Rufus Choate, and James Savage, "talking and reading, and having quite a nice time." Shaw particularly respected Savage as "one of the best officers, and a real brave fellow."[60]

In addition to keeping up his correspondence with family and friends back home, Shaw also followed military developments elsewhere. At the time, the nation was gripped by the Trent Affair—a diplomatic crisis that threatened to drag Britain into America's Civil War. On November 8, the USS *San Jacinto* had intercepted the British mail steamer *Trent* and arrested Confederate commissioners James Mason and John Slidell, who were sailing to Europe seeking recognition for the Confederacy. Now both diplomats sat in Fort Warren's cold cells in Boston Harbor while Britain demanded their release and a formal apology. Shaw recognized the explosive potential of the crisis. He hoped "the Government will probably wake up" to the danger of fighting both the Confederacy and the British Empire simultaneously. But he also prepared for the worst, suggesting that a military draft might become necessary if "all Europe will be drawn into this before it is finished."[61] Escalating tensions between the two nations, in what became known as the Trent Affair, were alleviated with the release of the prisoners in January 1862, though the Lincoln administration never apologized.

Shaw and his parents also watched developments along South Carolina's Sea Islands with intense interest. In early November 1861, Admiral Samuel F. Du Pont's fleet of seventy-five warships carrying 12,000 troops smashed into Port Royal Sound, seizing an ideal refueling station for the Union blockade and a staging area for their coastal operations. The assault triggered a plantation exodus. Du Pont faced minimal resistance taking Beaufort as terrified slaveholders fled inland, abandoning some of the South's wealthiest estates and roughly 10,000 enslaved people who suddenly found themselves free. Thousands more freedom seekers poured into the city from surrounding areas, creating an unprecedented refugee crisis and opportunity. News of the victory sparked fierce debate in Shaw's muddy Maryland camp. Officers struggled to understand why the War Department was not immediately reinforcing Du Pont to exploit Confederate panic throughout the region. "I know of a whole division, which instead of shivering in the mud of Maryland," one frustrated officer wrote, "would gladly be pursuing a panic-stricken multitude with fire and sword."[62]

Back in New York City, Frank Shaw began collecting clothing and other supplies for the Black community on the islands through the National Freedman's Relief Association. The organization raised money and support to "appoint suitable teachers to instruct the Freedmen in industrial and mechanical arts, in the rudiments of education, the principles of Christianity."[63] Josephine summed up the dramatic change in her diary: "Who one short year ago would have imagined that we should have shiploads of cotton picked by paid negroes?"[64] By March 1862, the first wave of volunteers from Boston and New York were headed to Port Royal to carry out their mission.

Encamped in Maryland, Shaw observed these distant military triumphs with growing frustration, hoping rumors about a southward deployment would prove true. The regiment relocated to a more comfortable camp near Seneca, Maryland, where they awaited orders for permanent winter quarters while the local countryside was "depopulated of geese and turkeys" in preparation for Thanksgiving.

November 28, 1861, dawned bright and unseasonably warm. Shaw joined his comrades for morning worship, followed by the governor's Thanksgiving Proclamation, a turkey shoot, and an elaborate feast that attempted to recreate New England tradition in a Maryland field. The officers' mess featured turkeys, geese, plum pudding, apple pies, nuts, raisins, and apples served in a tent "gorgeously lighted with candles" stuck on "bayonets serving for candlesticks."[65] The good cheer and food offered a brief respite from the daily drudgery of military life, but it also served as a reminder of just how much the men missed their families and loved ones back home.

In early December, the regiment was finally ordered into winter encampment on the southwestern side of Frederick, Maryland, near the Baltimore Turnpike. The landscape boasted sloping hills and valleys "with its bright, white farm-houses, and thrifty with its generous barns."[66] The move placed the regiment in a much healthier location, but the proximity to the town forced Shaw and his fellow officers to redouble their efforts to control the sale of alcohol to the soldiers and maintain discipline. The short ride into Frederick did, however, afford Shaw some welcome distractions. At the top of the list was the opportunity to spend time with "two young ladies." "In the evening," Shaw excitedly recalled in a letter to his mother, "there was a great deal of playing on the piano & chorus singing, in which latter we all howled, & made as much noise as we could." Shaw relished his time with the women. "I had hardly realized before that for 5 months we had been living like gypsies & seeing only men. I had really not spoken to a lady since we left New York."[67]

Frederick's residents had resisted secession despite Maryland's divided loyalties. Only 4 percent had voted for Southern Democrat John Breckenridge in 1860. The town's small enslaved population and strong economic ties to the North fostered hopes of avoiding armed conflict entirely. Shaw was struck by their warm reception, a sharp contrast to Baltimore's violent hostility eight months earlier. An elderly resident predicted that "there was no doubt that the slaves in this State would be emancipated if the question were to be decided to-morrow by vote of the people." "I was rather astonished at this," Shaw confessed to his father. The man explained that many Frederick residents, "like him, would never own a slave, though well able to buy them"[68] It was a reminder of how much the war had changed the outlook of Marylanders in such a short time, and it may have signaled to Shaw the direction that things would go if the war continued.

December's mild weather left some wondering whether McClellan had squandered another offensive opportunity, but Shaw's Christmas Eve passed like any other evening, apart from having to place two drunken soldiers in the guard tent. He spent the night reading over toast and coffee, a stark contrast to the family celebrations he would have enjoyed on Staten Island. The Christmas message of "peace on earth, good-will toward men" was more difficult to embrace in the midst of war. Shaw could only hope his family remembered him in their prayers and that this would be their last Christmas apart. "It began to snow about midnight," he wrote the next day, adding with bitter humor, "I suppose no one ever had a better chance of seeing 'Santa Claus,' but, as I had my stockings on, he probably thought it not worth his while to come down to the guard-tent."[69]

Shaw's attempt at a little lighthearted humor masked a hard reality that had settled in for many of the men in the 2nd Massachusetts. "Here, we have made up our minds that we shall have much more soldiering to do than we expected when we started."[70] Shaw's restless ambition reflected the army's broader frustration as 1861 ended. While he remained committed to Union victory, he feared the war would conclude before he could prove himself in combat. His efforts to discipline enlisted men had succeeded, but the leadership skills that would earn him the promotion and respect he craved could be demonstrated only under enemy fire. That test would come soon enough.

FIVE

What War Really Is

The town of Frederick, Maryland, where the 2nd Massachusetts remained in winter quarters in early 1862, offered few distractions. Social events, a brief visit from his family, and service on a court-martial punctuated long periods of boredom for Shaw. At the end of January 1862, Shaw and Charley Morse exchanged the drudgery of camp for a brief furlough to Annapolis, where they were reunited with Maj. Greely Curtis and Capt. Henry Higginson at the camp of the 1st Massachusetts Cavalry Regiment. A Baltimore stopover reminded them of how deeply Confederate sympathies ran in Maryland. Two "aristocratic looking and very richly dressed" ladies spotted their blue uniforms and reacted with theatrical disgust: They gave "their dresses a slap and swept off to the further side of the sidewalk, giving us the widest berth possible as if we were the plague," Morse wrote.[1] The "oysters and ale" imbibed in Baltimore and comradery in Annapolis could not hide the fact that a good deal of hard work still lay in Shaw's and Morse's future.

After ten months in uniform, Shaw had not yet drawn his pistol or raised his sword in anger. The ultimate test of his leadership and manhood—where courage mattered most and careers were forged—remained tantalizingly out of reach. But 1862 would change everything. Armies were stirring across multiple theaters after months of stalemate, promising battles that would dwarf 1861's limited engagements. The coming campaigns would shatter Shaw's assumptions about civilized warfare and force him to confront what total victory might require. As Union forces penetrated deeper into Confederate territory, thousands of enslaved people fled to federal lines, their desperate exodus undermining both slavery and the Southern war effort. These freedom seekers were transforming military camps into humanitarian crises, forcing reluctant commanders to choose between returning human property and harboring strategic assets. Lincoln could no longer ignore slavery's central role in sustaining Confederate resistance. Each escaped slave who reached Union lines weakened the enemy's labor capacity while strengthening the federal intelligence networks.[2]

Shaw's letters home captured his confusion as the war's moral landscape shifted beneath him. Frank and Sarah Shaw devoured each letter from their son, finding vindication for their abolitionist beliefs in his reports of slavery's collapse wherever Union armies advanced. Yet these same letters revealed the chasm between Shaw's military concerns and his parents' moral crusade. Shaw described military movements and camp conditions while his parents searched for signs of his spiritual awakening—evidence that their son was finally grasping the war's deeper purpose. His detached observations about "contraband" refugees contrasted sharply with their passionate conviction that each escaped slave represented a blow against human bondage.

Shaw and the rest of the 2nd Massachusetts left the relative comfort of their winter quarters around Frederick on February 27, 1862, bound for Harpers Ferry and other towns and villages that they had marched through the previous year. Some of the townsfolk came out to bid the soldiers goodbye, including "young ladies" who "waved handkerchiefs from windows."[3] Recent news of Gen. Ulysses S. Grant's victories at Forts Henry and Donelson, along the Tennessee and Cumberland Rivers, and the capture of Roanoke Island off the coast of North Carolina just a few weeks earlier buoyed the men's spirits as they boarded the railcars to cross the Potomac River back into Virginia. Unfortunately, Lincoln did not have the same success with Gen. George McClellan, who seemed to find an unending list of excuses as to why the Army of the Potomac could not also go on the offensive at the beginning of the new year. Lincoln finally ordered him to move no later than February 23—George Washington's birthday.[4]

Few people in the regiment had any knowledge of their final destination, but Morse believed it "should be Winchester." The regiment's experience in the lower Shenandoah Valley the previous year had left many of the men with a "good healthy hate for Charlestown and all its neighborhood."[5]

The war had clearly taken a toll on nearby Harpers Ferry. The town was marked by blackened walls along with the ruins of the old armory and destroyed bridges. "The sin of Secession has brought with it a curse. . . . If Harpers Ferry is a fair example of what Secession has done for Va.," observed Brig. Gen. John Sedgwick, "God help her!" McClellan and his staff were also in town to coordinate movements with General Banks. Banks's two divisions, numbering 20,000 men, were tasked with maintaining control of the lower Shenandoah Valley and preventing Stonewall Jackson's force from reinforcing the Confederates defending Richmond. After a brief stay, the 2nd Massachusetts moved on to Charlestown.[6]

Shaw's return to Charlestown revealed how deeply Union occupation had poisoned civilian relations. Locals cursed federal soldiers from behind shuttered windows, while the streets lay nearly deserted. Residents feared the Yankees might torch their town at the slightest provocation.[7] The few Confederate cavalrymen patrolling in and around town were quickly dispersed. The only threat that remained, Shaw jokingly mused, came from "a large body of pigs, turkeys, chickens & ducks" that attacked several companies of the 2nd Massachusetts on the day of their arrival. "As some of the secession animals & fowls met their death in the affray," Shaw jokingly informed his sister, "it was no sin to eat them."[8] While Shaw could justify the killing of wild animals as self-defense, he begrudgingly accepted and enforced orders to protect the private property of local civilians, despite their open hostility.

The regiment's return to Charlestown once again placed Shaw among the buildings and other landmarks associated with John Brown. Soldiers reflected on Brown's actions and his role in precipitating the conflict, and they mailed home mementos associated with his trial and execution. Reminders of Brown could be seen and heard. The bell on the church that called locals to rally against Brown's raid three years earlier now called the regiment to Sunday mass.[9]

Shaw and his fellow officers made themselves comfortable in the office of Andrew Hunter, the prosecutor who had sent John Brown to the gallows. They ransacked "piles of letters and papers," discovering correspondence from Virginia Governor Wise, former President Buchanan, and even Shaw family friend Lydia Maria Child. Shaw sent home "scraps" of sermons as war souvenirs, likely written by Brown's Kansas associates. Child's letter requesting permission to visit Brown in his cell should have stirred memories of his parents' reverence for the martyred abolitionist, but Shaw remained unmoved by the connection. Shaw justified ransacking Hunter's private papers not by defending Brown's antislavery cause but by pointing out that Hunter was a "traitor" and "one of the early Rebels" serving in the "Virginia Secession Legislature."[10] Forced entry by Union soldiers into private residences and the subsequent ransacking of the homes became increasingly common in 1862 as frustration with recalcitrant civilians mounted.[11]

On March 12, the regiment encamped just outside Winchester, Virginia. Shaw and Morse took the opportunity to explore the town that remained just out of the army's grasp the previous summer. Winchester was now a "tumble-down" and "decayed" town, and its residents were just as disloyal as their neighbors in Charlestown. One woman refused to sell an officer eggs and milk, explaining that "she wouldn't sell a Yankee anything that would give him any comfort at any price, and if she had had [a] gun in her house she would have fired it at our troops as they came up if it had been the last act of her life!" More disturbing were the rumors that the skulls of Northern soldiers had been sold in Winchester for ten dollars apiece and that Confederate "officers had spurs made of our men's bones." Shaw did not know what to make of these stories, but they quickly spread throughout the army and no doubt fueled even more hatred toward the civilian population. Though the practice of collecting human remains on Civil War battlefields—whether as trophies of war and as a symbolic "acts of domination"—was rare and shocking to most people, to Shaw it reinforced his view of the local civilians as little more than a "pack of rascals" who "are treated too well."[12]

The volatile relationship between civilians and the Union army was eclipsed by the main military threat in the area around Winchester, which remained under control by Maj. Gen. Thomas J. "Stonewall" Jackson's Confederates. His winter encampment around Winchester served dual strategic purposes. The Shenandoah Valley fed Confederate armies throughout Virginia with wheat, grain, and cattle; destroying this agricultural lifeline could cripple Southern logistics. More ominously, the Valley offered Jackson a natural invasion route toward Washington and Baltimore, threatening the Union capital with the same Confederate forces that had already embarrassed federal armies once.[13]

By early March, Shaw recognized that Shenandoah Valley operations would be dictated by larger strategic movements to the east. McClellan had lost overall command after his chronic refusal to attack, but Lincoln retained him as head of the massive Army of the Potomac—a compromise that satisfied no one. McClellan's new plan bypassed a direct assault on Richmond through central Virginia in favor of an amphibious flanking movement. His 100,000-man army would establish a new base at the tip of the Virginia Peninsula, between the York and James Rivers, advancing on the Confederate capital from the east. Meanwhile, Maj. Gen. Irvin McDowell's 40,000 troops, positioned near Fredericksburg, would strike Richmond from the north in coordinated assault.

As McClellan's armada sailed down the Potomac on March 17, Jackson unleashed the campaign that would make him legendary. Less than one week later, on March 23, Jackson's forces, numbering 17,500 men, clashed with Banks's army at Kernstown, near Winchester. Despite being outnumbered, Jackson launched a bold attack; but he was ultimately forced to retreat. The combined casualty count between both armies was relatively light compared with what was to come.[14]

Jackson's lightning strikes against Banks's and Frémont's eight-thousand-man force in the Shenandoah Valley created strategic havoc far beyond their tactical impact. Jackson's mobile Confederate division repeatedly outmaneuvered and defeated the larger Union armies, turning the Shenandoah Valley into a theater of federal humiliation. Jackson's victories achieved exactly what Confederate strategy required. Lincoln panicked about Washington's security and diverted troops meant for McClellan's Peninsula campaign to defend the capital and the Shenandoah Valley. Each federal regiment held back was one less available to capture Richmond, turning Jackson's small force into a strategic multiplier that negated the Union's numerical superiority. The result was predictable friction between Lincoln and McClellan, each blaming the other for insufficient support. Lincoln accused McClellan of moving too slowly while demanding more troops; McClellan, in turn, blamed Washington for withholding reinforcements that he claimed were essential for victory.[15]

Shaw and the 2nd Massachusetts arrived too late for the Kernstown fighting. A damaged bridge over the Shenandoah River had slowed their march, but a visit to Winchester revealed that its courthouse had been transformed into a hospital where "20 dead men [were] laid out, with the capes of their overcoats folded over their faces" to greet visitors. Shaw felt relieved not to recognize any corpses but found it "strange to see the dead & wounded Ohio men & Virginians lying there side by side." Doctors scrambled across blood-soaked floors treating Union and Confederate wounded equally, while assistants piled severed limbs behind the building like cordwood. Gangrene's stench penetrated everything within the building's interior. The dying received what comfort the overworked medics could provide. Shaw absorbed these scenes at arm's length, "looking about, as if I had lived all my life among the dead & wounded men." He spared his family the worst details but shared a sobering observation: "There is one thing about which every man who has been in a battle seems to be pretty sure and that is that he doesn't want to go into another if he can avoid it. I have no doubt though that this feeling wears off after a man has had more experience in fighting."[16]

The regiment spent the following weeks chasing shadows deeper into the Shenandoah Valley, seeking an enemy who refused to be pinned down. By April 5, the 2nd Massachusetts had reached Edinburg, south of Winchester, where Shaw discovered the frustrating reality of fighting Stonewall Jackson. The Confederate general had transformed warfare into psychological torture for his Union foe. Jackson's forces executed feints and diversions that kept Union commanders guessing his true intentions while forcing Banks into constant defensive postures. Confederate cavalry appeared where least expected, struck federal supply lines, then vanished before reinforcements could respond. Jackson's men seemed to materialize from mountain passes before quickly melting back into the Virginia countryside.

With warmer temperatures, the Shenandoah Valley exploded in color and smells. The Blue Ridge and Massanutten Mountains loomed on their left and right as the 2nd Massachusetts marched farther south. The men marveled at the miles of rolling hills and steep peeks as well as at the emerald-green wheat fields and blossoming peach and cherry trees.[17] Shaw characterized the Valley between Edinburg and New Market as "the most beautiful part of the country we have been in." The layout of the farms and their "neat" arrangement reminded him of the German countryside. "If I could get a hold of a lot of Confederate money, at a cheap rate," he speculated, "I would buy some land down here."[18]

As Banks's force penetrated deeper into the Shenandoah Valley, fugitive slaves arrived in unprecedented numbers—hundreds, possibly thousands, fleeing bondage from distances that dwarfed the previous year's exodus. Word of the federal advance had apparently reached enslaved communities as far south as Augusta County, Virginia, nearly one hundred miles from Winchester.[19] Congressional action had finally clarified the confusion plaguing field commanders since the previous summer. A March 13, 1862, resolution prohibited officers from returning freedom seekers "who may have escaped from any persons to whom such service or labor is claimed to be due." The penalty for violation was swift and could include dismissal from military service following a court-martial conviction.[20]

As was the case during the 2nd Massachusetts's stay in Harpers Ferry the previous summer, the close interaction of Union troops with enslaved people challenged assumptions among the soldiers about slavery and African Americans generally. While many individuals were running away from plantations and smaller farms, others were fleeing the Confederate army, which routinely seized enslaved people in the Shenandoah Valley to labor in support of the war effort.[21] Wherever the 2nd Massachusetts moved, they were accompanied by Black men, women, and children. One woman by the name of Peggy worked for a time as an assistant cook before passage was arranged for both her and her daughter to Massachusetts.[22] Peggy was one among countless freedom seekers who were mandated to work as a result of Banks's Special Order No. 50, which allowed for their employment in the quartermaster department. Freed people found work as teamsters, loading and unloading wagons, and in camp generally, performing a wide range of chores.[23]

A small number of soldiers who had embraced abolitionism before the war did everything in their power to encourage and support enslaved people to rebel against their masters. Others harbored deeply racist or paternalistic views that prevented them from appreciating the difficult calculations that African Americans were forced to make in a region where both armies were constantly on the move. Officers like Wilder Dwight struggled to understand why some enslaved people refused to abandon their homes after their enslavers had fled in the face of the arrival of the Union army. "Why will he not . . . learn to make free with *himself*?" Dwight wondered.[24] Perhaps their decision to remain on the property was itself a form of resistance and an assertion of their freedom to choose as well as an indication that they saw the land as their own, where they had toiled and raised families.

These encounters impacted soldiers differently. "I have changed some of my notions on the slavery questions," Charley Morse admitted to his father. He suggested that the "country is cursed by it and made comparatively useless by the institution," but he sympathized little with individual slaves, "except in occasional cases." Morse characterized the enslaved as a "happy lazy thoughtless set one of them not accomplishing more work in a day than a white laborer would in a couple hours." Morse rejected claims that whippings were common, believing instead that slavery and race relations were relatively benign in Virginia.[25]

By contrast, the regimental chaplain, Alonzo Quint, was moved by the plight of the enslaved and reevaluated his admittedly conservative beliefs. Quint prefaced his comments by noting that he was "no fanatic" on the issue of slavery and emancipation and that he had "never even voted a Republican ticket." However, the time he had already spent on Virginia's "slave soil, in localities where slavery assumes its mildest type," had made him feel "that the whole system is infamous." Slavery, according to Quint, was just as damaging to white people in the way it "perverts the conscience, warps the intellect," and "brutalizes the heart." Contrary to Morse, Quint insisted that slaves were anything but content with their situation and, more importantly, yearned to be free.[26]

Shaw understood his family's hunger for stories about how the movement of the armies impacted enslaved people. The emotional scenes that other officers shared in letters home—desperate families fleeing bondage, children clinging to their mothers as they sought federal protection—could have formed the shared moral purpose Frank and Sarah craved with their son. Instead, his letters during this period contain harsh words about officers whom he believed were unqualified to lead men as well as about the severe lack of discipline that he believed plagued the army. Shaw also continued to express an interest in joining the regular army or being assigned a role on General Frémont's staff, suggesting his continued preoccupation with advancement in rank.[27] One encounter with freedom seekers, however, broke through Shaw's usual silence on slavery.

What made this particular encounter so unusual was the fact that the individuals in question appeared to Shaw to be white. Shaw described the father and his "two little curly haired boys" as "handsome people as you would find." Intrigued by these apparent "white slaves," Shaw interrogated the man for two hours. "There he stood in front of us & talked . . . as eloquently as any educated man I know," Shaw reported with obvious surprise. "The simplicity of his language made it all the more impressive." Despite being illiterate, the man could have passed for a "well to do" and "remarkably intelligent" mechanic in Shaw's estimation. The attention to the man's demeanor highlights Shaw's cultural assumptions about race. Shaw and others peppered the man with questions. Was anyone in his family ever sold? Did his father live on the same plantation as he did? The man's story revealed slavery's most brutal contradiction when Shaw realized that "his Master was his Father & that it had often been a bitter pill to swallow when he had been badly treated by him to think that it was so."[28]

There is no evidence that Shaw's interaction with this man extended beyond this single conversation. Although many officers in Banks's corps were sympathetic with the plight of the enslaved and took steps to assist them, whether providing food or arranging for transportation north, at no time did Shaw offer to help this man and his family. But for the fact of the man's complexion, it is likely that Shaw would not have taken any interest in his story or his family's plight. Their phenotypical whiteness made them a curiosity to Shaw, nothing more. At no point did Shaw exhibit the same interest in darker-complexioned slaves, who suffered the same indignities and lived with the same fears. Neither is there any evidence that Shaw ever spoke out against or prevented others from assisting freedom seekers.

It is undeniable that Shaw abhorred slavery and that he looked forward to its eventual destruction; but unlike his parents, that did not translate directly into his understanding of how the war should be fought.[29] Shaw, like many of his fellow officers in his regiment, appreciated the extent to which the movement of thousands of freedom seekers undercut the Confederate war effort by depriving it of much-needed labor. He also likely anticipated mobilizing the services of African Americans more directly against the Confederacy. But as of the spring of 1862, Shaw's commitment to restoring the Union and defeating the Confederacy did not include demanding the end of slavery or a harder military policy toward Southern civilians and their property. His resistance stands in contrast with a growing number of officers and enlisted men whose personal experiences with enslaved men, women, and children translated into increased calls for harsh retribution against recalcitrant Confederates.[30]

The apparent absence of Shaw's interest in the plight of the enslaved stood in sharp contrast to the intense focus of his parents and sisters. Josephine celebrated the end of slavery in the District of Columbia on April 16, 1862. Every development, however small, she wrote was seen as the "direct work of God" in "Freedom's cause."[31] In New York City, Frank continued his work organizing aid for the contraband population along the Sea Islands of South Carolina.

In camp, Shaw closely followed news of military progress elsewhere as the 2nd Massachusetts, along with the rest of Banks's force continued to pursue

Jackson through the Shenandoah Valley, some days clocking close to twenty hours on foot.[32] In early April, Shaw learned that Grant had defeated a Confederate force under the command of Gen. Albert Sydney Johnston at Shiloh, close to the Tennessee–Mississippi border. It was the bloodiest battle to date, with just under 24,000 combined casualties. Farther south, on April 25, Union forces under the command of Maj. Gen. Benjamin Butler captured New Orleans. With McClellan's large army set to move on Richmond, the Confederacy appeared to be on the brink of annihilation.

A few weeks later, rumors swirled through Shaw's camp that "Richmond is in our possession." While the news was celebrated, it must have come as a surprise to Shaw, who had previously expressed concern that McClellan's movements were "being hampered" by Lincoln and his administration and unjustly criticized in the newspapers.[33] The reports of Richmond's fall, of course, proved to be premature. "Little Mac's" army was still miles from the Confederate capital. His decision to lay siege to Confederate forces outside Yorktown in early April cost his army valuable time. It would take the Army of the Potomac close to one month to finally arrive at Williamsburg, located just a few miles west of Yorktown. McClellan only just maneuvered his formidable host into position around Richmond on May 18, five days after Shaw had learned that the city had been taken.

No doubt Shaw welcomed the stream of positive news concerning the nation's military progress, but it also likely left him conflicted. There was the chance that the war might end before he would have the opportunity to demonstrate his leadership and fighting skills on the battlefield. Josephine sympathized with her brother's situation, noting that he "would feel dreadfully to come home without seeing a battle."[34] In a letter to his mother, Shaw acknowledged that his "desire to have a battle is a purely selfish feeling." He reminded himself of Colonel Gordon's remarks that the "number of orphans, widows, and childless people, is increased by the sending of one more regiment into a battle."[35] Not surprisingly, Shaw's knowledge of the very real costs of battle did not prevent him from continuing to seek an appointment to a general's staff or an assignment in the regular army. He remained as restless as ever.

That restlessness also prompted Shaw, once again, to pursue the possibility of raising a regiment of Black soldiers with Major Copeland. It is unclear why Shaw agreed to align himself with Copeland after the two had made such little progress on the issue the previous summer. There is no evidence that Shaw had brought up the subject of Black military enlistment with his family or friends in the interim. Copeland, by contrast, had never abandoned the idea, given his strong abolitionist views. Perhaps Shaw sensed a change in sentiment in Washington owing to recent military policies related to slavery, including Congress's decision to abolish slavery in the nation's capital. Copeland had also heard that Gen. David Hunter and Gen. Rufus Saxton in South Carolina were in the process of forming Black regiments and had inquired with Secretary of War Edwin Stanton if he could do the same, promising that his men would be "ready for service in three weeks after permission is granted me."[36] Adding to Copeland's optimism, Banks granted both Copeland and Shaw a leave of absence to travel to the capital to pursue their plan. According to Shaw, Copeland hoped to "enlist men in the North, who have had the courage to run away, and have already suffered for their freedom" as opposed to recruiting directly from contraband camps.[37]

On May 19, 1862, Shaw informed his father that he was in Washington, DC, with Copeland, that he was promised a major's commission in the new regiment, and that a meeting had been scheduled with Secretary Stanton. Shaw's parents were likely thrilled with the news, even if they might have wondered whether his motivations aligned with their own.

Copeland's preliminary meetings with Massachusetts congressmen revealed the political obstacles ahead; every member discouraged him from pursuing Black military service, citing its deep unpopularity. This reception foreshadowed disaster with Stanton. Copeland had fundamentally misread the political moment. While other abolitionist officers had already approached Stanton about organizing Black regiments, the secretary of war's position remained deliberately ambiguous. Stanton was a political chameleon, championing emancipation when meeting with radicals like Butler while adopting "pragmatic politics" with conservatives like McClellan. More critically, Stanton understood the constitutional reality that Copeland seemed to ignore. The decision to arm Black men belonged exclusively to the president, not to subordinate officials. Until the president was ready to embrace such a revolutionary step, even sympathetic cabinet members could not act unilaterally.[38]

Few people outside the abolitionist community were openly calling for the enlistment of African Americans. In response to a question from his father about whether Black men would be accepted as soldiers in integrated regiments, Shaw responded optimistically that "the men would object [to] it very strongly at first, but they would get accustomed to it in time." This integrated vision of the US Army was even more extreme compared with the more acceptable policy of racially segregated regiments; but Shaw cautioned his father that "there would undoubtedly be great dissatisfaction, if we should enlist blacks and put them into the volunteer regiments now."[39]

Lincoln's administration faced impossible political constraints. Maintaining border state loyalty while avoiding the alienation of white Northerners who feared Black military service required the achievement of a delicate balance that precluded taking radical steps toward arming enslaved people. Even Northern Black communities remained skeptical about military service after their patriotic offers in 1861 had been contemptuously rejected. Shaw discovered this political reality while searching for support among his fellow officers of the 2nd Massachusetts. The same Harvard-educated men who criticized Union military leadership balked at the prospect of Black soldiers serving alongside them. Their class prejudices, which Shaw had already made abundantly clear, were bad enough without adding former slaves to the mix.[40]

It is therefore unsurprising that Copeland's and Shaw's mission failed. With Stanton's rebuff there was little more the two could do. Since 1861, little appears to have changed in Shaw's attitude toward the raising of Black soldiers. Shaw saw an opportunity in organizing Black regiments, both in terms of their military effectiveness against the Confederacy and in terms of the possibility of his own personal advancement through battlefield command. While his commitment to the project seemed genuine, his motivations remained fundamentally selfish rather than moral. He wanted to lead Black troops not because he believed in racial equality but because such a command might offer him an opportunity to advance in rank. Though there is little reason to doubt his commitment to the project, it is also the case that Shaw never took any independent initiative to campaign to raise a regiment of Black soldiers. Once again, he seemed content to support Copeland's efforts and to embrace any advance in rank—if the mission proved successful.

Shaw's Washington furlough allowed him a precious visit to Staten Island for family time and dental care before returning to duty. The Shaws were just finishing tea when footsteps echoed across the piazza. "The door opened and Rob stood there," Josephine recorded excitedly in her diary, later describing his visit as a "dream." Shaw savored these relaxing days wrapped in family warmth, but the Shaws never wasted opportunities for serious discussion. His parents and sisters undoubtedly interrogated him about the failed Washington mission with Copeland and countless other war-related topics. Shaw likely expressed his continued frustration at not having the opportunity to fight and his lack of success in gaining a promotion or transfer out of the 2nd Massachusetts.[41]

While Shaw enjoyed precious family time on Staten Island, Copeland's Washington rejection triggered a decisive act of self-destruction. Attempting to support Governor Andrew's recruitment appeals, he published a newspaper letter blaming the Shenandoah Valley's military failures on Secretary of War Stanton—a direct assault on his own chain of command. The damage was immediate and irreversible. General Banks erupted in fury, describing Copeland as a "species of demon, more resembling in appearance and mind the Infernal spirit than any man I have seen." Banks immediately dismissed him from his staff and discharged him from the army in August, ending Copeland's military career in disgrace.[42] Though Shaw continued to speak in support of Copeland in his private correspondence, he may have suspected that Copeland's troubles were due, in part, to his persistent advocacy of Black enlistment.

As Shaw made his way back to the regiment on the morning of May 22, 1862, Union and Confederate forces maneuvered into a position to decide who would control the Shenandoah Valley. Jackson's defeat of Frémont's force at McDowell on May 8 had placed him in a position to advance on the rest of Banks's force farther north. Four days later, one of Banks's two divisions was ordered east to reinforce McClellan, providing Jackson with an opportunity to strike the Union's depleted force defending the approaches to Winchester at both Front Royal and Strasburg. Both positions collapsed on May 23, forcing Banks to consolidate his two divisions around Winchester. Late in the evening on May 24—a little more than twenty-four hours after leaving his loved ones back home on Staten Island—Shaw was reunited with the 2nd Massachusetts, just as Confederates maneuvered into position for an attack.

The regiment had skirmished with the Confederates throughout the afternoon and were exhausted. Shaw was immediately assigned to command a picket line, "firing at intervals all night long," in anticipation of an attack that all knew would commence at first light.[43]

The Confederate assault opened early the following morning against the Union left around Camp Hill. After numerous failed attempts to seize the position, Jackson turned his attention to the Union right and Bowers Hill, where the 2nd Massachusetts and the rest of Gordon's brigade defended from behind a stone fence the approach to Winchester along the Shenandoah Valley Turnpike. For close to two hours Shaw and his men held their ground, though it was clear to everyone that they were outnumbered and dangerously exposed. Gordon's brigade began to fall back as a result of a withering Confederate fire and maneuver around their right flank. "As we passed off the hill," Dwight recalled, "the enemy rose on its crest. Their cracking and whistling fire followed us closely." Dwight quickly tore up an unmailed letter home rather than see it fall into enemy hands. Another officer in the 2nd Massachusetts noted, "It was cruel to see our poor fellows shot through the back and pitch forward on their faces as we marched down the hill."[44]

As Shaw joined the mass of retreating soldiers he "felt a violent blow and a burning sensation," but managed to keep moving. Only later did he learn that his watch had deflected a bullet that may have hit a soldier next to him.[45]

By early afternoon, Banks's entire force was in full retreat through the streets of Winchester. Shaw blamed the 29th Pennsylvania Infantry Regiment and 27th Indiana Infantry Regiment, both of which had been positioned to the right of the 2nd Massachusetts, for not standing firm, but there was little they could have done to stem the Confederate tide. As difficult as it must have been to extricate themselves from advancing Confederates, the 2nd Massachusetts was now forced to navigate its way through a hostile town. Colonel Gordon recalled that, "Males and females vied with each other in increasing the numbers of their victims, by firing from houses, throwing hand grenades, hot water, and missiles of every description."[46]

Though far from a disorganized retreat, Shaw recalled that the 2nd Massachusetts "lost a great many men in the streets of Winchester" as bands continued playing "John Brown's Body" and "Yankee Doodle." Elements of the regiment managed to form up to cover the Union retreat at various intersections, only to be quickly surrounded and compelled to give way "in good order." Shaw described the retreat as a "neck and neck race." Both his pistol and his sword were still with the rest of his luggage, forcing him to guide his men through town with a "toy-sword" that he had procured from a drummer boy. To make matters worse, civilians, "women as well as men," fired on the retreating soldiers from behind second story windows and doorways. "I hope that town will be destroyed when we go back there," Shaw exclaimed. "We had time to burn part of it while the fight was going on."[47]

The battle proved to be a decisive Confederate victory. Banks lost nearly a third of his force as well as a significant number of supplies, not to mention the humiliation of a 32-mile retreat that ended only after crossing the Potomac River into Maryland. Meanwhile, Jackson was not only celebrated as a liberator by the white civilian population of Winchester, he also managed to further disrupt McClellan's plan to consolidate Union forces, part of his ongoing campaign against Richmond.

Shaw stood his first test of battle remarkably well. He offered few details on the violence he witnessed that day in a letter penned to his father from Williamsport, Maryland, on May 27—an indication of just how far Banks's force had retreated following their defeat at Winchester. It was not until the end of the letter that Shaw commented on his close brush with death. Countless stories abound of pieces of equipment as well as Bibles deflecting bullets and pieces of shrapnel away from their intended targets. For Shaw it was his watch that may have saved his life or prevented a serious injury. "The first thing I thought of," he admitted, "was how you all would have felt if I had been left on that infernal pavement and it seemed as if I could see you all standing on the piazza just before I came away."[48] Shaw mailed the watch home as a memento, providing his family with a physical link between the battlefield and the home front. Josephine surveyed the damage as a reminder of just how close her brother had come to death.[49] The sight and feel of her brother's watch animated her "soul" as she imagined the "noble fellows advancing, retreating, charging and dying, just how, when and where they are ordered."[50]

Reports that Wilder Dwight was missing and presumed captured, along with the regiment's two surgeons, only added to the sense of gloom that now hung over the 2nd Massachusetts. Shaw's company alone lost one man killed, eight wounded, and two taken prisoner out of a total of fifty—a 20 percent casualty rate.[51] Shaw praised the performance of the men under his command, "who behaved well and obeyed all orders promptly." The men's performance in battle also provided Shaw with a clear justification for the strict disciplinary measures that he had long advocated. Though he applauded his own men, Shaw cast blame for their defeat on Stanton's shoulders and his mismanagement of military affairs in the region.[52]

The suddenness of the blow and close call with death left Shaw "wondering why" he "wasn't lying on the ground." Soldiers struggled to come to terms with such close calls on the battlefield and with the randomness of death and serious wounding. Charley Morse may have shared his own observations with Shaw:

> The thing that strikes everybody most forcibly after a battle is how it can be possible for such a small proportion of the bullets to produce any effect; you are standing with your platoon in line we'll say, and a whole company at less than a hundred yards aim and fire their pieces at you. The balls strike the guns, go through clothes, between legs, under the arms, between the fingers, in every direction round the head, and two or three men at the most are hit, it is very singular I don't pretend to understand it.[53]

Ultimately, Shaw had little time to reflect on the vagaries of war. By June 10, Banks's force had recrossed back into Virginia toward Winchester. The return of Dwight and one of the regimental surgeons was a great relief to Shaw given the rumors of "the barbarity of the rebels" concerning the treatment of prisoners that swirled through camp. Shaw, however, had unexpectedly come to acknowledge Jackson as a "good man" and went on to praise his conduct in the recent campaign, "For he has escaped everything, when it seemed almost impossible."[54] Jackson had respected Union prisoners of war and the law of exchange, and he had accomplished everything he was tasked with, though his advance in pursuit of Banks toward the Potomac River left his army vulnerable to attack.

However, this praise did not extend to the civilian population. The 2nd Massachusetts and the rest of Banks's corps reentered Winchester "in close order and band playing so that there should be no chance of men's falling out and committing any outrages" against civilians. Shaw reported that the men obeyed orders; but given their experience of having to retreat through these very same streets just a few days earlier, he may have privately celebrated the news that one home had been burned by soldiers in nearby Martinsburg. For many of the men, including Shaw, the interaction with enslaved people and a defiant white civilian population continued to challenge their belief that the war could be fought strictly between the two armies. The "*citizens* of the towns we have passed through seem to hate us much more bitterly, as a general thing," Shaw informed his mother.[55] By June 25 the regiment was encamped near Front Royal. From Shaw's perspective, everything appeared "to be at a stand-still," but as he admitted to his mother, "Perhaps it is a lull before the storm."[56]

Shaw could not have known just how accurate his description would soon prove to be. By the end of May, McClellan's Army of the Potomac had finally completed its slog up the Virginia Peninsula to the "Gates of Richmond" itself. Three Union corps were positioned north of the rain-swollen Chickahominy River, while two additional corps lay exposed to its south. On the last day of May, Confederate Gen. Joseph E. Johnston took advantage of this situation and struck the two Union corps south of the river before they could be reinforced. The attack failed to dislodge the Union forces and cost both sides a combined 11,000 casualties. The most notable loss for the Confederacy was General Johnston himself, who fell wounded on the field. In response, President Jefferson Davis chose his military adviser, Gen. Robert E. Lee, to take command. Given his previous performance earlier in the war in western Virginia, few people anticipated that Lee would do more than order his men to fortify their positions and await an assault by McClellan, which never seemed to materialize.[57]

Shaw, still encamped near Front Royal, took advantage of the lull to catch up on writing letters to the families of soldiers wounded in the fight at Winchester, and he waited patiently for news about the situation around Richmond. He also considered and accepted an offer from Brigadier General Gordon, who had recently been promoted, to join his staff as an aide-de-camp—a position that would also allow Shaw to remain close to his friends in the 2nd Massachusetts. Charley Morse was "glad for him but sorry for us," as "he is one of the best fellows in the regiment and one of my most particular friends."[58]

Back outside Richmond, Lee wasted little time in assuming the offensive against McClellan's much larger army. News of the fighting proved a major disappointment for Shaw and the rest of Banks's army. In one week, Confederate Gen. Robert E. Lee, now with the support of Jackson's corps from the Shenandoah Valley, managed to push McClellan safely away from Richmond in a series of costly attacks that began at Mechanicsville on June 26 and culminated at Malvern Hill on July 1. What came to be known as the Seven Days' battles proved costly for both sides in both dead and wounded. Though McClellan's Army of the Potomac remained a viable threat—perhaps even more so now, given Confederate losses—Lee's aggressiveness unnerved the Union general, who chose to consolidate his forces along the James River at Harrison's Landing, where he would soon abandon the Virginia Peninsula altogether.[59]

Frank, Sarah, and the girls were also disappointed by the news coming out of Richmond. They mourned the dead, but as Josephine wrote in her diary, the family also remained committed to their faith that the ultimate course of the war was in "Our Father's hands and if it is good for us to suffer we must bear and it matters little what the end is."[60]

McClellan retained strong support among the junior officers who found it easier to blame distant politicians than question their beloved commander's failures. Contradictory reports from Richmond allowed Shaw and others to deflect responsibility from McClellan's overestimation of Confederate strength and hesitation in the face of opportunity. Shaw's letters home offered vague accusations rather than specific analysis, claiming the government failed to manage the war "with a very firm hand" or enlist sufficient troops. Rather than examine McClellan's delusions about Lee's numerical superiority, Shaw retreated to familiar complaints about military discipline, soldiers who "disobey orders, desert, and strike their officers," and the practice of electing unqualified company commanders. Shaw's frustration boiled over in letters home: "If I were sure of having a perfectly disinterested and patriotic man, what a good thing it would be to appoint a dictator in time of war. I begin to think I had rather have one at any rate, than see things go on as they do now."[61]

His parents, by contrast, were under no such illusions. Sarah admitted to being "greatly depressed" over the outcome of the fighting around Richmond and disappointed, specifically in McClellan. "We fear treachery in the Generals of our army, and weakness in our administration."[62]

Adding to Shaw's frustrations was an overall dissatisfaction with his new assignment. His responsibilities as an aide to Gordon involved little more than ensuring that "the different regiments and batteries . . . get under way at the proper time and in the proper order" while on the march. When they halted, Shaw directed each unit to where they would encamp. Other than the endless amount of paperwork to complete, Shaw "had so little to do, that I feel as if I were nothing but an 'orderly.'"[63] One thing that he appreciated was that the general tended to locate his headquarters close to the 2nd Massachusetts; but ultimately, Shaw looked forward to returning to his old regiment with a promotion to the rank of captain.[64]

In Washington, DC, Lincoln also took advantage of the lull in fighting by creating a new department in central Virginia for Gen. John Pope, who had come off a string of well-publicized victories—as a result of his capture of Island No. 10 on the Mississippi River—at New Madrid in Missouri. Pope's newly created Army of Virginia brought together the armies of Nathaniel Banks, Irvin McDowell, and Franz Sigel. With a strength of roughly 50,000 men, the Army of Virginia was tasked with threatening Richmond and protecting the Shenandoah Valley and the capital. Pope announced his arrival to his troops with a speech that infuriated many, especially McClellan. "Let us understand each other." "I have come to you from the West," he boasted, "where we have always seen the backs of our enemies."[65] Pope's braggadocio likely stung Shaw as it did others. Pope was one of the few superior officers about whom he made "disparaging remarks" in his personal correspondence. "I think that he is bold and rapid, but likely to lay himself open," he admitted to his father. "His proclamations and orders haven't done him much credit yet."[66] Shaw also admonished Pope for his criticism of McClellan and Frémont, who chose to resign rather than serve under his command.

Pope's General Orders No. 5, announced on July 18, 1862, directed the Army of Virginia to "subsist upon the country"; while his General Orders No. 7, issued the same month, held civilians who lived near the sites of guerrilla attacks responsible for damages. Citizens who refused to take the oath of allegiance could be forcefully removed from their homes and relocated beyond Union army lines. Those who took the oath but who later chose to violate it ran the risk of being treated as spies and even subject to execution.[67] Pope's orders outraged Confederates, including Robert E. Lee, who described him as a "miscreant." Rather than a decisive change in military policy, however, Pope's orders reflected a gradual shift away from a conciliatory, or limited, war policy that had been ongoing throughout 1862, toward a "harder" approach that more directly targeted civilians and their property. The order stripped central and northern Virginia farms bare causing further suffering for Confederate civilians and limiting the base of supplies available to the Army of Northern Virginia even further.[68]

Though Radical Republicans supported Pope's aggressive policies, especially those surrounding slavery and emancipation, Shaw attempted to walk a fine line. On the one hand, Shaw worried about the impact on army discipline of Pope's order "forbidding any commander to place a guard over private property in this department."[69] At the same time, Shaw had clearly become frustrated with the civilian population's defiance, though at no time did he declare them to be enemy combatants. The memory of the regiment's retreat through Winchester and the sight of civilians shooting from behind windows and doors was still fresh in his memory. The confiscation of property owned by civilians suspected of aiding the Confederacy did not trouble Shaw, and he took little notice of soldiers confiscating the enemy's resources for military purposes. He also admitted to having a "good deal of fun" watching Gordon harass and threaten civilians with arrest if they refused to sign a "parole" admitting to their support of secession and the Confederacy.[70] What Shaw feared most was uncontrolled pillaging and plundering that threatened to turn the army into an ineffective fighting force—the very behavior that he believed hard training and strict discipline helped to mitigate against. One thing was clear to him. The continued stubbornness of the civilian population coupled with recent military setbacks demanded a more consequential and less conciliatory policy toward them.

It was not simply the new military orders that ushered in a more aggressive posture toward Confederate civilians. During this same period, the Lincoln administration approved new policies that pushed the nation closer to emancipation. After abolishing slavery in the capital in April, Congress passed the

Second Confiscation Act on July 17, 1862, which proclaimed that any person committed of the crime of treason would have his slaves "declared and made free." It further stipulated, "All slaves captured from such persons [engaged in rebellion against the government of the United States] or deserted by them and coming under the control of the government of the United States; and all slaves of such persons found on [or] being within any place occupied by rebel forces and afterwards occupied by the forces of the United States, shall be deemed captives of war, and shall be forever free of their servitude, and not again held as slaves."[71] The act also allowed for the confiscation of Confederate property through court action and the recruitment of African American soldiers into the army.

Five days later, on July 22, Lincoln read a draft of his Preliminary Emancipation Proclamation to his cabinet. In it he outlined an even stronger policy that would free enslaved people in states that remained in rebellion once the order was enacted. Members of his cabinet advised the president that he should hold off on announcing the new policy until after a military victory rather than risk looking politically weak.

Although Shaw's parents applauded the Second Confiscation Act and accommodated themselves to the political realities that the president faced, like most abolitionists they remained frustrated with Lincoln. "Hesitancy is excusable in such a mighty question as the sudden emancipation of our poor slaves, even as a military necessity," Sarah admitted, "but I wish Mr. Lincoln would dare to do right, and trust that our Heavenly Father would see that no evil should come of it."[72] Their commitment to the end of slavery rested on a providential view of events. "Every defeat opens hundreds of blind eyes to the fact that slavery is at the bottom of all," Sarah wrote to a correspondent in Ireland. She could not comprehend that the sacrifice being made by "thousands of noble, brave young men"—including her own "darling son"—"in the field along with their mothers and wives back home was for anything other than 'some great end.'"[73] Shaw remained more sanguine as he contemplated events and the inevitable fighting that would surely come. "There is no doubt that good will ultimately come of this war; that slavery will disappear, and the country be eventually united; but I begin to doubt whether we shall accomplish it by force of arms."[74]

Shaw would soon face devastating proof of the army's vulnerability. Rather than wait for McClellan's renewed Richmond offensive, Robert E. Lee launched his own campaign to relieve the Confederate capital, destroy the

Cedar Mountain and battlefield, ca. 1863. On August 9, 1862, Shaw and the 2nd Massachusetts engaged Confederates under the command of Gen. Thomas "Stonewall" Jackson at Cedar Mountain. The Confederate victory allowed Jackson's men to continue north culminating in another victory at Second Manassas in late August. Shaw mourned the loss of a number of his fellow officers and helped to prepare their bodies for shipment home. *Photograph by Andrew J. Russell. Courtesy Library of Congress.*

"miscreant" Pope, and potentially invade Maryland or Pennsylvania to exploit Northern war weariness before the November midterm elections. Pope's three corps stretched from the Blue Ridge Mountains to the Rappahannock River, a line that Lee immediately targeted. The Confederate commander dispatched Jackson with 14,000 men toward Gordonsville, at Pope's center, later reinforcing him with A. P. Hill's division. On August 6, with temperatures approaching 100 degrees, Pope marched south into Culpeper County to capture the railroad junction. Three days later, Jackson's and Banks's corps collided at Cedar Mountain in a battle that would shatter Shaw's remaining illusions about war's nature.[75]

August 9 dawned brutally hot and humid. Gordon's brigade had received minimal rest before being posted on an eminence on the Union right, near the Orange-Culpeper Road, overlooking the Brown farm. Heat claimed its first casualties before the fighting even began. Several men collapsed from exhaustion, including one new recruit who died from the scorching temperatures.

Both armies endured hours of artillery bombardment that turned waiting into torture. Late afternoon brought the order to attack, and Shaw marched with the rest of the regiment into dense woods toward an open field. To their left, Brig. Gen. Samuel Crawford's brigade was already engaged and being systematically destroyed, "cut to pieces" by Confederate volleys that dropped men in rows.

The 2nd Massachusetts, along with the 3rd Wisconsin Infantry Regiment and 27th Indiana, was ordered to take a position behind a snake-fence and lie down until Confederates drew nearer. In short time the enemy was engaged. Shaw spotted Harry Russell, who was "pulling his moustache and looking over the field, the bullets whistling thick around him." Not five minutes after leaving Harry to order up artillery, the regiment found itself in a deadly crossfire. Colonel Andrews praised the calmness of his officers during the battle: "The enemy having gained our right, their fire became so destructive that the right was obliged to fall back, my right company losing its captain and more than half of its men." Ultimately, they accomplished little on the battlefield before being ordered to abandon the field. The order very likely saved Shaw from having to endure the "hottest fire" from the enemy.[76] A few companies managed to fire off a couple rounds, but within minutes the entire brigade was in full retreat.

Shaw estimated that the regiment was not under fire for more than thirty minutes, but the results were deadly. The regiment went into battle at Cedar Mountain with 474 men, and of these 120 were killed or wounded, along with 37 missing. Of the 22 officers, only 8 emerged from the battle unscathed. Four had been captured; and Shaw was saddened to learn that Harry Russell was counted among the 5 commissioned officers wounded, including Samuel Miller Quincy, who had been severely wounded and left for dead on the battlefield. Overall, the Union suffered 2,353 casualties compared with the 1,338 casualties of the Confederates.[77] Despite the fact that Confederates had achieved a tactical success, Lee chose to abandon the field and continue with offensive operations into northern Virginia.

For Shaw, Cedar Mountain was a rite of passage, an initiation into the horrors of battle. In the days following the battle he wrote no fewer than four letters detailing the events of August 9, which suggests that he replayed it over and over in his mind. Unlike the fight at Winchester, Shaw could see for himself the aftermath of the fight in all its horror and human carnage that littered the battlefield. The following day, Shaw walked the field with Gordon

Four of Shaw's fellow officers and close friends who were killed during the battles of Cedar Mountain and Antietam. *Clockwise from left:* Maj. Wilder Dwight, Capt. Richard Chapman Goodwin, Maj. James Savage Jr., and Capt. Richard Cary. The loss of so many close friends made it easier for Shaw to contemplate leaving the 2nd Massachusetts at the end of 1862. *Collection of the Massachusetts Historical Society.*

and later shared with his mother the agony of discovering the bodies of his friends. "The first man I recognized was Cary," he wrote sadly. "He was lying on his back with his head on a piece of wood. He looked calm and peaceful, as if he were merely sleeping; his face was beautiful, and I could have stood and looked at it a long while."[78] And then, in quick succession, Shaw discovered the body of Capt. William B. Williams, followed by Richard Chapman Goodwin, Edward Gardner Abbott, and Stephen George Perkins.

Shaw accompanied the bodies into Culpeper, where he helped to pack them in charcoal for the short trip to Washington, DC, and then home to their families. Before closing the metallic coffins Shaw "took a lock of hair from each one, to send to their friends." He could barely contain his sadness. He wept for the families, many of whom he knew personally. "Oh! It is hard to believe that we shall never see them again, after having been constantly together for more than a year."[79]

Back on Staten Island, Shaw's parents wrote to the families of the fallen expressing their sadness and grief, while Josephine listed the names of the dead in her diary. She noted that Richard Cary's wife, who lived nearby, "cried bitterly" after hearing the news of the loss of her husband. She had been preparing to travel to Culpeper to nurse her husband after learning that her husband had only been wounded. Now she assumed the task of raising their little girl alone.[80]

The scene was repeated in homes across the country. The summer campaigns had taken an awful toll, and it was clear to most everyone that the war was far from over. Shaw's grief quickly turned to anger and vengeance. "I long for the day when we shall attack the Rebels with an overwhelming force and annihilate them," he wrote to the sister of Harry Russell. "May I live long enough to see them running before us hacked to little pieces."[81]

Shaw would soon have that opportunity. Lee was poised to strike once again in northern Virginia and likely to cross the Potomac River, if feasible. The fate of the nation and slavery hung in the balance.

SIX

It Was the Greatest Fight of the War

News of the Union forces' August 9 defeat at Cedar Mountain reached the Shaw family at their Nahant summer retreat the next morning, shattering the seaside calm with reports of the dead and wounded. Frank Shaw had expected some "great blow" would fall, but nothing had prepared the family for the devastating toll among Boston's elite families.[1] The Shaw family members were relieved to hear that their son and brother had, once again, emerged from battle unharmed.

Back in Virginia, Shaw worried about his close friends, especially Harry Russell, who was missing and presumed to have been taken to Richmond as a prisoner. "I think of him all the time, and miss him at every turn."[2] Despite having "undisputed possession of the battle-field," Confederates abandoned the field and continued their march north, leaving many wounded soldiers in farmhouses and other buildings.[3] Their movements and ultimate objective remained a mystery to Shaw and his comrades. Following Jackson's victory at Cedar Mountain, Lee learned that McClellan was in the process of transferring troops from the peninsula, presumably to link up with Pope's force in northern Virginia. With the Confederate capital now safe, Lee began moving the rest of his troops north to unite with Jackson and defeat Pope's army before he could be reinforced by McClellan.

Shaw struggled to maintain contact with his family as Pope's army stumbled through a series of humiliating retreats. From Culpeper, the 2nd Massachusetts advanced to the Rapidan River only to fall back behind the Rappahannock by August 20, another federal withdrawal that handed Lee the initiative.

The next nine days dissolved into a nightmare of constant movement, with the regiment rarely camping anywhere for longer than a single day. Cut off from supply wagons, the men endured Virginia's scorching sun, torrential rains, choking dust, and clinging mud while subsisting on raw corn and stolen apples. The army was disintegrating through exhaustion and hunger while Lee maneuvered his forces for another devastating blow. Charles J. Mills joined the regiment as a replacement officer after Cedar Mountain, arriving without personal baggage or adequate bedding. Shaw offered his Harvard classmate a "corner" of his blanket during the cold, damp nights, a small gesture of humanity amid the systematic breakdown of military organization.[4]

Despite their recent defeat, the hardships of constant marching "up & down the Rappahannock" did little to dampen Shaw's spirits. He longed for another battle and remained confident that "we fight better than they, and, with an even force, would come out best."[5] Reports of Confederates nearby and the sounds of artillery and musketry in the distance were a clear indication that hard fighting lay ahead.[6]

While Shaw and Pope's officers stumbled through their exhausted retreat, Lee executed a masterpiece of strategic deception. On August 25, he launched Jackson's corps on a daring flanking maneuver—a wide clockwise arc around Pope's right that would sever federal supply lines and trap the Union army between Confederate forces. Jackson's lightning strike achieved complete surprise. His men torched federal supply depots and severed rail lines at Manassas Junction, the same ground where federal forces had fled in humiliation thirteen months earlier.

Between August 28 and 30, 1862, the two armies clashed on or near the old Bull Run battlefield resulting in another decisive Confederate victory. Union casualties topped 16,000, while Confederates suffered roughly 9,000; but, with the former now in disarray, Lee was in an ideal position to cross the Potomac River into Maryland. The 2nd Massachusetts and the rest of Banks's forces were held in reserve on the extreme left of the Union line and were spared having to endure another bloody fight. In the days that followed, Shaw and many of his comrades tried to understand why an entire corps had not been ordered into the fight, but Banks's men had suffered greatly at Cedar Mountain and the subsequent marches only wore the men out even further.[7] They likely would have made no difference to the outcome of the battle.

The defeat at Second Manassas (Second Bull Run) was made worse by the knowledge that the regiment was "just where we started from" six months earlier at the beginning of March. Shaw fell back on a well-worn explanation to explain the army's most recent defeat. "We shall never do much until we get a very different army from what we have now," Shaw exclaimed in a letter to his father. "Until the government finds that it is worth their while to get competent officers & attend themselves to the organization of the army & not allow it to be made a private speculation for Governors of States." The resulting lack of discipline was all too apparent in men skulking from the battlefield and the roads lined with "stragglers."[8]

On September 2, the news that McClellan had been appointed to reorganize the troops around Washington, DC, was greeted by loud cheers of joy among the soldiers—one of the few bright spots at such a low point for the Union cause. Shaw remained supportive of McClellan despite concerns expressed by many in Washington and in the ranks that McClellan had intentionally delayed the transfer of his army to support Pope against Lee's offensive.[9] Accusations of "treason" were expressed by some Radical Republicans such as Michigan's Zacharia Chandler.[10] These doubts, including McClellan's political conservatism, were shared by Shaw's family back home—a gulf between him and his parents that would only grow wider. As far as Shaw was concerned, McClellan's return was just the element of stability and leadership that the army needed if it had any hope of thwarting Lee's decision on September 4 to cross the Potomac River into Maryland.

In just eight weeks, Robert E. Lee had shattered Union strategy, driving McClellan from Richmond's gates back to Washington's defenses; Lee was now poised to invade the United States.[11] Lee gambled everything on Maryland's loyalty, crossing the Potomac with his battered army based on the fatal assumption that Marylanders had been forcibly prevented from joining the Confederacy in 1861. But this optimism about Marylanders' loyalty was dampened almost immediately upon the army's arrival in Frederick. The same residents who had welcomed Shaw's regiment the previous winter turned their backs on the Confederate forces, slamming shutters and emptying the streets as Lee's ragged columns marched through their town. As one historian observed, "Most residents of Frederick regarded not Lee but the Union army . . . as their liberator."[12]

Despite Maryland's cold reception, Lee pursued multiple strategic objectives beyond simple invasion. Virginia's farmers desperately needed uninterrupted harvest time after months of armies trampling their fields and consuming their crops. More ambitiously, Lee believed a decisive Confederate victory in Maryland—or even in Pennsylvania—could shatter Northern morale just weeks before the November midterm elections. Finally, Lee hoped further battlefield success would convince Britain to recognize Confederate independence and intervene militarily against the Union.[13] Lee's was just the kind of bold leadership that Shaw hoped McClellan might exhibit in the coming campaign.

Along with the news of McClellan's return, Shaw learned that the 2nd Massachusetts, now under the command of Col. George L. Andrews, had been assigned to the 3rd Brigade of the 1st Division of the newly formed XII Corps under the command of Maj. Gen. Joseph K. Mansfield. In addition to the 3rd Wisconsin and 27th Indiana, the 3rd Brigade was bolstered by the 13th New Jersey Infantry and 107th New York Infantry. Officers in the 2nd Massachusetts were horrified to learn that the New Jersey boys had been rushed into the field and had not been properly drilled in the loading and firing of their weapons. What mattered most to Shaw, however, was that his regiment was now officially part of the Army of the Potomac.[14]

Shaw welcomed the respite at Rockville after weeks of brutal marching. The arrival of regimental wagons reunited soldiers with personal belongings they had not seen in more than three weeks of constant movement. Men eagerly washed away the accumulated filth that announced an army's approach miles downwind and changed into clean clothes for the first time in recent memory. Campfires crackled with renewed life as soldiers enjoyed proper meals and caught up on long-delayed correspondence with families who had received no word during the chaotic retreat from Virginia. Shaw finally slept under canvas rather than sharing corners of threadbare blankets with his fellow officers.

By September 11, the Army of the Potomac was moving west toward Frederick to confront Lee's army. The men were impressed with the rolling hills, patches of wood, and well-kept farms of central Maryland. Charles Mills described it as "paradise compared with Virginia."[15] Shaw likely heard the news that just outside Frederick a soldier nearby in the 27th Indiana had come across a paper wrapped around some cigars intended for one of Lee's commanders; the papers provided the Union army with valuable information concerning the Army of Northern Virginia's movements and campaign plans.

Thinking that he would have plenty of time to maneuver unmolested by McClellan, Lee divided his already outnumbered army by sending Jackson's entire corps of 25,000 men to capture Harpers Ferry and secure a Confederate line of retreat, if needed. The remaining Army of Northern Virginia continued west toward Hagerstown, leaving Lee dangerously exposed should McClellan move quickly enough to exploit the separation. McClellan was, in fact, on the move. By September 15, the 2nd Massachusetts had passed through South Mountain's gaps, where Lee had tried unsuccessfully to block Union pursuit the previous day. War's debris littered the mountainside—abandoned equipment, bloodstained rocks, hastily dug graves—a clear indication that another battle was imminent. The regiment bivouacked near Keedysville that night, then moved closer to the sleepy village of Sharpsburg along Antietam Creek, where Lee was desperately trying to concentrate his scattered forces. Shaw could see Confederate positions on the ridgeline across the creek, close enough to distinguish individual enemy soldiers preparing defensive works.

That evening Shaw sought out his close friend William Forbes, stationed nearby with the 1st Massachusetts Cavalry. They shared letters from home by firelight. Shaw read aloud letters from Josephine and Nellie, who were still enjoying their family vacation at Nahant while their brother prepared for battle. "We lay on his blanket before the fire, until 10 o'clock, and then I left him, little realizing what a day the next was to be; though a battle was expected, and I thought, as I rode off, that perhaps we shouldn't see each other again."[16]

There was little opportunity to sleep. Overnight, the brigade was marched roughly three miles across the Antietam Creek and came to a rest on a wheat field. "Our pickets fired all night, and at daylight we were waked up by the artillery," Shaw recalled.[17]

Lee's army clung to undulating ridgelines west of Antietam Creek, his forces still dangerously divided and outnumbered. With Jackson's corps racing north following the Union surrender at Harpers Ferry on September 15, Lee desperately needed time to reunite his scattered forces around Sharpsburg before McClellan could exploit the Confederate's weakness. McClellan's battle plan was simple and promised a decisive victory if executed properly. A simultaneous three-pronged assault would prevent Lee from shifting reinforcements along his interior lines to threatened sectors. McClellan was well aware that the Potomac River, winding its way in the army's rear eliminated

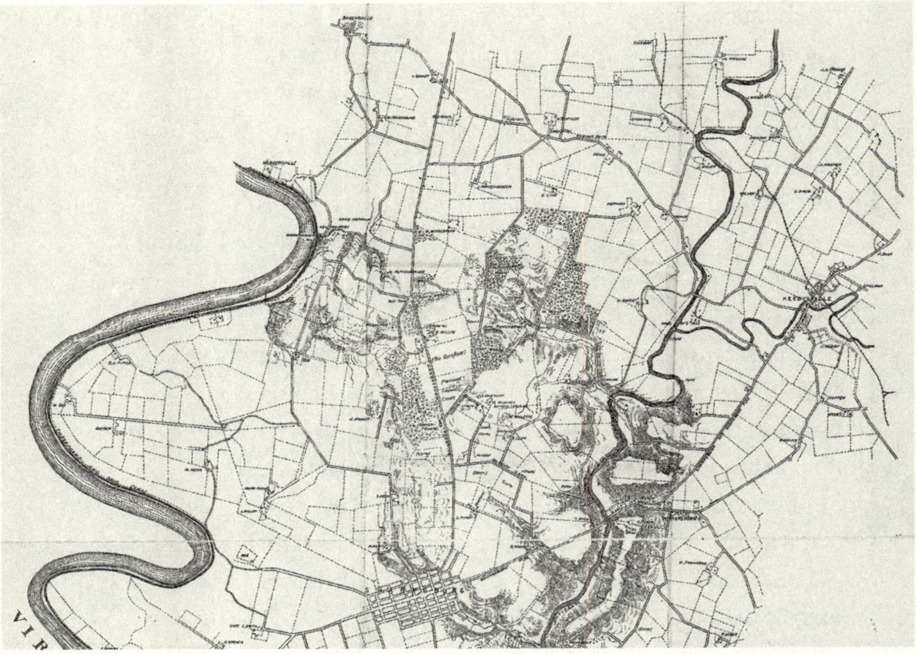

Map from 1894 showing the area around Sharpsburg, Maryland. The 2nd Massachusetts took part in the morning phase of the battle of Antietam, along the Hagerstown Pike, which ran north out of the town of Sharpsburg. The regiment saw fighting in what eventually came to be known as the cornfield as well as in support of Maj. Gen. John Sedgwick's advance into the West Woods near the Dunker Church. *Courtesy Library of Congress.*

any easy retreat options. Any significant breakthrough could trap and destroy the entire Army of Northern Virginia.

As morning fog lifted, Shaw gazed across Maryland's pastoral landscape that boasted orchards heavy with fruit, tall cornfields ready for harvest, freshly plowed fields, scattered woodlots, and rolling meadows. Zigzag or split-rail fences along the Hagerstown Pike divided the countryside into neat parcels, creating the timeless pattern of American agricultural prosperity. Under different circumstances, such scenery might have inspired poetic reflection on nature's beauty or America's bounty. Shaw's military training, however, had transformed his vision. Orchards became cover for advancing infantry, cornfields concealed enemy movements, and fence lines channeled attacks into killing zones.

The battle that unfolded on September 17, 1862, eventually enveloped the entire area around Sharpsburg and turned the cornfields, apple orchards, and farm lanes red with blood; but for Shaw and his regiment, the battle occupied a small area of farmland north of town. At around 8 a.m., the 2nd Massachusetts was ordered to march south along the Hagerstown Pike as part of a broader movement involving two Union corps to gain a plateau around the Dunker Church, the religious home of a group of pacifist German Baptist Brethren. Shaw's regiment held the brigade's right flank, with the 3rd Wisconsin and 27th Indiana extending the line leftward. The 2nd Massachusetts moved briefly through David Miller's apple orchard before advancing into his towering cornfield to support the other regiments, whose casualties were mounting fast, on an exposed knoll. Inside the corn rows, visibility dropped to mere yards as stalks higher than a man's head created a maze of green tunnels. Shaw could hear the Wisconsin and Indiana regiments being torn apart by Confederate volleys, but he could see almost nothing through the dense crop. When Alfred Colquitt's Georgia and Alabama brigades counterattacked into the cornfield, the battle became a deadly game of cat and mouse.

For thirty minutes, Shaw and his men fought an invisible enemy in the agricultural labyrinth. Muzzle flashes erupted from corn rows without warning, men screamed and fell among the stalks, and officers shouted contradictory orders while trying to maintain unit cohesion in terrain that fragmented every formation.

The results of the fighting were evident to Shaw as the regiment marched through the cornfield. "It was full of their dead and wounded, and one of our sergeants took a regimental colour there, belonging to the Eleventh Mississippi." "Beyond the cornfield," Shaw continued, "was a large open field, and such a mass of dead and wounded men, mostly Rebels, as were lying there, I never saw before; it was a terrible sight, and our men had to be very careful to avoid treading on them; many were mangled and torn to pieces by artillery, but most of them had been wounded by musketry fire."[18] Wilder Dwight eventually got ahold of a captured Confederate banner and rode along the line of the 2nd Massachusetts to the cheers of everyone. Charley Morse recalled, "The whole field before [us] was literally covered with dead and dying."[19]

For a brief moment, their hatred of the enemy, which had been so clearly articulated by Shaw following the battle of Cedar Mountain, was set aside as he watched his men stop to share their canteens with the wounded and place them in "easy positions." "There are so many young boys and old men among the Rebels," he observed, "that it seems hardly possible that they can have come of their own accord to fight us, and it makes you pity them all the more, as they lie moaning on the field."[20]

Whatever feelings of sympathy emerged among the men quickly passed as the regiment was ordered to a position at the edge of the East Woods. As the 2nd Massachusetts shifted to its new position, Maj. Gen. John Sedgwick's division swept across their front to assault the West Woods. "It was a grand sight," Shaw recalled, "and they looked as if they couldn't be repulsed." "They were in three lines," wrote Morse, "and looked splendidly"[21]

Shortly thereafter, Sedgwick's division "received . . . a most terrible musketry-fire, and finally had to fall back." The brigade was ordered to march toward the Hagerstown Pike to support what Sedgwick believed to be friendly troops that had reentered the West Woods. Elements of the 2nd, along with the 13th New Jersey to their right, just south of the Miller cornfield, scaled the fences along the Hagerstown Pike, but the site of the brigade's colors captured the enemy's attention. Instead of coming to the support of their comrades, Shaw and the rest of the brigade had marched straight into Brig. Gen. Robert Ransom's North Carolinians who were lying in wait in the woods. A hail of Confederate bullets from the woods forced Shaw and the rest of the brigade to abandon their position. Of the Confederates, Lt. John A. Fox later wrote, "They loaded and fired as cooly as ever." He watched "man after man fall dead or wounded, while we inflicted but little injury upon the enemy."[22] Morse was hit by a spent ball, which "laid me on my back for a moment, and raised a pretty black & blue spot."[23] At about this same time, Shaw was struck by a "spent ball in the neck, which bruised, but didn't break the skin."[24]

The scale of the fighting witnessed during the first few hours of the battle could have constituted an entire battle unto itself, but it was just its first phase. By late morning, the fighting shifted south to the center around a farm lane that is remembered to this day as "The Bloody Lane." Later in the afternoon, the Union's IX Corps, under the command of Maj. Gen. Ambrose Burnside, crossed a bridge that would eventually bear his name and advanced within sight of the town of Sharpsburg, only to be pushed back by the timely arrival of Lee's Confederates from Harpers Ferry.

Once the fighting ceased, Shaw took stock of the regiment's losses, which included 12 killed, 56 wounded, and 2 missing. Also counted among the dead was General Mansfield, who was killed, "to the great regret of us all," while personally leading troops on the field in the East Woods.[25] Shaw could only begin to grasp the scale of death across the two armies; it would take days to tally the names of the dead and wounded. Fewer than twelve hours of fighting cost the Army of the Potomac more than 12,000 casualties, while the Confederate losses numbered roughly 10,000 in killed, wounded, and missing combined. Shaw characterized the day's fighting as "the greatest fight of the war," and it remains to this day the bloodiest day in American history.

The Confederate dead scattered along the Hagerstown Pike.
This photograph was taken just a few yards from where the 2nd
Massachusetts maneuvered in support of Sedgwick's advance into
the West Woods on the morning of September 17, 1862.
Photograph by Alexander Gardner. Courtesy Library of Congress.

As was the case following Cedar Mountain, Shaw experienced the lengthy casualty list through the loss of or injury to close personal friends. His growing list now included Charles J. Mills, Francis W. Crowninshield, and James Francis, all of whom were wounded. The toughest loss for Shaw was Wilder Dwight, who fell during the regiment's support of Sedgwick's assault in the West Woods. Dwight started the day by penning a letter to his mother, only to be interrupted by orders to advance. Following his fatal wounding, Dwight continued his now bloodstained letter, the life literally draining from his body: "Dearest mother, I am wounded so as to be helpless. Good bye if so it must be[.] I think I die in victory. God defend our country. . . . Give love to father & all my dear brothers."[26]

Once darkness overtook the battlefield, Shaw noted that the "crickets chirped, and the frogs croaked, just as if nothing unusual had happened all day long, and presently the stars came out bright." Charley Morse and Shaw found a spot on the field to lay down to rest. They talked about their homes and families "among the thousands of dead about us."[27] Charley recalled that he and Shaw "slept within fifty feet of a pile of fourteen dead rebels, and in every direction about us they were lying thick."[28]

Shaw awoke early the next morning fully expecting the battle to continue since Lee's men remained in place. But those orders never came, leaving the Army of Northern Virginia the opportunity to recross the Potomac River "undisturbed" later that evening. Lee's escape left Shaw and others perplexed. On the one hand, his confidence in McClellan's leadership remained high. The soldiers, Shaw asserted "will fight under him better than under any one else, is proved by the difference between this battle and those about Manassas." On the other hand, he found it hard to believe that retaining control of the battlefield was all McClellan "wanted." In fact, control of the battlefield was all that McClellan apparently needed to claim victory and celebrate his success. Although Lee had failed to achieve all the goals set out at the beginning of the campaign, he managed to refocus the seat of war away from Richmond; and although severely battered, the Army of Northern Virginia remained intact. McClellan's failure to pursue him more vigorously allowed Confederates to gather stragglers, rest, and recross the Potomac to continue with offensive operations as the opportunity presented itself.[29]

McClellan's failure to pursue Lee after Antietam widened the gulf between Shaw and his family to a dangerous chasm. Frank and Sarah had grown disgusted with McClellan's Democratic politics and opposition to emancipation; they directly questioning their son about why his commander appeared to be incapable of destroying Lee's retreating army.

Shaw's defense of McClellan revealed the length to which he would go to defend his embattled army commander. He dismissed his family's criticisms, falling back on familiar complaints about army discipline and citing the "thousands of stragglers between here and Alexandria" as evidence of Union weakness. More troubling, Shaw urged his mother to judge McClellan purely on his ability to "obey orders and carry out plans," not on whether he was "inspired with the same faith in principles that you have." "If we have a man of military ability," he asserted, "we have what we need."[30] Political convictions, moral commitments, and the war's deeper purpose were irrelevant to Shaw as long as generals could execute tactical maneuvers effectively. The gulf between Shaw and his family widened further into mid-October, following Abraham Lincoln's September 22 formal issuance of the Preliminary Emancipation Proclamation.

There can be little doubt that Shaw's continued faith in McClellan was a disappointment to his parents, but his response to Lincoln's proclamation initially raised questions as to whether he fully shared their commitment to ending slavery. Lincoln had announced to his cabinet earlier that July that he was planning to issue a proclamation that would give the Confederate states until the end of 1862 to end the rebellion and return to the Union. If they failed to do so, slaves (with a few exceptions) would be freed throughout the Confederacy—in areas not yet occupied by the Union army. Lincoln had agreed to wait for a military victory before announcing the new policy rather than risk looking politically weak. Five days after the battle of Antietam, the proclamation was made public.

Though abolitionists like the Shaws lamented the fact that the proclamation would not be applied immediately—that it gave the rebelling states the opportunity to return to the Union with slavery largely intact; that it only applied to states still in rebellion; and finally, that it reiterated support for compensation and colonization—the family was thrilled with the news.[31] The proclamation, wrote Sarah to a correspondent overseas, "is in God's providence that we shall never rest until Slavery is entirely destroyed, & that this is the first step towards it."[32] "God bless Abraham Lincoln," Josephine wrote in her diary; but she also noted that while her parents welcomed the news, her mother believed that the proclamation did not go far enough.[33] In addition, Josephine was devastated by the news of Dwight's death, especially after having spent time with the fallen major earlier that summer in Nahant. The proclamation likely offered her some reassurance that his death was for a higher purpose.

Her brother, however, was much more skeptical about the proclamation's likely impact. "For my part, I can't see what *practical* good it can do now," he admitted to his mother. "Wherever our army has been, there remain no slaves, and the Proclamation will not free them where we don't go." Just as concerning to him was the likely response of the Confederate government, which he believed would "issue a proclamation threatening to hang every prisoner they take" and quickly turn the conflict into a "war of extermination." As for the proclamation's impact on the enslaved population, Shaw worried that their "condition . . . will not be ameliorated . . . if they are suspected of plotting insurrection, or trying to run away." Shaw likely knew that his response would disappoint his mother, so he was quick to reassure her that he believed Lincoln's proclamation was "the right thing to do, but that, as a war measure, the evil will overbalance the good for the *present*."[34]

Shaw acknowledged the Emancipation Proclamation's moral justification but remained fixated on strategic calculations rather than humanitarian imperatives. His primary concern was not human freedom but military efficiency. The question that ultimately mattered was whether emancipation would accelerate Union victory or prolong an already devastating conflict. Many soldiers shared his skepticism about whether freeing enslaved people would help or hinder the war effort. Shaw's pragmatic evaluation revealed how completely combat had trumped moral considerations.[35]

The attempt to reassure his parents that he had not abandoned his antislavery principles proved insufficient. In a subsequent letter dated October 10, 1862, Shaw found himself once again attempting to explain to his mother that he believed the president's proclamation to be an "act of justice," but that "as a war-measure" he still did not "see the immediate benefit of it," and that "much of the moral force of the act has been lost by our long delay in coming to it."[36] This was essentially a restating of his original position and likely did little to bridge the gulf between the two.

Shaw's concern that the proclamation would allow "evil" to "overpower the good" was shared by many of his fellow officers in the 2nd Massachusetts. Initially, Charley Morse maintained "that no change would be produced by it"; but he eventually admitted that it was the "beginning of a great reform." European nations would be less likely to officially recognize the Confederacy as an independent nation. The Union army was also likely to benefit from Confederate soldiers abandoning the army to protect their homes and families from "servile insurrection" that they believed would follow as news of the new policy spread throughout the South.[37] As we have already seen, Alonzo Quint's views on the subject of emancipation evolved early in the war, but in March 1862 he had expressed the concern that "if 'general emancipation' were now made the object of this war, I fully believe that our armies would melt away." He had gone on to assert, "Our men are fighting for the flag, not for the abolition of slavery. . . . General emancipation would add untold horrors to what already has horrors enough—WAR." Quint's views eventually softened, and he later acknowledged, "The more I see, the more I believe in the feasibility of emancipation"; though he also admitted that such a measure would be accompanied by numerous "obstacles."[38]

There is little doubt that Shaw shared Quint's views on emancipation and Lincoln's proclamation with fellow officers in the regiment and that he likely gave serious consideration to their thoughts as well. Resistance to emancipation in the army took many forms and collectively point to Lincoln's own reluctance to directly confront the subject. As one historian has correctly observed, "The cause of Union united Northern soldiers; the cause of emancipation divided them."[39]

Frank and Sarah should not have been surprised by their son's position on emancipation. He had never expressed much interest in the welfare of escaped slaves when the regiment was stationed in the Shenandoah Valley, nor did he ever explicitly state that the war was being fought primarily to end slavery. Shaw's focus from the beginning of his enlistment had been on preparing himself and his men for battle, defeating the Confederacy, and in the process, advancing his own prospects through promotion. Though the results of the fighting at Antietam had resulted in a Union victory, there was no indication that the war was any closer to being concluded. On the contrary, in addition to Lee's offensive into Maryland, Confederates had also invaded the border state of Kentucky before they were turned back at Perryville at the beginning of October. Shaw had no doubt that more fighting was in his future and, perhaps more importantly, he understood that the war could still be lost.[40]

Out of respect for his mother, Shaw attempted to explain himself one more time on the subject of emancipation and to offer her reassurance. "You must have thought, from my late letters, that I was degenerating sadly from the principles in which I was brought up; but an ordinary mortal must be somewhat affected by his surroundings, and events which you look at in one way from a distance, often seem very different when you are in the midst of them. The man at a distance is more apt to be impartial."[41] Shaw pleaded for his mother's understanding, insisting that he had not abandoned the antislavery principles taught to him as a child, but that from his perspective it was anything but clear on how best to prosecute the war and bring it to a successful conclusion. He wanted his mother to exercise a little empathy and to appreciate the confusion, uncertainty, and mortal danger that clouded every decision.

The incessant debate with his family over the war had taken a toll on Shaw. More than anything else, Shaw wanted his parents to cease discussing the president's proclamation with him, and he characterized as "sensible" McClellan's "order cautioning officers and soldiers to refrain from discussion of the President's acts."[42] In a letter written at the end of October 1862, Shaw pleaded with Josephine to refrain from "making any more remarks on the conduct of the War." The "subject is one, of which I am heartily sick."[43]

A few days after Antietam, the 2nd Massachusetts was ordered to take up a new position at South Mountain, near Harpers Ferry. The once familiar and picturesque landscape now looked desolate as the "trees had all been cut down and the old paths obliterated" by the constant movement of armies.[44] The new encampment was likely a welcome change, given the continued work of treating the thousands of wounded in and around Sharpsburg and the reminders of the great battle clearly evidenced on the battlefield and throughout the town itself. Shaw, along with Charley Morse and a few other officers, organized a mess and managed to find a "good cook, who can make a good coffee . . . can cook eggs in any way very nicely, and can also make pies and pudding, to roast and broil a stew is child's play for him."[45] Shaw used the lull in military activity to catch up on paperwork and the drilling of new recruits.

The regiment was also reviewed by the president in their new encampment as he made his way to Sharpsburg to encourage McClellan to cross the Potomac River and continue his pursuit of Robert E. Lee. One soldier in the 2nd Massachusetts thought it "funny" to "have the good old President ride smiling along so close that I could have touched him with my bayonet."[46] The relative inactivity left plenty of time for Shaw and Morse to saddle up their horses for the twenty-mile ride to Sharpsburg to spend time with friends or a relaxing excursion into Pleasant Valley. Soon the first indications of bright colors in the foliage along the mountains, and the first snowfalls signaled the coming of winter.

Shaw also enjoyed a brief, but welcome reunion with his family in New York City for the marriage of his sister Susie to Robert Minturn, who worked in the shipping commission house of Grinnell, Minturn and Co. The ceremony, along with the polished silverware, heated rooms, good cheer, and sophisticated dress, offered Shaw a stark reminder of the life and privilege he had left behind. On his return to camp, Shaw learned that the regiment had been ordered to return to Sharpsburg.[47]

The news of McClellan's firing the day after the congressional midterm elections on November 4, 1862, was welcome news in the Shaw home; but throughout the Army of the Potomac there was little confidence in Gen. Ambrose Burnside, who was chosen as his replacement. Concerns on the home front that the Army of the Potomac's rank and file would fight only under McClellan were quickly dispelled. The regimental chaplain for the 2nd Massachusetts responded that such notions were "perfectly foolish." "Our men fight for *their* country, not for a *man*."[48] Shaw certainly would have agreed, but he failed to see what Burnside had "ever done to merit the position."[49] The change at the top of the military chain of command, along with the deteriorating weather, convinced Shaw that the army's inactivity would continue indefinitely.

The relative inactivity of the army left Shaw considering a transfer out of the regiment. This was not the first time Shaw considered joining a new unit and assignment. Throughout his time in the army, Shaw was on the lookout for a command and responsibility befitting his class. In early October Shaw had been offered and rejected a position on the staff of his former tutor Frank Barlow, now a brigadier general and rising star in the Army of the Potomac. More enticing was the opportunity to join a new cavalry unit that was being organized in Massachusetts at that time. Shaw had heard about it through his cousin John Murray Forbes. Charles Russell Lowell was purportedly going to command the unit, with Caspar Crowninshield—Shaw's former Harvard roommate currently serving in the 1st Massachusetts Cavalry—serving at the rank of major. Life in the cavalry would present a number of challenges for Shaw, given his lack of experience in such a unit, but his biggest concern had to do with rank. After being promoted to the rank of captain following the battle of Antietam, Shaw was now one of the more experienced officers in the 2nd Massachusetts and was unwilling to "accept any position below that of 4th Captain"; and he expressed doubt that the new cavalry unit could "guarantee that to me."[50]

Harry Russell's return to the 2nd Massachusetts, following his parole from Libby Prison in Richmond, made Shaw's decision much easier. Even though many of his friends were no longer present, having been wounded or killed, Shaw was still attached to his regiment. "A man is or should be very loath to leave a regiment in which he has gone through as much as we have in this," he explained to his sister. "I have had a great many discontented moments, when I have thought I wanted to change, but when it came to deciding, I never went—Excepting on to Gordon's staff & then I was delighted to be back."[51] Shaw would remain with his regiment for the time being.

Another reason for Shaw's hesitancy to transfer to a new unit may also have been due to his developing relationship with Annie Haggerty. The two had maintained a regular correspondence over the previous two years and had, on occasion, spent time together during his visits home. Shaw kept a photograph of Annie, and his mother sent no fewer than four pictures of him in uniform to Annie's mother. Details of their relationship are difficult to discern given the absence of much of their correspondence. Sometime after Antietam Shaw proposed to Annie.[52] It took two weeks for Annie to respond, but it likely was not what Shaw hoped to hear. "She didn't say 'yes,' outright,"

Shaw reported to his mother, but he remained confident "that it will come [out] all right in the end."[53]

Annie may have worried about the stability of a marriage begun in the midst of an uncertain war. Her husband would be away for an indefinite period of time, and there was no guarantee that Shaw would survive the war. Annie likely knew of the strains the war placed on marriages in her own network of friends, and wives in mourning dress offered stark reminders of the grief that possibly awaited her if she agreed to marriage. There is also the likelihood that Annie harbored doubts about Shaw's long-term prospects, given the difficulty he experienced deciding on a career before the war. As has already been discussed, Shaw briefly considered a military career before the war. Shaw was evidently unclear in his response to her inquiry about his plans on possibly "staying in the army after the war." He admitted to not having thought about it "for a good while," but beyond a commitment to remain in the army until the end of the war, he was unable to offer a firm response.[54]

The close relationship between Shaw and his mother may also have left Annie wondering whether their marriage would be intruded upon in any way. In a letter to Annie, Shaw admitted that he "felt wicked when I told you I wanted to see you even more than Mother; I have always loved her more than any one else in the world, and I think she has me, from the sacrifices she has made for me, and for which I can never repay her."[55]

Finally, Annie may have also picked up on Frank's and Sarah's concerns about a wartime marriage. Though Annie hailed from a wealthy New York family that had made its fortune in the shipping industry, as had the Shaws, the Haggerty family did not trace their roots to Boston's Brahmin community. Whether the Shaws had any misgivings in this regard, however, is unlikely, given the Haggertys' reformist commitments. Frank and Sarah may have feared that marriage would prove a distraction to their son's military duties and preferred that the young couple wait until after the war. "Wartime romances were conducted," as one historian has written, "in an impassioned environment—one in which meetings between young women and their soldier beaux during furloughs or other short periods of time away from the war could ignite smoldering feelings into permanent commitments."[56] Shaw was ultimately relieved to hear from his mother that she approved of the match and that he would be a "fortunate fellow to get her."[57] Any lingering doubts Shaw may have had about Annie's ultimate acceptance of his proposal were probably dispelled in a letter that has since been lost. The couple chose to keep their engagement confidential, sharing the news only with close family members.

Shaw's positive spin on what he believed to be Annie's impending acceptance of his proposal and Harry Russell's return to the regiment proved to be the only bright spots for him as 1862 came to a close. Shaw and Russell shared a "very comfortable cubby-house together, with an open, brick fireplace, and all the modern conveniences."[58] The Army of the Potomac remained in encampment because of the weather and the appointment of General Burnside as the new overall commander, whom Shaw and many others believed to be unqualified. Shaw's decision to stay in the 2nd Massachusetts also signaled that his military prospects would remain in limbo for the foreseeable future. The return of the regiment to Sharpsburg at the end of November 1862 reminded Shaw of the many close friends that he had lost at Cedar Mountain and Antietam. "There is hardly a tree near without several bullets and cannonballs in it," Shaw noted on one of many rides around the battlefield. "The place is full of graves; thirty or forty men together in some of them, often without a board to mark the place." Decaying horses were still "scattered about, for a distance of four miles."[59]

The regiment's celebration of its second Thanksgiving away from home proved to be a "very quiet affair" due to the absence "from the table [of] so many faces which were there last year at this time." Shaw could not help but use the occasion to reflect on the fate of his friends. "It is very strange and unfortunate," he observed in a letter to Annie, "that the officers that have been killed were the very best we had, both as comrades and as military men. . . . No doubt, after a man is dead his virtues only are remembered, but in our case the dead ones really were the best."[60] Shaw's melancholy was magnified by a lingering concern that their deaths would ultimately prove to be in vain, given the continued inaction of the Army of the Potomac and the broader state of military affairs.

Burnside's November 15 order to move the Army of the Potomac toward Fredericksburg may have lifted Shaw's spirits, but the 2nd Massachusetts remained stranded in Maryland while the main army departed. Burnside's plan promised the kind of aggressive movement Shaw had long craved. The general hoped to cross the Rappahannock River on pontoons, maneuver around Lee's right flank, and position his army between Richmond and the Army of Northern Virginia. The strategy depended entirely on speed and coordination, qualities the Army of the Potomac had rarely demonstrated. While Burnside's men reached Falmouth, opposite Fredericksburg, in just two days, the critical pontoons took an additional week to arrive. That delay gave Lee the time he needed to recognize Burnside's intentions and respond accordingly.[61]

Lee's army used the week-long delay to transform Fredericksburg into an impregnable fortress. Confederate engineers carved gun emplacements into Marye's Heights while infantry dug trenches and built stone walls that would channel Union attacks allowing Lee's men to take full advantage of their positions. When Burnside finally ordered the river crossing on December 11, his soldiers had to fight street by street through Fredericksburg before facing the real horror two days later. Burnside launched wave after wave of assaults against prepared Confederate positions. On the Confederate right, Union forces briefly penetrated Jackson's line before being hurled back with devastating losses. The main attack focused on James Longstreet's corps defending the stone wall below Marye's Heights—a position so strong that Longstreet reportedly told Lee, "If you put every man on the other side of the Potomac on that field to approach me over the same line, I will kill them all before they reach my line." The Army of the Potomac suffered roughly 12,500 casualties while the Confederates suffered roughly half that number, with little gained for Burnside.[62]

Shaw learned of the defeat while encamped forty-five miles north of Fredericksburg at Fairfax Station with much of the rest of the XII Corps. The 2nd Massachusetts had left comfortable cabins to face "some very hard weather" that included "rain, snow, and cold" with little more than their tents and a couple of blankets that Shaw and Russell fastened together to stay warm.[63] Shaw likely worried about his friends in the 20th Massachusetts, which had taken part in the street fighting in Fredericksburg, before joining the assault the following day.[64]

But it was the loss of his cousin Theodore Parkman on December 16, 1862—the result of a friendly fire during a skirmish at Whitehall, North Carolina—that hit Shaw hardest. Parkman had left home only the previous month to join the 45th Massachusetts Infantry Regiment. His loss after such a short period made little sense to Shaw given that he had largely escaped serious wounding after eighteen months away from home and having participated in more than one major battle. "It must be all chance; for if he had lived," Shaw believed, "he would probably have done more good in the world than I ever shall."[65]

As for the loss of his cousin and the late-year battle, there was little more that Shaw could say other than to acknowledge that war is a "terrible thing that so many lives should have been lost for nothing."[66] It should come as no surprise that Shaw was feeling disillusioned as the year came to a close. He had witnessed too many military setbacks in 1862 and had mourned the loss of too many friends. In a letter to his sister just a few days before Christmas and a few weeks before Lincoln's Emancipation Proclamation was to be enacted, Shaw expressed his frustrations with the war's lack of progress:

> They say that "Uncle Abe" is on the verge of lunacy. I don't wonder at it. I am afraid now there is a danger of the government backing down. I had rather stay here all my life (though in this case, I should pray for a short one) than give up to the South. The most satisfactory ending to me, would be to have them brought to their knees, and then kicked out, and allowed to set up for themselves within certain limits. I would have them hemmed in on all sides by free States, and not allowed a chance of extending.[67]

Shaw must have known that his parents would read or at least hear about the content of this letter, and he may even have anticipated their disappointment. After reassuring his mother that he had not abandoned his abolitionist principles, the question of emancipation appeared to be of little concern to him as the year came to an end. Shaw was willing to see the war end with a defeated, but independent, Confederacy left to govern itself with slavery still largely intact. His conviction that slavery could be contained by a cordon of free states harkened back to a position embraced by many Republicans before the war; but much had changed since then that rendered such a view a surrender of principle by his parents. Perhaps Shaw recognized that his was an untenable position, and perhaps he was simply using the opportunity to vent his frustrations.

The year 1862 had been transformative for Robert Gould Shaw and the rest of the nation. Through it all, Shaw struggled to come to terms with the shifting landscape of war. He finally experienced the chaos and violence of battle, and although he stood the test well, he mourned the loss of a number of close friends whose comradeship he had relied on for support. He had witnessed thousands of African Americans flock to the Union army along the roads and pathways of Virginia's Shenandoah Valley, forcing Republicans in Congress to approve policies that gradually eroded the institution of slavery. Lincoln's Preliminary Emancipation Proclamation moved emancipation to the center of the nation's wartime agenda, but it also widened an already significant gulf between Shaw and his parents over how the war should be conducted. The war would soon assume a revolutionary character in the new year, one that would continue to undermine the institution of slavery, in part, through the recruitment of African Americans into the US Army. The only question that remained was whether Shaw would embrace and contribute to achieving these new wartime goals.

SEVEN

I Feel Convinced I Shall Never Regret Having Taken This Step

January 1, 1863, dawned cold, cloudy, and gloomy in Boston, but the city's abolitionist elite gathered at Music Hall in anticipation of Lincoln's promise to sign the Emancipation Proclamation. The orchestra performed Mendelssohn's *Hymn of Praise* and Beethoven's Fifth Symphony for an audience that included literary giants Oliver Wendell Holmes, John Greenleaf Whittier, Henry Wadsworth Longfellow, and Harriet Beecher Stowe. The event's program proclaimed the significance of the occasion: "This first day of the new year will prove the complement of the 4th of July 1776, and a new era in the history of the Republic, when the soil of America, hallowed anew by the sacrifice of so much heroic blood, shall no longer be trodden by the foot of a slave."[1] Boston's abolitionists understood they were witnessing the moral revolution they had advocated for decades. The proclamation would transform Lincoln's war to preserve the Union into a struggle to destroy slavery. When word arrived that Lincoln had indeed signed the Emancipation

Proclamation, a "storm of enthusiasm followed. . . . Shouts arose, hats, and handkerchiefs were waved, men and women sprang to their feet to give more energetic utterances to their joy."[2]

Across town at Tremont Temple, located across the street from Park Street Church, where William Lloyd Garrison had delivered his earliest abolitionist speeches, Frederick Douglass joined fellow Black abolitionists William Wells Brown, William Cooper Nell, Rev. Leonard Grimes, and Charles Lenox Remond, along with a crowd that was estimated at three thousand. Garrison, once a close mentor and now rival of Douglass's, chose to remain at Music Hall, thus avoiding an uncomfortable encounter on what promised to be a joyous occasion. Douglass's anxiety grew with each passing hour as the crowd increased in size and cheered the many speeches delivered that day. Douglass knew that there was always the chance that Lincoln would back down from signing the proclamation. Perhaps the Confederacy had agreed to return to the Union in the final hours of 1862, or Lincoln's own understanding of military necessity might have shifted, rendering the proclamation unnecessary or even counterproductive in his mind. "Every moment of waiting chilled our hopes, strengthened our fears." Finally, "a face fairly illumined with the news he bore, exclaimed in tones that thrilled all hearts, 'It is coming! It is on the wires!'" Douglass and the crowd could barely contain themselves upon the realization that Lincoln had kept his promise. "Joy and gladness," Douglass wrote, "exhausted all forms of expression from shouts of praise to sobs and tears." After midnight, the crowd moved across the Boston Common to continue the celebration at Grimes's Twelfth Street Baptist Church, where freedom seekers had long sought protection.[3]

One thousand miles to the south, in Port Royal, South Carolina, a large interracial crowd gathered at Camp Saxton, which served as the training ground for the 1st South Carolina Colored Infantry Regiment. The roads "were thronged" with visitors that included military officers and other dignitaries as well as the many teachers and other reformers who had traveled to the Sea Islands to work with the thousands of formerly enslaved men, women, and children after the Union navy had occupied the area in November 1861.

Charlotte Forten, a young Black school teacher from Salem, Massachusetts, took a ferry from St. Helena Island to take part in the festivities. "As I sat on the stand [and] looked around on the various groups," she later recalled in her diary, "I thought I had never seen a sight so beautiful. There were the black soldiers, in their blue coats and scarlet pants, the officers of this and other regiments in their handsome uniforms, and crowds of lookers-on, men, women and children grouped in various attitudes, under the trees. The faces

Emancipation Day in South Carolina, 1863. Hundreds of freedpeople joined Northern reformers, along with soldiers of the 1st South Carolina Colored Infantry Regiment, on Port Royal Island to celebrate Lincoln's signing of the Emancipation Proclamation on January 1, 1863. The lithograph appeared in *Frank Leslie's Illustrated Newspaper*. *Courtesy Library of Congress.*

of all wore a happy, eager, expectant look."[4] Silence hung over the crowd as Lincoln's Emancipation Proclamation was announced. Regimental flags were presented to Col. Thomas Wentworth Higginson and his 1st South Carolina. Higginson was moved by the ceremony, he recalled, but what followed was "so utterly unexpected and startling." Almost on cue, the largely Black audience began singing "My Country tis of Thee." Higginson was moved to tears: "I never saw anything so electric; It made all other words cheap; it seemed the choked voice of a race at last unloosed. Nothing could be more wonderfully unconscious; art could not have dreamed of a tribute to the day of jubilee that should be so affecting; history will not believe it; and when I came to speak of it after it ended, tears were everywhere."[5]

The celebrations at Camp Saxton continued well into the evening. For Forten it had been a "grand, glorious, day," one that justified a cautious optimism about the future. "The dawn of freedom which it heralds may not break upon us at once," she anticipated, "but it will surely come, and sooner, I believe than we have ever dared hope before."[6]

No celebrations marked the first day of the new year for the 2nd Massachusetts camped at Fairfax Station. Shaw spent New Year's Day making routine "rounds" through winter quarters, speculating on what the coming year might bring to the "history of the world, if the Emancipation Proclamation is really what we hope it is." Shaw's attitude toward Lincoln's proclamation remained unchanged since Antietam—cautious, calculating, and emotionally detached. Writing to his mother, he admitted he did not always "appreciate" the proclamation's significance or believe that 1863 would prove a "great year . . . for the negroes and the country."[7] The contrast with Boston's and Port Royal's jubilant celebrations was stark and revealing. While his parents and their circle celebrated the day as the moral climax of their lifelong crusade, Shaw treated it as just another day requiring military duties. The proclamation that represented divine justice to his family registered as little more than a possible future that would depend on a wide range of factors. Other issues occupied his attention.

Shaw anticipated another "failure" in response to news that Gen. Joseph Hooker was likely to replace Ambrose Burnside as commander of the Army of the Potomac.[8] With the new year, Shaw finally admitted that George McClellan had "not [been] rapid enough in carrying out his plans" at Antietam, and especially in his failure to pursue Confederates after they had abandoned the field. Volunteering was close to a standstill, while the "peace faction" of the Democratic Party stood to gain influence as a result of the Union's military defeats and especially from the signing of Lincoln's proclamation. All this added to a bleak picture of military affairs in the East for Shaw and others. "If a peace is patched up with the South," Shaw opined, "I don't believe it can be a permanent one, and the war goes on for another eighteen months, other nations are likely to be drawn into it."[9]

Meanwhile, the regiment remained in winter quarters, "comfortably housed in log-huts, with fireplaces." Shaw shared his cabin with Harry Russell, the two biding their time reading newspapers, Charles Dickens's *Bleak House*, and William F. P. Napier's history of the Napoleonic Wars in Spain and Portugal. Shaw no doubt relished the opportunity to share a passage from the book with his mother in which the author admonishes people who criticize military affairs from afar and who "detail with great accuracy the right method of executing the most difficult and delicate operations of war."[10] In a letter to Annie Haggerty he described his cabin as "palatial" and anticipated a "comparatively pleasant winter"; but he also expressed his hope to secure a furlough to visit his fiancée and family, though he admitted, "I do not see any chance of it now."[11]

That wish was fulfilled when on January 22, Shaw traveled north on a ten-day furlough to spend a few days with Annie in Lenox before spending time with his family on Staten Island. Shaw clearly relished the memory of the private moments that he and Annie shared. "I have thought a great deal of you—indeed almost all the time since I left Lenox—and of my visit to you," Shaw wrote, "especially the last part of it."[12]

Memories of Annie, however, were overshadowed by the clear lack of enthusiasm and antiwar sentiment that Shaw overheard in "public conveyances and hotels," which led him to speculate "that the war may very possibly come to a more sudden end . . . unless there is a great change in the feelings of the people."[13] Shaw's skepticism was reinforced when he returned to the regiment's new camp at Stafford Court House and learned of Burnside's most recent failed offensive.[14] On January 20, as Shaw prepared to leave camp, Burnside ordered the Army of the Potomac to cross the Rappahannock River west of Fredericksburg in an attempt to flank the Confederate army, still positioned just south of town and guarding the roads to Richmond. Though the army's initial movements were encouraging, the rain quickly made the roads impassable and all but brought an end to what would come to be known ignominiously as Burnside's "Mud March"—the humiliation made worse by the taunting of Confederates from across the river in Fredericksburg.[15]

While waiting for transportation in Washington, DC, Shaw received an unexpected offer to join Maj. Gen. Samuel P. Heintzelman's staff as commander of the capital's defenses. The opportunity forced Shaw to weigh familiar calculations about abandoning the 2nd Massachusetts for staff duty. The position offered clear advantages. Shaw would be joining "a very nice staff" with better living conditions and reduced combat risk. But he also worried about his reputation among fellow line officers, fearing they would view him as "enjoying a pleasant position, by making their duty heavier." Shaw's mere mention of the offer revealed his continued restlessness and career anxiety. Despite claiming little serious consideration of such offers, he was clearly evaluating every opportunity for advancement or transfer that crossed his path. His engagement to Annie Haggerty and survival through the battles of Cedar Mountain and Antietam had not settled his professional ambitions. If anything, they had intensified his desire to find a position that offered both advancement and relative safety.

The new year had thus far mirrored the end of 1862, with the regiment confined to camp and with military affairs at a standstill. Ultimately, any new assignment would have to come with a significant promotion in rank and a responsibility befitting his class and military experience for him to consider leaving the 2nd Massachusetts.

As Shaw returned to his regiment, Massachusetts Governor John Andrew's plan to raise his own regiment of Black soldiers—made possible by the Emancipation Proclamation—finally came to fruition. A lawyer with abolitionist sympathies, Andrew was elected to his first term as governor in 1860. Historian Allan Nevins described Andrew as "an aggressive, generous, choleric little man, the Miles Standish of the Bay State . . . far-sighted, fearless and unwearied . . . emotional and impulsive; he was tactless, and his fierce bluntness made many enemies."[16] Though Andrew and Lincoln shared many of the same political goals, their personalities and tactics often brought them to loggerheads, no more so than over the issue of emancipation and Black enlistment. From the earliest days of the war, Andrew had called on the Lincoln administration to move against slavery and open enlistment to African Americans as a means not only to fill state quotas but also to demonstrate their willingness to fight to save the Union.[17]

Secretary of War Stanton notified Governor Andrew that he had one hundred days to complete the unit's recruitment and that the funding for organizing and outfitting the regiment would have to come entirely from the Commonwealth. Andrew thus faced a number of challenges from the start, including having to recruit men from outside Massachusetts to make up for the state's limited number of African Americans of military age. He also acknowledged the deep and widespread racism among the majority of the white population that would cast doubt about every stage of the organization of the new regiment. Of all the decisions that needed to be made by Andrew, none was more important than the selection of white officers to command the first Black regiment raised in the North. The regiment would be counted as a regular volunteer regiment from Massachusetts, thus assuming its place in the sequencing as the 54th Massachusetts as opposed to the 1st Colored Massachusetts Troops.[18]

It was not just a matter of finding the right military officers. Andrew needed officers that hailed from families whose commitment to abolitionism was unwavering and who would provide support during challenging moments and the inevitable doubts that would likely emerge as a result of the nature of this endeavor. Andrew proposed Robert Gould Shaw to serve as the regiment's colonel and Capt. Norwood Penrose Hallowell of Philadelphia as lieutenant colonel. Andrew knew of Shaw's parents from their involvement in a wide range of reform movements in Boston and New York; and he was aware of Frank Shaw's work with the National Freedman's Relief Association, which supplied aid and support as well as education to the thousands of formerly enslaved people along the Sea Islands of South Carolina.

Norwood Penrose Hallowell grew up in a prominent Quaker family. His father was part-owner of a firm that imported silk. More importantly for Andrew, the Hallowells were passionate abolitionists, whose summer home served as a stop on the Underground Railroad. During the war, the family established a hospital for recuperating soldiers. In January 1863, Hallowell was serving as a captain in the famed 20th Massachusetts, having distinguished himself at the battle of Ball's Bluff early in the war and later seeing action at the battle of Glendale and Antietam, where his left arm was shattered by a bullet.[19]

Rather than write Shaw directly with the offer, Andrew solicited the help of his parents in convincing their son to accept the appointment. Why he did this is a bit of a mystery. Andrew was aware that Shaw had shown interest earlier in the war in Major Copeland's plan to organize a Black regiment. Perhaps he appreciated the gravity of the decision that he was asking a young man like Shaw to make and that it might take the support and even pressure of his parents to seal the deal.

In his letter to Frank Shaw, the governor described the regiment as "perhaps the most important corps to be organized during the whole war." Andrew's description of the type of officers he sought forced both parents to assess their son's merits. Was he, in the words of Andrew, "of firm Anti-Slavery principles, ambitious, superior to a vulgar contempt of color, and having faith in the capacity of Colored men for military service"? The governor also placed a certain amount of pressure on Frank's and Sarah's own sense of honor by stressing that the officers recruited for this regiment "must be necessarily gentleman of the highest tone and honor," hailing from "those circles of educated Anti-Slavery Society, which next to the colored race itself have the greatest interest in the success of this experiment."[20] Both parents likely interpreted the governor's description as a test not only of their son's abolitionist principles but of their own as well. Shaw's decision would reflect either positively or negatively on their own worth as parents and their commitment to the abolitionist cause.

Frank decided to personally deliver Andrew's offer to his son in camp at Stafford Court House. He arrived in the camp of the 2nd Massachusetts on February 3, 1863. It was a time of year that Charley Morse described as "miserable," with the "men huddled up in their little shelters trying to keep warm over smoky fires."[21] The mud and slush that had hampered the Army of the Potomac's recent movements were ankle-deep, and in many places even knee-deep. Frank was relieved to find his son comfortable and in good health when he handed him the letter from Governor Andrew.

Upon realizing that the governor had already contacted his father, Shaw may have been mildly amused by the governor's attempt to pressure him into accepting the offer.[22] What would have stood out to Shaw, first and foremost, was not the reference to a "Colored Regiment" but the promise of a promotion to the rank of colonel. This would be the highest jump in rank of any opportunity for advancement that Shaw had entertained since joining the army. The brief letter concluded abruptly with the expectation that Shaw would "reply to this offer at the earliest day consistent with your ability to arrive at a deliberate conclusion on the subject."[23]

Any analysis of Shaw's decision to eventually assume command of the 54th Massachusetts must proceed by acknowledging that he had sought out or considered promotions on a number of occasions while he was still with the 2nd Massachusetts. Like many others, he was ambitious and yearned for a rank and assignment befitting his class and experience; with every offer he received, he always ran through the pros and cons in his mind and sought the advice of family and friends in the regiment and elsewhere. He would do the same with this current offer before responding to the governor.

Shaw likely sought the counsel of his father, who no doubt shared his mother's hopes for him and the work that she believed he was called to do. Sarah viewed the opportunity to command Black soldiers as a vindication of principles that she and Frank had attempted to instill in all their children from an early age. Having clashed with her son numerous times over the question of slavery and emancipation, most recently in response to Lincoln's Emancipation Proclamation, Sarah also likely viewed her son's command of Black soldiers as a way to finally unite the family around the cause of abolitionism and to solidify its place in the vanguard of the broader antislavery movement.

At first, Shaw informed his father that he would accept the offer, but by the time Frank was ready to return home, he had reversed course. Frank immediately telegraphed a short message home informing the family, "Rob declines. I think rightly," though Frank did not explain why he had taken his son's side.[24] It is not known if Shaw consulted with anyone else in the roughly twenty-four hours it took for him to decline the governor's offer. On February 4, Shaw wrote to Annie informing her of his father's departure and of his decision. While he acknowledged the governor's offer as a "great honor," Shaw admitted that his acceptance would have been only out of a "sense of duty," which suggests that he did not view the command of Black soldiers as constituting solely a moral question. Shaw maintained that he had "good practical reasons" for rejecting the offer, but beyond wanting the "liberty to decide what to do when" his three-year enlistment had "expired," those reasons remain unclear. What it reveals, however, is that Shaw continued to approach the war and his place in it in pragmatic terms. The question that ultimately mattered most was what would best advance *his* career and *his* prospects for future advancement and recognition.

Annie had already inquired as to whether her future husband planned to remain in the army after the war—a question that likely weighed heavily on Shaw as their wedding day approached. After his experience with Major Copeland the previous May, trying to convince the Lincoln administration to support the raising of a Black regiment, Shaw may have wondered whether the government would provide sufficient support to Black regiments and their white officers. Both Gen. David Hunter and Gen. John Frémont had attempted to enlist Black soldiers earlier in the war, only to be rebuffed by Lincoln—though by the latter half of 1862 the tide was clearly beginning to shift. In August 1862, Gen. James Lane, a former US senator, recruited African Americans he had come across during raids into Missouri and Arkansas into the 1st Kansas Colored Volunteers. Although Lane's actions were not authorized by Lincoln, Secretary of War Stanton did not order him to cease his activity. The following month, the 1st Louisiana Native Guard was mustered into service in New Orleans. And as we have already seen, Gen. Rufus Saxton appointed Thomas Wentworth Higginson to command the 1st South Carolina in November of 1862.[25]

Even with the decision to raise Black troops more generally following the Emancipation Proclamation, Shaw may still have harbored doubts whether the Lincoln administration would see this project through, given the intense public scrutiny as well as the many unknowns surrounding the future course of the war and its potential impact on Black military service and on the reputation and careers of officers like himself who accepted command of these new regiments.

It was also known to Shaw that many white Northerners did not support Black equality and protested compulsory military service that now forced them to serve in a war for Black freedom. Lincoln's proclamation and its authorization of Black enlistment was widely criticized both on the home front and in the army. The *New York Times* summarized the arguments against enlistment for its reader: "1) That the negro will not fight; 2) It is said that whites will not fight with them,—that the prejudice against them is so strong that our own citizens will not enlist, or will quit the service, if compelled to fight by their side,—and that we shall thus lose two white soldiers for every black one that we gain." Finally, critics asserted that not enough Black men of military age will volunteer to fight.[26] Charles Francis Adams Jr., the grandson of President John Quincy Adams and son of US diplomat Charles Francis Adams, eventually accepted command of the 5th Massachusetts Colored Volunteer Cavalry, but initially harbored strong prejudice against African Americans and their ability to fight. "As to being made soldiers, they are more harm than good," argued Adams. "It will be years before they can be made to stand before their old masters, unless . . . some leader of their own, some Toussaint [L'Ouverture] rises, who is one of them and inspires them with confidence. Under our system and with such white officers as we give them, we might make a soldierly equal to the native Hindoo regiments in about five years." A corporal in the 74th New York Infantry, admitted matter-of-factly to his sister, "We don't want to fight side by side with the n——. We think we are a too superior race for that."[27] Such views were pervasive throughout the junior officer corps as well as the rank and file.

At first it appeared that Shaw was at peace with his decision. In the same letter to Annie in which he attempted to explain his decision not to accept the governor's offer, he quickly moved on to answering Annie's question on whether he was a practicing Unitarian, his preference for the name "Robert" over "Rob," and his response to the news about the replacement of Ambrose Burnside with Joseph Hooker. Even after he made his decision, however, Shaw could not ignore the fact that he worried his mother was going to be disappointed and convinced that "I am shirking my duty."[28]

As Shaw had anticipated, his mother was devastated by the news of her son's refusal to accept Governor Andrew's offer. Sarah immediately wrote to Andrew after receiving a telegram from her husband notifying her of the decision. She thanked the governor for the "honor" that he bestowed on her son and shared that his "decision has caused me the bitterest disappointment I have ever experienced. . . . It would have been the proudest moment of my life & I could have died satisfied that I had not lived in vain." In an attempt to try to explain her son's decision, Sarah curiously assigned blame to Frank, claiming that her son had a "habit inherited by his father of self-distrust in his own capabilities."[29] It is unknown whether Frank was aware that his wife held this opinion of him.

Within hours, however, Shaw had reversed course and notified his father to immediately inform Andrew that he had accepted his offer. The governor was no doubt pleased by Shaw's reversal, but he balked at the young officer's hesitation and, in response, suggested that he accept the lieutenant-colonelcy under Hallowell, who had immediately accepted the governor's offer and who was already making his way to Boston. Shaw declined the step down in rank—an indication of just how important he considered the rank of colonel to be—and the governor returned to his initial offer of command.[30]

The depth of Sarah's disappointment in her son was matched only by the joy she experienced after learning that he had reversed course. "No words written or spoken can ever make you understand the deep and holy joy that your acceptance of this call has given me." "God rewards a hundred-fold every good aspiration of his children," she wrote to her son, "and this is my reward for asking my children not [for] earthly honors, but [for] souls to see the right and courage to follow it. . . . Now I feel ready to die, for I see you willing to give your support to the cause of truth that is lying crushed and bleeding."[31] Shaw may have been overjoyed to receive his mother's approval, but at the same time it also underscores the increased tension in their relationship that likely would have resulted had he remained committed to his initial decision. Arguably, rejecting the governor's offer to take command of Black soldiers in a war of liberation would have been an embarrassment as well as an emotionally crushing disappointment for Shaw's parents. For now, however, Sarah relished the thought that her son had finally seen the light and was committed to fighting for a higher principle. The truth was much more complicated. As Charles Russell Lowell recognized at the time, "Bob Shaw is not a fanatic."[32]

Shaw weighed the same practical considerations that had guided his judgment of earlier opportunities of advancement in the army. Other than Charley Morse, it is difficult to know who, if anyone else, Shaw may have consulted between initially rejecting and ultimately accepting the governor's offer. Morris Copeland and James Savage were ardent abolitionists, but they were no longer around—the latter having succumbed to his wounds received at Cedar Mountain; while Harry Russell, Greely Curtis, and Dr. Lincoln Stone merely held antislavery views and did not necessarily support the enlistment of Black soldiers. On the positive side, "Going for another three years is not nearly so bad a thing for a colonel as a captain," he explained to Annie.[33] Furloughs would be easier to come by, something that the couple relished, given their impending marriage. The training of the 54th Massachusetts would also bring him—at least for a time—closer to his fiancée.

If Shaw had any hesitation about proving "that a negro can be made a good soldier," he was encouraged by conversations in camp with Morse, who supported the enlistment of Black men as a "military measure" and expressed "hope it will be entirely successful." As far as their training was concerned, Morse could see "no reason in the world why black troops raised in this country shouldn't be as good as those used by the English and French. I always argue that any men who have enough understanding to obey orders implicitly, where they are led by brave officers can make good soldiers. I think negroes could be much more easily disciplined than most white men."[34] Shaw likely viewed the training of Black men as no greater a challenge than the training of Irish recruits, whom he also believed lacked discipline or, for that matter, the mass of volunteer soldiers, whose poor behavior he had witnessed firsthand on numerous occasions. Concerns about popular support for Black enlistment also appear to have abated for Shaw, who was now convinced that "after a little thought" most "sensible men in the army" will "say that it is the best thing that can be done; and surely those at home, who are not brave or patriotic enough to enlist, should not ridicule, or throw obstacles in the way of men who are going to fight for them."[35]

In addition to his family, the approval of his friends no doubt added to Shaw's confidence that he had made the correct decision. Henry Lee Higginson, now serving in the 1st Massachusetts Cavalry with Greely Curtis and stationed near Fredericksburg, welcomed a final visit from Shaw before he headed to Boston and celebrated his announcement as "great news, indeed a real event in all our lives." Higginson noted the strong connections that existed between himself, Shaw, Morse, and Curtis: "We four had marched from Boston together, and were held together by strong bonds."[36] An acquaintance of Morse took the time to write to Shaw: "Rest assured you have done a good thing. I could not myself do what you and Hallowell have done, and so I respect it the more." The author was confident that history would one day "justify your course" and "all will confess that you were right, and wonder how the world could have been so wrong."[37]

Promotion to a higher rank, the approval of his friends, command of his own regiment, and proximity to Annie all proved attractive to Shaw. He likely agreed with Morse and others who balked at the idea of Black enlistment "as an abolition measure or as a means to elevate the black race"; but he also, perhaps for the first time in his life, caught a glimpse of a broader purpose for himself.[38] "You know how many eminent men consider a negro army of the greatest importance to our country at this time," he mused to Annie. "If it turns out to be so, how fully repaid the pioneers in the movement will be, for what they may have to go through! And at any rate I feel convinced I shall never regret having taken this step, as far as I myself am concerned; for while I was undecided I felt ashamed of myself, as if I were cowardly."[39]

It is tempting to view this moment as a significant turning point in Shaw's military career; and it has been what many people later viewed as a watershed moment in his journey to fully embracing the abolitionist principles of his parents through the command of Black soldiers. William James captured this moment in Shaw's life for his audience at the dedication of the Shaw Memorial in Boston in 1897: "Whatever doubts may have beset him, they were over in a day, for he inclined naturally toward difficult resolves. He accepted the proffered command, and from that moment lived but for one object, to establish the honor of the Massachusetts Fifty-fourth."[40] James's heroic portrait was exactly what mourning audiences wanted to hear—a tale of instant moral transformation and noble purpose. But the evidence suggests Shaw's decision was far more complex and self-interested than this memorial rhetoric implied. Shaw did not experience a sudden conversion to his parents' understanding of the war's ultimate purpose; he saw an opportunity that combined career advancement with social distinction.

James was surely correct, however, in his assessment of Shaw as committed to his new assignment: preparing the men of the 54th Massachusetts for battle and for the challenges they would face along the way. With his promotion in rank to colonel and command of one thousand men came a host of new responsibilities for Shaw, attention to which would go far in his ability to "establish the honor" of the regiment. At the same time, James's depiction of Shaw as having placed the doubts about his decision to accept the governor's offer permanently behind him were made decades after the Civil War and must be understood as part of the postwar mythmaking surrounding the young colonel. Rather than view his acceptance of command of the 54th Massachusetts as the fulfillment of his destiny, we should view it for what it probably meant to Shaw in that moment: an opportunity to advance his military career, prove his worth as an officer, and contribute in a meaningful way to the defeat of the Confederacy and the preservation of the Union.

His doubts about his decision would repeatedly surface in the coming months. Few people in 1861 had anticipated a long war; and even fewer people imagined or desired the creation of an interracial army in 1863. Like the rest of the nation, Shaw now found himself on uncharted ground. How he would respond to the command of a Black regiment was anything but certain.

EIGHT

They Feel as Big as All Creation—and Look Very Well

Shaw wasted little time in assuming the responsibilities of his new rank as colonel of the 54th Massachusetts. Bidding goodbye to his comrades and leaving the camp of the 2nd Massachusetts for the final time, Shaw arrived in New York on February 11, 1863, to a warm but brief embrace from his family. Sarah was likely relieved that her son had not "wavered" in his decision since last hearing from him.[1] From there, Shaw traveled on to Boston, where he arrived four days later to meet with Governor Andrew in the State House on Beacon Hill. Shaw and the governor quickly turned his office into a war room from which they could direct the raising of the new regiment from the ground up.

Shaw was likely overwhelmed by the challenges that lay ahead, but he was encouraged by his first few meetings with the governor. "His views about the regiment are just what I should wish," Shaw enthusiastically reported to his father.[2] To Annie Haggerty, he wrote, "Governor Andrew's ideas please me extremely, for he takes the most common-sense view of the thing. He seems inclined to have me do just what I please."[3]

The most pressing concern was in the selection of suitable volunteers to serve as officers in the 54th Massachusetts. Governor Andrew was determined that his regiment "shall be commanded by officers who are eminently gentlemen" with known abolitionist sympathies. They also had to be from Massachusetts. To that end, Norwood Hallowell took charge of interviewing prospective candidates. Years after the war Hallowell recalled the interview process, asking candidates to discuss the "orthography of the word 'negro.'" If the candidate "spelled the word as though it was pronounced *darky*," Norwell explained, he "was admitted," but if he "spelled it as though it was 'n——'" the candidate was "rejected."[4]

John W. M. Appleton, a Harvard graduate who was living in West Virginia at the start of the war, had returned to Boston where he served on garrison duty in Boston Harbor until his discharge in 1862. Appleton welcomed Lincoln's Emancipation Proclamation and wasted little time in applying for a commission in Col. Thomas W. Higginson's regiment of freed and runaway slaves in South Carolina before accepting a commission as a lieutenant in the 54th Massachusetts. Appleton firmly believed that African Americans would fight for their liberty, and he hoped to do his part in supporting the cause.[5] William H. Simpkins, who was serving as a sergeant in the 44th Massachusetts Infantry in New Bern, North Carolina, in 1863 became the captain of Company K of the 54th. Like Shaw, Simkins struggled with his decision, admitting that it was "no blind leap of an enthusiast, but the result of a considerable hard thinking." And like Shaw he was clear-eyed about the risks to his career and public perception. "It will not at first, and probably will not be for a long time, an agreeable position for many reasons too evident to state," Simkins continued, "and the man who goes into it resigns all chances in the new white Regiments, that must be raised."[6]

Cabot Jackson Russell also accepted a commission as captain in the 54th. The eighteen-year-old admired John Brown to such an extent that he slept under Brown's portrait following the failed Harpers Ferry raid in 1859. In 1862, Cabot Russell left Harvard in his freshman year to join the 44th Massachusetts Infantry. Despite having applied to command a company in the 54th, Russell worried that Black men were too "awkward" and "dull of apprehension" to be properly trained as soldiers. He acknowledged the raising of the 54th Massachusetts as an "experiment" and believed, like Simkins and others, that it would take time for the nation to accept Black troops; once they "prove the efficacy of black troops," however, Russell believed, "I think they will hail them, as drowning men catch at straws." Russell fervently maintained that the "right sort of men" needed to step up to this challenge. "I came out here, not from any fancied fondness of a military life," he admitted in an attempt to explain his decision to his family, "but to do what I could to help along the good cause. . . . Why should I not stretch my patriotism a little further and accept a commission in a Negro Regt?"[7]

Garth Wilkinson "Wilkie" James, the younger brother of William and Henry James and a close friend of Cabot Russell's, had been "brought up in the belief that slavery was a monstrous wrong, its destruction worthy of a man's best effort, even unto the laying down of his life." Years after the war he recalled the "sharp rebukes" that he and his comrades in the 44th Massachusetts, who had chosen to join a regiment of Black soldiers, were subject to "from the men with whom they had fought side by side on the various fields of North Carolina." James was enough of an idealist at this point to hope to believe that the loyalty of African Americans to the nation through military service would eliminate such racist outbursts.[8]

Five additional men from the 44th Massachusetts signed on, including Charles Tucker, Willard Howard, Henry Littlefield, Edward Jones, and George Pope. The officer corps of the 54th—like those of 2nd and 20th Massachusetts—were bound together by a set of shared values and hailed from families who were closely aligned with one another through marriage, business, and education. They expressed many of the same concerns as Shaw about their reputations after agreeing to sign on, and they even harbored some doubts as to whether this experiment would succeed. But these young officers also expressed views on race that were decidedly more progressive than those of their commanding officer.

While Governor Andrew prioritized recruiting officers sympathetic to enslaved people and committed to abolition, Shaw's concerns remained purely military. What mattered to him was the selection of men who could transfer hard-won battlefield experience to new recruits and enforce the strictest of discipline he believed essential for military effectiveness. The case of New Bedford native James W. Grace serves as a reminder of the steps Shaw would take to maintain the integrity of the regiment's officer corps. A few weeks into the organization of the regiment, Shaw learned that Grace had instigated a petition calling for his promotion to the rank of captain based on the claim that he had raised one hundred men for the regiment. Shaw informed Governor Andrew that Grace, then serving as a first lieutenant in Company C, had in fact raised no more than forty men for the regiment; but what troubled Shaw most was that the petition undercut his own control over the regiment. Even at his current rank, Grace outranked "officers, who have been in service since the beginning of the war and who are, in no wise, his inferior in point of capacity." Shaw maintained that while Grace had made some progress, he had no intention of recommending him for promotion. "As you know," he reminded the governor, "a man may be a most estimable citizen and a very poor soldier; and however well able his fellow townsmen may be to judge of him in the former capacity, in the latter their opinion does not carry so much weight."[9] The governor eventually relented in the face of Shaw's persistence in the matter.

The only question that remained was whether African Americans would answer the governor's and the nation's call, and that was out of Shaw's control. Back home on Staten Island, Annie Shaw had her doubts, writing to her cousin that while the rush to enlist at the beginning of the war demonstrated a strong commitment on the part of African Americans to the Union, "a good many have felt indignant at being excluded & say that they will not go now."[10] Governor Andrew wasted little opportunity in sounding out Black men of military age in Massachusetts and beyond.

Even before Shaw arrived in Boston, Andrew had organized a committee to help with enlistment. George L Stearns, a wealthy manufacturer from nearby Medford headed up the committee. Stearns had embraced abolitionism after marrying a niece of Lydia Maria Child. During the fighting in "Bleeding Kansas," in the mid-1850s, Stearns had purchased rifles for Free-Soilers to ensure the territory entered the Union as a free state, and in 1859 he had financed John Brown's Harpers Ferry raid through the Secret Six. Other enlistment committee members included Richard P. Hallowell, the brother of Norwood Hallowell. Richard had made a fortune in Boston as a wool merchant. After Brown's execution, he traveled to Virginia to bring the martyr's body back North. Shaw's cousin John Murray Forbes, another Brown supporter, also joined the committee as well as reformers William I. Bowditch and Frank Shaw. The committee also benefited from the financial resources of leading businessmen such as Amos A. Lawrence and James B. Congdon.[11]

While Shaw relished the approval and the "good words" he received from his close friends and family regarding his decision to assume command of the 54th, Boston's Black population remained ambivalent and cautious about rushing to the colors. Annie was not far from the truth in her doubts about whether Black men would join.

Just days before the Emancipation Proclamation was signed, Confederate President Jefferson Davis announced a proclamation of his own targeting Black soldiers. Davis maintained that Lincoln's proclamation was intended to "excite servile war within the Confederacy"—a fear that had long animated Southern slaveholders and non-slaveholders. In response, he declared that Black Union soldiers captured while armed would not be treated as ordinary prisoners of war but would be turned over to state authorities to be punished under state laws as insurrectionists. White officers who served with them would likewise be treated harshly.[12]

On February 16, 1863, a broadside appeared in Boston newspapers: "TO COLORED MEN! Wanted—Good men for the 54th Regiment of Massachusetts Volunteers, of African descent." Another broadside encouraged African Americans to enlist and prove that they were "not inferior in Courage and Patriotism to White Men."[13]

At a "spirited and enthusiastic" recruitment rally the next day at Joy Street Baptist Church, in the heart of Boston's Black neighborhood on the north slope of Beacon Hill, African American leader Henry Highland Garnett inquired defiantly, "What have black men to fight for in this war?" Before the Civil War, Robert Morris tried unsuccessfully to organize a Black company in the Massachusetts Volunteer Militia as a means to challenge racist assumptions about African Americans and as a claim to the rights of citizenship.[14] As the first Black lawyer to try a case in Massachusetts, Morris had helped to desegregate the city's public schools. Like other Black leaders, Morris understood that the nation needed Black recruits because white recruitment had fallen off since the beginning of the war. Garnett and Morris also knew that many white Americans approved of Black recruitment to offset the looming Conscription Act and the threat to their own sons. As a result, leaders like Morris and Garnett believed that conditions should be attached to calls for Black soldiers, namely that they should be commanded by Black officers. William Wells Brown demanded "Equality first" before supporting enlistment.

The "golden trumpet of abolitionism," Wendell Phillips, acknowledged the injustice of not commissioning Black officers but nonetheless encouraged the Black community to embrace the moment: "God has given the black race its first great historic chance for writing its name high in the history of ages,

Recruitment poster for the 54th Massachusetts. Early efforts to attract recruits to the 54th Massachusetts proved challenging. Black Bostonians had volunteered in 1861 only to be rebuffed by the Lincoln administration. As a result, Governor Andrew was forced to recruit from outside the state to fill the regiment's ranks. *Collection of the Massachusetts Historical Society.*

and in the struggle I know the blacks will bear a great part; that they will fight and fight well." "If you cannot have a whole loaf," he asked, "will you not take a slice? That is the great question for you to decide." John S. Rock, one of the first African Americans to earn a medical degree, reminded Phillips that his community did not have the luxury of "living entirely for posterity" and that "a loaf of bread to-day is worth a barrel of flour next year."[15] Rock eventually came around to a more nuanced view that included support for enlistment, but the damage had been done.

Before the war, Robert Morris had been able to rally roughly one hundred men in his unsuccessful bid to organize a Black militia company. During the rush to war in the spring and summer of 1861, more than one hundred Black Bostonians volunteered to defend the Union, but by 1863 enthusiasm had dried up. Of the one thousand men who would eventually volunteer to serve in the 54th, fewer than forty resided in Boston.[16]

Shaw had little patience for these principled stands that only made his job more difficult. He had a regiment to organize and needed Black bodies. In a letter to the governor, Shaw admitted that "the influential colored men of Boston . . . have done us more harm th[an] good." Shaw showed no curiosity about what the war meant to African Americans or how decades of systematic oppression might shape their response to military service. He never considered how disenfranchisement, exclusion from public office, and a long history of discrimination and racial violence might create skepticism about whether wearing a uniform would actually expand civil rights.[17]

In response to the lackluster support among Boston's Black residents, Governor Andrew invited William Wells Brown, who worked closely with Frank Shaw in New York, and Charles Lenox Remond to join the recruiting committee. After establishing a recruitment office in Buffalo, New York, Stearns hired Frederick Douglass to encourage volunteers in nearby Rochester. While Douglass was also disappointed by the failure to commission Black officers, he encouraged Black men of military age to volunteer. "Shall colored men enlist notwithstanding this unjust and ungenerous barrier raised against them? We answer yes," he stated in *Douglass' Monthly* in March 1863. "Go into the army and go with a will and a determination to blot out this and all other mean discriminations against us. To say we won't be soldiers because we cannot be colonels is like saying we won't go into the water till we have learned to swim."[18] Douglass urged his readers to "get an eagle on your button and a musket on your shoulder as soon as you can, and when that is done all the devils in Jeff Davis's dominions cannot keep you out of citizenship."[19]

Robert Hamilton, the editor of the New York *Anglo-African*, stated the matter more bluntly, inquiring of his readers, "Can you ask any more than a chance to drive bayonet or bullet into the slaveholders' hearts?"[20]

As recruiters fanned out across the country, preparations were made to begin training the regiment at Camp Meigs—named after quartermaster Gen. Montgomery C. Meigs—in Readville. Located just a few miles outside Boston and situated along the Neponset River and a rail line, the site would facilitate the arrival of both new recruits and supplies. Camp Meigs had been established in July of 1861 as one of thirty-nine training camps. It encompassed 139 acres and included barracks, stables, officers' quarters, a hospital, kitchens and nearby water sources for cooking and bathing.[21]

The first recruits for the 54th disembarked at Readville on February 21, 1863, and walked the short distance to camp to begin their transition from civilians to soldiers. The camp was relatively quiet compared to the flurry of activity it saw at the beginning of the war, when men rushed to volunteer. Shaw and the governor encouraged recruiters to enlist the help of a "surgeon to examine them [the recruits] before" they arrived at camp—to minimize the cost of transportation if a recruit was deemed unfit for military service.[22] More importantly, choosing the men carefully, according to Shaw, would result in "a very sound set." While some recruiters complied with this request, the two-dollar commission earned for each man who joined guaranteed that some less qualified men slipped through. It was thus the job of Dr. Lincoln R. Stone, who had previously served in the 2nd Massachusetts, to review the recruits once they arrived at Camp Meigs. In the first few weeks, Stone rejected 132 of the first 500 men. The attention to the regiment's health, according to one historian, resulted in the organization of "the most highly selective regiment of the war."[23]

Once given a clean bill of health, the recruits were required to bathe before being issued uniforms and receiving an assignment to one of ten buildings, which had been completed only a few months earlier. Field, staff, and company officers were quartered nearby. New recruits arrived daily. "We have got 30 men out at Readville," Shaw wrote enthusiastically to Charley Morse just a few days after the camp opened, "all washed & uniformed. . . . They feel as big as all creation—and look very well."[24]

The first recruits arrived from within the Commonwealth of Massachusetts. Only twenty-seven men came from Boston. The old whaling town of New Bedford, where Frederick Douglass once made his home, sent

A Black Union soldier with his wife and children, ca. 1863–1865. Recruitment for the 54th Massachusetts took place throughout the North, pulling men from families like this one who had long experienced discrimination and racial violence in their communities. Military service offered an opportunity for these men to prove their bravery and secure their place as citizens in a reconstructed nation. *Courtesy Library of Congress.*

thirty-nine, and thirty-three men arrived from the Berkshire region in the western part of the state. In total, 133 men volunteered from the Bay State. Because recruiters fanned out far and wide, the regiment eventually represented a wide swath of the Black population across the Northern states, in addition to Canada and the Caribbean. Pennsylvania topped this list, sending 294 men; New York sent 183; and 155 arrived from Ohio. Sixty-four men made the trip to Readville from Michigan, along with fewer than fifty men each from Illinois and Indiana. Just under forty former slaves, hailed from states below the Mason-Dixon Line.[25]

The average age of the men in the regiment was 24.3 years, though a number of recruits either did not know their age or lied during their examination. Elijah G. Biddle was one of the first to enlist from Boston at age seventeen, and America C. Tabb was fifty-seven when he volunteered. A thorough health examination did not prevent Peter Vogelsang from volunteering at age forty-six. His acquaintance with Frank Shaw in New York City, where he was working as a clerk, may have influenced his decision to enlist. Within weeks of joining, Vogelsang was appointed sergeant of Company H. Recruits were also categorized based on skin color, including, "black," "dark," "brown," "dusky," "medium," "mulatto," "colored," "light," "yellow," and "white"—a testament to the racialized language of the time and a belief among many that skin color reflected intelligence and moral character.[26]

Recruits younger than seventeen were assigned as musicians or drummers. About half of the recruits described themselves as farmers. Roughly 10 percent identified as laborers, though their occupations varied widely. While barbers, seamen, waiters, boatmen, and teamsters topped the list, the regiment also included cabinetmakers, a dentist, a druggist, and five students. A few of the men stood out because of their personal backgrounds and stories.[27]

George E. Stephens was born in 1832 to a fairly prosperous middle-class family living in Philadelphia's free Black community. Stephens pursued a number of occupations, including cabinetmaker, journalist, sailor, soldier, teacher, and businessman. Unlike many of the men in the regiment and free Black people generally during the antebellum period, Stephens was highly educated, well read, and politically astute. By the eve of the Civil War, he had become a leading voice within the African American community as a correspondent to the New York *Weekly Anglo-African*. He continued publishing his reports after he first volunteered to accompany an officer to war as the man's personal servant, then worked as a recruiter for the 54th, and eventually served as a sergeant in the regiment.[28]

James Henry Gooding was born into slavery in North Carolina in 1838. Following the purchase of his freedom by a man who may have been his father, Gooding arrived in New York City in 1846. There he enrolled as a student in the Quaker-run Colored Orphan's Asylum. Gooding eventually moved to New Bedford, Massachusetts, where he married and worked in the whaling industry. As one of the earliest recruits in the 54th Massachusetts, Gooding also kept the Black community of New Bedford apprised of the training and eventual service of the regiment in the pages of the *New-Bedford Mercury* newspaper.[29]

Like many of the men who joined the 54th Massachusetts, Stephen A. Swails grew up with the constant threat of racial violence and white mobs that assailed the Black working-class families in the Tow Hill neighborhood of Columbia, Pennsylvania. One of his earliest experiences was listening to the shouts of racial epithets and the sounds of broken glass as a white mob terrorized his neighborhood for four days in October 1834. Like Gooding and

Stephens, young Swails managed to get an education while his family moved around and eventually settled in Elmira, New York, in 1855. Swails was living in Cooperstown, New York, and working as a waiter in a hotel when it was destroyed by fire in 1862. After that, he worked briefly as a canal boatman before volunteering to fight in the 54th. He eventually becoming the first African American commissioned as an officer in the US military.[30]

Frederick Douglass recruited more than one hundred men from towns and villages throughout western New York and the Hudson Valley. That number included his sons Charles and Lewis, who arrived at Camp Meigs in late March 1863, along with fifty additional recruits, all accompanied by Douglass himself. Charles recalled his pride at being the first to enlist in Rochester on February 9, while Lewis described for his future wife, Amelia Loguen, the excitement and pride that he and his fellow recruits felt as they sang "John Brown's Body" in the railcars traveling to Boston.[31]

The motivation of the men who volunteered varied as much as their places of origin and personal backgrounds. Some were motivated by a deep sense of honor, a desire to prove their worth as men, and a belief that as African American men, they had a duty to answer their nation's call. "We do not deserve the name of freemen," asserted George Stephens, "if we disregard the teachings of the hour and fail to place in the balance against oppression, treason and tyranny, our interests, our arms, and our lives."[32] Wesley Furlong, who had been working as a steward in New Bedford stated with the confidence of a man more mature than his twenty-four years: "The black man must put down this war." For Furlong, the war was an opportunity to fight "for the liberty of his race and to prove himself a man."[33] Others were motivated by the federal government's promise to pay each volunteer thirteen dollars per month—a sum equal to that of white soldiers.

Despite their differences, the men of the 54th Massachusetts were bound together by their race. Many were united by slavery, either as a lived experience or as one passed down from elders to a younger generation born and raised in the North. Many of the men had experienced or been the targets of racial violence or had internalized the humiliations of white racism that relegated them to second-class status. Finally, and perhaps most importantly, every man in the regiment was united around the uncertainty of whether military service would fundamentally alter their place in a reunited nation.

Despite the challenges that many of the volunteers had faced and overcome before arriving in Readville, Shaw took little notice of what set this regiment apart from the men he had previously commanded. He casually referred to the progress in enlisting men as the "darky" and "n—— concern."

In a letter to his father, he characterized some of the earliest recruits as "not the best class of n——s," and he went as far to refer to himself as a "n—— colonel."[34] Shaw's racist assumptions extended beyond casual prejudice to embrace the pseudoscientific theories that Harvard professor Louis Agassiz used to justify white supremacy. When Shaw observed what he believed were longer heels among some of his Black soldiers, he saw confirmation of Agassi's claims about fundamental anatomical differences between races—supposed evidence of a "natural hierarchy" that placed white people above Black people in human development.[35]

Such language was commonplace throughout mid-nineteenth-century America and especially in the army; but it also speaks to the gulf between Shaw's lived experience and this new crop of men, whose experiences and views of the war differed sharply from his own. Shaw's lack of any deep interest in the men now beginning to fill out the regiment points to how little interaction Shaw had had with African Americans up to this point in his life.

In her tribute to Shaw following his death, reformer and family friend Lydia Maria Child recalled an incident at Readville in which "two intelligent, well-bred, coloured strangers, who brought letters of introduction" joined Shaw for dinner. At some point, the two men described for Shaw the discrimination they had faced because of their race. According to Child, Shaw replied, "All gentlemen are the same to me whatever their complexion may be."[36] Childs's story is a reminder of how quickly Shaw was recast as a civil rights warrior following his death. But this story is unsupported by any additional evidence and stands in sharp contrast to Shaw's own racial outlook at the time.

Even for reformers committed to the end of slavery, like Shaw's own father, interactions with African Americans often revealed racial animus. After entering Frank Shaw's New York City office to volunteer to assist former slaves, Paschal B. Randolph and another Black individual recalled being "rudely" ushered to wait in the hallway without any opportunity to explain themselves. The two left the office, "positively assured that our color alone was the pretext for the insult."[37]

We should remember that Shaw had never taken an interest in any enlisted men since volunteering with the 2nd Massachusetts in 1861. His understanding of his social class and the conviction that his responsibility as an officer was to prepare men for battle by reinforcing strict disciplinary measures left Shaw with neither room nor inclination to get to know the men under his command. Preparing the 54th for active service remained a priority for Shaw, especially in light of any lingering doubts he may have harbored as to whether

Black men could be trained for the challenges of military life and the intense scrutiny that the regiment was likely to receive from much of the public.

Shaw remained in Boston to confer with Governor Andrew on matters related to enlistment and logistics while the organization and training of the regiment in Readville was left to his second in command. In addition to his regular meetings with the governor, Shaw enjoyed dinner and small parties on most evenings with friends as well as visits with his extended family. These visits were a welcome distraction from the many public-relations events he was required to attend, none of which he particularly enjoyed. On March 4, he met with a "committee of ladies" who had expressed interest in providing assistance to the regiment. In describing one event to his sister, Shaw admitted, "If I could possibly have bolted, I should have made the attempt, but it was useless. . . . I was brought forward, as to the slaughter, in a terrible perspiration, and If I had not been able to recover myself, while I was being introduced to the audience, I don't know that I should have pulled through." Shaw, however, pulled through and enlisted the aid of the group to help raise funds to purchase various "articles the men were in need of."[38]

Though he may not have enjoyed these fundraising events, they served an important purpose. They helped to raise money for additional supplies such as socks, towels, handkerchiefs, thread, needles, and many other articles necessary "for the benefit of the colored soldiers" not otherwise provided by the state or federal government. More importantly, working with social clubs that included many of the elite and powerful families of Boston provided a forum via which Shaw could highlight the progress of the regiment and cultivate support that could be called upon in the future, if needed. News that a ladies group was soliciting funds for a flag for the 54th raised hopes that both the white and Black residents of Boston would eventually rally around the regiment once it was ready to depart for the front.[39]

Not every Boston social club, however, was eager to welcome Shaw or to support the efforts of raising a Black regiment. Founded in 1852, the Somerset Club was located on Beacon Hill, near Shaw's childhood home; its members hailed from some of Boston's most elite Brahmin families. During the Civil War, the club split along political lines, especially over the issue of slavery and emancipation. One member was forced to retract his comments when he toasted "Jeff Davis's health" during a social gathering.[40] Shaw's March 1863 visit to the club—just weeks after members had celebrated Gen. George B. McClellan as their hoped-for 1864 presidential candidate—revealed a nest of "bloody Copperheads." These radical Democrats opposed both emancipation and Black military service with venomous intensity, making Shaw's presence as commander of a Black regiment potentially explosive. Shaw navigated the hostile environment carefully, relieved that "no one made any disagreeable remarks" during his visit. Writing to Charley Morse afterward, Shaw suggested that some members deserved a thorough "soaping down for their treasonous sympathies."[41] The visit served as an important reminder that while Shaw's family and close friends expressed support for his new command, many in Boston and throughout the nation remained hostile to enlisting Black soldiers.

Shaw arrived in Camp Meigs permanently on March 3 and was generally pleased with what he saw. On observing Shaw in camp, one correspondent wrote, "He is a slight but compact in figure, with light hair and mustache, and without a beard."[42] The weather remained cold, and the snow forced the officers to drill the men inside three empty barracks. The enlisted men drilled on average five hours per day, while the noncommissioned officers were drilled separately. "My regiment is making pretty good headway. We have nearly 150 men in camp and they come in pretty past. There are several among them, who have been well drilled, & who are acting sergeants. They drill their squad with a great deal of snap, and I think we shall have good soldiers."[43] In addition, Shaw observed that their "barracks are in better order, and more cleanly" than any other regiment he had witnessed thus far, and during the first two weeks in camp only two cases of drunkenness had been reported.[44]

By the end of March 1863, the regiment numbered approximately 450 men and now occupied ten large barracks. The snow was "still deep" but had melted some, allowing the regiment to drill on the open field, though the mud proved to be a hindrance.[45]

The daily routine for the 54th Massachusetts followed that of most other regiments during their roughly eighty days spent in training at Readville. The day typically began with the sharp sounds of reveille bugle before sunrise at 5:30 a.m., followed by a short prayer service, in which many of the men participated. By 7:00 a.m. the barracks had been cleaned, and the soldiers dressed for breakfast. Following barracks inspection, the men engaged in up to five hours of drills that included long marches with full packs and instruction on how to march and maneuver as one cohesive group. Additional drills followed lunch until dinner. Whatever free time the men enjoyed during the evening hours was spent writing letters or taking advantage of reading lessons

Colonel Shaw, 1863. Shaw initially rejected Governor John Andrew's offer to take command of the 54th Massachusetts. In this photograph, Shaw poses in a studio wearing his colonel's uniform and holding his Pattern 1850 Foot Officer's Sword.
Courtesy of Zachery A. Fry, private collection.

offered by volunteers, in song with the accompaniment of instruments, or in small prayer groups.[46] "They all seem contented," observed one soldier, "and appear in the best spirits. . . . We have drill morning and afternoon, and the men are taking hold with a degree of earnestness."[47]

Though Shaw expressed satisfaction with the early organization and training of the regiment, even admitting to his mother that "they learn all the details of guard duty and Camp service, infinitely more readily than the Irish," he admitted a preference for recruits from the country versus the city. Shaw shared this preference with Hallowell, who confided to a fellow officer that the 54th included "some of the worst reprobates of Northern cities."[48] Shaw never clarified his preference, but it likely reflected widely held beliefs about the vices of urban life as well as a reminder of the resistance to enlistment evident in some quarters of Boston's Black community.

Shaw's preference for recruits from rural areas likely stemmed from his belief that they would be less rebellious and more compliant than their urban counterparts, who had endured more intense forms of racial discrimination. Shaw understood that the level of discipline that needed to be instilled in the 54th that would have to exceed that of most white regiments to satisfy the public's doubts and fears. From the very beginning of the war, as we have already seen, Shaw placed a high priority on the importance of discipline, even coming into conflict with his family over his embrace of extreme disciplinary measures. This, however, did not prevent Shaw from instituting the same strict methods he had imposed on the men of the 2nd on those of the 54th Massachusetts. Years after the war, Hallowell recalled that "unruly members" of the regiment "were stood on barrels, bucked, gagged, and, if need be, shot; in fact, treated as white soldiers were in all well-disciplined regiments." Though Hallowell also approved of these methods, it did not take long for rumors to surface once again from family members and members of the public. Shaw brushed these rumors aside, insisting, "I shall continue to do what I know is right . . . and you may be perfectly certain, that any reports of cruelty, are entirely untrue. I have treated them much more mildly, than we did the men of the 2d." Despite Shaw's claims to the contrary, concerns persisted. The surgeon-general of Massachusetts inquired as to what punishments had been "inflicted" on the men, which eventually led the commander of Camp Meigs to order Shaw to stop "severe and unusual punishments."[49]

Desertions crept up steadily between March and the end of April 1863. Shaw noted to his father that somewhere between seventeen and twenty men were absent without leave.[50] It is difficult to know to what extent, if at all, this development was a result of Shaw's strict disciplinary measures.

Capt. John Appleton and other officers were routinely assigned with locating "wayward troopers," which suggests that the frequency of desertion may have been higher than Shaw had reported. Appleton was acutely aware of what he characterized as a "very stringent discipline" imposed on the regiment, but he went even further, acknowledging, "I have never known a Regiment where the officers were under as strict discipline as the 54th."[51]

Shaw understood that his regiment and his own ability to mold them into a cohesive fighting force was under constant scrutiny from both Black and white visitors. A reporter with the *Anglo-African* scrutinized every aspect of camp life. "Their cookhouses and cooking utensils were as clean and neat as a new pin. Their quarters also were as tidy as any I saw." And in drill, "Every man turned upon his heel in place like clock-work, and throwing his eyes right or left as the order might happen to come from his officer."[52] "They marched well, they wheeled well," observed another correspondent, "and there was about their whole array an air of completeness and order and *morale* which as I have not seen surpassed in any white regiment." This same reporter speculated that among the crowd of admiring spectators included "many who within the last two years have declared that they would not fight for or with the negro and would not have the negro fight for them and did not believe he could fight or would, and that if the rebellion couldn't be put down by white soldiers, it sought not to be put down at all."[53]

As the regiment continued to fill up, dress parades provided Shaw with an opportunity to showcase the developing skills of his men and the results of his strict disciplinary measures. At least one person speculated that "any doubts or prejudices" present while observing one particular dress parade must have been "dispelled." "A finer line or a better manual . . . has never been seen on that field."[54] Even some of the white soldiers training at Camp Meigs were forced to rethink some of their assumptions about whether Black men could be transformed into soldiers. One soldier admitted that he had indeed "been wrong about the black regiment here." He "used to think that blacks were a shiftless lot," but he eventually acknowledged their skill as soldiers. "Real friendly fellows too, when you give them half a chance and get to know them. I don't reckon I'll think the same about blacks again."[55]

But there were deeper concerns that occupied Shaw's attention. In addition to Jefferson Davis's proclamation promising to treat Black soldiers as slaves in rebellion and their white commanders as accomplices, many white Northerners, including even those who supported Black enlistment as a war measure, worried about the threat that Black enlistment posed to the nation's racial status quo. Military service, many feared, would lead to racial equality.

Frederick Douglass himself reinforced this fear. "Once let the black man get upon his person the brass letters U.S.; let him get an eagle on his button, and a musket on his shoulder," he told a crowd in Philadelphia in the summer of 1863, "and there is no power on the earth or under the earth which can deny that he has earned the right of citizenship in the United States."[56] These words, intended to encourage the Black community to continue to support the war effort, were interpreted by many white Northerners as the first step toward "negro equality." The rights of citizenship would lead to race mixing and a breakdown in the racial order of the North. "If ever the Anglo Saxon American citizen forsake their manhood so far as to come on a level with the 'American citizen of African descent,'" insisted one writer to a Michigan newspaper, "we will deserve to be forsaken by our Maker forever."[57]

In addition to his own questions about the ability to train Black men for military service, Shaw was most certainly sensitive to the fears of many across the country about the implications of Black enlistment. In addition to reading newspapers, Shaw could call up his own memories of the many conservative voices from the 2nd Massachusetts and from among his close friends in the 20th Massachusetts, who had expressed reservations about the changing nature of war and especially emancipation. These fears had been amplified since the release of the Emancipation Proclamation, and Shaw likely acknowledged that his men would face them directly once the regiment was deployed. The strict discipline imposed on the men of the 54th by white officers sent a signal to concerned onlookers that Black men could be controlled and managed. In doing so, Shaw hoped to assuage some of the fears attached to the thought of Black men with guns—a development that many viewed as both a revolutionary and a dangerous step.[58]

The responsibilities involved in overseeing the organization of a new regiment would have been enough to monopolize the attention of most colonels, but Shaw was also committed to marrying Annie Haggerty before the regiment departed from Boston. As was the case with their decision to become engaged, the question of marriage remained a thorny issue for both the Shaw and the Haggerty families. Shaw wrote to his mother on March 27 inquiring "*exactly*" what she and his father thought about his marrying Annie, which suggests that he was well aware of their reservations. Both his parents believed that marriage would prove to be too much of a distraction from his responsibilities to his new regiment.[59] Shaw's correspondence suggests that Sarah was more vocal in her protestations. Shaw had finally fulfilled his mother's wishes in assuming a role that could help bring about the end of slavery. Marriage to Annie threatened to undo what Sarah viewed as a close partnership of mother and son in pursuit of this shared goal.

Shaw did his best to reassure his parents that this was the most opportune time for marriage. "If I thought that being married were going to make me neglect my duty, I should think it much better never to have been engaged." He denied any interest in having Annie accompany him on active duty—a concern expressed by his mother—after having seen how difficult it was for other married couples in the field. Not knowing whether he would return, Shaw did not want to leave without marrying Annie. "The chances of my coming home in six months are very small; for, if we are put on the service we expect, we shall get into the interior before long. Indeed, one reason for my wishing to be married is, that we are going to undertake a very dangerous piece of work, and I feel that there are more chances than ever of my not getting back. I know I should go away more happy and contented if we were married."[60] Though Shaw expressed concern about whether he would be able to apply for a leave of absence at some point, the prospect of not returning at all must have been apparent to everyone.

Annie's parents expressed similar concerns about a wedding so close to Shaw's departure, but his insistence that he would "feel very much dissatisfied and discontented" to leave having not married appears to have been enough to gain the approval of Annie's parents as well.[61] A date was set for the second of May in New York City. Both Shaw and Annie planned on a "quiet" ceremony that included family and a few close friends.

Meanwhile, back in camp, the regiment continued to expand, numbering 700 men by the third week of April. The Ladies' Committee donated funds to pay for a music instructor for a proposed regimental band. The regiment also reached its quota of line officers and other personnel. All the men were now outfitted with Enfield rifles, and with the fast approach of spring, the regiment was now able to drill on the fields on a daily basis.[62]

Shaw also learned that Secretary of War Stanton and Governor Andrew planned to deploy the 54th to New Bern, North Carolina, to serve under Edward A. Wild, who was organizing a brigade of Black regiments. Wild, a thirty-eight-year-old native of Brookline, Massachusetts, had served as a doctor in the Turkish army during the Crimean War. Promoted to colonel of the 35th Massachusetts Infantry, Wild had his left arm amputated after being wounded for the second time at Antietam. After assisting in recruiting for the 54th, Wild was promoted to brigadier general and eventually raised two regiments of Black soldiers, who became known as "Wild's African Brigade."[63]

The impending deployment of the 54th Massachusetts, however, brought Shaw and the governor into direct conflict with one another for the second time. Governor Andrew hoped to deploy four companies of the 54th to North Carolina to join Wild, with the remainder of the regiment to follow once their organization was complete. Shaw explained to the governor that this was a bad idea. First, the "moral effect" for the people of Boston "of seeing a well armed, well drilled and well disciplined regiment march would be lost entirely." He also believed that the "pride" of the officers and men would "be very much lessened" as a result of such a plan. Many of the men, according to Shaw, still needed additional training, especially in the handling of their rifles. Shaw went on to explain to the governor, "We should cut a sorry figure in our present condition, in the midst of the old troops at Newburn, and it is of much importance to make a favorable impression on the white troops from the very beginning."[64]

Then there was the concern about how the regiment might perform in battle "before we had reached a good state of discipline, or a feeling of mutual confidence between officers and men had arisen." The results, Shaw mused, "might be disastrous to the whole undertaking."[65] He hoped to convince the governor to wait until the regiment was at full strength and had completed its training; but if the plan moved forward, Shaw directed Andrew to relieve him of command of his regiment.

There is no record that Shaw ever discussed his ultimatum to the governor with his parents, but there can be little doubt that Frank and especially Sarah would have been disappointed that their son was even considering abandoning the regiment and the broader issues that they believed were at stake. For Shaw, however, the governor's plan to send the regiment to North Carolina "piecemeal" threatened to undo the weeks of rigorous training and undercut the integrity of his command.

Shaw's concerns had their intended effect. Governor Andrew responded immediately reassuring Shaw that the regiment would not be sent "off in detachments" but "all together," when ready.[66] The incident speaks to the close working relationship between the two, but it is also the case that Shaw likely anticipated the governor's acquiescence rather than risking the political fallout of losing his young colonel over the question of the regiment's preparedness for active duty.

Shaw and Annie married on May 2 in the Church of the Ascension, a Protestant Episcopal Church on Fifth Avenue and Tenth Street in New York City; they were surrounded by family and close friends. Not wanting a "Show Wedding," Shaw chose to wear civilian clothes rather than his military uniform. Annie wore her travel dress and carried a bouquet of flowers. If family members harbored any doubts about the marriage, they were set aside as Rev. Cotton Smith led the ceremony and the young couple pledged their lives to one another. Following the ceremony, the bride and groom, along with the rest of the wedding party, made their way uptown to the Fifth Avenue Hotel to continue the celebration. The next day, Shaw and his new wife entrained to Lenox, to the Haggerty family home, for a brief honeymoon.[67]

Nestled in the Berkshire mountains, the small peaceful town of Lenox offered a brief and welcome respite for Shaw from the demands of military life. By early May the new foliage was quickly spreading across western Massachusetts, signaling the start of spring. Their week together was the longest uninterrupted time the two had spent together since the beginning of their courtship. Shaw and Annie spent their days riding horseback or traveling through the countryside together by carriage. The Haggerty home included a "nice garden," and a pine grove nearby provided the setting for daily "pleasant walks."[68]

For Shaw, the war was never far from his mind. The start of spring meant the beginning of military operations for the Army of the Potomac and his friends in the 2nd Massachusetts. "How I wish I were to take my share in this campaign," he wrote to Charley Morse from Lenox, "and that my future fighting were to be (if there is any in store for me) might be done alongside my old companions."[69] While in Lenox, Shaw learned of another Union defeat at the hands of Robert E. Lee at Chancellorsville, just a few miles west of Fredericksburg, in central Virginia during the first week of May.

Shaw's "angelic mood" was shattered when he learned, via telegram, that Governor Andrew planned for the 54th to depart Boston on May 20, just ten days after his planned return to camp.[70] The disappointing news was made worse upon learning that a new regiment was to be organized with the overflow of recruits from the 54th. Governor Andrew convinced Norwood Hallowell to take command of the 55th Massachusetts, while his brother, Edward Needles Hallowell, was promoted and remained with the 54th as Shaw's new second in command. Shaw was forced to cut short his honeymoon because of the changed timeline for the regiment's departure and the disruption to his chain of command.[71] The memories of the week Shaw shared with Annie quickly faded into the background as the two traveled back to Readville, where they would take up residence at a boarding house. Preparations for the regiment's departure needed to be addressed, and matters related to the shuffling of command demanded Shaw's attention as well.

Shaw returned to a regiment that had reached its full capacity. The men had completed their transformation from civilians into soldiers. Military drills and the routines of camp life were now second nature. Most importantly, the men had bonded with another, forming an esprit-de-corps that would help to maintain morale in the face of the dangers that awaited them once deployed.

Their pride was on full display for the presentation of the regimental colors on May 18, 1863. Extra railcars were added to accommodate the regiment's friends and families who had flocked to Readville to witness the ceremony. Shaw's parents were unable to attend, but the crowd included leading abolitionists such as William Lloyd Garrison, Wendell Phillips, Josiah Quincy Jr., and Frederick Douglass. A large contingent of African Americans from Boston and the surrounding community, perhaps as many as two thousand, made the trip to witness the historic ceremony.

Just before noon, the sound of the regiment's new band cut through the noise and anticipation of the large crowd. Shaw ordered his men to form a hollow square, allowing for the various parties to occupy its center to assist with the transfer of flags. Four standards were presented, including the national flag, presented by the Colored Ladies Relief Society, and the state colors; then came a banner, the gift of the recruiting committee of the 54th, bearing a picture of the Goddess of Liberty, with the motto, "Liberty, Loyalty and Union." The final flag, a cross on a "heavenly deep blue of rich silk," bearing the inscription "In Hoc Signo Vinces" (In This Sign Thou Shalt Conquer) was presented by Mary Traill Spence Putnam, the mother of Willie Lowell Putnam, who had been fatally wounded in 1861 at the battle of Ball's Bluff.[72]

Following a brief prayer by Rev. Leonard Grimes, Governor Andrew addressed the men of the 54th Massachusetts and the rest of the crowd. The governor was overwhelmed by the sight of the regiment now standing at attention before him—a dream he had lived with from the earliest days of the war. The formation of the 54th, Andrew urged, "marks an era in the history of the war, of the Commonwealth, of the country, and of humanity." "I stand or fall," he went on to say, "as a man and a magistrate, with the rise and fall in history of the Fifty-fourth Massachusetts Regiment." Addressing Shaw directly, the governor acknowledged, "I know not, Sir, when in all human history, to any given thousands of men in arms, there has been committed a work at once so proud, so precious, so full of hope and glory, as the work committed to you."

Never comfortable addressing an audience, Shaw offered a few words in response: "May we have an opportunity to show that you have not made a mistake in entrusting the honor of the State to a colored regiment,—the first State that has ever sent one to the war." Shaw concluded his remarks by congratulating the officers and men of the regiment for "their untiring fidelity and devotion to their work from the very beginning." For the men of the regiment, it was an awe-inspiring day to be surrounded by a large crowd of Black and white well-wishers and the governor. Following the ceremony, the governor handed Shaw a telegram notifying him that his regiment was to report to Maj. Gen. David Hunter at Hilton Head on the coast of South Carolina. News of the regiment's new assignment quickly spread. "Most of the men are eager to go to their destination," reported the *Boston Journal*, "some saying they have accounts to settle in that vicinity."[73]

Following a slight delay in their initial departure date, Shaw issued orders on May 27 for the regiment to pack their knapsacks and be in line, ready to leave camp early the next morning at 5:00 a.m. The regiment was finally shipping out. A great excitement filled the air in camp that evening not only because the men realized that they would be leaving Readville for good, but also because it had been decided that rather than heading straight to the wharf to embark for South Carolina, the regiment would parade through downtown Boston.

As the train lunged forward toward Boston on May 28, the men of the 55th Massachusetts cheered their departing comrades, wishing them well in their new adventure.[74] Large crowds began arriving in Boston that morning from all over the surrounding area to bid farewell to the 54th. Many were no doubt curious as to what one thousand Black men under arms and in uniform looked like.

At 9:00 a.m. the regiment arrived at the Providence Railroad Station, a block south of the Public Garden and Boston Common. A blue sky and warm temperatures greeted the men as they formed up in ranks. Led by mounted police and a drum-and-fife corps, the parade route followed a circuitous route through town along Boylston, Essex, Federal, Franklin, Washington, School, and Somerset Streets before finally reaching the Massachusetts State House atop Beacon Hill. Storefronts were decorated with red, white, and blue bunting. One observer recalled, "The cheers on the march were almost incessant, and flags and handkerchiefs were waved along the whole line of march." "Everywhere," according to Daniel F. Childs, the regiment was "greeted with enthusiastic applause" from the city's Black and white residents.[75] In many places along the route, the crowds spilled into the streets, making it difficult for the regiment to pass.

Shaw led his men on horseback, passing the homes of prominent abolitionists like Theodore Parker and Wendell Phillips. William Lloyd Garrison watched from Phillips's balcony, "his hand resting on a bust of John Brown, tears streaming down his face." Shaw saluted the longtime editor of the *Liberator* as he passed by. For Boston's small community of abolitionists, the parade was the culmination of years of struggle and setbacks. Many had been the victims of mob attacks and had witnessed firsthand the return of fugitive slaves such as Thomas Sims and Anthony Burns. William Cooper Nell, one of the city's most prominent Black abolitionists, watched the parade from the Old State House and site of the Boston Massacre, the very spot where Crispus Attucks, the first Black martyr of the American Revolution fell. Nell thought of Sims and Burns and could not help but contrast this "shameful past with the glorious present,—a thousand armed colored American soldiers en route for the land of slavery, marching down State Street, the band playing, and the soldiers singing 'John Brown,' all indicating the free, the happy future, as within a seeming hailing distance,—I could not help mentally exclaiming, 'Glory enough for one day; aye, indeed, for a life-time.'"[76]

William Wells Brown, who had helped recruit the men of the 54th Massachusetts, addressed an excited audience gathered for the annual meeting of the New England Anti-Slavery Society, which coincided with the parade. Brown was emotionally overcome by the sight of the 54th marching through his city. "These men go to the South, not only to put down this rebellion," he reminded his audience, "but to destroy that system of slavery which caused the rebellion. We are to have a new Union. And the black man is one of the forces which are to produce it."[77]

Shaw was conspicuous atop his horse as he gloried in the celebration erupting all around him. "I can never forget the scene as Colonel Shaw rode at the head of his men," recalled the poet and pacifist John Greenleaf Whittier. "The very flower of grace and chivalry, he seemed to me beautiful and awful, as an angel of God come down to lead the host of freedom to victory."[78] Anna Cabot Lowell noticed Shaw's "pleasant smile & expression" as well as "his hair & blue eyes" that "contrasted with the ebony hue of his soldiers."[79] Another observer could not "help contrasting his fair hair and delicate refined features with the dusky faces of his soldiers, and I thought of him as the type of Anglo-Saxon race offering itself in sacrifice for the African."[80] Even in this moment, white onlookers could not help but lace their observations without reference to race.

By 10:00 a.m., Shaw and his men had arrived in front of the State House, where the governor, the executive council, and with a group of dignitaries that included Senator Henry Wilson reviewed the regiment. From there it was but a few steps to Shaw's childhood home at 44 Beacon Street. Shaw's sister Ellen watched from behind a window while her mother, Annie, and her two other sisters cheered as Shaw approached. Frank, meanwhile, waited for the arrival of his son on the Common. Ellen recalled that her brother "looked up and kissed his sword." He had "the face of an angel and I felt perfectly sure he would never come back."[81] Sarah beamed with pride as their eyes met. Standing in the home where her son had spent his first few years may have reminded Sarah of the long journey that brought the two of them to this point, despite their sometimes-fraught relationship over the question of slavery and emancipation. In this moment, however, there was only tears of celebration.

Finally, the regiment wheeled left through the Charles Street gate and on to the Boston Common, where Shaw led his men in a short drill to the cheers of the crowds. The exercises offered the entire regiment the opportunity to demonstrate that no other unit surpassed the 54th in "excellence of drill" as well as in "discipline" and "dignity."[82] Spectators crowded on Flagstaff Hill to get a view of the regiment. According to one reporter, "Thousands of persons viewed the spectacle with immense satisfaction."[83] A little after noon, the regiment walked the final length of their scheduled march to Battery Wharf to the tune of "John Brown's Body." The crowds continued to line the streets not wanting them to depart without expressing one final cheer. One soldier responded to the enthusiastic crowd that they were "gwine down to see Jeff," and that they would "fix up de rebels."[84] As Shaw and his men marched down State Street, they passed Thomas Sims, the formerly enslaved man who years earlier had been dragged down this same street in chains, forced aboard a ship, and returned into bondage under the hated Fugitive Slave Act. Now he stood as a free man watching armed Black soldiers march toward a steamer that would carry the regiment south to destroy the very system that had once reclaimed him.[85]

The presence of a large police force is a reminder that the response to the 54th was not uniformly positive.[86] Authorities had prepared for trouble from Boston's white working class, who viewed armed Black men as threats to their economic status and racial privilege. The city's "roughs" had reportedly planned to disrupt the parade or attack the soldiers, continuing their long history of violent conflict with African Americans over jobs and social position.

But hostility crossed class lines that day. At the exclusive Somerset Club, members hissed audibly and drew their curtains in disgust rather than witness a thousand uniformed Black soldiers marching through their beloved Boston.[87] Hisses and jeers could be heard occasionally throughout the march. Two Black women were attacked as they followed the regiment through the streets. But these incidents did little to dampen the mood of the crowds or the regiment itself. While most of the newspaper coverage of the parade was positive, the Irish-run *Boston Pilot* predicted that Black soldiers "are not yet fit to lead for such a great nation as this the noble career of arms." "They are as fit to be the soldiers of this country, as their abettors are to be its statesman. ... *Twenty thousand negroes on the march would be smelled ten miles distant*."[88]

As the regiment neared Battery Wharf, along Commercial Street in the city's Irish North End neighborhood, a small group attacked and spat on Lewis Douglass, the son of Frederick Douglass.[89] Shaw had likely heard of this incident, but he chose not to let it dampen the joyous occasion. In the years that followed, few people had any interest in recalling the few exceptions to what was a triumphant display of patriotism and devotion to the Union by all parties involved. The officers and men of the regiment enjoyed a few final moments milling about with their friends and families before storing their rifles away and climbing on board the steamer for the journey south.

Shaw's family, along with Annie, likely accompanied him to Battery Wharf to see him off. This was the third time that Shaw bade farewell to family before going off to war, but that fact certainly did not make it any easier. After returning to their summer home on the North Shore, Sarah acknowledged in a letter to Lydia Maria Child, "The future does look dark. . . . Our dear boy has gone with his regiment . . . and my heart sinks when I think of it."[90]

As painful as his separation from his parents and sisters was that day, Shaw must have found it especially difficult to say goodbye to Annie. They had been married for less than a month, and Annie had no way of knowing when or even if her husband would return. As the sun began to set, the steamer carrying the 54th Massachusetts untied from the docks and settled into the calm waters of Boston Harbor. At some point, Shaw turned away from the faint outlines of the waving crowds and skyline and looked out toward the open sea and the work that lay ahead.

NINE

I Do Not Like to Degenerate into a Plunderer and Robber

The steamer *De Molay* carried the 54th Massachusetts into the Atlantic on what began as a "very smooth" voyage toward their South Carolina destination. The 1,300-ton vessel, built in Medford and commissioned by the US Quartermaster Department, was relatively new and well-maintained, with "perfectly clean" decks free of the "disagreeable odours" that might have made close quarters unbearable. For many soldiers, this was their first ocean voyage and opportunity to experience the vastness of the Atlantic Ocean. While the inevitable "rolling and pitching" of the ship eventually sent many to the guardrails to find relief, Shaw enjoyed the fresh sea air, clear weather, and hot temperatures under the shelter of "a fine large awning over the quarter-deck."[1]

The relatively calm voyage was punctuated by a few violent incidents between the men, one of whom "was badly stabbed in the face with a bayonet." Captain Appleton recalled that "some liquor had been brought on board," which no doubt contributed to the fighting, but by and large they "huddled on deck and below singing and chatting."[2] Shaw used his time to write to loved ones back home and to reflect on the events of the past few months. At the beginning of 1863, Shaw had been sheltering in winter quarters in Virginia, unsure of what the future would bring. Now, he was not only newly married but in charge of a regiment of African American volunteer soldiers. "I hope I shall never forget," he wrote to Annie, "the happy days we have passed together since then, and that I shall always look back on them with the same pleasure as now." He regretted that it would likely "be a long time before we find ourselves driving about Berkshire again."[3]

Whatever sadness Shaw felt being separated from Annie was overshadowed by the memory of the regiment's triumphant march through Boston just a few days earlier, "amidst a greater enthusiasm than has been seen since the first three-months troops left for the war." Shaw had overcome his "own doubts and fears" as well as the "sneering and pitying remarks" of others during the regiment's training at Readville. He found encouragement in the performance of his men thus far, even if his observations of them were sometimes racist in character. The opportunity to reflect on recent events left Shaw feeling grateful: "Truly, I ought to be thankful for all my happiness, and my success in life so far; and if the raising of coloured troops prove such a benefit to the country, and to the blacks. . . . I shall thank God a thousand times that I was led to take my share in it."[4]

After a brief stop in Cape Hatteras, North Carolina, the *De Molay* continued south into warmer waters. The air became increasingly "soft and balmy," and a "few porpoises and a shark or two followed the ship," providing entertainment for all on board.[5] On the morning of June 3, 1863, the regiment sailed past Charleston Harbor. Shaw gazed out at the blockading fleet and caught a glimpse of the top of Fort Sumter, now largely in ruins and in Confederate hands. He may have been able to see the numerous church spires that dotted Charleston, the city viewed by many as the seat of the rebellion.

A flurry of activity ensued as soldiers packed knapsacks, rolled blankets, and wrote letters to loved ones back home as the *De Molay* continued to hug the sandy shores of South Carolina for the final leg of its journey. Shaw's focus likely turned to the task at hand. He knew little about military affairs in what was known as the Department of the South—a district that encompassed the states of South Carolina, Georgia, and Florida—given that his new orders arrived just prior to the regiment's embarkation from Boston.

At Hilton Head, Shaw reported to Maj. Gen. David Hunter. The fifty-nine-year-old Hunter was politically connected and one of the oldest generals in the US Army. Hunter dyed his mustache and wore a poorly fitted wig in order to make himself look younger. He was known to have a volatile temper and rarely backed down from a fight. A graduate of West Point, Hunter had once been assigned to protect President Lincoln after his inauguration. But then he was severely wounded while leading his division at the First Battle of Bull Run. After recovering sufficiently from his injury, Hunter was reassigned to the Department of the West and became second in command to General Frémont in Missouri. While Hunter privately agreed with Frémont's controversial August 1861 proclamation freeing all slaves in his district belonging to Confederates, he maintained that it was flawed as a military order. Hunter stayed on for a few additional weeks after Frémont was removed from command; but by the end of March 1862, he was in Port Royal, South Carolina, to take command of the Department of the South.[6]

Two months later, Hunter began enlisting freedmen in what became the 1st South Carolina Colored Infantry Regiment, and he issued his own general emancipation order declaring slaves in Georgia, South, Carolina, and Florida free. As was the case with Frémont, Lincoln rescinded Hunter's emancipation order so as not to upset the border slave states, but he looked the other way when it came to the enlistment of Black soldiers. Shaw was unamused by Hunter, writing to his mother that he "doesn't impress me as being a great man."[7]

From Hilton Head, the regiment was ordered to report to Col. James Montgomery, who commanded the 2nd South Carolina Colored Infantry Regiment in nearby Beaufort. Once the *De Molay* reentered Port Royal Sound en route to Hilton Head, Shaw and the regiment looked out on a vast fleet numbering roughly seventy ships, including the frigates *Wabash* and *Vermont,* several monitor gunboats, and a French steamer. The sight was a small snapshot of the US Navy's efforts to blockade the Atlantic coast and starve the Confederacy into submission. As the steamer entered the Beaufort River, the men caught their first glimpse of the dense foliage and wildlife that hugged the shores of Parris and Saint Helena Islands. An occasional break along the tree line at Port Royal revealed endless acres of the valuable sea island cotton for which the region was famous as well as the extravagant plantation homes that reflected hundreds of years of accumulated wealth built on the backs of the enslaved, who lived in "long rows" of small cabin-sized homes.[8]

The regiment first set foot on South Carolina soil on the early morning of June 4, just outside Beaufort. The smell of wisterias, wild white lilies, and yellow jessamine filled the air. There were few people to greet the men as they marched along Bay Street into town before bivouacking on the nearby Thompson plantation, close to the camps of both the 1st and 2nd South Carolina. "Sandy streets shaded with fine oaks crossed one another at right angles," recalled Capt. Luis Emilio. The town boasted some "fine old houses and gardens . . . churches public buildings, and a spacious green."[9]

The stillness of the morning, however, masked the revolutionary changes that had taken place in and around Beaufort since the US Navy first entered Port Royal Sound in November 1861 and occupied many of the surrounding coastal islands. Wealthy slaveowners quickly abandoned their plantations and fields and followed the retreat of a small Confederate force assigned to defend the region. Though their flight included a small number of enslaved men and women, thousands of others cast a shadow on their masters' assumption that their human property would remain loyal in the face of "Yankee" aggression. Instead, the enslaved men and women embraced their freedom by claiming food, farm animals, and the land itself. Strict boundaries between master and slave, long maintained by the lash, were quickly shattered as bare feet kicked open the front doors of plantation homes to take ownership of clothing, furniture, liquor, and other luxury items. Others took out their anger by destroying the contents of the homes that their labor made possible, and in some cases the homes went up in flames. In his description of Beaufort, one naval officer wrote, "The stores were stripped of their contents and private dwellings are in the greatest disorder, furniture broken, beds ripped open and their feathers scattered . . . books, valuable books lying about in the yards and streets, torn, mutilated; in the houses all is disorder."[10]

Confederate retreat from Beaufort triggered jubilant celebrations throughout the Sea Islands as enslaved people embraced their sudden freedom. But Washington, DC, viewed these scenes with alarm rather than joy. Officials feared that the collapse of plantation discipline would create chaos as food supplies dwindled and planting season approached without organized labor. The legal status of 10,000 newly freed people created an unprecedented crisis that demanded an immediate federal response. Military commanders, Lincoln's administration, and Northern abolitionists all recognized the Sea Islands as a crucial test case for a postslavery labor system and Black citizenship. For abolitionists, the situation offered the perfect laboratory to prove their theories about Black people's capacity for freedom and self-governance. They saw an opportunity to demonstrate that formerly enslaved people could become productive citizens rather than the dependent burden that slavery's apologists predicted. Military officials worried more practically about maintaining cotton production and preventing a social breakdown in the occupied territory.[11]

Treasury Secretary Salmon Chase saw the Sea Islands as an opportunity to refill federal coffers depleted by war costs. He hoped to employ thousands of formerly enslaved people as paid laborers farming cotton, with the profits flowing to the federal government. Chase dispatched Edward L. Pierce, a committed antislavery attorney from Massachusetts who had supervised contraband labor at Fortress Monroe, to manage this ambitious experiment. But Pierce's vision extended far beyond treasury revenues. He planned to eliminate corporal punishment, reunite separated families, and establish schools for Black children, transforming the islands into a laboratory for free labor principles. The American Missionary Association reinforced this humanitarian mission by sending Rev. Mansfield French to coordinate the education efforts. Both men believed the federal government bore the responsibility to prepare formerly enslaved people for citizenship in a postwar biracial democracy.

In early March 1862, the first wave of missionaries from Boston and New York City—dubbed "Gideonites" by some critics—arrived in Port Royal. The following month, a group of reformers from Philadelphia, led by Laura Towne joined their colleagues. Towne, educated at the Female Medical College of Pennsylvania, was a trained homeopathic physician and had built a career educating underprivileged children. Along with her friend Ellen Murray, the two quickly established a school on the Oaks Plantation on nearby St. Helena Island, in a church constructed by slaves for their masters.[12]

The challenges facing Sea Island reformers were overwhelming and complex. Despite their good intentions, most had never ventured into the Deep South; nor had they ever interacted directly with enslaved people. The majority of educators were white, middle-class women whose ideas about African Americans ranged from paternalistic sympathy to genuine egalitarian commitment—but all were operating from a theoretical knowledge base rather than from lived experience. More immediately dangerous were the Confederate forces that remained active in the region. Artillery thunder rolled across the water from nearby islands, while "reports of rebel boats stealing by" reminded everyone that this humanitarian experiment was unfolding in a war zone. Reformers trying to establish schools and reunite families did so under constant threat of Confederate raids that sought to recapture the very people they sought to help.[13] The heat and mosquitos, along with the threat of disease, were a constant concern, especially during the summer months. While many of the educators found their work with the freedmen to be rewarding, others experienced frustrations deciphering the freedpeople's distinct dialect as well as their cultural and religious practices. The reformers' own ideas of freedom and uplift often conflicted with the choices and beliefs of the individuals committed to exploring the first few steps of freedom on their own terms. This perception of defiance among the freedmen often brought them in direct conflict with the military as well, whose leadership expected all able-bodied men to work the land to guarantee a large cotton harvest for the benefit of the federal government.[14]

By late 1862, more than two thousand Black children attended schools across St. Helena, Ladies, Port Royal, Hilton Head, and Parris Islands—a stunning educational achievement in the heart of former slave territory. Reformers like Laura Towne quickly learned to navigate the delicate balance between military objectives and missionary goals, working to prevent conflicts that might destabilize relations with formerly enslaved communities. The transformation unfolding in the Port Royal region was genuinely revolutionary, far exceeding the Lincoln administration's original conservative goal of simply preserving the Union.

Shaw and the 54th Massachusetts disembarked in Beaufort with little understanding of their role in this complicated and ongoing effort to protect and guide this newly emancipated population on their first steps into freedom. The landscape of war in South Carolina differed dramatically from what Shaw had experienced in Maryland and Virginia. With so few Confederates in the immediate vicinity, there was little opportunity to engage in the type of campaigning that Shaw had experienced over the previous two years. Up to this point, Shaw had spent relatively little time reflecting on the conditions of the enslaved; but now he found himself commanding a regiment of Black soldiers amid thousands of formerly enslaved men, women, and children. General Hunter likely reiterated to Shaw what he had communicated to Governor Andrew back in Boston, that the regiment would take part in a "system of operations which will rapidly compel the Rebels either to lay down their arms and sue for restoration of the Union or to withdraw their slaves into the interior, thus leaving desolate the most fertile and productive of their counties on the Atlantic seaboard." Questions, however, remained about what these "operations" would entail.[15]

In Beaufort, Shaw reported to the military governor of the Department of the South, Gen. Rufus Saxton. A West Point graduate, Saxton's life before the war had overlapped with the Shaw family in numerous ways. In addition to being born in Massachusetts, Saxton was also an outspoken abolitionist, a supporter of the Brook Farm experiment, and an admirer of Charles Fourier. During the opening campaigns of the Civil War, Saxton quickly rose to the rank of brigadier general. He won the Medal of Honor for his successful defense of Harpers Ferry during the Shenandoah Valley Campaign in 1862, before being assigned to the Department of the South.[16]

Shaw was likely pleased by the enthusiastic welcome he received on the first day by Col. Thomas Wentworth Higginson. Shaw was familiar with the Unitarian minister, abolitionist, and politician. Higginson's commitment to ending slavery had been demonstrated years earlier through his membership on the Boston Vigilance Committee, which aided fugitive slaves; through his work with the New England Emigration Society to ensure that Kansas entered the Union as a free state; and most notably, through his membership in the Secret Six, which provided financial support to the abolitionist John Brown. In 1862, Saxton tapped Higginson to command the 1st South Carolina.[17]

Higginson was able to answer many of Shaw's questions about the military situation in and around Beaufort as well as about the work that he and his regiment would be required to undertake. The two discussed the fighting capabilities of Black soldiers. Decades after the war, Higginson recalled that Shaw had suggested, "that while I [Higginson] had shown that negro troops were effective in bushfighting, it had yet to be determined how they would fight in line of battle." Though Higginson pushed back on his skepticism, Shaw concluded, "It would always be possible to put another line of soldiers behind a black regiment, so as to present equal danger in either direction."[18] Higginson may have been surprised by the suggestion that bayonets might be necessary to motivate the men of the 54th Massachusetts to face the enemy, but he also recognized that Shaw had been in command of his regiment only for a few months and had yet to witness Black soldiers in action.

Despite their differing views on the fighting abilities of Black soldiers, the two shared a good deal in common. Both men had been raised among the cultural elite of Boston's Brahmin class, which instilled in both Higginson and Shaw a strong sense of their own superiority over most other people. Both men singled out Southern slaveholders for causing the war rather than the poor and vast yeomen population, who were goaded into fighting it for the slaveholders' benefit. Both men believed that proper leadership was essential to maintaining discipline and the fighting readiness of the rank and file. Finally, and perhaps most importantly, Higginson and Shaw maintained "that it was through warfare that a civilized people demonstrated their high moral values."[19]

Shaw also briefly met his brigade commander, Col. James Montgomery. The gulf between Montgomery on one side and Shaw and Higginson on the other could not have been wider. Montgomery was born in 1814 and raised in Ashtabula County, Ohio. He possessed little in the way of formal education but became a preacher and schoolteacher in Kentucky before moving to Missouri to become a farmer. A Free-Soiler at the time, Montgomery objected to slavery on economic grounds; but he was later radicalized as the fighting on the Missouri-Kansas border increased in the mid-1850s. In 1857 he organized free-state men into a "self-protective company," which he used to intimidate and force proslavery men out of the Kansas Territory. Montgomery's antislavery stance was infused with a rigid moral and religious code: "It is always right *to do* Right. And I am right sure it is right to 'Break every yoke, and let the oppressed go free.' It [is] right because God commanded it, 'And shall not the Jud[g]e of All the Earth do right?'" Montgomery's crusade against slavery led him, on occasion, to partner with John Brown to harbor freedom seekers and punish their enslavers before the latter left to carry out his raid against Harpers Ferry in 1859.[20]

By the beginning of the Civil War, Montgomery had been transformed into a religious zealot who would "fight a holy war against slavery and a war of vengeance against slaveholders."[21] Early on, he was commissioned as colonel of the 3rd Kansas Infantry. Unlike most people in the army, Montgomery called for the recruitment of African American soldiers at the very beginning of the war. After reporting to the Department of the South in January 1863, Montgomery was authorized by Saxton to raise a second regiment of Black soldiers from among the population of freedmen. Though Montgomery believed that he was engaged in a religious crusade to end slavery, he also embraced deeply racist views of African Americans, believing them to be a race of savages, conditioned by generations of enslavement.[22]

Shaw likely pressed Montgomery for details about his regiment's recent operations. Montgomery had perfected hit-and-run tactics using shallow-draft steamboats to strike coastal targets before Confederate forces could organize effective resistance. In February 1863, he had led the 2nd South Carolina twenty-five miles up the St. Mary's River along the Florida-Georgia border, seizing building materials and other valuable supplies. A few weeks later, Montgomery returned with a larger force to announce the Emancipation Proclamation to enslaved communities and recruit as many men as possible for military service. On March 25, the regiment executed an even more ambitious expedition, traveling up the St. Mary's River to Palatka, Florida, and "returning laden with wagons, mules, cotton, forage, freed slaves, and fifteen prisoners."[23] Positive reports of the successful repulse of Confederate attacks during the expedition strengthened the Lincoln administration's commitment to recruit Black troops in other theaters of operation.[24]

Along the way, Montgomery formed a close partnership with the famed Underground Railroad conductor Harriet Tubman, who arrived in Port Royal in May 1862 at the suggestion of Governor Andrew. The governor believed that Tubman would be invaluable in collecting information from escaped slaves and other sources that would prove valuable to military planners. Montgomery may have met Tubman in 1860, and the two would have easily bonded over their shared friendship with John Brown and their commitment to ending slavery.[25]

Montgomery's most audacious raid unfolded along the Combahee River on June 1, 1863, just days before Shaw's arrival. Local enslavers had grown complacent, believing Union forces could not penetrate so deeply into Confederate territory. Montgomery hoped to liberate as many enslaved people as possible for potential military recruitment and to clear Confederate torpedoes that blocked Union gunboat navigation. Harriet Tubman's intelligence proved invaluable, guiding Montgomery to torpedo locations and plantation sites where enslaved communities awaited liberation. Minimal Confederate resistance allowed the expedition to cast a wide net across the river's plantations. Montgomery's forces systematically destroyed the economic infrastructure of slavery, burning hundreds of acres of crops, rice mills, cotton warehouses, storehouses, and plantation mansions with General Hunter's explicit approval. Roughly 800 men, women, and children crowded onto Union gunboat decks for the return voyage to Beaufort. Many would become soldiers, others would join the Sea Islands labor experiment, but all had been transformed from Confederate assets into Union refugees in a single day's operation.[26]

Montgomery's expeditions struck fear in area's plantation owners, who were forced to flee farther into the interior, often with little warning. Every retreat left additional slaves and other valuable property behind. Newspapers throughout the North celebrated Montgomery's efforts. "This expedition reflects great credit upon Col. Montgomery and the men of his command," reported the Philadelphia *Inquirer*. "He has destroyed property of the enemy estimated at a million dollars, proved himself a capable commander, and that the negro troops can be made efficient soldiers."[27] Rev. Daniel Foster, who served as the chaplain of the 33rd Massachusetts Infantry Regiment—also known as the Abolition Regiment—traveled to Beaufort to secure an officer's commission under Montgomery. Though unsuccessful, he left a positive

Led by Col. James Montgomery and Harriet Tubman, the raid up the Combee River freed roughly 800 people just days before the arrival of Shaw and the 54th Massachusetts to Beaufort, South Carolina. *Harper's Weekly*, July 4, 1863. *Courtesy Library of Congress.*

account of the man, writing, "What Stonewall Jackson was to the rebels, he is fitted to be on our side at the head of an adequate colored force."[28]

Montgomery's tactics, however, were not without its critics. Higginson described Montgomery as a "singular mixture of fanaticism, vanity, and genius." "His hatred of control," continued Higginson, "makes it hard for him to believe that a regiment which is well drilled can be fit for action. . . . He thinks me straight-laced and red-tapish—I think him fitter to command a hundred men than a thousand." All of this was driven home for Higginson when he learned that Montgomery "had one of his own men shot without trial . . . for desertion, & was about to shoot two more" before cooler heads intervened.[29]

Shaw's initial impressions of Montgomery were formed by the pair's brief meeting as well as by his conversations with Higginson. "He is an Indian in his mode of warfare," Shaw shared with his father, "and though I am glad to see something of it, I can't say I admire it." In a letter to his mother, Shaw described Montgomery as a "strange compound." "He allows no swearing or drinking in his regiment & is anti-tobacco—But he burns & destroys wherever he goes with great gusto, & looks as if he had [sic] quite a taste for hanging people & throat-cutting whenever a suitable subject offers."[30]

It is important to point out, given the controversy that would soon ensue between the two men, that Shaw was eager to attach his regiment to Montgomery's command. He was aware of Montgomery's mode of warfare, including the destruction of private property, and Shaw had some understanding of his command style and his volatile personality. Shaw certainly witnessed the celebrations in Beaufort among the hundreds of newly liberated slaves, brought back by Montgomery and Tubman from the Combahee River expedition, who were now being sheltered in many of the town's churches and other available spaces. Just as important, the men in the 54th Massachusetts caught a glimpse of the key role that they would likely play as liberators in upcoming military operations. Ultimately, Shaw hoped to get his men into the field "as soon as possible," and he was enthusiastic, admitting, "Montgomery is a good man to begin under."[31]

Late on June 8, 1863, the 54th Massachusetts boarded the *De Molay* for the eighty-mile voyage south to St. Simons Island, where Montgomery's 2nd South Carolina awaited them. Despite some rough seas, the steamer reached the island's southern tip by dawn, disembarking Shaw's regiment near the ghostly remnants of Confederate earthworks that enslaved hands had been forced to build. The soldiers marched passed these abandoned fortifications to Pike's Bluff, an abandoned plantation where they established camp near Montgomery's forces. Shaw commandeered the plantation mansion as his headquarters, writing to Annie about the island's haunting beauty despite the decay of war and abandonment. "You would be enchanted with the scenery here," Shaw told his fiancée. "The foliage is wonderfully thick, and the trees covered with hanging moss, making beautiful avenues wherever there is a good path; it is more like tropics than anything I have seen."[32]

Shaw's peaceful appreciation of St. Simons Island's landscape ended abruptly, on the morning of June 11, when Montgomery arrived with urgent orders. Montgomery inquired how quickly the 54th Massachusetts could be ready for an expedition. Shaw's immediate response—thirty minutes—revealed his hunger for combat action after weeks of training and travel. Shortly thereafter, Shaw's regiment joined five companies of Montgomery's 2nd South Carolina and a battery of the 3rd Rhode Island Artillery aboard the steamers *Harriet A. Weed, Paul Jones,* and *John Adams.* The small flotilla navigated the maze of brackish creeks and tidal streams feeding into the Altamaha River, carrying Shaw toward his first joint operation with Montgomery's battle-tested veterans at the small town of Darien, Georgia.

The men of the 54th Massachusetts caught their first view of the carefully laid out rice fields with their embankments, levees, and tide gates that controlled the introduction and removal of water from the fields. Though now abandoned, the backbreaking labor, performed by tens of thousands of enslaved people, that was needed to maintain these fields for the benefit of their enslavers was not difficult to envision. As the boats neared Darien they passed a small portion of the roughly one thousand acres of Pierce Butler's abandoned rice plantation. It was another reminder for Shaw's men that they were waging war not only on the Confederacy but on slavery itself.[33]

By 1863, Darien was a shadow of its former prosperity. The town's population had dwindled to roughly 500 residents served by 1,500 enslaved people who maintained what remained of the local economy. During the 1840s and early 1850s, Darien had thrived as a commercial hub, shipping rice, Sea Island cotton, and lumber north and overseas before railroad expansion redirected trade through Savannah's superior port facilities. War had drained the town of fighting-age men, who had either volunteered for local units like the McIntosh Guards, the Forest Rifles, and the McIntosh Cavalry or been swept up by Confederate conscription. Among those who remained were the blockade runners, who used Darien's strategic harbor as a departure point for their attempts to pierce the Union naval blockade.[34]

The first indication of the Union expedition's approach to Darien was the sound of the shells they lobbed randomly into and around the sleepy town, just before noon. Capt. John Lane who was commanding a small detachment of Confederate cavalry responsible for the defense of the county, sighted the gunboats and steamers from a thicket near the ridge, just outside the town, to which most of the remaining inhabitants had fled in anticipation of the enemy's arrival.[35] According to Shaw, "The town was deserted, with the exception of two white women and two negroes."[36]

One of the first shells fired from the gunboats set a portion of the town ablaze, and the fire was already quickly spreading as the men disembarked from the boats along the wharves. Warehouses located near the riverfront were filled with rice and resin, while the rest of the town contained three churches, jail, courthouse, and school. A main road ran parallel to the river, with a host of smaller roads "shaded with mulberry and oak trees of great size and beauty."[37] The 54th Massachusetts formed up in the center of town and was ordered to confiscate "all the furniture and movable property to be taken on board the boats."[38] One of the officers recalled that the men quickly returned with "every species and all sorts and quantities of furniture" including "sofas, tables, pianos, chairs, mirrors, carpets, law-books . . . china sets, tinware," to name just a few of the items removed.[39] Eighty bales of long staple cotton, worth approximately $30,000, were also confiscated farther up the river and brought aboard a schooner that was set to sail for the Bahamas.[40]

In contrast with his previous expeditions, only a small number of enslaved people followed Montgomery's men to the wharves. An elderly Black woman named Nancy, who had been born in Africa, refused to climb aboard. All these years later, the horror of having been kidnapped and forced to endure the Middle Passage may have still been fresh in her mind.[41]

Once it was clear that the town had been "disembowelled," Montgomery turned to Shaw and "in a very low tone" informed him, "I shall burn this town." Shaw refused to take part personally in the firing of the town, but one of Shaw's companies was ordered by Montgomery to assist the 2nd South Carolina. There was little that Shaw could do to prevent the town's complete destruction. Montgomery justified his actions by explaining to Shaw that "Southerners must be made to feel that this was a real war, and that they were to be swept away by the hand of God, like the Jews of old."[42]

Montgomery himself torched the last building as the men continued loading their plunder onto the transports. Very little of the town had been spared. Commercial buildings, private homes, and even St. Andrew's Episcopal Church succumbed to the flames. "The heat was so intense," recalled Captain Emilio, "that all were driven to the farther side of our boat, and gun barrels became so hot that the men were ordered to hold them upward."[43] At one point during the raid, Shaw and Captain Appleton walked through a private residence, "which was well furnished, but found nothing of use." The two crossed paths in one room "and sadly gazed at the family portraits . . . doomed to the flames."[44] The sun set before the expedition headed out again, but the lack of visibility forced the expedition to anchor nearby. Flames continued to sneak through the dense smoke emanating from the burning resin in the warehouses. To pass the time the men on board continued to fire an occasional shell into town to encourage the flames further.

Shaw and the 54th returned to their camp on St. Simons by early afternoon the following day. After getting settled and with the events of the previous day still spinning in his head, Shaw wrote both to Hunter's adjutant inquiring whether Montgomery had specific orders to burn Darien as well as to Governor Andrew to make clear that while the "men themselves behaved very well," the orders to torch the town came directly from Montgomery. Shaw wanted it known that he opposed these orders and that what transpired "is sure to bring discredit on the coloured troops if persisted in."[45] Shaw also returned to the letter he had started writing to Annie before the regiment's abrupt departure. As he described what took place, Shaw warned Annie not to "breathe a word" of what he had written before he decided what, if any, official action was to be taken.[46]

What troubled Shaw about the Darien expedition was the intentional burning of the town as the two regiments were preparing to depart. Unlike Shaw's experience the previous spring during the retreat of the 2nd Massachusetts through the streets of Winchester, Virginia, "not a shot had been fired" against the Union troops by the civilians in Darien. Montgomery's Old Testament justification for burning the town and his belief that his men were not bound to the rules of regular warfare greatly troubled Shaw. "If we had fought for possession of the place, and it had been found necessary to hold or destroy it, or if the inhabitants had done anything which deserved such punishment, or if it were a place of refuge for the enemy," he explained to Annie, "there might have been some reason for Montgomery's acting as he did; but as the case stands, I can't see any justification."[47] As far as Shaw was concerned, the unnecessary suffering of the innocent and defenseless had no military justification and fell outside any ethical understanding of the accepted rules of war.

Montgomery, by contrast, maintained that his actions fell well within the expectations of his superiors; but on June 9, General Hunter issued an order to "avoid any devastation which does not strike immediately at the resources or material of the armed insurrection which we are now engaged in the task of suppressing." Montgomery was to continue to welcome fugitive slaves into his lines, and the confiscation of food, cattle, and other personal property could continue as well, but he was to avoid escalating the conflict before the "wickedness and folly of the enemy" justified a harsher policy.[48] It is unclear whether Montgomery was aware of this order before the start of the Darien expedition. In his own defense, Montgomery highlighted the Confederacy's proclamation to execute captured Black soldiers and their white officers as a sufficient justification for his actions.[49]

In addition to his concerns about the rules of war, Shaw also worried about the impact of the raid on the reputation of Black troops, and on the 54th Massachusetts specifically, "and of those connected with them."[50]

Newspapers throughout the country published firsthand accounts and commentary about the Darien expedition, but their assessments of whether the burning of the town was justified almost always came down along political lines. The *Hartford Weekly Intelligencer* characterized the Darien raid as the "Barbarous Fruits of Abolitionism," while a correspondent for the New York *Daily Tribune* stated unequivocally, "These bold, rapid, and successful expeditions of Col. Montgomery are spreading terror throughout the entire coast and are compelling the Rebels to abandon their rice and cotton fields and all the smallest villages which would be at all likely to be visited by him."[51]

Shaw feared that continued participation in what he called "this barbarous state of warfare" would undermine his regiment's training and destroy the military discipline he had worked months to instill. The experience in Darien also led Shaw to worry about his own reputation, which had always been of considerable concern to him throughout his time in the army. Shaw expected that his advancement through the ranks and increase in responsibility would come with an improvement in his reputation. "For myself, I have gone through the war so far without dishonour, and I do not like to degenerate into a plunderer and robber,—and the same applies to every officer in my regiment. There was not a deed performed, from beginning to end, which required any pluck or courage."[52] Honor, for Shaw, would be won only by leading his men in battle against Confederates on the battlefield as he had done at Antietam. For Shaw, the burning of Darien pointed to a widening of the conflict that he had resisted from the beginning of his military service. Now he was being forced to participate in it directly.

Not all the officers involved in the raid shared Shaw's concerns about what had transpired at Darien, but there is no evidence that he sought out their opinions. The 2nd South Carolina's Capt. William Lee Apthorp recalled that the town "had been a good while deserted and used as a rendezvous for guerillas, and belonged entirely to full-blooded rebels all in arms against us." "What better warrant," he concluded, "did we need for its destruction?"[53] Writing to his wife, Appleton noted that Montgomery "is one of our kind that believes in making the enemy pay the way." Appleton was disgusted by the sight of a whipping post in front of the town jail and kept its keys as a "trophy."[54]

There is also no evidence that Shaw attempted to solicit the views of the rank and file. This is not at all surprising. As has already been noted, Shaw never formed a close bond with enlisted men and that certainly would not change with a regiment composed of Black men. If he had, Shaw would have quickly noticed a substantial gulf between their assessments of the Darien raid and his own.

This was the regiment's first experience in hostile territory. Many of the men likely thought about the risks they had assumed, given the Confederacy's recent proclamation stipulating that captured Black soldiers would be executed or sold into slavery. James Henry Gooding offered the readers of the *New-Bedford Mercury* a concise overview of the expedition, including details about the scope of the "fruits of the expedition," but he blamed the ensuing debate on an "opposition press" bent on using Darien to confirm the worst fears that much of the public harbored about the use of Black troops and as a justification for those who continued to push for the overseas colonization of Black Americans. The "Copperhead press," Gooding maintained, intentionally exaggerated Darien's economic importance, supposedly "rivaling New York, in commercial importance, and the peer of Rome and Athens, in historical value" not only to discredit Black soldiers, but as a means to instill fear among white Northerners of the consequences of emancipation.[55]

Reporting for the New York *Weekly Anglo-African*, George Stephens characterized Montgomery as an "active and brave leader." "No sooner does he accomplish one object than he has already inaugurated the necessary steps for the accomplishment of another." Rather than viewing the Darien raid as a violation of the rules of war, Stephens emphasized "spreading terror to the hearts of the rebels throughout this region" as one of the regiment's most noteworthy accomplishments. In addition to the cattle, pigs, poultry, and other confiscated items carried away, Stephens took special pride in the "first rebel flag" captured by Montgomery's company.[56] Decades after the war, a veteran of the 2nd South Carolina testified in his pension file affidavit that his "first battle was in Darien," which suggests that many of the enlisted men who took part, especially those recently liberated from slavery, viewed the destruction as an appropriate response.[57]

Frederick Douglass responded to the condemnation of the burning of Darien by also pointing out that the Confederate proclamation "made lawful every possible form of retaliation . . . which is likely to bring them to their senses the most speedily." "A few more raids like that of Col. Montgomery, will do more than all the soft talk of a thousand presses about the 'rules of civilized warfare' to bring Jefferson Davis and his rebel crew to their senses."[58] Douglass's sharp response to the critics of Montgomery's tactics reflected the hard work that he had put into encouraging African Americans to enlist as well as his very personal concern for the safety of his two sons, who were serving in the 54th Massachusetts.

Neither Gooding, Stephens, nor Douglass for that matter mentioned Shaw by name or expressed his dissatisfaction with what transpired in Darien, which suggests acknowledgment that the 54th was ultimately under Montgomery's command and that the operation unfolded according to his direction. Their accounts also suggest that, by and large, the men of the 54th Massachusetts approved of the raid and their participation in it. It is not that they were unconcerned about the regiment's reputation or about serving honorably, but that their understanding of their role in the operation differed sharply from that of their colonel. Their view of what took place was also informed by a clear-eyed understanding of the risks they incurred as soldiers and their shared beliefs in what they were fighting against.[59]

The 54th had been in the Lowcountry for a little over a week, and during that time they had seen the outcome of Montgomery's exploits along the Combahee River that resulted in the liberation of hundreds of enslaved people and the confiscation of enslavers' property. Shaw failed to acknowledge that from the point-of-view of the men under his command, the Darien expedition was their opportunity to hammer their own nail into the coffin of the "Slaveholders' Rebellion."

Back on St. Simons Island, Shaw expressed no regrets in his letters home about assuming command of the 54th Massachusetts. It had been months since he expressed his doubts about the impact of Lincoln's Emancipation Proclamation, and Shaw now viewed the "overgrown plantation" and "empty house" occupied by his regiment as a "harbinger of freedom to the slaves, and every lover of his country, even if he have no feeling for the slaves themselves, should rejoice."[60]

But in his private moments, alone with his thoughts, there is every reason to believe that Shaw harbored regrets about having accepted Governor Andrew's offer to command a regiment of Black soldiers. Darien represented a serious blow to the role Shaw anticipated that he and his regiment would play in his new command. He was still under the direct command of Montgomery, and Shaw likely anticipated future raids similar to what had transpired in Darien. Such assignments, in his mind, would threaten the discipline of his regiment, but more importantly, they would bring Shaw no closer to the respect and honor that he hoped to experience in his new rank. The prospect of finishing the war engaged in uncivilized warfare must have been horrifying for Shaw to consider after everything he had been through.

TEN

My Men Are Capable of Better Service than Mere Guerilla Warfare

The regiment's return to St. Simons Island offered Shaw his first extended stay in one place since arriving in the Lowcountry roughly ten days earlier. He resumed regular correspondence once again with his family and close friends; but the respite from active operations made Shaw increasingly restless. His former friends and comrades in the 2nd Massachusetts were now engaged in another costly campaign season in central Virginia that had the potential to change the tide of the war. But there appeared to be little prospect for battlefield glory or opportunity to help bring the Confederacy to its knees as long as Shaw and his regiment remained under the command of James Montgomery. In contrast with how the men under his command viewed their work in Darien, Shaw maintained that "these little miserable expeditions are of no account at all" to the broader course of the war. Speaking as much for himself as for those under his command, Shaw was convinced: "My men are capable of better service than mere guerilla warfare."[1]

Shaw's feelings of isolation on St. Simons stemmed from more than just the distance from active operations. While he took some satisfaction in the regiment's role in liberating enslaved people through military raids, he remained disconnected from the broader reconstruction efforts transforming the Sea Islands. The educational and economic programs uplifting thousands of formerly enslaved people around Port Royal—work his own parents were passionately supporting from New York—held no interest for him. The schools, labor experiments, and family reunifications that represented his parents' deepest hopes for racial equality registered with Shaw as peripheral concerns unrelated to his military duties.

St. Simons Island was largely abandoned by the time Shaw and his regiment arrived. Before the war, the island's economy had been fueled by hundreds of enslaved laborers, who cultivated thousands of acres of long staple cotton across fourteen plantations. Five hundred formerly enslaved people, including Susie King Taylor, continued to call the island home after Confederates abandoned it in February 1862. Taylor established a school on the island until the freedpeople were relocated to Hilton Head and Fernandina, Florida, nine months later. Taylor was in Beaufort when the 54th arrived in early June and taught a number of the men in the regiment "to read and write, when they were off duty."[2]

Shaw was impressed with St. Simons's natural features. An array of scents emanated from the shrubbery, grass, and trees. Gentle breezes swept the island from the marsh and open sea. The sound of the waves lapping the sandy shores competed with the call of a wide array of birds and the "hum of insects," that Shaw first initially mistook for "a vessel blowing off steam."[3] Despite the constant rain, Shaw enjoyed exploring the island along a well-laid shell road that ran from one end to the other. The ruins of Fort Frederica, founded by Governor James Oglethorpe in 1736 and located at the center of the island, were still visible and a reminder of the colony's initial efforts to prevent slavery from taking hold.

Deserted homesteads and once grand plantation homes abounded. Shaw visited the former plantation home of Pierce Butler at the island's northern end. As he walked the grounds and talked with the few elderly freedmen who chose to remain, Shaw recalled the stories told by Butler's former wife, the actress Fanny Kemble (during the Shaw family's stay in Sorrento, Italy), about the horrors she witnessed while living at Hampton Plantation. Shaw was surprised to learn that a few of the freedmen fondly remembered Kemble.

One man "named John wanted me to tell her I had seen him."[4] A few recalled for Shaw the sale of 436 enslaved people, including close family members and friends, by Butler on March 2 and 3, 1859, in what would prove to be the largest sale of enslaved people in American history. The sale, which took place in Savannah, was referred to as the "Weeping Time" or "Weeping Day."[5]

Stories of families violently split apart for profit left Shaw confused about what he perceived to be the freedmen's continued loyalty to their former enslavers. "These [individuals] were all born and bred on the place, and even selling away their families," Shaw wrote to Annie, "could not entirely efface their love for their master." "Isn't it horrible to think of a man being able to treat such faithful creatures in such a manner."[6] Shaw's assessment is revealing. What horrified Shaw about Butler's treatment was not the violation of another person's desire to be free but the betrayal of people whom he believed were naturally disposed to remain "faithful." Regardless of what stories these elderly individuals chose to share with Shaw about life under the lash, his paternalism left little room to consider their own attempts to secure their freedom in the past or the possibility that they decided not to risk offending a stranger who had such a close connection with their former master.[7]

Shaw's blindness was particularly striking given the revolutionary transformation unfolding around him daily. Thousands of enslaved people had gained their freedom largely through military expeditions led by Black soldiers, the very men Shaw now commanded. Acts of self-emancipation were occurring constantly throughout the region as people seized their own liberation, yet in his letters home, Shaw rarely acknowledged these events or their implications for the future of the region and the nation. Shaw was witnessing one of the largest rebellions in American history not through violent uprising but through systematic flight to Union lines and through an embrace of military service against former masters. Every formerly enslaved soldier in his and other Black regiments operating along the Sea Islands represented an act of self-determination. Their presence in federal uniforms proved that enslaved people possessed the courage, intelligence, and patriotism that slavery apologists claimed they lacked.

News of Brig. Gen. Quincy Adams Gillmore's appointment to replace Major General Hunter offered Shaw little encouragement. Gillmore, an Ohio native and former West Point instructor, had earned recognition for forcing Fort Pulaski's surrender near Savannah in 1862, but his lukewarm attitude toward Black military service troubled those who understood the broader significance of Black troops' involvement. "General Gillmore, I hear, is not a friend to black troops," Shaw confided to his sister-in-law, revealing his own troubling indifference to this threat. "But I don't mind that, for as long as there are so few regiments of them here, they may as well lie quiet as not."[8]

With no Confederate opposition on the island, Shaw caught up with his personal correspondence, read Emil Schalk's newly published *Campaigns of 1862 and 1863*—an early attempt to evaluate the first two years of the war—and he instituted strict discipline across his regiment to maintain morale and to prepare his men for a battle that he hoped would come at some point soon. In the case of an extended stay on the island, Shaw broached the possibility of having his family visit "after the hot weather is over."[9]

The regiment's inactivity and isolation quickly ate at Shaw's self-doubt in his ability as a leader. "I am placed in a position where, if I were a man of real strength and ability," he confided with his mother, "I might do a great deal, but where, under present circumstances, I am afraid I shall show that I am not of much account."[10] Shaw continued to replay the events of June 11 over and over in his mind. He wrote to Charles Russell Lowell asking for his opinion on what had occurred in Darien and inquired with Charley Morse as to whether he agreed that the burning of the town was "contrary to all rules of warfare."[11] But it was not simply the events in Darien that occupied Shaw's attention and contributed to his lack of self-confidence. It was Montgomery himself.

The "Kansas Bushwhacker" continued to perplex Shaw in the weeks that followed the Darien expedition. He evaded easy description, but Montgomery appeared to be perfectly suited for his current command. According to Shaw, Montgomery "seems the only active man in this Department." "He is very prompt & active, never lying idle, if he can help it, for more than three days at a time," Shaw admitted to Lowell. "When delayed and disappointed, he is wonderfully patient & calm, never letting a word escape him & putting through what he undertakes in spite of everything. I never met a man who impressed me as being more conscientious."[12]

From Shaw's vantage point, Montgomery was a mass of contradictions. "He is not what one would call a 'Kansas Ruffian,'" Shaw noted to his father, "being very quiet and reserved, & rather consumptive looking"; but when he speaks, Shaw continued, "His language is very good & always grammatical."[13] At first glance, Montgomery appeared to Shaw more as a "school-master or parson." "The only thing that shows the man, is that very queer roll or glare in his eye—and a contraction of the eyebrows every now & then, which gives him rather a fierce expression." During one extended conversation with Shaw,

Montgomery began crying as he recalled the violence in the Kansas Territory and the "utter desperation & hopelessness in which they began their fight against the [proslavery] Border Ruffians." The more time Shaw spent with Montgomery, the more he began to enjoy his company and listening to his personal stories. Shaw ultimately admitted to his mother, "I have taken a great fancy to him."[14]

Montgomery embodied the moral conviction and sense of purpose that had eluded Shaw throughout his pampered but aimless youth. While Shaw had drifted through European travel, Harvard studies, and vague fantasies about military service or western farming, Montgomery had committed his life to the defining moral struggle of their generation, first fighting slavery's expansion in Kansas, then working to destroy it entirely. The contrast was stark and humbling. Shaw had spent his twenties searching for direction while Montgomery had found his calling in the most dangerous and principled work imaginable. Where Shaw had chosen comfort and social advancement, Montgomery had chosen moral leadership that required genuine sacrifice and physical courage.[15] Montgomery's antislavery convictions and willingness to risk his life in order to make other men free, years before the start of the Civil War, had animated him during the first two years of the conflict while Lincoln and much of the rest of the nation still resisted calls for emancipation and the arming of Black men. Regardless of whether Shaw agreed with Montgomery's methods, it was impossible for him not to acknowledge that Montgomery's military exploits in the Lowcountry reflected a deep commitment to ending slavery and deep sense of purpose.

Shaw received welcome orders on June 23 to return the 54th Massachusetts to Hilton Head. Though Gillmore's intentions remained unclear, Shaw suspected that the general planned to establish positions on the coastal islands south of Charleston Harbor, a perfect launching point for attacks against Fort Sumter and the city itself. Shaw eagerly anticipated real combat that might restore his regiment's reputation after the Darien controversy. National military developments suggested that the summer of 1863 would prove decisive. Lee's army was once again moving north, following his Chancellorsville triumph, and Grant's relentless siege of Vicksburg along the Mississippi River was gradually coming to fruition. Shaw took particular interest in Lee's northern offensive, having long argued that "the North must feel the war much more than they have before it is ended."[16]

Two days later, on June 25, the regiment disembarked amid a rainstorm on St. Helena Island, just to the north of Hilton Head, and camped in a cotton field close to the water and some swampy ground that boasted a few trees, shrubbery, and as a number of plantations and dense woods nearby. The island hummed with activity as regiments from New Hampshire, Pennsylvania, and New York prepared for military operations. Despite the incessant rain and lightning, which killed one man in another regiment and wounded several others, the regiment managed to settle in for what appeared to be another extended stay.[17]

Shaw reported to Brig. Gen. George C. Strong and was once again assigned to Col. Montgomery's "Colored Brigade." Born in Stockbridge, Vermont in 1832, Strong had graduated from West Point in 1857. He served as a lieutenant of ordnance on Gen. Irvin McDowell's staff at the First Battle of Bull Run in 1861. Rising rapidly through the ranks, he then served on the staffs of Gen. George B. McClellan and Gen. Benjamin Butler. In 1862, he commanded two expeditions along the coast of Mississippi and was commissioned brigadier general of volunteers in November 1862 before arriving in the Department of the South in mid-June 1863.[18]

In addition to the movement of troops, St. Helena buzzed with the labor of thousands of freedmen now working for wages on the many plantations that dotted the island. At the Penn School, just a few miles from the encampment of the 54th Massachusetts, children attended school in the Brick Church, where they learned spelling, writing, grammar, diction, history, geography, arithmetic, and music.[19] Shaw's visit to the Penn School marks one of the few times he acknowledged the revolutionary impact of the Port Royal Experiment. He wrote enthusiastically to his family about taking part in a "colored abolitionist meeting" on a nearby plantation. "There were collected all the free slaves on the island, listening to the most ultra abolition speeches that could be made, while two years ago their masters were still here, the lords of the soil and of them. Now they all own something themselves, go to school and to church and work for wages!" "Such things," he observed, "oblige a man to believe that God isn't very far off."[20]

Shaw's assessment of the radical changes he witnessed on St. Helena, however, did not translate to his personal interactions with the island's freedpeople. In these moments, Shaw continued to embrace the same tired and demeaning characterizations of African Americans that he had shared with his family going back to his first foray into Virginia in July 1861. "Whatever the condition of the slaves may be, it does not degrade them, as a bad life does most people," he observed "for their faces are generally good." Shaw attributed this "to their utter ignorance, and innocence of evil." He interacted "with a good many" of the freedpeople around the island, but his conversations only served to reinforce his paternalistic and racist sentiments. "Whatever their habits of life may be, they certainly are not bad or vicious," he observed "they are perfectly childlike it seems to me, and are no more responsible for their actions than so many puppies."[21]

This racist outlook reflected widespread attitudes at the time, including those of the many reformers working to educate formerly enslaved people around Port Royal. These humanitarian workers had come south with the intention of proving Black capacity for citizenship, yet many carried the same prejudices that undermined their mission. The psychological toll of confronting their own assumptions proved overwhelming for some. Living among formerly enslaved people who demonstrated intelligence, dignity, and capability that contradicted racist stereotypes created a cognitive dissonance that many were unable to resolve. Rather than abandon their prejudices, some abandoned their work instead, returning north after brief service. One observer coined the term "Plantation Bitters" to describe reformers who had arrived with confidence in their racial theories only to become disillusioned when reality challenged their preconceptions. These failures reflected not the inadequacy of formerly enslaved people but the inadequacy of white expectations that assumed Black people needed extensive guidance to function as free citizens.[22]

Shaw's application of such derogatory language to his own soldiers revealed his hierarchy of racist assumptions. He distinguished between Northern free Black men, whom he viewed as partially civilized through proximity to white society, and formerly enslaved people, whom he considered closer to their supposed natural state of dependence and inferiority.[23] Shaw's limited acknowledgment that his soldiers fought for full citizenship rights in a reconstructed America certainly did not extend to the formerly enslaved people he encountered on St. Helena Island. Evidence suggests Shaw viewed the island's Black inhabitants as fundamentally different from—and inferior to—his Northern recruits, and unworthy of serious consideration as future citizens.[24]

Throughout the regiment's service in the Lowcountry, the potentially volatile issue of pay loomed constantly overhead. As early as March, while the unit was still encamped at Readville, Shaw had heard troubling rumors that the men might not receive the full thirteen dollars per month they had been promised. Those concerns proved well founded. On the very day the regiment reached Beaufort, Secretary of War Edwin Stanton issued an order setting the pay for Black soldiers at just ten dollars a month as originally stipulated in the Militia Act of 1862. Worse, an additional three dollars were withheld as a clothing deduction—a fee not required of white troops and that reduced the men's actual pay to seven dollars per month. Shaw's response revealed an unexpected moral backbone. He "refused to allow them to be paid" under these discriminatory terms until Governor Andrew could clarify whether Massachusetts troops were exempt from this federal policy. Shaw declared the unequal pay an obvious "injustice" and insisted the regiment "should be mustered out of the service or receive the full pay which was promised them."[25]

It was also rumored that the Black soldiers would be armed with pikes rather than with rifles, a proposal that Shaw attributed to someone who was "looking for a means of annihilating negro troops altogether." Shaw worked behind the scenes to clarify the army's intentions for his soldiers, and the rumors were soon quelled. But the problem of unequal pay lingered and threatened to undo the discipline and training that Shaw and his fellow officers had worked so hard to instill and which he hoped to put to use in the near future. For now, there was little that Shaw could do beyond hoping that the governor's letters to President Lincoln and Secretary Stanton would yield positive results.[26]

For the men in the regiment, the betrayal by the federal government undercut their sense of manhood and justice; and it also directly impacted their families back home, who depended on the military's promised monthly payments to make ends meet. James Henry Gooding captured the sting of betrayal by inquiring directly of President Lincoln, "Are we Soldiers, or are we Laborers?" He implored the president to acknowledge that if Black men had done "a Soldier's duty," they deserved "a Soldier's pay."[27] Lincoln never responded. For now, the men in the 54th would go without pay. Little did they know that it would not be until June 1864 that Congress finally passed legislation authorizing equal pay retroactive to the beginning of 1863.[28]

Shaw's frustrations over his regiment's unequal pay was alleviated somewhat by visits to the Oaks Plantation, just a few miles from the regiment's encampment, where the teachers at the Penn School lived and worked. Shaw likely met Laura Towne and Ellen Murray, but he was especially impressed by Charlotte Forten, who had arrived in late October 1862. Born the same year as Shaw, Forten had been raised in a prominent and affluent Black family in Philadelphia. Rather than send her to one of the city's segregated schools, Charlotte's father had her home schooled until she was old enough to attend the Salem Normal School in Massachusetts. There she prepared for a teaching career, which eventually led to her volunteering to work among the reformers on the Sea Islands. Though Forten at first struggled to adjust to her "restless" children, she soon grew to embrace her students and her mission. "It is wonderful how a people who have been so long crushed to the earth . . . can have so great a desire for knowledge, and such a capability for attaining it."[29]

Forten caught Shaw's attention as well as the attention of a number of other officers in the regiment. "She is quite pretty, remarkably well educated, and a very interesting woman," Shaw confided to his mother.[30] The two enjoyed conversation over tea on a "moonlit piazza" and even attended what locals called a praise meeting, consisting of prayer, loud singing, and dancing. For her part, Forten described Shaw as "one of the most delightful persons I have ever met." "There is something girlish about him, and yet I never saw anyone more manly. To me he seems a thoroughly lovable person. And there is something so exquisite about him." "I have seen him but once," Forten confided to her diary, "yet I cannot help feeling a really affectionate admiration for him."[31]

Shaw accompanied Forten, along with Major Hallowell and a few other officers in the regiment, to the Fourth of July celebration at the Brick Church, where hundreds of freedmen gathered in the churchyard under "some magnificent old oaks, covered with the long, hanging, grey moss." Shaw described the colorful dresses and turbans worn by the women in a letter to his mother back home. "A little black boy read the Declaration of Independence" after which a group of children sang a rendition of "My Country."[32] Forten promised to transcribe the hymns for Shaw's mother. The speeches and hymns delivered during the ceremony celebrated not only the nation's birthday but the promise of a new beginning for thousands of freedpeople in a reunited nation.

Two days later, Shaw entertained Forten in camp, following a dress parade by the regiment. Forten described the men as "splendid looking" and "an honor to the race." A few of Shaw's men sang for his guest. The evening ended with the two talking in private. Shaw informed Forten that it was likely that the regiment would be ordered to Charleston and added, "I do hope they give *us* a chance." He wanted his troops to prove themselves "as brave soldiers as though their skins were white."[33] At the end of the evening, Forten once again

Charlotte Forten, ca. 1870. Shaw first met Forten when he and his regiment were encamped on St. Helena Island in June 1863. They met numerous times and quickly formed a friendship characterized by mutual admiration and intellectual exchange. Following the assault on Fort Wagner, Forten traveled to Beaufort, South Carolina, to care for the wounded of the 54th Massachusetts. *Photograph by Charles Milton Bell. Courtesy New York Public Library Digital Collections.*

shared in her diary, "Tonight he helped me on my horse, and after carefully arranging the folds of my riding skirt, said, so kindly, 'Goodbye, if I don't see you again down here, I hope to see you at our house.'"[34]

There is no question that Shaw and Forten enjoyed one another's company. Shaw may even have been physically attracted to her, but characterizing their relationship as anything more than a brief friendship must remain speculation. On the one hand, it is worth pointing out that Shaw wrote about his interactions with Forten in a letter to his mother, perhaps knowing that this information would not be related to Annie. On the other hand, Shaw made no mention of Forten in a long letter to Annie, written on July 6, just days after his first meeting with her. It is also worth noting that while Forten acknowledged in her diary that Shaw spoke "lovingly" and "tenderly" about his mother, there is no indication that he brought up the subject of his wife with her.[35]

Shaw likely viewed Forten as a pleasant distraction from the responsibilities and rigor of military life. She was the first woman Shaw had encountered since arriving in South Carolina in whom he could confide and discuss topics he cared about. Despite her race, Forten's education and family background approximated and served as a reminder of Shaw's own upper-class community. Finally, Shaw's infatuation with this Northern born African American woman is another indication of his own racial biases that served as a barrier to his interactions with the freedpeople on St. Helena Island and the surrounding area.

After bidding farewell to Forten on the evening of July 6, Shaw wrote to Brigadier General Strong expressing his disappointment at being left behind as the brigade prepared for the coming campaign against Charleston. Shaw respected Strong and believed that his brigade commander understood the importance of including the 54th in military actions and giving his soldiers the opportunity to fight alongside white men, which would serve as an "incentive to them . . . to do their best."[36] Just as importantly, he stated that he wanted to serve under someone other than Montgomery to demonstrate that his "men are capable of better service than mere guerilla warfare."[37]

On July 2, Shaw received orders from Strong to join his brigade in Alfred Terry's 1st Division of the X Corps. Seven companies prepared for immediate departure with minimal supplies—rubber blankets and basic rations of less than a pound of meat, hardtack, coffee, sugar, and salt. A small contingent remained to guard the camp while the main force boarded the steamers

Chasseur and *Cossack* for the forty-mile voyage north to Folly Island. The Atlantic remained turbulent from a recent offshore storm, making for a rough passage that tested the soldiers' sea legs once again. After midnight on July 9, the steamers approached Stono Inlet at Folly Island's southern tip. "The sea was running very high all the time," Shaw wrote to Annie, describing conditions that likely left many soldiers seasick and miserable in the cramped quarters below deck.[38]

Shaw and his rain-soaked men looked out from the deck of their transport on an inlet "full of transports, loaded with troops, gunboats, and supply vessels." General Gillmore, only weeks into his new assignment as commander of the Department of the South, had amassed roughly ten thousand infantry, supported by artillery and engineers, for his planned assault that would hopefully result in the capture of Charleston. The "cradle of secession" was protected by a ring of Confederate forts, including Forts Sumter, Moultrie, and Johnson as well as by gun emplacements on Sullivan's Island and Castle Pinckney, all of which guarded the entrance and approaches to the city.[39] Gillmore put in place an abbreviated island-hopping campaign that necessitated the capture of Folly, James, and Morris Islands.

The maze of islands and salt marshes guarding Charleston Harbor created numerous challenges for Union commanders attempting to position troops and artillery for an assault. Folly Island stretched northward as a narrow sand spit toward Morris Island, where Confederate Gen. P. G. T. Beauregard had established a deadly defensive network. Fort Wagner commanded Morris Island's southern approaches, while Fort Gregg controlled its northern tip, and both positions offered clear fields of fire across the harbor entrance. To the west lay James Island, a labyrinth of tidal creeks, salt marshes, and narrow waterways that channeled any attack into predictable corridors where Confederate artillery could concentrate devastating fire. The Stono River separated James Island from the mainland, creating another natural barrier that limited Union approach routes while providing Confederate defenders with secure communication and supply lines.[40]

While two regiments had already disembarked from the brigade for James Island, the 54th remained on board throughout the day on July 10. Most of Gillmore's force, however, had already crossed the channel from Folly to Morris Island for a planned assault against Fort Wagner. That afternoon, Shaw went ashore and found a house from which he could see "Fort Sumter, our Monitors, and the spires of Charleston." His blood was racing after learning "the news of the fall of Vicksburg, and of Robert E. Lee's defeat" at Gettysburg the previous week. Having experienced countless disappointments in the past, Shaw cautioned his wife that the end was not near and that he anticipated "the next mail will probably tell us that Lee has got away with a good part of his army."[41]

The 54th finally disembarked from their transport for James Island on July 11. In the distance they could hear the heavy bombardment of Fort Wagner that preceded Gillmore's first frontal assault, which was severely repulsed. Shaw anticipated a "regular siege" of Wagner to follow, which meant that at least for now, his regiment would be forced to settle in for yet another extended encampment with little to show for it.

As they waited for orders, news of the horrendous casualties from Gettysburg filtered in, including those from the 2nd Massachusetts, which saw heavy fighting along Culp's Hill on the first and last days of the battle. Among the fallen was Shaw's former Harvard classmate Maj. Charles Redington Mudge. News of his fallen comrades in the 2nd Massachusetts and his own regiment's inactivity, once again, left Shaw questioning his decision to take command of the 54th. "I should have been Major of the Second now if I had remained there, and lived through the battles," he confided to Annie. "I had rather have that place than any other in the army. It would have been fine to go home, a field-officer in that regiment."[42]

The sound of artillery and offshore bombardment of Morris Island was increasingly drowned out as the men in the 54th shared the news of widespread racial violence in faraway New York City. The city had already been a hotbed of social and economic unrest by the time the Conscription Act was passed in March 1863. The working class, many of whom were recent Irish immigrants, faced harsh living conditions, low wages, and high unemployment rates. They viewed the draft as affecting them disproportionately, while wealthier residents could afford to pay substitutes to take their places. Many Irish immigrants, who made up a large portion of the city' population, were particularly resentful of the draft and the war, viewing it as a conflict that primarily benefited wealthy elites and abolitionists. Additionally, there was competition for jobs between Irish immigrants and African Americans.

The violence exploded on July 13, 1863, as draft protests transformed into one of the worst racial massacres in American history. Organized mobs systematically hunted African Americans through Manhattan's streets, lynching men from lampposts, burning homes and churches, and beating children to death for the crime of being Black. The rioters targeted every symbol of Black presence in the city. They burned the Colored Orphan's Asylum, forcing 233 terrified children to flee through back exits while the mob destroyed their sanctuary. African American churches, businesses, and homes became funeral pyres as white mobs attempted to eliminate Black New Yorkers through coordinated terrorism. Government authority collapsed as rioters seized control of entire neighborhoods. They attacked draft offices, newspaper headquarters, and wealthy Republican homes while police either fled or joined the violence. For five days, Manhattan belonged to the mob as they enacted their vision of a white-only city through systematic murder. Federal troops rushed from Gettysburg, where they had just defeated Lee's Confederates and finally restored order through military occupation of America's largest city.[43]

First Sgt. Robert Simmons faced every soldier's nightmare in not knowing whether his family was safe. His sister Susan Reed, her two children, and their mother, Margaret, found themselves caught in the racial terror that had engulfed Manhattan. When Margaret attempted to evacuate the children to safety, Susan rushed to deliver laundered clothing to clients, hoping to save their possessions from destruction. At some point, their eldest son, seven-year-old Joseph, became separated from his grandmother and was severely beaten by the mob. He died of his wounds the next day. For many of the men in the 54th, the news of the riots was a stark reminder of their firsthand experience of racial violence and discrimination in their communities across the North before the war.[44]

Simmons knew nothing about the fate of his loved ones as the 54th moved into position on James Island, where they were likely to meet Confederate resistance. Four companies of the 54th Massachusetts were on picket duty near Grimball's Landing on the night of July 15. The 10th Connecticut Infantry took up position on the regiment's left, with its left flank anchored close to the Stono River. A swamp, however, created a dangerous gap between its right and the left flank of the 54th. The 2nd South Carolina and 104th Pennsylvania Infantry took up a position to the 54th's right, on the ground of the Legare Plantation.[45]

Confederates began probing the Union pickets early the following morning. Scattered rifle fire could be heard up and down the line. As dawn neared, Confederates lobbed a few shells that landed harmlessly behind the picket line. At daylight, roughly 1,400 Confederates, supported by artillery, began their assault opposite the 10th Connecticut, but soon spread down the line. Capt. Cabot Jackson Russell of the 54th's Company F did his best to hold his men in place. "As their force advanced on our right," recalled Pvt. James Gooding, "the boys held them in check like veterans; but of course they were falling back all the time, and fighting too."[46] There were moments that Confederates thought they had finally broken through only to find that the 54th had managed to form up again in time to fire another volley into their ranks. After holding the Confederate advance for up to an hour, the regiment's pickets finally gave way and headed back toward the 54th's main line.

Though the engagement was brief and involved relatively few men, the fighting was no less intense for those involved. Ordered to support the left flank of the advance pickets, Sergeant Simmons recalled, "The bullets fairly rained around us; when I got there the poor fellows were falling down around me, with pitiful groans."[47] A mounted Confederate officer twice lunged at Captain Russell with his sword, only to have his third swing deflected by the bayonet of Preston Williams, who managed to shoot the determined enemy in the neck. His actions likely saved Russell's life. Sgt. James Wilson of Company H defended himself against five Confederates with his bayonet and managed to kill four of his attackers before being overtaken and killed. Peter Vogelsang found himself surrounded by Confederates at one point during the engagement, but he somehow managed to avoid serious injury and continued to lead his men in battle. The 54th's casualties included fourteen killed, seventeen wounded, and twelve captured. Reports of the execution of captured Black soldiers echoed throughout the camp.

As the remnants of the picket line took up position with the rest of the regiment, Captain Emilio noticed "some of the wounded limping along unassisted, others helped by comrades. . . . One poor fellow, with his right arm shattered, still carried his musket in his left hand." By then the rest of the units deployed had prepared for the inevitable assault, but other than a few exploding shells and falling branches, it never materialized because the Confederates realized that they would then be in range of federal gunboats along the Stono River and Big Folly Creek.

The delaying action on the part of Shaw's men afforded General Terry ample time to organize the rest of his division, but more importantly, it provided valuable minutes for the men of the 10th Connecticut to extricate themselves from their vulnerable position. "But for the bravery of three companies of the Massachusetts Fifty-Fourth (colored)," one Connecticut soldier wrote, "our whole regiment would have been captured. . . . As it was, we had to double-quick in, to avoid being cut off by the rebel cavalry. They fought like heroes."[48] Appleton expressed the thoughts of many of the regiment's officers: "In this first fight with the enemy, their stubborn courage filled the officers with joy."[49] Another officer praised his men's fighting prowess before concluding, "My men did nobly."[50]

After the battle, Shaw sent out squads of men to collect the wounded and dead from the battlefield. A few of the bodies appeared to have been mutilated by Confederates, but a closer look revealed that their condition was the result of the work of fiddler crabs and other insects. Rumors and evidence of the execution of Black soldiers as well as a report in the *Charleston Daily Courier* notifying the public of the capture of fourteen Black soldiers was a disturbing reminder of the unique dangers Black soldiers faced on the battlefield. Shaw heard reports that "some prisoners were shot," but he dismissed these stories as the words of "frightened men." While a few men in the 54th may have met their deaths at the hands of vengeful Confederates who refused to accept their surrender, there is little evidence of the scale of executions that would take place in 1864 at places like Fort Pillow, Tennessee, and at the Crater in Petersburg, Virginia.

The men in the regiment were thrilled with their performance. "It is not for us to blow our horn," Gooding boasted, "but when a regiment of white men gave us three cheers as we were passing them, it shows that we did our duty as men should."[51] Newspaper coverage reinforced their positive assessment of their first battle. "Not myself a believer in the arming of negroes, free or contraband, as soldiers," wrote a correspondent with the Democratic-leaning journal the *New York Herald*, "I must do this regiment the credit of fighting bravely and well. . . . The rebels attacked them with a cry of 'No quarter,' and they accepted the condition of the fight. . . . The Massachusetts negro regiment is evidently made of good stuff, if they are darkeys, and no better fighting can be asked for than they did on James Island when so furiously attacked at their pickett station."[52]

"You don't know what a fortunate day this has been for me, and for us all," Shaw proudly reported to Annie. Shaw was thrilled with the performance of his men. Any questions whether the men in the 54th needed bayonets at their back in order to fight were dispelled once and for all. Not only had his men stood their ground, they demonstrated their bravery and skill in front of a regiment of white soldiers, who now applauded for saving them from capture or worse. Shaw welcomed General Terry's message in which he applauded the bravery of Shaw's men. Terry singled out the 54th in his official report for its "steadiness and soldierly conduct" and highlighted that it had "met the brunt of the attack."[53] Most importantly for Shaw, he could begin to put the "Darien affair" behind him.[54]

ELEVEN

I Do Not Believe I Shall Live Through Our Next Fight

Shaw had no time to savor his regiment's performance on James Island as attention immediately shifted back to Morris Island for another assault on Fort Wagner following the July 11 defeat. In the brief lull between operations, Shaw scribbled hasty letters home, his disorientation evident when he gave Annie the wrong date for the recent skirmish, a sign that exhaustion and adrenaline had scrambled his sense of time.[1]

On the night of July 16, the 54th Massachusetts moved off James Island amid a severe thunderstorm.

> It thundered and lightened, and rained hard all night, and it took us from 10 p.m. to 5 a.m. to come four miles. Most of the way we had to march in single file along the narrow paths through the swamps. For nearly half a mile we had to pass over a bridge of one, and in some places, two planks wide, without a railing, and slippery with

rain,—mud and water below several feet deep,—and then over a narrow dike so slippery as to make it almost impossible to keep one's feet. It took my regiment alone nearly two hours to pass the bridge and dike. By the time we got over, it was nearly daylight.[2]

The regiment arrived on Cole Island as the sun dawned and peeked through the remaining storm clouds. Shaw and the rest of his rain-drenched regiment took advantage of the opportunity to rest and catch a few hours of sleep in preparation for further transport to Folly Island. The men had no change of clothes and relied on what little rations they had prepared days earlier. Shaw nibbled on a few stale crackers. "There is hardly any water to be got here and the sun and sand are dazzling and roasting us."[3] Just before midnight the regiment boarded the transport *General Hunter*, yet again in the middle of a thunderstorm, for the brief ferry ride to Folly Island.

As the regiment disembarked on the morning of July 18, Shaw spent a few moments conversing with Ned Hallowell and a few other officers before wandering off to take advantage of a few minutes of quiet contemplation. Eventually Hallowell found Shaw looking "sad" and perhaps even unwell. The thought of dying in battle was never far from Shaw's thoughts. He had witnessed too many battles and walked the fields, where he came face-to-face with the mangled bodies and cold stares of the dead. At Cedar Mountain and Antietam, Shaw had helped to prepare the remains of friends for shipment home to their families. Shaw understood that death or serious wounding was possible and that there was no reason to believe he was exceptional in his ability to avoid losing his life up till now. Since arriving in the Lowcountry, Shaw had desperately sought a combat assignment for his regiment. Now, having fought a minor engagement with the enemy on James Island, Shaw confronted the sight of the wounded and dead from his own regiment. It was impossible for him to look away and avoid the fact of his own mortality.

Shaw and Hallowell sat in silence for some time. In response to Hallowell's concerns, Shaw finally shared his deepest fears: "O Ned! If I could only live a few weeks longer with my wife, and be at home a little while, I think I might be happy; but it cannot be; I do not believe I shall live through our next fight." There was little that Hallowell could do for his friend but sit by his side in support, perhaps harboring doubts about his own prospects for survival as well. Eventually, Shaw emerged from his funk to join his men on the beach, resigned to whatever fate awaited him, his face now "perfectly cheerful." There was work to be done.[4]

At some point during the morning, Shaw penned a final letter to Annie admitting that "he had not a wish ungratified."[5] Around noon the regiment arrived at the northern tip of Folly Island, which offered the men their first view of Morris Island, with Fort Wagner still off in the distance. The two islands were separated by a narrow inlet. Soldiers and freedmen worked feverishly through the midday sun and heat to offload military cargo and direct transports shuttling additional troops onto the island.

Morris Island was not much to behold. It stretched just over three miles in length and varied in width from only twenty-five to as much as one thousand yards and boasted a "succession of irregular sand hills and ridges," from just a few feet to forty feet above ordinary high-water level. The island was bordered on the east by the Atlantic Ocean and to the west by swampy marshes, shaped by the outflow of the Ashley River to the ocean. According to one Union military report, the island was little more than "an irregular mass of sand" influenced by the "continued action of the wind and sea."[6]

The 54th Massachusetts waited at the water's edge, while Gillmore's artillery and offshore gunboats unleashed devastating fire against Fort Wagner. From their position, the soldiers watched shells burst in brilliant flashes that shrouded the Confederate fortress in dense smoke, a spectacular but ominous prelude to what was clearly another assault in preparation. The pyrotechnic display offered little reassurance to soldiers who had already witnessed how quickly Confederate positions could spring back to lethal life once Union infantry advanced within range. By 5 p.m., Shaw's regiment had crossed to Morris Island with 625 men and 22 officers, the reduced numbers reflecting the casualties from James Island and the detachment left guarding their camp back on St. Helena Island.[7]

Shaw directed his men to a clearing on the beach, where they unburdened themselves of their packs and enjoyed a few welcome minutes of rest while they awaited further orders. Shaw and a few others found amusement in the behavior of fiddler crabs swarming on the beach. Appleton made note of "the fine air, bright sun, broad flat beach with white shallow waves rippling up on one side, and on the other hand the ranges of hills with lines of spectators looking towards Wagner." A fellow officer broke the calm and beauty of the afternoon by inquiring of Appleton, "I wonder how many of us will be here tomorrow night."[8]

The march north began with a shouted "Forward!" that shattered the temporary quiet. Shaw's regiment trudged through abandoned camps, through

Photograph of Fort Wagner ca. 1863–1864, showing its defensive palisade and the open ground that the 54th Massachusetts had to cross as it faced artillery and small arms fire. While the 54th and a few supporting regiments managed to gain a foothold, stiff Confederate resistance eventually forced their retreat. *Collection of the Massachusetts Historical Society.*

brackish tidal pools, and alongside the remains of a lighthouse recently destroyed by Confederate fire but still functioning as a Union signal station. Shaw rode ahead to report to General Strong as the bombardment's thunder became deafening. Cresting the final bluff, he surveyed the artillery spread across the island's width: forty-two siege guns and field pieces—mortars, rifled Parrots, and Wiard rifles—all maintaining a relentless fire against Fort Wagner, 1,600 yards distant.[9]

From his elevated position, Shaw studied Wagner's formidable defenses with growing apprehension. The fort's palmetto-log walls, reinforced with compacted sand and turf, could absorb tremendous punishment while allowing rapid repairs between bombardments. Wagner's 210-foot sea face mounted three guns protected by traverses, while the 600-foot land face bristled with five additional pieces, all shielded from enfilading fire. The fort's armament was impressive: fifteen to twenty guns of various calibers, including a massive 10-inch Columbiad, a 32-pound rifle, a 42-pound Carronade, two naval guns, and four smoothbore 32-pounders. Two field guns commanded the sea approaches through narrow embrasures that protected the crews while maximizing their fields of fire. Most ominously, Wagner's garrison numbered roughly 1,300 Confederate veterans, including the 51st and 31st North Carolina Infantry Regiments supported by the 63rd Georgia

Infantry and the 1st South Carolina Regular Artillery, all under Brig. Gen. William Booth Taliaferro's experienced command.[10]

Shaw watched the naval bombardment unfold with devastating precision to his right. Single-turreted ironclad monitors, wooden-hulled gunboats, and the massive USS *New Ironsides*, under the command of Adm. John A. Dahlgren, pounded Wagner's sloping parapets with concentrated fire. The flagship *Montauk* used the rising tide to close the distance with the beach, maximizing the destructive power of its guns against the Confederate earthworks. An average of fourteen shells per minute crashed into Wagner, with one observer counting twenty-seven impacts in a single sixty-second period. Shaw watched 11-inch shells from the *New Ironsides*'s dual 8-gun broadsides strike Wagner's walls, some deflecting skyward while others exploded within the fort's interior or burst above the ramparts.[11] If Shaw had given any thought to taking part in an assault against Fort Wagner, the bombardment and explosions of sand, mud, and timbers may have given him some hope of success.[12]

Shaw found General Strong at his headquarters; Strong had himself just returned from a meeting with his division commander, Gen. Truman Seymour, and Brigadier General Gillmore. Strong informed Shaw of Gillmore's intention to launch another assault against Fort Wagner in just a few short hours at dusk. Gillmore preferred an engineering solution and a more formal siege to dislodging Confederates inside the fort, but observations of the continued bombardment boosted his confidence. Col. Haldimand S. Putnam, who commanded the second of Seymour's two brigades, believed that the assault was doomed to fail. When Putnam returned to his headquarters he confided to one of his officers, "We are all going into Wagner, like a flock of sheep."[13]

Seymour assigned Strong with the task of leading his brigades in the assault on Fort Wagner. The only question that remained was which of his four regiments would lead the attack. Months after the assault, *New York Tribune* correspondent Nathaniel Paige claimed to have overheard a discussion between the two men. "Well, I guess we will let Strong lead," Paige recalled the division commander saying, "and put those damned n——s from Massachusetts in the advance." "We may as well get rid of them one time as another."[14] It is certainly possible that Seymour uttered those words, as such views were not uncommon throughout the army, but as one historian has pointed out, despite the fact that Seymour shared some of George McClellan's views on the war, including on emancipation, he had moved freely among the freedmen in and around Port Royal, "where he promised to fight for them and their children."[15] In his after-action report, Seymour praised

The Seige [*sic*] *of Charleston*, August 1863, colorized lithograph by Currier & Ives. The assaults on Morris Island that took place in July 1863 were part of a broader effort to capture the city of Charleston. Fort Wagner can be seen as the center of the island with Fort Gregg just to its north. Fort Sumter is located at the entrance of Charleston Harbor, while the city itself can be spotted at the top left corner. *Courtesy Library of Congress.*

the 54th Massachusetts for its conduct on James Island. He went on to claim that the regiment "was in every respect as efficient as any other body of men" and that "it was one of the strongest and best officered, there seemed to be no good reason why it should not be selected for the advance."[16]

Strong may have shared with Shaw Seymour's suggestion that the 54th lead the assault, even if he did not share Seymour's sentiment, but Strong still left the final decision up to Shaw. "You may lead the column, if you say 'yes.' Your men, I know, are worn out; but do as you choose." Shaw admired Strong and appreciated the confidence that Strong now extended to him and his regiment. In one of his final letters, Shaw expressed relief that he was no longer under the immediate command of James Montgomery.[17] Despite the condition of his men, Shaw did not want to disappoint his brigade commander, and given the struggle Shaw had faced in securing a combat assignment, he likely understood that this might be an opportunity that would not come around again soon. Most importantly, Shaw wanted to demonstrate the fighting capabilities of his men, especially after their performance two days earlier on James Island, all of which would reflect positively on his own skill and character as a commanding officer. From the very beginning of the war, Shaw had envisioned himself in just this position. A high-profile and successful assault against Fort Wagner and eventual capture of Charleston would, once and for all, turn the page on the 54th's participation in the Darien raid.

Shaw did not hesitate in his response to Strong's offer, recalled Captain James. His face "brightened up" and without responding officially to Strong's invitation, Shaw turned to his adjutant and ordered him to bring the regiment immediately to the front. James never forgot these words. Shaw's "countenance seemed to change immediately and in what he said there seemed to be such an undercurrent of life and hope for the regiment." It almost appeared "prophetic of something good to come."[18]

The ferocious bombardment of Fort Wagner may have led Shaw and the other officers slated to join the assault to believe that the Union high command had devised a carefully coordinated plan. It had not. Military leadership had apparently learned nothing from the failed July 11 assault. They still underestimated Fort Wagner's strength, and they had made no effort to study the treacherous terrain that an attacking force would need to cross. No preparations had been made to clear obstacles from the assault route. Shaw's regiment received no intelligence about the hillocks, ridges, sand drifts, and shell craters that would fragment their advance even before it reached the fort. Most catastrophically, the men of the 54th were given no guidance for navigating the deadly bottleneck directly in front of Wagner—a narrow twenty-five-to-thirty-yard corridor squeezed between Vincent Creek and salt marsh on the left and the rapidly narrowing beach on the right as flood tide reduced their maneuvering space.[19]

Adding to the list of challenges, the regiment was expected to attack without skirmishers and engineers familiar with the ground. Neither Shaw nor any of his officers was shown a map of the fort, and those men who somehow reached the fort would have to scale its walls without ladders.[20] But the larger problem was that Gillmore failed to recognize that while Fort Wagner had been "pounded into an almost shapeless mass" in places—with its "parapet, traverses, scarp, and counter scarp" badly damaged—the bastion's sand-and-palmetto construction remained intact and maintained its defensive capacity. Inside, many of the fort's defenders awaited the inevitable assault and remained largely unscathed by taking shelter in one of two bombproofs or behind the fort's traverses and embrasures.[21]

Among the many civilian observers on Morris Island that day was Edward Pierce. Shaw and Pierce had dined together on more than one occasion on St. Helena Island and had last seen one another just two days earlier on James Island, following the regiment's brief engagement. After briefly talking, Shaw handed Pierce some private letters and papers, which he requested be sent to his father in the event he did not survive the assault.[22]

At about 6 p.m. Major Hallowell arrived with the regiment at the forward position. The men of the 54th Massachusetts were worn and weary, having marched six miles across Folly Island followed by a slow march up Morris Island. They had gone without a hot meal for two days and two stormy nights before arriving at the jump-off point, and there was no time for a final meal with less than an hour remaining before the assault would commence.[23] Captain Emilio recalled that Shaw looked striking in his uniform. He wore light-blue trousers topped by his close-fitting staff officer's short jacket, with silver eagles on his shoulders. A buff-colored silk stash was tied around his waist, along with sword-belt that now contained the English sword gifted to him by his uncle, George Russell.[24]

Once the bombardment ceased at 7 p.m., the regiment moved beyond the siege line and defensive palisades and took a position past an advanced lookout station. Fort Wagner was clearly visible 1,500 yards ahead. Shaw may have heard a group of gunners shout "some insulting remarks" in the direction of his troops, but Strong clearly did and responded angrily that if anyone uttered another word of disparagement, "he should be placed in the front of the assault."[25]

Hallowell inquired if Shaw planned to send his personal items to the rear, but unlike his correspondence, he chose to retain his "pocket-book" that contained official identification papers. Shaw went into battle wearing two rings, one included the carving of a dove, with his name and the words "from his mother" inscribed inside, and his heavy gold chain and gold watch also inscribed with his name.

The regiment was formed into two lines of battle consisting of five companies each. Shaw commanded one wing while Hallowell led the other. The 6th Connecticut Infantry along with the 9th Maine Infantry would follow to take advantage of any breach in Wagner's defenses; both regiments were familiar with the terrain, having participated in the previous assault against

Wagner. Additional regiments—close to 6,400 men in all—were positioned farther to the rear.

The men fixed bayonets and were ordered to keep their rifles uncapped. As the 54th Massachusetts formed up, Strong addressed the men. He acknowledged that they were tired and hungry but urged them to remember that "the men in the fort are tired too." He encouraged them to refrain from firing their weapons, but to "go in and bayonet them at their guns." Strong then pointed to the color-bearer asking, "If this man should fall, who will lift the flag and carry it on." Standing nearby and pacing impatiently in anticipation of what was to come, Shaw removed the cigar from his lips and responded confidently: "I will."[26]

Shortly thereafter, Shaw approached Hallowell to inform him that he planned to "go in advance of the men with the National Flag," and he instructed Hallowell to "keep the State flag" with his men. He then likely spoke his final words to Hallowell, "We shall take the fort, or die there. Good bye!" Hallowell recalled that Shaw "seemed happy and cheerful; all of the sadness" that he had expressed earlier that morning "had left him." Shaw, he believed, "felt ready to meet his fate."[27]

Shaw now walked casually among the men as he positioned himself in front of the regiment. Private Gooding observed that Shaw's manner, which was usually "cold, distant, and even austere" toward his men was now "more unbending." He reminded his men of "how the eyes of thousands would look upon the night's work they were about to enter on." "Now boys," he insisted, "I want you to be MEN!" The seriousness and perhaps even the nervousness in Shaw's tightly compressed lips was magnified by what Gooding observed to be a "slight twitching of the corners of the mouth, like one bent on accomplishing or dying."[28] Emilio, who was positioned farther back, noticed that Shaw's "cheek had somewhat paled," and he, too, noticed his twitching but believed it "plainly showed . . . his expressed determination to take the fort or die" in the attempt.[29]

At approximately 7:45 p.m., Shaw took his position a few paces in front of the first series of low midline sand hills pointing toward the fort. The men jumped to attention. His orders: "Move in quick time until within a hundred yards of the fort; then double quick and charge!"[30] Shaw ordered, "Forward!" as darkness began to envelop the beach. An ominous silence settled over the battlefield during the initial advance, but the assault immediately devolved into confusion as the two wings became hopelessly entangled, the result of soldiers breaking their ranks to avoid the salt marsh pressing from the left and the surf encroaching from the right. Men stumbled through the funnel of sand, some collapsing from exhaustion, others frantically seeking solid footing on terrain that appeared designed to fragment their formation. Despite a level of confusion that would have shattered less disciplined units, the 54th Massachusetts held its course and continued its advance. The regimental colors provided the only fixed point in a swirling mass of blue uniforms struggling across treacherous ground in the gathering darkness.[31]

Confederate seacoast artillery located at nearby Fort Sumter, Fort Johnson, and other batteries in Charleston Harbor opened up on Shaw and his men once they moved onto the open ground in full view of Fort Wagner. Officers and men did their best to dodge and duck the 32-pound shells that fell short and ricocheted overhead. Shaw ordered his men to continue at the double-quick once Wagner's defenders opened fire. "The flash of hand grenades and musketry from the parapets of Wagner, the renewed storm of grape and canister from her remorseless guns," James remembered, "and all individuality vanished from the line behind me."[32]

Edward Pierce watched the advance from the observation tower near Strong's tent. "The intervening distance between the place where the line was formed and the Fort," he wrote, "was run over in a few minutes. . . . When within one or two hundred yards of the Fort, a terrific fire of grape and musketry was poured upon them along the entire line, and with deadly results. It tore the ranks to pieces and disconcerted some. They rallied again, went through the ditch, in which was some three feet of water, and then up the parapet."[33] Shaw led his scattered companies through the wide moat, now waist-deep with water, to the base of the escarpment.

Capt. George Pope of Company I followed closely behind Shaw during the initial charge and had him "in plain view" until he was "lost in smoke & darkness" near the outer slope of the fort.[34] Ned Hallowell spotted Shaw for the last time "as he sprang into the ditch, his broken and shattered regiment following" his lead.[35]

Shaw and the men did their best to find cover, but it quickly became clear that their position was untenable as the Confederates easily found their mark with small arms fire and close-range artillery. Sensing this, Shaw pulled himself out of the moat and up the 30-foot escarpment, followed closely by Pope and the remnants of his company, all the while cheering and shouting. Shaw waved his sword high above his head to rally his men and quickly climbed the steep slope amid a withering fire, shouting, "Onward! Boys," and, "Come on, boys," and "Rush on, rush on, boys! . . . Forward, Fifty-fourth!"[36]

Though the smoke and darkness obscured his view, Pierce could still make out the raising of the flag on the parapet, "where it remained for a few minutes." "Here they melted away before the enemy's fire, their bodies falling down the slope and into the ditch."[37] Outlined against the night sky by red cannon flashes and sheets of musketry fire, Shaw stood defiant on the parapet for a few moments still trying to rally his men forward into the fort.

The fighting quickly descended into close hand-to-hand combat as men screamed wildly, parrying bayonet thrusts and swinging their rifle butts. It was "push, and punch, and shuv," recalled one Black soldier.[38] Bodies on both sides dropped, riddled with bullets and other ghastly wounds, falling back into the ditch, adding to the deepening pool of blood or behind the parapet and into the fort itself. Lewis Douglass also attempted to rally the men, shouting, "Come, boys, and fight for God and Gov. Andrew!" as shells and musketry fire continued to do their deadly work creating room for additional men to take their place and continue the push forward.[39]

As he continued to rally his men, Shaw was cut down, shot through the head and chest by multiple bullets. Wilkie James saw him fall as did Pvt. Thomas Burgess, who fell badly wounded nearby. As he attempted to crawl away, Burgess grabbed Shaw's boots to pull him along, but "there appeared to be no life in him." Shaw's body fell lifelessly down onto the platform behind the parapet, falling close to the body of a Black sergeant, possibly that of Andrew Benton.[40]

Captain Russell witnessed Shaw's death moments before Confederate fire brought him down near his colonel's body, wounded in the leg and chest. As Russell lay bleeding on Wagner's rampart, Captain Simkins and Sgt. Stephen Swails from Company F crawled through the deadly crossfire to reach him and offered to carry him to safety. Russell refused evacuation, perhaps understanding that movement would only draw more Confederate attention to his rescuers. After Simkins and Swails helped straighten Russell's wounded legs to ease his pain, a Confederate bullet tore through Simkins's body, killing him instantly beside the man he had tried to save. Swails found himself alone with two fallen officers, unable to rescue either because of the "withering fire and hand grenades" that Confederate defenders were hurling from Wagner's interior.[41]

The few eyewitness accounts of Shaw's death indicate that he was felled by musketry fire, but after the war, Pvt. John Pinson, who served in the 27th South Carolina Infantry, claimed to have bayonetted Shaw during the fight. Pinson's story was passed down through his family and supported by J. Y. Pitts, who served in the same regiment as Pinson and claimed to have witnessed the act.[42] It is certainly possible that Shaw's death was the result of having been bayonetted, given the nature of the fighting at the height of the battle. It is also possible that Shaw was bayonetted after being shot and falling to the ground, which would confirm eyewitness testimony. Unfortunately, Shaw's body was not recovered in time to determine the exact cause of his death. It is impossible to confirm these accounts, but it is worth acknowledging the extent to which Pinson's account contrasts with the popular perception of Shaw's death at Fort Wagner that would later be highlighted and even celebrated in poetry, fiction, music, illustrations, and eventually the movie *Glory*.

Despite Shaw's absence, small groups of the 54th Massachusetts continued their desperate assault along Wagner's 210-yard eastern face, nearest the fatal bottleneck that had channeled their approach. Surviving officers—Hallowell, and Captains Appleton, Jones, and Pope—led fragments of companies in futile attempts to penetrate the Confederate interior; but Wagner's defenders continued to unleash tightly packed canister and solid shot, hurling the attackers back from the ramparts they had fought so hard to reach. Appleton continued to struggle to dislodge Confederate defenders around him while desperately searching for reinforcements that would never come. A bursting shell struck him "heavily" in the chest with jagged fragments, dropping him among the dead and wounded men who littered the ground. As Appleton assessed his serious wounds, he looked back at the "heaps of bodies, dead and dying" that marked the regiment's sacrifice. In the ditch below, corpses lay "like stepping stones," "dark objects in the track of our crossing."[43]

At about the same time, Sgt. William H. Carney of Company C was scaling the wall close to where Shaw fell, when the color-bearer carrying the Stars and Stripes fell. Carney immediately sprang into action, grabbed the flag, and carried it up the slope, planting it on the parapet. There the flag remained for a short time until he was forced to retreat, along with the rest of the regiment. Sliding down into the ditch, Carney climbed over the dead and wounded collected below. Shortly thereafter, he was struck in the left hip and fell but managed to continue on his hands and knees, all the while still grasping the flag. Shrapnel tore into Carney's body a second time, yet he pressed forward with help from a New York soldier until reaching scattered remnants of his regiment. Only then did Carney surrender the flag to an officer, declaring with fierce pride that the "old flag never touched the ground." Shortly thereafter, Carney lost consciousness and awoke the next day aboard a steamer bound for a hospital in Beaufort, permanently crippled and neurologically impaired. In 1900, Congress would eventually award Sergeant Carney the

Medal of Honor for this act of bravery. He would be the first African American to be so recognized.[44]

In a little over an hour the fight was over. Additional regiments failed to turn the tide of the battle and may have, in all the confusion, accidentally fired on some of the men from the 54th. Men from all the regiments stumbled back, many of them wounded, all of them exhausted. Adding insult to injury, drunken artillerymen allegedly prevented the retreating soldiers from passing to the rear.[45] A reporter observed, "The battle is over; it is midnight; the ocean beach is crowded with the dead, the dying and the wounded. . . . Faint lights glimmer in the sand-holes and rifle pits where many a poor and bleeding soldier has lain down to his last sleep."[46]

The scale of the regiment's loss became increasingly clear as the survivors gathered together under the command of Captain Emilio, one of the few officers to return from the fight unscathed. Emilio reformed the regiment to guard against a counterattack that never materialized.[47]

Of the 650 men who followed Shaw against Wagner's ramparts, 272 became casualties—nearly half the regiment's strength. Three officers, including Shaw, and thirty-one enlisted men lay dead on the beach. Eleven officers and 135 men suffered wounds that would mark them for life, and 29 men had been captured, 14 of whom would die in Confederate prison camps. Sixty-three men remained missing, perhaps drowned in the rising tide and carried out to sea, buried in shell craters, or vanished as a result of a direct hit by a Confederate shell.[48] The 54th suffered the brunt of the casualties, but the two brigades that took part in the attack suffered an additional 1,500 casualties. Colonel Putnam, who had expressed doubt the assault would succeed, was killed at the head of his brigade. Both General Seymour and General Strong were wounded, the latter eventually succumbing to his thigh wound. Confederate casualties were significantly lighter at 222, including four officers; the heaviest losses were confined to the artillerymen and the 51st North Carolina Infantry.[49]

Amid the smoke and confusion of battle, it was not clear to all Confederates defending Wagner that they were engaged in a desperate struggle against an entire regiment of Black soldiers. As the sun rose, however, it became clear to everyone what they had been up against just a few hours earlier. A correspondent from the *Charleston Daily Courier* painted a bleak scene for his readers: "The ground in front of the Battery was thickly strewn, but in the ditch around the work the dead and wounded, white and black, were literally piled together—men lying every conceivable attitude, with every conceivable expression on their countenances, their limbs bent into unnatural shapes by the fall of twenty or more feet—the fingers rigid and outstretched, as if they had clutched at the earth to save themselves—pale, beseeching faces, looking out from among the ghastly corpses, with moans and cries for help and water, and dying gasps and death struggles."[50]

The men of the 54th Massachusetts awoke the next morning to the sight of the Confederate flag flying defiantly over Fort Wagner. Many no doubt worried about the fate of wounded comrades who had been left behind once the assault was abandoned. Were they still alive? Were they acknowledged as legitimate prisoners of war by their Confederate captors? How were they being treated? Black soldiers had every reason to fear retaliation, given Confederate threats to execute Black prisoners and the role that Shaw and the 54th Massachusetts had played in the burning of Darien as well as in the many additional violations of the rules of war that Confederate authorities believed had been committed under white commanders such as James Montgomery. "Unofficial reports say the negroes have been sold into slavery," wrote one newspaper correspondent, "and that the officers are treated with unmeasurable abuses." More than one source claimed that Shaw had been taken prisoner and "hung by a Charleston mob." Back on Morris Island, however, the fate of Shaw's body was much clearer.[51]

Shaw's body still lay where it had fallen, just below the parapet. One Confederate recalled seeing his body "carried through our lines" and "stripped of all his clothing save vest and drawers." The body was briefly relocated by four men in a burial party to one of the two bombproofs, where it was displayed. Adding to the desecration of his body, Shaw's watch, chain, and other personal items were stolen.[52]

In the morning General Gillmore, under a flag of truce, rode out to confer with Confederate General Taliaferro about an exchange of prisoners—especially the Black soldiers, whom Gillmore insisted "were to be treated like all others"—the condition of the wounded, and the retrieval of bodies for burial. Gillmore also sought confirmation as to whether Shaw was dead or wounded and learned later that day from Gen. Johnson Hagood, who arrived to replace Taliaferro, that Shaw was indeed among the dead. Hagood refused to honor the "widely accepted" custom of returning the bodies of fallen officers through the lines so they could be given a proper burial, telling Gillmore that if Shaw had been in command of white soldiers he would have given him an "honorable burial," but owing to the circumstances, Shaw had been buried "in the trench with his n——s."[53]

The Confederate commanders refused to allow the Union forces to retrieve their dead, fearing intelligence gathering about Wagner's damaged defenses. Burial details performed the grisly work of disposing of hundreds of corpses scattered around Wagner's ramparts. Bodies were unceremoniously dumped into hastily dug pits or shell craters, stacked like cordwood and covered with thin layers of sand. No distinction was made between officers and enlisted men. Shaw's body was thrown into a communal trench, six feet wide and four feet deep, along with his soldiers, white and Black alike. The Confederate treatment of the Union dead violated both military custom and basic human decency. Proper burial was a fundamental obligation that armies had honored even in the most bitter conflicts, but Hagood's racism and logistic expedience trumped any respect for the courage his enemies had displayed.[54] Any future assault against Fort Wagner would entail Union soldiers being forced to march over the bodies of their comrades.

A clear message had been sent by Confederates in their handling of Shaw's body. Stripping Shaw of his uniform and placing his body in a mass grave with Black soldiers, where it would quickly deteriorate and be rendered unidentifiable, sent the clear message that Confederates did not recognize Shaw as a legitimate US officer and considered him instead as the leader of a servile insurrection and a direct threat to the nearby civilian population of Charleston. Given the rarity of interracial burial sites across the North and the South, "indiscriminately dumping a white officer's body in a mass grave of black volunteer soldiers," according to one historian, "represents the greatest display of disdain that the Confederacy could muster toward the dead."[55]

Despite their failure to take the fort, the men and officers in the 54th Massachusetts could take pride in their efforts. Lewis Douglass, who spoke for many in the regiment, wrote home to his wife, Amelia, with a sense of pride, declaring, "This regiment has established its reputation as [a] fighting regiment not a man flinched, though it was a trying time." If "we had a hundred thousand colored troops," Douglass stated confidently, "we should put an end to this war."[56]

James Gooding also was proud of his regiment's performance, but he seethed at the way Shaw's body was treated, "not even the commonest respect paid to his rank." The corporal would later take part in an effort to raise funds to send Shaw's body back to his family. "They all declare that they will dig for his body till they find it. They are determined that this disgrace shall be counteracted by something noble."[57] George Stephens described Shaw as "the bravest of the brave."[58] In the wake of the assault of Fort Wagner, Sgt. Albanus Fisher, a laborer from Montgomery County, Pennsylvania, recommitted himself to the struggle. "I still feel more Eager for the struggle," he declared, "for now I wish to have Revenge for our galant Curnel."[59]

The bravery of the regiment was on full display back in the six Beaufort hospitals that were available to nurse the hundreds of wounded from the battle. The 54th was assigned to Hospital No. 6. An outbuilding behind the prominent home-turned-hospital quickly was converted from a kitchen into a makeshift morgue.[60] Freedmen who had welcomed the 54th just weeks before transported wagonloads of food to the hungry men—an acknowledgment of their sacrifice and recognition of the efforts made by Black soldiers to liberate slaves throughout the Lowcountry. Edward Pierce observed that the "men of the regiment are very patient, and where their condition at all permits them, are cheerful. . . . They expressed their readiness to meet the enemy again, and they keep asking if Wagner is yet taken."[61]

On St. Helena Island, Charlotte Forten learned of the battle and unconfirmed reports that Shaw had been killed in the assault. "It is too terrible, too terrible to write," she confided to her journal. "We only hope it may not be true. That our noble, beautiful young Colonel is killed and the reg[iment] cut to pieces!" Eventually, Forten left to join Harriet Tubman and others in Beaufort to nurse the wounded. There she mended soldiers' uniforms and assisted them in writing loved ones back home, all the while hoping that Shaw had somehow survived. Forten and the rest of the wounded received confirmation of his death a few days later, on July 24. The news hit hard, but Forten was confident that it was a "glorious death." She fondly recalled the time they had spent together just a few short weeks earlier, but also acknowledged Shaw's "young wife, so late a bride" as well as for his mother "who rejoiced in the position which he occupied as colonel of a colored regiment. . . . His death is a very sad loss to us."[62] Forten would eventually send the transcriptions of the hymns that the two had heard sung at the prayer sessions to his mother.

Back on Staten Island, Shaw's parents, sisters, and wife Annie waited desperately for news of their loved one.

TWELVE

Our Hero Has Received at the Hands of the Rebels the Most Fitting Burial Possible

The Shaw family huddled together in their Staten Island home hoping for the best but fearing the worst as they awaited news of the fate of their beloved son and brother. Family and friends gathered around the Shaws to comfort and help them deal with the waves of grief and uncertainty that overcame them during those first few days after the assault on Fort Wagner. "The same sun no longer shines for me, the same flowers no longer bloom," Sarah wrote to a correspondent in Europe.[1] Shaw's sister Josephine spent long hours alone in her bedroom. Back in Lenox, Annie's parents did their best to shield her from the often-contradictory newspaper reports about the assault and the fate of her husband of less than two months. Annie eventually joined the Shaw family to mourn together. A visitor to the Shaw's home in early August reported that Annie "was sorry she has no hope of a child," but bore "her trial beautifully."[2]

When the war began, abolitionist families like the Shaws had embraced Lincoln's administration and worked tirelessly to push the nation toward emancipation. They had understood the cruel mathematics of their cause. The longer the conflict raged, the more likely military necessity would deliver the final blow to the institution of slavery. Frank and Sarah Shaw had celebrated both the Emancipation Proclamation's revolutionary impact and their son's decision to command the 54th Massachusetts as vindications of their lifelong crusade. Now the very war they had prayed would continue until slavery's complete destruction had claimed their only son's life.

Despite rumors that their son had been only "slightly wounded while inside the rebel works" and taken prisoner, it became increasingly clear to Frank and Sarah that Rob had not survived.[3] By then, condolence letters began to pour in from close friends and family. Senator Charles Sumner could hardly believe that Shaw had been killed but insisted in a letter to the grieving parents that his "heroism is enhanced by the cause in which he fell and the companions by whom he was surrounded." "I mistake much," Sumner predicted, "if this incident does not take a place in history and also in art."

Journalist and author Charles A. Dana encouraged Sarah to remember that her son was destined to "fill a bright place among the martyrs of liberty," while Frank Shaw's niece, Alexander Agassiz, took comfort in knowing that her cousin "died in a noble cause." "His grave," she predicted, "will be to him a monument such as few men have."[4] While caring for the wounded soldiers in the 54th in Beaufort, Charlotte Forten found time to write the Shaws to share with them that the men's "attachment to their Colonel was beautiful to see. I believe there was not one who would not willingly have laid down his life for him."[5]

These sentiments were echoed across the abolitionist press, which quickly turned Shaw into a martyr for the cause of emancipation and racial equality by emphasizing the fact that he had been buried with his Black soldiers. The abolitionist community encouraged the nation to see Shaw's death as indisputable proof that "antislavery idealism" had been decisive in bringing about emancipation and freedom for African Americans.[6] The *National Anti-Slavery Standard* predicted that the "wide grave on Morris Island will be to a whole race a holy sepulchre." "Neither death nor the grave have divided the young martyr and hero from the race for which he died, and a whole people will remember in the coming centuries, when its new part is to be played in the world's history, that 'he was buried with his n——s!'" Though many believed that Confederates acted out of malice in burying Shaw with his Black soldiers, the *Boston Courier* insisted that "it could be no indignity for the heroic youth," who sought to "vindicate the claims of the black man, thus to share the grave of the true men who had followed him." One newspaper editorial asked its readers, "Could any man, whose heart is with liberty, wish him a more honorable sepulchre?"[7]

When Frank and Sarah learned that efforts, led by Lincoln Stone and Edward Pierce, were underway to locate his grave and have the body disinterred they immediately relayed the family's wishes that his grave should not be disturbed.[8] A few weeks later, on August 24, Frank expressed the same wish to General Gilmore in South Carolina. In a letter to Lydia Maria Child, Frank explained the family's position—echoing much of what had already been written in the press—stating that the "rebels" had given their son "the most fitting burial possible." "They buried him with his brave devoted followers, who fell dead over him and around him. The poor benighted wretches thought they were heaping indignities on his dead body," he explained, "but the act recoils on themselves, and proves them absolutely incapable of appreciating noble qualities. They thought to give an additional pang to the bruised hearts of his friends; but we would not have him do it, we would not have his body taken away from those who loved him so devotedly, with whom and for whom he gave up his life."[9]

Shaw's parents' decision not to disturb the burial site was not simply a direct response to Confederate "malice"; it also proved to be one of the earliest attempts to shape the meaning and memory of their son's military service. In their hands, Shaw was recast as an abolitionist crusader, whose death sealed his commitment to his men, the end of slavery, and equal rights for all African Americans—all embodied in his final resting place on Morris Island. Frank and especially Sarah found a way to channel their grief by transforming their son into the reformer that they had always hoped he would become. In their hands, all the rough edges could now be smoothed over, and disagreements over fundamental questions about the nature of the war, including emancipation, would be forgotten or at least minimized. This reinvention of Robert Gould Shaw would make it possible for Sarah to write to a friend overseas after the war that her relationship with her son had been "without a shadow."[10] The public would come to believe that abolitionism had truly been a family affair.

Focusing on the higher purpose and significance of Shaw's and his men's sacrifice at Fort Wagner served a number of purposes for many Northerners, especially within the abolitionist community. It proved a distraction from lingering questions about the performance of the men in the 54th and the decision to order the assault in the first place. Garth James described the assault on July 18 as "an ill-advised movement." He criticized the decision to mass troops, fully exposed, in front of a heavily fortified Confederate position. There was no chance of surprise, and the timing of the assault at dusk guaranteed that darkness would significantly decrease the chance of a successful outcome. "The fact is," James concluded, "the whole tragedy was a totally inconsistent maneuver."[11] An officer in one of the supporting regiments concluded that their "repulse . . . was entirely owing to our not being promptly sustained."[12] Those who questioned the wisdom of the assault provided evidence for those who believed that Black soldiers were being used as cannon fodder by the military and the federal government.

For other observers throughout the army, the repulse of the 54th reinforced doubts about the wisdom of enlisting Black men. Maj. Henry Livermore Abbott, who served briefly in the 2nd Massachusetts and was acquainted with Shaw, concluded, "He was too good a fellow to be sacrificed for an experiment, & an experiment I think that has demonstrated n——s won't fight as they ought."[13] Suggesting that the assault was futile or that Shaw had died in vain challenged any attempt on the part of his parents to turn their son into a martyr for emancipation and the Black race.

The 54th Massachusetts's heroism at Fort Wagner deepened rather than healed America's racial divisions. Democratic newspapers, terrified that attention to Black prisoners of war and unequal pay would fuel demands for racial equality and citizenship, launched a coordinated campaign to discredit the regiment's performance.[14] A report in the Democratic *Buffalo Courier*, purportedly from an officer on Morris Island, who claimed to have witnessed the assault, stated that the men "ran away as fast as they could, and came near demoralizing the whole attacking force." A Pennsylvania paper insisted, "One of the greatest outrages ever offered to people on earth has been that of the Lincoln administration, in uniforming and arming Negro troops and demanding their equal consideration with the volunteer citizenry soldiery of the Republic! Oh! The offense is rank! It smells to high heaven!"[15]

Such accounts pointed to the deep political divide over emancipation and Black enlistment in the summer of 1863. Military victories at Gettysburg and Vicksburg buoyed the hopes of many, but the violence experienced by African Americans in New York City, Boston, and elsewhere over the draft was a stark reminder to Shaw's parents and the abolitionist community that progress on the emancipation front and the continued push toward the end of slavery and racial equality remained uncertain.

Just as Col. Elmer Ellsworth had become a martyr to the Union and helped to rally Northerners at the opening of the Civil War, Frank and Sarah's decision to valorize their son by leaving him on Morris Island, constituted another powerful symbol of Northern unity. According to one historian, it proved that, "Northern whites were righteous enough for victory; and the burial was a physical manifestation of the eternal brotherhood between blacks and whites that had to be realized on Earth."[16]

Frank and Sarah lent their support to Military Governor Rufus Saxton's plan to erect a monument in honor of Shaw on Morris Island. In language that was both paternalistic and condescending, Saxton implored the Black soldiers and freedmen in his department to "cherish in your inmost hearts the memory of one who did not hesitate to sacrifice all the attractions of a high social position, wealth, and home and his own noble life, for the sake of humanity." Apparently forgetting that Black soldiers were being paid less than white soldiers, Saxton encouraged them to "honour themselves" and Shaw's "glorious memory" by donating "the first proceeds" of their labor as freemen to his proposed monument.[17]

Frank followed the fundraising progress and urged Saxton to include on the monument the names of the officers and enlisted men "who fell and were buried" with his son.[18] Money quickly poured in from freed people as far away as St. Augustine, Florida, as well as from the Black regiments stationed throughout the area. The 1st South Carolina regiment alone donated $1,000, while the "colored people" of Beaufort donated $300.[19]

Although an order was made for a piece of Massachusetts granite, the monument never came to fruition. James Gooding expressed the concerns of many in the 54th about the impracticality of dedicating a monument on Morris Island. For one, it would involve a "toilsome pilgrimage in order to look upon it," but he also warned that it would likely be "desecrated by unfriendly hands" after the war. Gooding and others preferred that the monument be raised in Massachusetts: "Let her have the first monument raised by black men's money, upon her good old rocks."[20] The funds that were earmarked for the monument were eventually applied toward the opening of a new school for Black children in Charleston named in honor of Shaw. Opened in 1868, the school included nine classrooms and could accommodate seven hundred students. The project was supported financially by the New England Freedman's Aid Society until it was handed over to the city in 1874.[21]

Back on Staten Island, Sarah devoted her time throughout much of 1864 to the publication of two works that memorialized her fallen son and the men of the 54th. In *Memorial: RGS* (1864), Sarah collected newspaper articles, letters, and other documents that immortalized her son and his regiment, beginning with Governor Andrew's offer for Shaw to take command of the 54th and ending with Congress's announcement "recognizing the absolute equality of all soldiers of the United States, without distinction of colour" and its intention to pay Black soldiers the same amount as white soldiers. Sarah claimed that the book was for "intimate friends only," but publication ensured that it would reach a wider audience. For a second book, *Letters: RGS* (1876), Sarah published a selection of Shaw's correspondence that left out some of his more embarrassing and racist observations about African Americans. Here Sarah was acting out of a desire to protect her son's reputation and reinforce a narrative that depicted him as an unwavering abolitionist, but she was equally concerned about protecting the reputation and memory of Black soldiers.

Finally, Sarah also completed an entry about her son for inclusion in the *Harvard Memorial Biographies* (1867), which was edited by Thomas Wentworth Higginson and intended to honor the school's students who lost their lives during the war. Unlike her previous two projects, Sarah's contribution exhibited much more of her own voice in the narrative alongside a selection of Shaw's letters. Sarah placed her son at the center of a war effort to destroy slavery and depicted him as "one of the many thousand young men who have fallen victims to that Moloch, American Slavery, or we may rather say, to whose victorious lives and deaths the Moloch, American Slavery, has fallen a victim." As she did with *Letters: RGS*, Sarah left out examples of Shaw's harsher references to African Americans that might compromise his commitment to his men and the broader cause of abolition. Sarah ended her narrative by reminding her reader of Shaw's final resting place alongside his Black soldiers at the base of Fort Wagner—a scene that many people had come to symbolize Shaw's military service around.[22]

These two books, along with the entry for *Harvard Memorial Biographies* signaled a clear commitment by Shaw's mother to control the narrative of heroic martyrdom that had so quickly emerged following his death. These texts also ensured that Shaw's leadership of the first Black regiment raised in the North and commitment to abolition and racial equality remained front and center.[23] The publications also guaranteed that Sarah could keep the public spotlight on the bravery and challenges faced by Black soldiers and the "moral progress of the cause" of abolition and racial equality. "The change of feeling about the colour'd race," Sarah mused in early 1864, "seems nothing short of miraculous."[24]

As a self-proclaimed keeper of her son's story, Sarah and the rest of the family kept close track of how his memory was being shaped in the art world. In May 1864, Boston hairdresser Christiana Carteaux Bannister announced that the Colored Ladies Sanitary Commission of Boston would sponsor a fair to benefit the 54th and 55th Massachusetts Infantry Regiments, the 5th Massachusetts Cavalry, and their families. To raise money, Bannister commissioned her husband, Edward Bannister, to paint a portrait of Robert Gould Shaw. The completed portrait was displayed at the fair framed around an embroidered banner reading "Our Martyr." Unfortunately, the fair was a failure; few tickets were sold, and the portrait disappeared. It is unknown as to whether any members of the Shaw family had an opportunity to view the portrait.

At the same time, the sculptor Edmonia Lewis, born to parents of both African American and Native American descent, was working on a bust of Shaw. After moving to Boston in 1863, Lewis completed portrait medallions of John Brown, William Lloyd Garrison, and Wendell Phillips as well as a small sculpture depicting William H. Carney's act of bravery at Fort Wagner holding up the national flag.

Members of the Shaw family, along with Sarah's confidante Lydia Maria Child, visited Lewis in her Tremont Street studio. While the family considered the bust an "excellent likeness" of Shaw, Child maintained that the sculptor lacked "genius" but possessed "a good deal of imitative talent." While Child at first discouraged Lewis from taking on Shaw as a subject, the final version "seemed to me to have many obvious defects, and yet, on the whole, it was better than I had expected." "Brought up among the Chippewas," Childs asked, "how *can* she know anything of the delicate proprieties of refined life?" Childs's doubts concerning Lewis's talents, however, did not prevent Sarah and the rest of the family from ordering copies of the work and having it photographed, "allowing the artist to sell copies for her own benefit."[25]

Amid their efforts to immortalize Shaw's military career, the family endured another wartime tragedy. In late 1862, Josephine Shaw become romantically involved with Charles Russell Lowell. The two became engaged on March 5, 1863, while Lowell was organizing his new regiment—the 2nd Massachusetts Cavalry—at Readville at the same time as Shaw was recruiting and training his regiment. During this period, Lowell and Shaw lived at the same boarding house, where they each enjoyed regular contact with their respective fiancées. Shaw's death was a huge blow to everyone, including Lowell, who attempted to console Sarah by observing "that his life had such a perfect ending." "I see now that the best Colonel of the best black regiment had to die," he wrote, "it was a sacrifice we owed,—and how could it have been paid more gloriously?"[26]

Rather than postpone their planned wedding, Josephine and Lowell exchanged vows on October 31, 1863, in Staten Island's Unitarian Chapel, offering a small glimmer of light and hope for the family during an otherwise dark period. Unlike Annie, Josephine chose to follow her husband into the field shortly thereafter, where he commanded a brigade in Gen. Philip Sheridan's Army of the Shenandoah. The two shared nine months of marriage before the war caught up with Lowell at the battle of Winchester on September 19, 1864. Lowell was killed by a sniper while leading a counterattack that ultimately routed Confederates under the command of Jubal Early. News of his death hit Josephine and the Lowells hard and once again sent the Shaw family into a period of mourning, no doubt reminding them of the pain of having lost their son just the year before. One month later Josephine gave birth to the couple's now fatherless child. Sarah lamented, "Truly, the sins of the fathers are visited upon the children."[27]

The Shaws found comfort, however, in their work helping to steer the nation toward the final abolition of slavery and in their support of the tens of thousands of formerly enslaved men, women, and children throughout the war-ravaged South. While Sarah focused on her efforts to remind the nation of her son's sacrifice, Frank continued his work with the National Freedman's Relief Association in support of freedpeople along the Sea Islands and elsewhere. He also promoted legislation that culminated in the creation of the Bureau of Refugees, Freedmen, and Abandoned Lands, commonly known as the Freedmen's Bureau.

All the family's activities through to the end of the war were focused on curating the memory of Shaw and honoring the continued bravery of African American soldiers in bringing the war to a conclusion. Unlike William Lloyd Garrison, who believed that the passage of the Thirteenth Amendment to the Constitution in 1865 marked the end of the abolitionist cause, the Shaws and others continued to work for the benefit of the freedmen and to "push a still-unredeemed North toward and expansive morally transformed Union."[28]

Frank and Sarah must have been pleased with the coverage of the regiment's return to Boston on September 2, 1865, after the men had been mustered out a few weeks earlier in South Carolina. The focus on Shaw's connection with the 54th endured despite the fact he had spent only six months training and leading the regiment in the field before his death at Fort Wagner. Without him, the regiment served for two more years, fighting at the battle of Olustee (Florida) in February 1864, at Honey Hill (South Carolina) in November 1864, and at Boykin's Mill (South Carolina) in mid-April 1865. Throughout this period the regiment continued to protest the government's unequal pay policy.

Following the defeat of the Confederacy, the regiment spent the next few months stationed in Charleston, South Carolina. The regiment's final Independence Day together during that first summer of freedom, in 1865, was spent in the now former "cradle of secession," Charleston. Cannon fire marking the national holiday could be heard from the many forts in and around the harbor, including at Fort Wagner, as troops paraded and listened to readings of the Declaration of Independence and the Emancipation Proclamation.[29]

After disembarking at Commercial Wharf, the Shaw Guards—a militia unit named in his honor—escorted the regiment over much of the route it had taken when it marched off to war fifteen months earlier. In addition to escorting the 54th Massachusetts on their return to Boston, the Shaw Guards took part in parades commemorating the anniversary of the Emancipation Proclamation and other anniversaries celebrated by the city's Black population. In 1874, the Shaw Guards accompanied the funeral procession of Charles Sumner and guarded his body as it lay in state for public viewing in the State House.[30]

Edward Hallowell, who assumed command of the 54th Massachusetts after Shaw's death, now led what remained of his regiment (numbering just under six hundred), toward the State House, where they were once again received by Governor John Andrew. A large number of people came out to welcome the regiment home. Veterans such as William Carney, who had experienced the city's send-off, marched proudly through the streets. Others like James Gooding had died at Andersonville, while still others lay in graves marking the regiment's two-year deployment. The regiment, along with Hallowell and especially the "battletorn colors," elicited "the most demonstrative applause." A reporter with the *Boston Evening Transcript* noted, "Rarely has more enthusiasm been elicited by the appearance of troops." Along Joy Street and the rest of the African American neighborhood of Boston "the enthusiasm was intense and the cheers were loud and long."[31]

By the end of the war, according to the *New York Daily Tribune*, Shaw would be "forever linked" with the 54th, "which he first commanded, and which he inspired with so much of his own gentle and noble spirit as to make it a perpetual legacy to the men who fought under and loved him." The *Boston Daily Advertiser* reminded its readers of the attempt to "dishonor" Shaw by "burying him in the common grave of his men" following a battle that proved to be the regiment's "baptism of success and lasting fame." Another newspaper took notice of Shaw's boyhood home on Beacon Street and of the balcony from which the family observed the regiment's celebrated parade in May 1863, which now exhibited a "neat American flag" that "hung closely to the staff, as though festooned with invisible crape, to indicate the family's loss."[32]

In the decades following the Civil War, Robert Gould Shaw and the 54th Massachusetts remained a touchstone of Civil War memory. Attention now focused on leveraging their memory to remind the nation not only of what it took to save the Union but also of a continued struggle to secure civil rights for African Americans, including the right to vote.

The return of the 54th to Boston inspired Republican Senator Charles Sumner to revive the idea of dedicating a monument in honor of Shaw. "The monument should be in Boston," Sumner wrote in a letter to the editor of a Boston newspaper on October 2, 1865, "where the martyr was born, and where the regiment was born also." As for where it should be placed, Sumner proposed that this "equestrian statue" should be located on "one of the stone terraces of the steps that ascend from Beacon Street to the State House," where the "regiment was equipped and inspired" and from where its "devoted commander rode to death."[33]

Sumner was moved by Shaw's bravery and sacrifice, but he also likely understood the monument as a rallying point and justification for Radical Republican plans to pass civil rights legislation. Governor Andrew's support and donation of $500 led to the formation of a committee of twenty-one prominent Bostonians that included Leonard Grimes, the pastor of Twelfth Baptist Church; Sumner, Edward Atkinson, a wealthy Boston cotton broker; and abolitionist Joshua Bowen Smith.

Born in 1813 in Pennsylvania to a mother of African and Native American ancestry and a British father, Joshua Bowen Smith had been educated in Philadelphia on a scholarship before moving to Boston in 1836, where he worked as a waiter. Within a few years, however, Smith made a small fortune with his own catering business, while at the same time becoming more involved in

Boston's abolitionist movement as a cofounder of the New England Freedom Association.[34]

Smith may have been the first person to propose a memorial just days after the colonel's death, demonstrating the immediate recognition of Shaw's symbolic importance. After the war, Smith claimed to have an intimate connection with the Shaw family, though evidence suggests a much more limited relationship. Though he likely encountered Frank Shaw while waiting tables at Boston restaurants, there is no documentation that he ever worked in the Shaw home or engaged in the dramatic conversations he would later describe with a young Rob Shaw before the state legislature: "As we were sitting there [on the Boston Common] I noticed that he looked intently at me, and presently he said, 'Smith, what makes your hands black?' 'Well, my boy, God made them so,' I replied. 'Well,' said he, 'if God made them so, why do people find fault with it?' 'Because they are bad,' I answered. He gazed at me a few moments without speaking and then said 'Smith, some day I'll fight for you.'"[35] Smith's story is almost surely a fabrication, but its message was significant. His imagined conversation with Shaw, and his sizable donation of $500 toward Sumner's monument fund served as a reminder of the sacrifices of Black soldiers at a time when Black political activists were campaigning for seats in the state legislature and rallying the public to advance civil rights causes in the Commonwealth and throughout the South.[36]

Regardless of the veracity of Smith's story, the Shaws were thrilled with the plans for a monument honoring their son to be placed at such a prominent location in Boston. Sarah wrote to Sumner thanking him for his efforts to memorialize her son. "How it takes me back to that beautiful day in May," she wrote, "which was the culminating point to the happiness & pride of my whole life."[37]

Sarah turned her own home into a memorial to her son's memory by displaying his personal possessions and other items connected to the 54th Massachusetts. The regimental flag hung proudly for a time in their hall. Shaw's writing table, antique bronze inkstand, and with pictures that he brought back with him from Europe were all lovingly displayed in the family guest room. Sarah also attempted to locate her son's personal effects that he had taken with him to South Carolina. The family was able to secure his sword, identified by its "beautifully Damascened with his initials surmounted by the U.S. Coat of Arms." Lydia Maria Child recalled that when Sarah showed her the sword she said, "This is the sword that Robert waved over his followers, as he urged them to attack."[38] For families like the Shaws, these sacred relics were a timeless and unquestionable reminder of their loved one's sacrifice and valor during the war.[39]

There were few direct challenges to Shaw's memory during the postwar period, but when they did emerge, Sarah took it upon herself to defend her son's legacy. In 1870, Sarah was reading a copy of the *New York World* when she came across an announcement signed by Rev. Robert F. Clute and his senior warden, William Robert Gignilliat, requesting financial assistance to rebuild the St. Andrew's parish house of worship in Darien, Georgia. Sarah no doubt recalled the significance of Darien as she continued to read, but she must have been startled and deeply disappointed when she came across the following sentence: "One June 11, 1863, without an engagement, the town of Darien, Georgia, was taken and burned by the United States Colored troops, Colonel Shaw, Fifty-fourth Massachusetts Regiment, commanding."

Sarah immediately wrote to the editor of *Harper's Weekly* to set the record straight. Publishing her response in *Harper's* guaranteed a wide readership and provided Sarah with a platform to highlight her fallen son's virtues. Sarah not only corrected the record by noting that Col. James Montgomery had been in command of the expedition but also included one of her son's letters in which he expressed his disgust about what had taken place in Darien and inquired among his superiors as to whether Montgomery had the authority to engage in such actions. Sarah then proceeded to write to Reverend Clute directly to clear Rob's good name. In addition to sending along a few of Shaw's letters demonstrating "how strongly he deprecated the act at the time, and how earnestly he endeavored by his remonstrances to prevent the repetition of such deeds," Sarah also suggested that had her son survived the war he "would have wished to contribute" to the rebuilding of the church.[40]

Reverend Clute's response and the posting of a correction in Darien's *Morning News* pleased Sarah immensely, prompting her to send a check for $500 for the rebuilding of the parish church and another for the same amount to the town of Darien. While her desire to assist the church and broader Darien community in their work to rebuild was sincere, the need to vindicate her son's memory was just as strong. "You see, my dear sir," Sarah wrote, "he was beloved in his family, and how glad we are that his dear name shall not be hated at the South." Having established a trustworthy connection with Reverend Clute, Sarah made one final request that any further publication of the church's appeal for funds leave out any mention of Shaw's name or that of the 54th.[41]

One year later, the St. Andrew's community commenced with the rebuilding of their house of worship, made possible by the mother of one of the Union officers, who took part (willingly or not) in the burning of their quiet town. One can only speculate as to how the veterans of the 54th would have responded to this act of generosity at the height of Reconstruction and racial violence throughout Georgia and the rest of the South.[42]

While the parishioners at St. Andrew's rebuilt their house of worship with the help of the Shaw family, African Americans throughout the former Confederacy struggled to build new lives as freedmen. Despite resistance from white Southerners, Reconstruction began with a good deal of promise. Frank initially had "confidence" in President Andrew Johnson, who assumed his role after Lincoln's assassination, maintaining "that he is as conscientious and honest a man as President Lincoln, and will, like him, endeavor to do the right as God gives him to see it."[43]

Even though Frank's faith in the new president quickly proved to be misplaced, Congress was able to pass constitutional amendments that guaranteed equal protection under the law, birthright citizenship, and the right to vote regardless of race. These new laws buoyed the hopes of the Shaws and others among their circle of friends. Military occupation throughout much of the South made it possible for Black men to vote and run for office. Large numbers of African Americans attended school for the first time. But throughout this period, racial violence was all too common and threatened to undo the progress that had been achieved. By the early 1870s even the federal government had initiated an investigation and held hearings to determine the extent of violence on the part of white terrorists groups like the Red Shirts and the Ku Klux Klan, who killed thousands of Black Americans for daring to challenge white home rule. The government prosecuted and convicted many of their members but abandoned the effort soon afterward.[44]

Activists like the Shaws continued to work to reshape the postwar South by rallying public approval for civil rights for the freedmen; but these commitments faced increasing challenges not just from recalcitrant white Southerners but from a Northern public and a Republican Party that increasingly became focused on other pressing issues. While African Americans throughout the South and their white allies continued to fight for civil rights and even managed to win some notable victories in certain places and stem the tide of white "redemption" in others, by the end of the 1880s the writing was on the wall.

Throughout this period, commemorative efforts centered around Shaw and the regiment continued. Robert Gould Shaw, William Carney, and the 54th were celebrated and memorialized in verse by both Black and white writers. In 1872, Irene LaBate, then a student at the Shaw Memorial School in Charleston, composed an essay in which she praised Shaw as "a voluntary sacrifice on the altar of Liberty for an enslaved race."[45] In 1883, James Monroe Trotter, who was born enslaved in Mississippi before joining the 55th Massachusetts, composed an ode to its sister regiment and Shaw on the anniversary of his birth:

> "To front of column, Massachusetts fifty-fourth!" Thus the order
> came.
> "'Tis what we wish!" their gallant Shaw exultingly did quick exclaim;
> "With most at stake, my men undaunted now do claim the hour
> To glorious victory gain, at least to show no fear of slavery's power."
> Momentous hour! A race on trial, which oft in this and other lands
> Had filled the deadly breach, had helped to burst foul slavery's hands!
> O shades of Attucks, Salem, Hannibal, O grant Toussaint,
> Thy valor's lost, thy fame is nought, if these now prove faint![46]

After the war, Trotter moved to Boston, where he became the first African American to be hired by the Post Office Department before being appointed Recorder of Deeds in Washington, DC, a position previously held by Frederick Douglass. Like many other veterans, the war proved to be a transformative experience for Trotter, who believed that the legacy of Black military service should be remembered alongside Revolutionary War heroes, such as Crispus Attucks and Peter Salem; the Carthaginian general, Hannibal; and Toussaint Louverture, the military leader of the Haitian independence movement.[47]

A number of pictorial representations of the assault on Fort Wagner appeared during this period in *Harper's Weekly* as well as a mass-produced lithograph in 1863 from the firm Currier & Ives. "The Gallant Charge of the 54th Massachusetts (Colored) Regiment," with its focus on Shaw and the national flag at center and surrounded by his men poised to breach Fort Wagner's defensive walls, served as the foundation for future prints.

In 1867, the illustrator Thomas Nast produced "Attack on Fort Wagner" for Evert A. Duyckinck's *National History of the War for the Union Civil, Military, and Naval.* Though Shaw is depicted inaccurately with sideburns, the print accurately highlights the confusion of nighttime fighting and close hand-to-hand combat. For Nast, this wartime scene fit into a larger body of work that

The Gallant Charge of the Fifty Fourth Massachusetts (Colored) Regiment, lithograph by Currier & Ives, September 1863. The artists quickly took advantage of the intense interest in Shaw and the 54th Massachusetts with this mass-produced lithograph of the assault on Fort Wagner. Shaw is clearly visible at the center, with sword unsheathed, at the very moment he was felled by enemy bullets. Very little of the physical dimensions of the fort are taken into consideration resulting in a highly inaccurate representation of the assault. *Courtesy Library of Congress.*

"emphasized freedmen's potential in American life" and reminded the American people of the wartime sacrifices that justified the rights and privileges of full citizenship for African Americans.[48]

In 1890, the Chicago-based print maker Kurz & Allison released the colored lithograph "Storming Fort Wagner." The choice to inaccurately set the assault on Fort Wagner, in full daylight, allowed the illustrator to more clearly depict details such as soldiers wrestling one another to the ground and Black soldiers plunging their bayonets into the chests of Confederate soldiers. The racialized nature of the fighting is vividly portrayed as it would be again with the release of *The Fort Pillow Massacre* in 1892, which depicts the Confederate massacre of US Colored Troops and defenseless Black civilians at Fort Pillow, Tennessee, on April 12, 1864. Kurz & Allison feature Shaw at the center of the action, sword unsheathed, leading his men into the fort at the very moment

Thomas Nast's *Attack on Fort Wagner* (1867) places the assault in complete darkness and highlights the confusion and close hand-to-hand fighting that took place. Though he is shown inaccurately with a full beard, Shaw is clearly visible leading his men into the fort.
Courtesy Library of Congress.

he is shot. William Carney stands defiantly next to him holding the national flag.[49]

The attention focused on Shaw in these mass-produced prints, however, did not always explain their popularity, especially among African Americans. The *Richmond Planet*, a Black newspaper founded by John Mitchell Jr. in 1883 offered the Kurz & Allison print to its readers. A small number of Black Virginians had served in the 54th, and Black soldiers had liberated the seat of the Confederate government in early April 1865 after it had been abandoned. Mitchell likely anticipated sales based on an interest in the depiction of Black soldiers and Carney rather than of Shaw and marketed the print accordingly. "Here is where the 54th Massachusetts regiment won undying fame. Colonel Carney is on the breast-works waving the flag of the union. Look at the Confederates. They pour shot into the colored troops. The rebel flag waves from the breast-works. Cannon belch forth their deadly contents. The colored troops do not falter."[50] The misidentification of Carney as a colonel renders Shaw's absence in the description that much more conspicuous but also speaks to racial pride among African Americans and an intense focus on Black soldiers at a time when their place in the nation's collective memory of the Civil War was beginning to recede. For Black Richmonders specifically, the memory of emancipation and Black military service was quickly being overshadowed by the dedication of Confederate monuments throughout the city, including one honoring Robert E. Lee in 1890.[51]

Closer to Boston, Shaw remained one of the most popular focal points in the commemoration of the Civil War that placed him at the center of a narrative of emancipation, the end of slavery, and Black military service. In 1878, Harvard's Memorial Hall was completed and dedicated. Though Shaw did not graduate with the class of 1860, his name was included on one of the twenty-eight marble tablets that honors the 136 students who died during the war. Close by, the names of Charles Russell Lowell and a host of Shaw's friends in the 2nd and 20th Massachusetts Regiments served as reminders to students of the bravery and sacrifice of those who came before.

A number of Grand Army of the Republic (GAR) posts were also named in honor of Shaw. The fraternal organization for veterans of the Civil War was established in 1866 and at its peak achieved a membership numbering 410,000, scattered in hundreds of posts across the country. New Bedford's contribution to the 54th was significant, so it is no surprise that in 1871 its African American veterans founded the Robert Gould Shaw Post 146. Additional posts named in Shaw's honor were established in Illinois, Kansas, Missouri, Ohio, Virginia, and even close to the Shaw home on Staten Island. The GAR exercised a great deal of political influence, most significantly through the federal pensions that were awarded to the aged and infirm veterans. Unlike most other fraternal organizations, many GAR posts were integrated, and African Americans enjoyed access to positions of leadership. The interracial cooperation, forged by the shared experience of war, arguably came closest to Sarah's efforts to remember her son as a champion of civil rights.[52]

Apart from the GAR, veterans in the 54th and 55th Massachusetts regiments honored Shaw through the establishment of the Robert G. Shaw Veterans Association in March 1881 and took part in numerous commemorative events in Boston's Black neighborhood. In 1882, Robert Smalls joined the festivities to mark the twentieth anniversary of his escape to freedom and the delivery of the Confederate vessel *Planter* to the Union navy in Charleston Harbor. The following year, the group gathered at Leonard Grimes's Twelfth

Kurz & Allison released *Storming Fort Wagner* in 1890. As with previous illustrations, Shaw stands at the center of the fighting at the moment he is struck by enemy fire. Standing next to him holding the national flag is William Carney, who was later awarded the medal of honor for ensuring that the flag did not fall into enemy hands. *Courtesy Library of Congress.*

Baptist Church to mark the anniversary of their former colonel's birth. Sarah Shaw attended and presented the group with two flags that had been given to the regiment at Camp Meigs shortly before their departure.[53]

Honoring Shaw during veterans' reunions and other commemorative events recognized his leadership and bravery but also kept alive a legacy of interracial cooperation. In an address at the first official meeting of the Massachusetts Colored Veterans Association in Worcester in 1886, Edward Hallowell singled out John Brown and Shaw as the "two figures who stand out in noblest relief." "By the earnestness of their convictions, the unselfishness of their characters, their championship of an enslaved race, and the manner of their death," proclaimed Hallowell, "all the conditions are given to make Brown and Shaw the best historical exponents of the underlying cause, the real meaning of the war."[54] African American veterans emphasized patriotic discourse and their wartime service at these events in hopes of achieving a number of political goals, including maintaining access to the ballot box and political office in Boston and beyond. They also rallied in response to rising concerns in the city, among white Bostonians, surrounding "miscegenation" and "amalgamation," and the increasing frequency of lynchings in the South.[55]

In the summer of 1887, Sarah read with approval of the planned "grand reunion of colored veterans" in Boston's Tremont Hall. On the first two days of August of that year—the anniversary of emancipation in the British West Indies—the veterans of the 54th and 55th Massachusetts infantry regiments and the 5th Cavalry gathered in Boston to recall and celebrate their shared history together. Attendees visited the grave of Governor John Andrew, who died shortly after the end of the war in 1867, and visited their old campground in Readville. Many of the participants eulogized Shaw, including William Carney, who spoke of him as a man "whom the colored race will never forget."[56]

Though the veterans invited Sarah, she was unable to attend. "If I were in Boston, or near," she wrote, "nothing would give me greater pleasure than to unite with the soldiers in celebrating that day." In closing her letter, Sarah reminded the veterans of the place of their military service and that of her son's in the long history of emancipation. "You do not remember as I do the day that England set us the example which we followed so many years later, with tears and grief mingled with our joy, that our land too was free from the great sin of slavery. . . . Pray think of me always as a sincere friend of your race."[57]

During the 1887 veterans gathering in Boston, James Monroe Trotter lamented the fact that Shaw's grave "is not nearer to us" so as to "be able to show our regard for him." By that point, however, the location of Shaw's final resting place was no longer clear. In 1865, the federal government disinterred the remains of many buried soldiers in and around Charleston, including those on Morris Island. Shaw's remains were likely relocated along with those of his men to the national cemetery in Beaufort, where they lie today in an unmarked grave.[58] The ruins of Fort Wagner and other wartime constructions on the island have since been lost to erosion.

By the 1880s, work was progressing on the Shaw Memorial at Charles Sumner's chosen site near the State House on Beacon Hill. The project had stalled following the deaths of both Sumner and Governor Andrew, but Edward Atkinson had maintained the committee's funds, accumulating roughly $16,000 over two decades. Atkinson's revival of the Shaw Monument represented a troubling shift in memorial control. His efforts effectively marginalized Joshua B. Smith's original proposal and excluded the Black community from the commemoration process they had initiated.[59]

In 1884, Augustus Saint-Gaudens was commissioned to create the equestrian monument of Shaw for the city of Boston. The Paris-trained sculptor had already completed a number of monuments to notable Civil War figures, including Adm. David Farragut, as well as a celebrated statue of Abraham Lincoln located in Chicago. Saint-Gaudens was thrilled with the commission to memorialize Shaw. He had been looking for an opportunity to carry out a monument in equestrian form and now, "I had found my opportunity."[60] The famed sculptor anticipated that it would take him two years to complete the project.

The focus on Shaw on horseback was quickly challenged by Sarah and the rest of the family, who "objected on the grounds that, although Shaw was of a noble type, as noble as any, still he had not been a great commander, and only men of the highest rank should be so honored" on horseback.[61] With the death of Frank Shaw in 1882, Sarah may have accompanied her daughter Josephine to the artist's studio to share their concerns with Saint-Gaudens. Sarah also hoped to see her son depicted as a champion of freedom and racial justice and encouraged Saint-Gaudens to find a way to include the Black soldiers of the 54th in the commissioned work.

Saint-Gaudens remained committed to an equestrian monument but eventually "fell upon a plan of associating" Shaw "with his troops in a bas-relief, and thereby reducing his importance." This decision likely pleased the Shaw family, who understood that his story was inseparable from his soldiers' sacrifice, but it added years to the project as Saint-Gaudens continually revised his ambitious design. The sculptor's obsessive attention to detail—from uniform buttons to canteens and rifles—further delayed completion as he pursued unprecedented authenticity. Saint-Gaudens sought Black models throughout New York City streets, eventually selecting twenty-three faces from forty candidates to represent the 54th Massachusetts in bronze. Many potential sitters viewed his requests with suspicion, as Saint-Gaudens recalled, some would "follow me as far as the door and then leave." Eventually, Saint-Gaudens had more than enough volunteers, including a few who claimed to have fought alongside Shaw at Fort Wagner.[62]

In addition to delays due to Saint-Gaudens's involvement with other projects, a number of questions lingered about the inscriptions that would adorn the monument. The Shaw family wanted the monument to include the names of the officers and the rank and file—an addition that Frank Shaw had insisted on when Rufus Saxton called to place a monument to Shaw on Morris Island back in 1863. "I want very much to have the names of all the men of the 54th killed at Fort Wagner & afterwards, put on the base at the back—it seems to me due the privates," Sarah wrote to the committee in 1886. She hoped to counter any "feeling that it is only men with rich relations and friends who can have monuments."[63]

In addition to his obsession with the accuracy of the soldiers and questions surrounding inscriptions, Saint-Gaudens had also decided to add an angel hovering over Shaw and his men, which he believed would "combine the ideal with the real."[64] In 1896 Ellen Shaw, now married to former Union Gen. Francis Channing Barlow, her brother's former Harvard tutor, visited Saint-Gaudens's studio to assess his progress. Her concern prompted Atkinson to write another letter to Saint-Gaudens stressing that "we are all appalled and disheartened, including Mrs. Shaw, the Committee and myself, by learning indirectly through Mrs. Barlow that you have again decided to reconstruct that angel."[65]

Each delay to the memorial's completion deepened the painful absence of public recognition for Black Union soldiers, creating mounting frustration for both the Shaw family and African Americans fighting to preserve the memory of their military service and emancipation. Saint-Gaudens's work on the memorial took place amid a flurry of Confederate monument dedications in public spaces across the South. While the earliest Confederate statues and memorials, dedicated during the immediate postwar period were located in cemeteries, by the 1880s they increasingly came to occupy more prominent spaces, including public parks, major intersections, and courthouse lawns. In 1884, the city of New Orleans dedicated a statue of Robert E. Lee atop a 60-foot-tall pedestal. Six years later, the former Confederate capital of Richmond dedicated a monument to Confederate general Robert E. Lee that attracted well over 100,000 attendees.[66]

By the beginning of the twentieth century, Confederate monuments systematically mythologized enslaved people's experiences during the war to justify the emerging Jim Crow system that relegated African Americans to second-class citizenship. These monuments created a fictional narrative of "faithful slaves" who supposedly supported the Confederate cause willingly, directly contradicting the historical reality of the widespread flight of enslaved people to the Union lines and their taking up military service against their former masters. The 1896 monument in Fort Mills, South Carolina, exemplified Southern propaganda with an inscription honoring the "faithful slaves who, loyal to a sacred trust, toiled for support of the army. . . . With matchless devotion, and with sterling fidelity guarded our defenseless homes, women, and children during the struggle for the principles of our Confederate States of America." A similar statue in Tyrrell County, North Carolina, was dedicated a few years later "In Appreciation of Our Faithful Slaves."[67]

The demand for Confederate monuments transformed memorial building from expensive custom projects into affordable mass consumption. Stone quarries throughout New England began producing standardized soldier statues in various poses that could be ordered through catalogs at prices that made widespread commemoration economically feasible for communities across the South. The United Daughters of the Confederacy seized this opportunity to launch an unprecedented campaign of Confederate mythologizing. Between 1900 and 1910, they dedicated hundreds of monuments in Southern public spaces, averaging twenty per year in a systematic effort to control Civil War memory through physical occupation of civic landscapes. This monument boom went far in cementing a Lost Cause mythology in the nation's collective memory. Mass production made it possible for even small towns to afford symbols that portrayed Confederate soldiers as noble defenders of constitutional principles rather than as armed rebels fighting to preserve slavery.[68]

In addition, reunions among former enemies and a popular memory of the war that celebrated sectional reconciliation and the bravery of the men in the ranks—irrespective of the side for which they had fought—threatened to confine the memory of emancipation and the story of Black Civil War soldiers to the African American community. It appeared that the public in the North and even in Boston risked forgetting about the military service of Black soldiers and of Robert Gould Shaw. John Murray Forbes was horrified to learn that prominent Bostonians "thought Robert Shaw was a fine colored fellow."[69]

During the summer of 1896, Saint-Gaudens completed the memorial—much to the relief of the committee and the Shaw family. After visiting his studio, Sarah wrote that Saint-Gaudens "has immortalized my native city, my dear son, and himself."[70] The artist had created a monument that honored both white leadership and Black sacrifice as equal partners in the struggle for freedom. The bronze relief depicts Shaw riding in perfect synchronization with twenty-three fully equipped soldiers, their drums and flags creating a sense of movement that enables viewers to almost hear the rhythmic sounds of hooves and boots, the metallic clank of canteens and equipment as the regiment marches toward destiny.

Saint-Gaudens captured the 54th Massachusetts during its triumph procession down Boston's Beacon Street on May 31, 1863, before they embarked to South Carolina. The sculptor's genius lay in freezing that moment of hope and determination before Fort Wagner's tragedy, allowing viewers to witness the regiment at the height of their promise rather than in the depths of their sacrifice. The memorial's power comes from its invitation to join the march. Saint-Gaudens positioned viewers as potential participants rather than as distant observers, challenging them to consider whether they possess the courage to follow Shaw and his soldiers toward the dangers that await. The bronze figures seem to step forward off their granite base, moving toward a future where racial equality might finally be achieved through sustained struggle.

Plans for the unveiling quickly took shape and the dedication was set for May 31, 1897. The Shaw family had little involvement in the ceremony, but both Sarah and Josephine recommended Harvard philosopher William James—the brother of Capt. Wilkie James, who had served with Shaw in the 54th—as principal speaker. The committee also invited Booker T. Washington to speak for his "race and people."

Following Frederick Douglass's death in 1895, Booker T. Washington emerged as the most prominent African American leader in the nation. The Tuskegee Institute founder promoted industrial education over liberal arts, teaching students practical trades rather than classical subjects. This approach reflected Washington's broader strategy of seeking economic integration for African Americans while avoiding demands for social and political equality. Washington articulated this philosophy in his landmark Atlanta Exposition address on September 18, 1895. Speaking to a predominantly white audience, he offered a compromise that would define race relations for decades: "In all things that are purely social we can be as separate as the fingers, yet one as the hand in all things essential to mutual progress."[71] Washington's message of compromise and accommodation was met with approval by Boston's white conservative-elite class but it divided the Black community.[72]

The evening before the dedication ceremony, African American veterans gathered at Twelfth Baptist Church, in Boston's West End, now led by Rev. Dolphin P. Roberts. A large portrait of Shaw hung next to the pulpit. "Tomorrow a monument will be dedicated to the memory of a man and his followers," Reverend Roberts declared, "who made for themselves a place

Augustus Saint-Gaudens's memorial honoring Shaw and the 54th Massachusetts was dedicated on May 31, 1897. It stands across from the Massachusetts State House on the Boston Common. It remained one of the only representations of Black military service during the Civil War until a monument to US Colored Troops was dedicated in the Shaw neighborhood of Washington, DC, in 1998. *Collection of the Massachusetts Historical Society.*

in the history of the nation. . . . There should be a clean tablet in the heart of every one of our race whereon can be inscribed a never-dying memorial to this young commander and his soldiers."[73]

The memorial's dedication dawned gray and somber, rain drumming against Boston's streets in a rhythm that seemed to echo the march of long-dead soldiers. Despite the weather, crowds pressed along the parade route while others watched from windows and balconies, drawn to witness this unprecedented moment in American memory. Two large American flags were stretched between two large elm trees flanking the memorial that Shaw may have attempted to climb as a young boy. Shortly before 9:00 a.m., roughly 150 veterans of the 54th Massachusetts gathered on Arlington Street alongside survivors from the 55th Massachusetts Infantry and 5th Massachusetts Cavalry. These elderly Black men, many now gray-haired and walking with canes, represented the living embodiment of the courage Saint-Gaudens had captured in bronze. Their presence transformed the dedication from artistic unveiling into sacred reunion between survivors and their fallen comrades.

Though Sarah and her daughters would certainly have been welcomed at the ceremony, they chose not to attend. They did, at the request of

Saint-Gaudens, send Shaw's nephews Hugh Minturn and Charles Lowell Barlow to assist with the unveiling of the memorial. Also absent from the ceremony was Annie Haggerty Shaw. Her marriage to Shaw was sadly brief, and Sarah had quickly emerged as the guardian of her son's memory. Annie may have struggled to find a welcoming place in the family after her husband's death. It also did not help that Sarah likely never fully approved of the timing of the marriage, just weeks before the departure of the regiment. By the 1890s, Annie had little connection to the Shaw family. She spent most of her time in France and Switzerland, leaving a sizable donation to a church in Geneva before returning to the United States. She died in her sister's home in Boston in 1907 at the age of 71, never having remarried.[74]

At 10 a.m., the chief marshal of the parade signaled the start of the procession for the roughly 3,500 participants. Seven carriages carrying the invited speakers and other honored guests wound their way through the streets of Boston toward the State House and the new memorial. Mounted police, cadets, seamen, militia units as well as the 7th New York Militia Regiment, which Shaw first marched with in 1861, followed along, but the stars of the parade were the Black veterans.

Saint-Gaudens recalled the approach of the few remaining men of the regiments as they neared the reviewing stand that included the governor and mayor. "Many of them were bent and crippled, men with white heads, some with bouquets, and, the inevitable humorous touch, one with a carpet-bag."[75] A reporter from the *Boston Herald* noted that the "marks of battle," still apparent on many of the aged veterans, "forced tears to the eyes of many who had thus brought vividly home to their minds the heroic event of which these men were part."[76] After being reviewed by Governor Wolcott, the battalion of survivors escorted him and his staff to the memorial. A little after 11:00 a.m., Robert Gould Shaw's nephews cut the cords still holding the American flags in place, revealing the memorial to the public for the first time. The crowds applauded as the governor accepted the memorial in the name of the city.

Following the unveiling, dignitaries, invited guests, and the public gathered in Music Hall to hear orations from William James and Booker T. Washington. A "shout went up" at the arrival of the 54th and the sight of the "old tattered battle flag aroused every heart."[77] The seating however, reflected a clear racial imbalance. Washington was the only Black man among the eighty-one dignitaries seated on the stage, and representatives of the 54th were seated to one side. Not one of the 423 tickets for the rows immediately in front of the stage was reserved for an African American. Instead, African Americans were expected to view the ceremony from the gallery.

Any notice of this racial discrepancy in the seating arrangements was likely overshadowed by the festive atmosphere as people packed the aisles and entryway. Following a short address by Governor Wolcott, the Harvard philosopher William James strode to the podium to deliver the official oration. James warned his audience of the dangers of forgetting the righteousness of the "Union cause" and the many acts of "civic virtue" and sacrifice that were needed for its preservation. The Shaw Memorial served as a reminder of "civic courage" and not simply to "battle instinct" and manly acts of bravery—a view that was gradually being embraced to foster sectional reconciliation.

James's remarks placed Shaw alongside the abolitionists, who "were the voice of the world's conscience" and "drove the South to madness." Shaw, according to James "recognized the vital opportunity: he saw that the time had come when the colored people must put the country in their debt." James implored his audience, and specifically the veterans of the 54th in attendance, to recognize the "lonely courage which he showed when he dropped his warm commission in the glorious Second to head your dubious fortunes, negroes of the 54th." The lesson that Shaw and his men left for the nation was the vindication of the nation's civic religion "that a man requires no master to take care of him, and that common people can work out their salvation well enough if left free to try." "What Shaw and his comrades stand for and show us," James declared, "is that in such an emergency Americans of all complexions and conditions can go forth like brothers, and meet death cheerfully if need be, in order that this religion of our native land shall not become a failure on the earth."[78]

Following the singing of "The Battle Hymn of the Republic," Booker T. Washington used the occasion to celebrate Shaw as a selfless hero, "altogether lovely," who "was willing to make himself of no reputation that he might save and lift up others." Shaw's sacrifice in abolishing slavery placed the burden of making meaning of freedom and realizing their potential squarely on the shoulders of Black Americans. "The full measure of the fruit of Fort Wagner and all that this monument stands for will not be realized until every man covered by a black skin shall, by patience and natural effort, grow to that height in industry, property, intelligence, and moral responsibility, where no man in all our land will be tempted to degrade himself by withholding from his black brother any opportunity which he himself would possess." The monument to Shaw and his men symbolized a work-in-progress. "What these heroic souls of the 54th Regiment began," Washington continued, "we must complete."[79]

Washington also used the occasion, no doubt to the consternation of some people in the audience, to encourage sectional reconciliation. "My heart goes out to those who wore the gray as well as to those clothed in blue, to those who returned defeated to destitute homes, to face blasted hopes and shattered political and industrial system." Returning to themes introduced in his Atlanta speech in 1895, Washington addressed William Carney, who had carried the regiment's national flag to the Music Hall. Washington encouraged the veterans to continue the fight begun during the Civil War and now "fight by the side of white men North and South . . . in the battle of industry, in the struggle for good government, in the lifting up of the lowest to the fullest opportunities." Once achieved, Washington was convinced, the "old flag, that emblem of progress and security which brave Sergeant Carney never permitted to fall upon the ground, will still be borne aloft by the southern soldier and northern soldier, and in a more potent and higher sense we shall all realize that 'The slave's chains and the master's alike are broken. The one curse of the races held both in tether; they are rising,—all are rising, the black and white together.'"[80]

Back on Staten Island, Sarah must have been overjoyed by the extensive newspaper coverage of the Shaw Monument's unveiling. One Massachusetts newspaper described it as "the most impressive record of the redemption of the nation from slavery, the raising of the negro from a chattel to a man, the elevation of the United States to the fulfillment of the Declaration of the Independence."[81] A year after the dedication, Sarah wrote to Saint-Gaudens, having heard that the memorial "is more & more appreciated there, and that there are people looking at it all the time." In response, Saint-Gaudens shared one bystander's admission of "having gone out of [his] way three times every fortnight for the last year just to see those soldier boys marching."[82]

Saint-Gaudens's memorial solidified in bronze, once and for all, Shaw's memory around the men of the 54th Massachusetts. For much of the next century it remained the most powerful reminder of the military service of Black soldiers during the Civil War, even as many white Americans turned toward a memory of the war that celebrated themes of reunion and the bravery of the soldiers on both sides without dredging up unpleasant reminders of the causes each side fought to defend. It would be one hundred years before another monument, honoring Black Civil War soldiers would be unveiled, this time in the historic Shaw neighborhood of Washington, DC.

Sarah Blake Shaw died on New Year's Eve in 1902 at the age of eighty-seven. She had spent her life championing a wide range of causes, most notably the abolition of slavery. The years after her son's death were filled with sadness, but Sarah was committed to transforming her son into the reformer and champion of African Americans that she always hoped he would become, but which, in life, he had never quite achieved. Now at the end of a long life, Sarah could rest easy, comforted by the belief that the nation now possessed an image of her martyred son that she had long envisioned, but one that Robert Gould Shaw neither anticipated nor sought for himself.

EPILOGUE

Through much of the twentieth century, Black Bostonians continued to rally around the Shaw Memorial and the memory of the 54th Massachusetts Infantry Regiment not merely as a means to counter the widely popular Lost Cause narrative and much of white America's embrace of reconciliation, but as a reminder of their military service and sacrifice and as a justification for their claims to citizenship and civil rights.[1] While the national struggle for civil rights was focused on the post-Reconstruction South, Black activists in Boston remained defiantly focused on a number of issues.

Despite its deep abolitionist and Black activist roots, de facto segregation remained the norm in Boston at the beginning of the twentieth century. Black residents faced exclusion from white neighborhoods, restaurants, theaters, and hotels. Job discrimination was rampant, with Black residents confined to low-paying, menial jobs such as janitors, porters, and servants. Though public schools were technically integrated, in practice, racial disparities were still clearly visible. Black children often attended poorly funded, overcrowded schools. Racial stereotypes remained strong among white residents and were reinforced in newspapers, literature, and popular culture. While new immigrants from places like Italy, Ireland, and Eastern Europe often found themselves targets of discrimination, they sometimes embraced anti-Black racism to distance themselves from African Americans in the social hierarchy.[2]

The Shaw Memorial provided a powerful reminder to Black Bostonians of the work that still needed to be done to achieve full citizenship and what previous generations had fought to achieve. On May 31, 1905, Harriet Tubman joined the Robert G. Shaw Veteran Association, the Robert A. Bell G. A. R. Post, and the Peter Salem Garrison Post at the Shaw Memorial as part of the city's Memorial Day activities. According to a reporter with the *Boston Herald*, Tubman "bent with the weight of years, gazed long and tenderly on the magnificent work of the sculptor and dropped a silent tear for the departed." Representative William L. Reed, "spoke of the daring of those of his color whenever the country's honor had been threatened, and prophesied for the honest black man a higher place in the country than the white man who was a traitor to the country that gave him birth."[3]

Four years later, in 1909, the place of honor was reserved for fourteen veterans of the 54th, who had fought with Shaw at Fort Wagner. The deteriorating political climate for African Americans in the South received a good deal of attention, especially reports of lynching and other forms of intimidation that had become all but routine in newspapers across the country. "The South will never consider the problem solved," asserted Rev. B. W. Farris of St. Paul's Baptist Church, "until they get the negro back into slavery and before they do that the heavens will fail." At just this moment the preacher raised his right hand and touched Shaw's sword on the memorial.[4]

For veterans of the regiment, a visit to the memorial could be an overwhelmingly emotional experience as memories of the war, including its horrors and sacrifices as well as pride of service, once again surfaced. Civil War veterans joined a parade through downtown Boston in August 1917 to honor Americans headed off to fight in another war, this time in Europe. As the procession made its way to the State House, a journalist observed an elderly Black man veer off to pay his respects to his old regiment, completely unaware that his comrades were about to salute the governor positioned on the reviewing stand. "'That's my regiment!' he cried, and his right hand came up to his hat brim." The veteran saluted Shaw and his comrades before being led to the base of the memorial, where he could sit with his memories for a few moments. Such visits became increasingly rare as veterans from the Civil War passed away.[5]

While there was little that Black Bostonians could do to counter monument dedications to and other public celebrations of the Confederacy, they did push back when confronted with it in Boston in 1915. In April of that year, *The Birth of a Nation* premiered at the Tremont Theatre just blocks from the Shaw Memorial, bringing D. W. Griffith's cinematic propaganda directly to the heart of abolitionist Boston. Based on Thomas Dixon Jr.'s novel *The Clansman*, the film offered a sweeping revision of Civil War and Reconstruction history that portrayed enslaved people (played by white actors in blackface) as intellectually inferior and sexually threatening to white women. Griffith's racist spectacle depicted Black politicians during Reconstruction as corrupt buffoons sitting in state legislatures drinking whiskey and eating chicken, reinforcing every stereotype that white supremacists used to justify Black disenfranchisement throughout the Jim Crow South. The film's climax presented the Ku Klux Klan as heroic saviors riding to defend "innocent" white women and "American values" as part of a narrative that transformed terrorist organization into patriotic defenders of civilization.[6]

Dixon's stated goal was "to revolutionize Northern sentiment" and as a result "transform every [white] man in my audience into a good Democrat." Bostonians refused to accept the film's racist assault on their history and dignity. In the weeks following its premiere, protesters led by William Monroe Trotter—the son of James Monroe Trotter—and the Boston NAACP chapter gathered beneath the Shaw Memorial to protest. On May 2, 1915, over two thousand demonstrators gathered just steps from the Shaw Memorial on the Boston Common to denounce both the film's racism and the lack of Black representation in local government. Rev. B. W. Swains warned "that a colored Ku Klux Klan might result," while another Black minister "declared that the negroes would choose the hospitals, jails, and even death, rather than to have 'The Birth of a Nation' continue its production." The film company's decision to promote the movie by parading white-robed horses and costumed Confederates through the streets of Boston led one Black minister to threaten to poison the animals.[7]

The Shaw Memorial proved to be a bulwark for Black Bostonians in countering the racist propaganda of Dixon's movie; but African Americans across the country found ways to use the memorial, one of the few public reminders of Black military service and sacrifice, to educate and inspire the next generation. Around 1920, photographer and sociologist Lewis Hine brought his camera to Atlanta to document African American communities with the same reformist vision that had made him famous nationwide. Hine had built his reputation exposing social injustice through powerful images of immigrants, the urban poor, and exploited child laborers in factories and mills across America. In Atlanta, Hine focused his lens on Black families for a photographic series he titled "Southern Negroes."[8]

Hine's camera captured a middle-class Black family in their modest living room, where education clearly held sacred status. The well-dressed husband and wife read to their two young daughters amid sparse furnishings of wooden chairs and a well-worn rug. The scene embodies the family's commitment to racial uplift through learning, transforming their humble

Lewis Hine photographed this family in Atlanta sometime around 1920. The decision to hang a popular print of the Shaw Memorial speaks to the place of both Shaw and the 54th Massachusetts in the Civil War memory of African Americans during the Jim Crow era and at a time when reunion and the Lost Cause had come to dominate the nation's memory of the Civil War. *Courtesy of the George Eastman Museum.*

home into a classroom where the value of literacy can be conveyed as both a survival skill as well as an act of resistance. Two small portraits on the mantelpiece reveal the family's ideological framework. Above the bespectacled father hangs what appears to be a portrait of Booker T. Washington's image, while the opposite portrait remains too blurred for identification, but may be one of civil rights leader W. E. B. Du Bois.

Occupying the place of honor above the fireplace hangs a Curtis and Cameron mass-produced print of Augustus Saint-Gaudens's Robert Gould

Shaw Memorial. The family's decision to display this particular image in their living room's most prominent location speaks to the profound meaning that Shaw and the 54th Massachusetts held in African American's collective memory at the time. Perhaps the couple had personal connections to the regiment—a father or grandfather who had served in the 54th or another US Colored regiment. But even without direct family ties, their choice to honor Shaw and the 54th reflects how deeply Black military service during the Civil War had become embedded in African American identity and aspiration.

The mass-produced print served multiple functions in this modest Atlanta home. It provided visual testimony to Black participation in the war that had saved the Union and destroyed slavery, offering proof that African Americans had earned their freedom rather than receiving it as a gift from benevolent white people. The image also served as inspiration for the family's own struggles, suggesting that the courage displayed at Fort Wagner could be channeled into the daily battles against Jim Crow segregation.[9]

The image of Robert Gould Shaw marching along with the men of the 54th Massachusetts, displayed so prominently above this family's mantlepiece in 1920, offered a stark reminder that the Confederacy lost the war and that it was still possible to reinvent and reimagine the American Republic.

By World War II, the story of Shaw and the 54th Massachusetts was already receding into the shadows of the nation's collective memory of the Civil War in favor of a more alluring narrative that united white Americans by minimizing or ignoring altogether the importance of emancipation and Black military service in favor of one that highlighted reunion and that left the myth of the Lost Cause largely intact. However, for African Americans, and especially for Boston's Black residents, the memory of Shaw and the 54th Massachusetts continued to serve as a touchstone of civic pride and as rallying point in their continued calls for civil rights and justice.

In March 1945, Ralph J. Banks, who served as vice president of the Boston Equal Rights League—founded by William Monroe Trotter in 1901—urged a Massachusetts legislative committee to adopt a Fair Employment Practice Act to counter discrimination in the workforce. If passed, the legislation would create a commission that would "settle complaints of discrimination on grounds of race, religious belief, color, national ancestry or origin." The issue at hand was clear to Banks: "You can't have a job in this state if you are a black man, in the ordinary course of events. . . . But we are human beings and we are going to eat." To drive his point home, Banks directed the committee's attention to the Shaw Memorial across the street from the State House: "You have given us monuments. You have given us the Shaw monument . . . but we can't eat monuments."[10]

As the nation commemorated the Civil War centennial between 1961 and 1965, Black history continued to be neglected and ignored. White Americans gathered on battlefields like Manassas to witness reenactments and cheer in response to Confederate victory. They consumed stories about larger-than-life figures and famous battles in the pages of *Life* magazine, and they played board games that allowed young and old to refight the war on the side of their choosing without having to deal with larger questions about the cause of the war and its legacy. Largely absent were any references to the role of Black Americans in helping to save the Union and destroy the institution of slavery. It was a narrative that shielded white America from having to confront the "unfinished work" of emancipation at the height of the civil rights era.

Black Americans reached back to the Civil War past to demand civil rights and the dignity that they believed had already been paid for 100 years earlier. In June 1963, following the assassination of civil rights leader Medgar Evers, just steps from his front door in Jackson, Mississippi, Black Bostonians rallied to honor the slain leader and "further the extension of democracy in America." They used the opportunity to register as many Black residents as possible to vote. Before gathering on the Boston Common to listen to an address from Massachusetts Attorney General Edward Brooke, the first African American elected to this position, the marchers stopped briefly in front of the Shaw Memorial.[11] A week before Martin Luther King Jr. shared his "dream" with America on the steps of the Lincoln Memorial, five hundred members of Alpha Phi Alpha had marched to the Shaw Memorial waving American flags to demand that the city desegregate its public schools. Charles Wesley, who in addition to serving as the fraternity's history director and president of Central State College, was only the third African American to earn a doctoral degree from Harvard University. Gathered in front of the memorial, Wesley declared, "We are having our call to arms to fight for freedom in the U.S."[12]

In April 1973, white students took ownership of the Shaw Memorial to protest the Racial Imbalance Law that mandated court-ordered busing. Students shouted that "no black student will come into Southie." One student managed to climb on top of Shaw's horse and held a sign in front of his face that read, "No Busing in Southie." Additional rallies took place during the decade, including one in 1979. A reporter with the *Boston Herald* mused that students were apparently unaware that the memorial "is a tribute to one of the nation's earlier instances of racial integration." Nor did they "notice that the troops behind Shaw on his horse were black."[13]

The gulf between the Civil War memories of white and Black Americans could not have been wider. It would take decades for this to change, spurred in part by the success of the movie *Glory* in 1989. While the history behind the movie may have long occupied a central place in the memory of the Civil War among African Americas, for much of the rest of the country it was a revelation.

Since then, Shaw and his Black regiment have gradually come to occupy a central place in a revived and widely embraced "emancipationist" memory of the war, supported by, among other things, an increased scholarly focus on the history of US Colored Troops and emancipation, the election of the nation's first Black president in 2008, and the commemoration of the 150th anniversary of the Civil War (2011–15), which was framed largely around the theme: "From Civil War to Civil Rights." This progressive narrative, in which the story of Shaw and the 54th Massachusetts figured so prominently, pointed to the possibility of progress on the racial front.

In recent years, however, even this memory of the war has been challenged. Recent incidents of racial violence—beginning with the murder of nine African American churchgoers in Charleston, South Carolina, in 2015 by an admitted white supremacist, and continuing through the police murder of George Floyd in 2020—along with the rise of white nationalism, have left many Americans wondering whether the United States has made any progress in combating racism. Some people have even argued that the American Civil War changed nothing; that we are fighting the very same battles that Americans fought in the 1860s; or that the country is fated to fight another civil war. There appears to be no clear place for someone like Robert Gould Shaw in such a pessimistic atmosphere and flattened historical timeline.

There is certainly no place for the mythical Shaw that Saint-Gaudens immortalized in bronze in Boston in 1897; but perhaps what we need now, more than ever, when we look back on our collective past, is a more nuanced gaze. Shaw was not an abolitionist. He did not leave home in 1861 to set men free, and it was not even his primary reason for accepting command of the 54th Massachusetts in 1863. There was nothing inevitable about the path that led Shaw to accepting the colonelcy of the regiment; rather, it was the result of events that he struggled to comprehend from the very beginning of the war, along with his own pursuit of promotion and respect. Once in command of Black soldiers, Shaw continued to raise doubts about the course he had chosen for himself.

But if we situate Shaw alongside the thousands of enslaved men and women who passed him on the roads and paths in Virginia and South

Carolina between 1861 and 1863 in search of freedom, and who eventually volunteered to fight for the United States; if we listen to the sometimes heated conversations between Shaw and his parents over the issue of emancipation and purpose of the war; and if we can fully understand the uncertainty and contingency of events during this same period, then we can begin to better appreciate what transpired on that sandy beach on July 18, 1863. Shaw could not have foreseen the significance of the moment when he ordered the 54th Massachusetts to commence its assault on Fort Wagner and the extent to which his sacrifice reinforced a conviction among Americans that in the midst of civil war, their nation could be transformed and reimagined.

All these years later it is still possible to catch a glimpse of Robert Gould Shaw's place in the sweep of events that ultimately led to the preservation of the Union, the end of slavery, and the struggle to create a biracial democracy. His and his men's efforts and sacrifice might still serve as an inspiration and as a reminder of what it will take to preserve the American Republic today.

NOTES

ABBREVIATIONS

AHS	Annie Haggerty Shaw
BECF	Shaw, *Blue-Eyed Child of Fortune*
CMA	Commonwealth of Massachusetts Archives, Boston
FS	Frank Shaw
GHS	Georgia Historical Society, Savannah
JSL	Josephine Shaw Lowell
MHS	Massachusetts Historical Society, Boston
OR	US War Department, *War of the Rebellion: The Official Records of the Union and Confederate Armies*
RGS	Robert Gould Shaw
RGSL-HU	Robert Gould Shaw Letters, Houghton Library, Harvard University, Cambridge, MA
SBS	Sarah Blake Shaw
SS	Susanna Shaw

INTRODUCTION

1. *National Anti-Slavery Standard* (New York), August 15, 1863, reprinted in Karcher, *Lydia Maria Child Reader*, 267–68.

2. This story is repeated in Peter Burchard's *One Gallant Rush*, 5. Joan Waugh was the first historian to point out the lack of evidence for this story. See Waugh, *Unsentimental Reformer*, 25, 248n32.

3. See Purcell, *Spectacle of Grief*, 45–94.

4. De'Ann Weimer, "After 126 Years, 19 Black Union Soldiers Receive Military Burial," UPI, May 29, 1989, www.upi.com/Archives/1989/05/29/After-126-years-19-black-Union-soldiers-receive-military-burial/7519612417600; Green, *Unforgettable Sacrifice*, 200–206.

5. It should be noted that by the beginning of the Civil War, whipping had been banned by the military as a form of punishment.

6. Director Ed Zwick discusses his attempt to avoid turning Glory into a white savior movie. See Zwick, *Hits, Flops, and Other Illusions*, 69–107. The Marable quote can be found in "Glory: Controversy, Commemoration, and Indifference in Charleston" (unpublished paper), in Edwin Gittleman Research Materials, MHS; Frank Jarrell, *Post and Courier* (Charleston), January 12, 1990.

7. Burchard, *One Gallant Rush*, xii.

8. Burchard, *One Gallant Rush*, 147.

9. Russell Duncan, *Where Death and Glory Meet*, 4.

10. Potter, *Impending Crisis*, 405–514.

11. The trajectory of Shaw's military career offers a case study for what historian Peter S. Carmichael refers to as "hard-nosed pragmatism." Rather than attempt to identify a consistent ideological root for why Shaw fought or why he persevered, we should try to better understand how he adapted to the changing ground conditions of war and how various factors often pulled him in different directions. Carmichael, *War for the Common Soldier*, 7–10.

12. Sternhell, "Revisionism Reinvented?," 241–42.

13. See Dabney et al., "Interpreting Race," 131–48; Rudy, "From Tokenism to True Partnership," 61–76.

14. Sternhell, "Revisionism Reinvented?," 242. The essay offers a thorough analysis of the relevant scholarship. See also Gannon, *Americans Remember Their Civil War*, 113–31.

CHAPTER 1

1. Quoted in M. W. Smith, *Beacon Hill's Colonel Robert Gould Shaw*, 36.

2. Seasholes, *Atlas of Boston History*, 27–29; Hardesty, *Black Lives, Native Lands, White Worlds*, 76–82.

3. Leamon, "Search for Security in Maine after Penobscot," 119–54.

4. Lt. John Wragg may have been John Ragg. Thanks to J. L. Bell for pointing this out to me.

5. Quincy, *Journals of Major Samuel Shaw*, 3–5.

6. On the quartering of British officers in private homes, see Zabin, *Boston Massacre*, 66.

7. Quoted in Foote, *Seeking the One Great Remedy*, 15.

8. Foote, *Seeking the One Great Remedy*, 16–17.

9. Francis Shaw, *Biographical Sketch of Robert Gould Shaw*, 14.

10. Foote, *Seeking the One Great Remedy*, 18; Smith, *Making Maine*, 14–17.

11. Quoted in Foote, *Seeking One Great Remedy*, 19.

12. Amory, *Proper Bostonians*, 20, 49, 209; Crawford, *Famous Families of Massachusetts*, 1:24e2, 2:163.

13. Foote, *Seeking the One Great Remedy*, 21.

14. Quoted in Foote, *Seeking the One Great Remedy*, 23; Donovan, *Joseph Coolidge Shaw*, 3–4.

15. Foote, *Seeking the One Great Remedy*, 25–30; Waugh, *Unsentimental Reformer*, 25.

16. Waugh, *Unsentimental Reformer*, 26.

17. Waugh, *Unsentimental Reformer*, 13; Barber, *View of Boston Common*, 160. On the transformation of the Boston Common, see Rawson, *Eden on the Charles*, 22–74.

18. O'Connor, *Civil War Boston*, 3; Clark, *City of Second Sight*, 26–28; Hirota, *Expelling the Poor*, 48–69.

19. Quoted in Russell Duncan, *Where Death and Glory Meet*, 4.

20. Bayles, *History of Richmond County*, 572.

21. The history of Transcendentalism is thoroughly explored in Gross, *Transcendentalists and Their World*. Quotes from Emerson are from Ralph Waldo Emerson, "The American Scholar," American Transcendentalism Web, accessed May 5, 2023, https://archive.vcu.edu/english/engweb/transcendentalism/authors/emerson/essays/amscholar.html.

22. Seasholes, *Atlas of Boston History*, 54–55; Brown and Tager, *Massachusetts*, 144–61.

23. Russell Duncan, *Where Death and Glory Meet*, 3; Sinha, *Slave's Cause*, 233–34; W. P. Garrison and F. J. Garrison, *William Lloyd Garrison*, 3: 79–80.

24. David Walker, *Appeal to the Colored Citizens of the World*.

25. On the history of Boston's abolitionist community, see Kantrowitz, *More Than Freedom*; Sinha, *Slave's Cause*; Hardesty, *Black Lives, Native Lands, White Worlds*.

26. Waugh, "It Was a Sacrifice We Owed," 57.

27. Quoted in Delano, *Brook Farm*, 34.

28. Frank Shaw, *The Harbinger*, July 12, 1845, typescript copy in Edwin Gittleman Research Materials, MHS.

29. Swift, *Brook Farm*, 256–57; Waugh, *Unsentimental Reformer*, 28–30; Gross, *Transcendentalists and Their World*, 561–62.

30. Frank Shaw, *The Harbinger*, September 13, 1845, and October 4, 1845, typescript copies in Edwin Gittleman Research Materials, MHS.

31. Swift, *Brook Farm*, 269–71; Foote, *Seeking the One Great Remedy*, 33; Moland, *Lydia Maria Child*, 64–66.

32. Crawford, *Romantic Days in Old Boston*, 52.

33. Waugh, *Unsentimental Reformer*, 14; Fredrickson, *Inner Civil War*, 13–14.

34. Waugh, *Unsentimental Reformer*, 34–35.

35. Russell Duncan, *Where Death and Glory Meet*, 6; Waugh, *Unsentimental Reformer*, 33–34.

36. Leng and Davis, *Staten Island and Its People*, 253–54.

37. Russell Duncan, *Where Death and Glory Meet*, 9.

38. RGS to SBS, June 3, 1850, in Higginson, *Harvard Memorial Biographies*, 173.

39. RGS to SBS, September 7, 1850, in Higginson, *Harvard Memorial Biographies*, 174.

40. RGS to SBS, September 17, 1850, RGSL-HU.

41. Waugh, "It Was a Sacrifice We Owed," 62.

42. Russell Duncan, *Where Death and Glory Meet*, 10. On the European Tour, see Kilbride, *Being American in Europe*, 124–66.

43. Quoted in Burchard, *One Gallant Rush*, 9.

44. RGS to SBS, November 13, 1851, and February 28, 1852, RGSL-HU.

45. RGS to SBS, March 15, 1853, RGSL-HU.

46. Quoted in Foote, *Seeking the One Great Remedy*, 64.

47. SBS to RGS, December 6, 1852, RGSL-HU; Louisa Jay Barlow, "Notes for a Biography of Rob Gould Shaw," n.d., RGSL-HU.

48. See Masur, *Until Justice Be Done*, 241–43.

49. Kemble, *Records of Later Life*, 40. On Kemble, see Clinton, *Fanny Kemble's Civil Wars*.

50. RGS to SBS, January 30, 1856, RGSL-HU.

51. Quoted in Burchard, *One Gallant Rush*, 11.

52. RGS to SBS, October 29, 1854, RGSL-HU.

53. RGS to SBS, December 26, 1855, RGSL-HU.

54. RGS to FS, March 5, 1856, RGSL-HU.

55. RGS to SBS, October 28, 1855, and December 26, 1855, RGSL-HU.

56. Waugh, "'It Was a Sacrifice We Owed,'" 62–64.

57. RGS to SBS, October 7, 1855, RGSL-HU.

58. RGS to SBS, January 30, 1856, RGSL-HU.

59. See Levine, *Spirit of 48*; Matthew Stewart, *Emancipation of the Mind*.

60. The story of Anthony Burns is the focus of Von Frank, *Trial of Anthony Burns*. See Woo, *Master Slave Husband Wife*, for the story of the escape of Ellen and William Craft. For a more focused look at how Boston responded to the Fugitive Slave Act and Kansas-Nebraska Act, see Kantrowitz, *More Than Freedom*, 205–14.

61. Quoted in Burchard, *One Gallant Truth*, 14; in addition, see Phillips, *American Negro Slavery*, 462–63.

62. Quoted in Russell Duncan, *Where Death and Glory Meet*, 13–14.

63. RGS to SBS, April 9, 1856, RGSL-HU; Russell Duncan, *Where Death and Glory Meet*, 19.

CHAPTER 2

1. RGS to FS, March 5, 1856, and March 6, 1856, RGSL-HU.

2. Welch, *Boy General*, 19–29.

3. See Wongsrichanalai, *Northern Character*, 22; Livia Gershon, "How Harvard Became Harvard," *JSTOR Daily*, April 11, 2016, https://daily.jstor.org/how-harvard-became-harvard.

4. Bundy, *Nature of Sacrifice*, 58–59.

5. Quoted in Wongsrichanalai, *Northern Character*, 26.

6. Foote, *Seeing the One Great Remedy*, 83.

7. Harvard University Presidential Committee, *Legacy of Slavery at Harvard*, 37.

8. Harvard University Presidential Committee, *Legacy of Slavery at Harvard*, 67–73.

9. Quoted in Bosco, "Harvard University and the Fugitive Slave Act," 232.

10. Quoted in Bosco, "Harvard University and the Fugitive Slave Act," 244.

11. Quoted in Von Frank, *Trial of Anthony Burns*, 17.

12. RGS to SBS, November 18, 1856, RGSL-HU.

13. Index to University Records, 1636–1870 and Sibley's Private Journal, 1847–82, drawer 56, Houghton Library, Harvard University, Cambridge, MA.

14. RGS to SBS, September 5, 1856, RGSL-HU.

15. Burchard, *One Gallant Rush*, 16–18.

16. RGS to SBS, February 28, 1858, RGSL-HU.

17. RGS to SBS, March 29, 1857, RGSL-HU.

18. RGS to SBS, October 31, 1857, RGSL-HU.

19. Quoted in Russell Duncan, *Where Death and Glory Meet*, 21.

20. Wongsrichanalai, *Northern Character*, 37, 81; *Cambridge Chronicle*, July 1860, reprinted in Harvard College, *Report of the Class of 1860*, 203–4.

21. RGS to SBS, November 18, 1854, RGSL-HU.

22. Woodard, *Union*, 130–31.

23. RGS to SBS, November 18, 1856, RGSL-HU.

24. On the public reaction to Dred Scott, see McPherson, *Battle Cry of Freedom*, 176–80.

25. Guelzo, *Lincoln and Douglas*, 57–64.

26. RGS to FS, March 24, 1858, RGSL-HU.

27. See RGS to SBS, October 31, 1857, RGSL-HU.

28. RGS to SBS, March 24, 1858, RGSL-HU; Burchard, *One Gallant Rush*, 21.

29. RGs to SBS, November 5, 1854, RGSL-HU.

30. RGS to SBS, December 9, 1858, RGSL-HU.

31. RGS to SBS, December 1, 1858, RGSL-HU.

32. William Howell Russell, *My Diary North and South*, 28.

33. Quoted in Burchard, *One Gallant Rush*, 22–23.

34. Wells, *Kidnapping Club*, 255–78.

35. Wells, *Kidnapping Club*, 259–60.

36. Digital History. "Abraham Lincoln, Cooper Union Address, February 27, 1860," accessed October 11, 2024, www.digitalhistory.uh.edu/active_learning/explorations/brown/public_lincoln.cfm.

37. Holzer, "Housekeeping on Its Own Terms," 4.

38. Quoted in Burchard, *One Gallant Rush*, 24–25.

39. RGS to SBS, November 18, 1860, RGSL-HU.

40. Quoted in Starobin, *Madness Rules the Hour*, 202–3.

41. See Swinton, *History of the Seventh Regiment*; Clark, *History of the Seventh Regiment of New York*; L. Gordon, "Novices in Warfare."

42. L. Gordon, "Novices in Warfare," 197.

43. Quoted in L. Gordon, "Novices in Warfare," 205; Groeling, *First Fallen*, 82–86.

44. Swinton, *History of the Seventh Regiment*, 17–21.

45. Russell Duncan, *Where Death and Glory Meet*, 44–45; RGS to SS, August 15, 1861, *BECF*, 128; RGS to SBS, August 30, 1861, *BECF*, 133.

46. Quoted in Burchard, *One Gallant Rush*, 25.

47. RGS to FS, March 28, 1861, RGSL-HU.

48. Quoted in Burchard, *One Gallant Rush*, 26.

49. McPherson, *Battle Cry of Freedom*, 266–75; Goodheart, *1861*, 136–83.

50. Quoted in Burchard, *One Gallant Rush*, 26.

51. RGS to FS, March 28, 1861, RGSL-HU.

52. Quoted in Burchard, *One Gallant Rush*, 26.

53. Quoted in Burchard, *One Gallant Rush*, 28. The term "ells" refers to a former measure of length, used mainly for textiles, locally variable but typically about forty-five inches.

CHAPTER 3

1. *New York Times*, April 20, 1861; Frost, *Rebellion in the United States*, 169–71.

2. Goodheart, *1861*, 209; Swinton, *History of the Seventh Regiment*, 237.

3. Swinton, *History of the Seventh Regiment*, 37.

4. *New York Times*, April 20, 1861.

5. Quoted in Russell Duncan, *Where Death and Glory Meet*, 26.

6. RGS to SBS, April 18, 1861, *BECF*, 73.

7. RGS to SBS, April 18, 1861, *BECF*, 73.

8. RGS to FS and SBS, April 23, 1861, *BECF*, 76–77.

9. RGS to FS and SBS, April 23, 1861, *BECF*, 77.

10. Quoted in Swinton, *History of the Seventh Regiment*, 76.

11. RGS to SBS, April 26, 1861, *BECF*, 80–81.

12. Quoted in Swinton, *History of the Seventh Regiment*, 111–12.

13. Dickens, *American Notes for General Circulation*, 21–22.

14. On the city's antebellum development, see Gugliotta, *Freedom's Cap*, 26–29; Asch and Musgrove, *Chocolate City*, 84–86.

15. Charles Lee Decker, "Washington Canal," National Park Service, accessed June 4, 2024, www.nps.gov/articles/history-archeology-of-dc-washington-canal.htm; Gugliotta, *Freedom's Cap*, 27–29.

16. Roberts, *Capital Dames*, 9–31.

17. RGS to SBS, April 26, 1861, *BECF*, 82.

18. Quoted in Gugliotta, *Freedom's Cap*, 380–81. On early wartime Washington, see Winkle, *Lincoln's Citadel*, 142–64; Goodheart, *1861*, 269–71.

19. Theodore Winthrop, quoted in *BECF*, 84n9.

20. RGS to SBS, April 26, 1861, *BECF*, 82.

21. RGS to SBS, May 2, 1861, *BECF*, 91.

22. On popular perceptions of Lincoln, see Fox, *Lincoln's Body*, 10–13; Reynolds, *Abe*, 479–82.

23. Quoted in *BECF*, 95n9.

24. RGS to SBS, May 10, 1861, *BECF*, 96.

25. RGS to JSL, April 30, 1861, *BECF*, 88.

26. On the importance of Union, see Gallagher, *Union War*, 33–37.

27. RGS to SBS, May 10, 1861, *BECF*, 96.

28. Shaw's commission as second lieutenant dates to May 28, 1861. His promotion to first lieutenant dates to August 10, 1861. *Public Documents of Massachusetts*, 196–98. On Gen. George H. Gordon, see Boatner, *Civil War Dictionary*, 19, 347; Wallace, *Framingham's Civil War Hero*, 9–38.

29. Wongsrichanalai, *Northern Character*, 107–11.

30. G. Gordon, *Brook Farm to Cedar Mountain*, 14; Dyer, *Compendium of the War of the Rebellion*, vol. I, 157; Bowen, *Massachusetts in the Civil War*, 113.

31. RGS to SBS, May 19, 1861, *BECF*, 101.

32. RGS to FS, May 21, 1861, *BECF*, 103.

33. Comey, *Legacy of Valor*, 9.

34. RGS to SBS, May 19, 1861, *BECF*, 101.

35. RGS to SBS, May 25, 1861, *BECF*, 103.

36. Comey, *Legacy of Valor*, 3–4.

37. Bledsoe, *Citizen-Officers*, 63.

38. Bledsoe, *Citizen-Officers*, 67–68.

39. Comey, *Legacy of Valor*, 5–6.

40. RGS to SBS, May 25, 1861, *BECF*, 104. On the history of anti-Irish sentiment in Boston and New York City before the Civil War, see Hirota, *Expelling the Poor*, chap. 1.

41. On the bias against the Irish among college-educated New Englanders in the officer corps, see Wongsrichanalai, *Northern Character*, 141–43.

42. Comey, *Legacy of Valor*, 6.

43. Comey, *Legacy of Valor*, 8–9.

44. RGS to SBS, June 9, 1861, *BECF*, 107.

45. RGS to SBS, June 9, 1861, *BECF*, 107.

46. On the relationship between Ellsworth and Lincoln, see Reynolds, *Abraham Lincoln in His Times*, 528–44; RGS to SBS, June 16, 1861, *BECF*, 109.

47. Cirillo, *Abolitionist War*, 25.

48. Foote, *Seeking the One Great Remedy*, 89–91.

49. William Stewart, *Philanthropic Work*, 13, 16.

50. Quoted in Wallace, *Framingham's Civil War Hero*, 35.

51. G. Gordon, *Brook Farm to Cedar Mountain*, 31.

52. Comey, *Legacy of Valor*, 10–11.

53. Comey, *Legacy of Valor*, 11.

54. William Stewart, *Philanthropic Work*, 14; Burchard, *One Gallant Rush*, 39.

CHAPTER 4

1. RGS to SBS, July 13, 1862, *BECF*, 112. The debate over civil liberties in wartime Maryland is explored in Frank J. Williams, "Abraham Lincoln, Civil Liberties, and Maryland," in Mitchell and Baker, *Civil War in Maryland Reconsidered*, 139–59.

2. From Thomas Jefferson's *Notes on the State of Virginia*, quoted in Boles, *Jefferson*, 173.

3. On the history of the Shenandoah Valley, see Wallenstein, *Cradle of America*, 49–55. On the history of slavery in the region, see Noyalas, *Slavery and Freedom in the Shenandoah Valley*, 10–24.

4. Long, *Civil War Day by Day*, 90–94.

5. RGS to SBS, July 23, 1862, *BECF*, 118.

6. Comey, *Legacy of Valor*, 17.

7. Comey, *Legacy of Valor*, 17–19; G. Gordon, *Brook Farm to Cedar Mountain*, 26–27.

8. RGS to SBS, July 21, 1862, *BECF*, 115–16.

9. Dwight, *Life and Letters of Wilder Dwight*, 63.

10. Burchard, *One Gallant Rush*, 41.

11. Responses to John Brown's Harpers Ferry raid can be found in Stauffer and Trodd, *Tribunal*, 77–228.

12. RGS to SS, July 30, 1861, *BECF*, 119.

13. RGS to SBS, August 8, 1862, *BECF*, 124.

14. McPherson, *Battle Cry of Freedom*, 348. On abolitionist views of McClellan, see Cirillo, *Abolitionist Civil War*, 131–32.

15. RGS to SBS, July 13, 1862, *BECF*, 113.

16. RGS to SBS, August 8, 1861, *BECF*, 124. The importance of discipline among the junior officer corps is thoroughly explored in Wongsrichanalai, *Northern Character*, 143–48; Bledsoe, *Citizen-Officers*, 18–23, 32–37, 43–44; Fry, *Republic in the Ranks*, 29–31; R. Mitchell, *Civil War Soldiers*, 57–59.

17. Foote, *Gentlemen and the Roughs*, 123.

18. SBS to JSL, September 11, 1861, *BECF*, 139.

19. SBS to SS, September 17, 1861, *BECF*, 141–42.

20. Quoted in Bledsoe, *Citizen-Officers*, 35–36. Bledsoe thoroughly explores the controversy surrounding electing officers in chapter 1.

21. RGS to SS, August 15, 1861, *BECF*, 128.

22. *New York Times*, July 27, 1861; McPherson, *Battle Cry of Freedom*, 328, 350.

23. RGS to SS, July 30, 1861, *BECF*, 119.

24. Quoted in Leonard, *Benjamin Franklin Butler*, 66.

25. This section relies heavily on Noyalas, *Slavery and Freedom in the Shenandoah Valley*, 45–49; and Hennessy, "Army of Virginia Confronts the 'Moral Spectacle' of Freedom," 36–64.

26. Comey, *Legacy of Valor*, 19.

27. Charlie Morse to Father, August 5, 1861, Charles F. Morse Papers, MHS.

28. Quint, *Potomac and the Rapidan*, 34.

29. RGS to SBS, July 18, 1861, *BECF*, 115.

30. RGS to SBS, July 21, 1861, *BECF*, 116.

31. RGS to JSL, July 31, 1861, *BECF*, 120.

32. RGS to Sidney Howard Gay, August 6, 1862, *BECF*, 123.

33. *Douglass' Monthly*, May 1861, quoted in Martin, *Mind of Frederick Douglass*, 60.

34. Few Northerners called for the enlistment of slaves as soldiers during the first year of the war, though newspapers were already reporting sightings of Black men carrying arms and constructing earthworks for the Confederacy. Such stories provoked calls for enlistment, including by Frederick Douglass. See Brasher, *Peninsula Campaign*, 50–74.

35. See Brooke, *"There Is a North,"* 295–305.

36. Copeland, *Statement of R. Morris Copeland*, 8.

37. RGS to FS, August 10, 1862, *BECF*, 125; RGS to Sydney Howard Gay, August 6, 1861, *BECF*, 123.

38. Stewart, *Philanthropic Work*, 18.

39. RGS to SS, September 17, 1861, *BECF*, 142.

40. Stewart, *Philanthropic Work*, 17.

41. RGS to SBS, August 30, 1861, *BECF*, 132.

42. Charlie Morse to Father, September 1861, Charles F. Morse Papers, MHS.

43. RGS to SS, August 15, 1861, *BECF*, 127.

44. RGS to FS, September 30, 1861, *BECF*, 149.

45. RGS to JSL, July 31, 1861, *BECF*, 121.

46. RGS to FS, August 10, 1861, *BECF*, 125.

47. RGS to FS, August 10, 1861, *BECF*, 127. Aunty Betty is not identified, but she could very well be the Black woman referenced in the letter.

48. Charlie Morse to Father, July 31, 1861, Charles F. Morse Papers, MHS.

49. RGS to SBS, July 21, 1861, *BECF*, 116. On the perceptions of white Southerners by college-aged men from New England, see Wongsrichanalai, *Northern Character*, 115; R. Mitchell, *Civil War Soldiers*, 91–107.

50. RGS to AS, September 23, 1861, *BECF*, 145.

51. RGS to AS, September 23, 1861, *BECF*, 144.

52. RGS to SBS, September 5, 1861, *BECF*, 137.

53. RGS to Ellen Shaw, September 26, 1861, *BECF*, 147.

54. RGS to George Curtis, October 8, 1861, *BECF*, 152.

55. On Ball's Bluff, see Morgan, *Little Short of Boats*. On the Twentieth Massachusetts at Ball's Bluff, see R. Miller, *Harvard's Civil War*, 51–83.

56. *Cape Ann Light and Gloucester (MA) Telegraph*, November 9, 1861.

57. RGS to SBS, October 22, 1861, *BECF*, 155.

58. Dwight, *Life and Letters of Wilder Dwight*, 134.

59. Officers and enlisted men mastered a number of "self-care" techniques in response to the changing weather and other environmental challenges. See Meier, *Nature's Civil War*, 99–125.

60. RGS to SS, November 15, 1861, *BECF*, 160–61.

61. RGS to SBS, November 25, 1861, *BECF*, 164.

62. RGS to SBS, November 25, 1861, *BECF*, 164; Dwight, *Life and Letters of Wilder Dwight*, 144.

63. On the National Freedman's Relief Association, see Rose, *Rehearsal for Reconstruction*, 41–42.

64. Steward, *Philanthropic Work*, 22.

65. RGS to FS, November 23, 1861, *BECF*, 163.

66. Dwight, *Life and Letters of Wilder Dwight*, 168.

67. RGS to JSL, December 8, 1861, *BECF*, 166.

68. RGS to FS, December 14, 1861, *BECF*, 167.

69. RGS to SBS, December 25, 1861, *BECF*, 169.

70. RGS to SBS, December 25, 1861, *BECF*, 168.

CHAPTER 5

1. Charles Morse to Robert Morse, January 31, 1862, Charles F. Morse Papers, MHS.

2. On the changing nature of the war in 1862, see Grimsley, *Hard Hand of War*, 23–68; Sheehan-Dean, *Calculus of Violence*, 2–132; Varon, *Armies of Deliverance*, 78–152.

3. G. Gordon, *Brook Farm to Cedar Mountain*, 101.

4. On military campaigns in early 1862, see McPherson, *Battle Cry of Freedom*, 392–405. The relationship between Lincoln and McClellan in early 1862 is analyzed in Rable, *Conflict of Command*, 101–31.

5. Charles Morse to Robert Morse, February 13, 1862, Charles F. Morse Papers, MHS.

6. Quoted in Rafuse, *From the Mountains to the Bay*, 38–41.

7. Charles Morse to RGS, March 2, 1862, Charles F. Morse Papers, MHS.

8. RGS to JSL, March 9, 1862, *BECF*, 180.

9. G. Gordon, *Brook Farm to Cedar Mountain*, 105.

10. RGS to SBS, March 3, 1862, *BECF*, 177.

11. Nelson, *Ruin Nation*, 72–87.

12. See RGS to SBS, March 14, 1862, *BECF*, 182; Charles Morse to RGS, March 15, 1862, Charles F. Morse Papers, MHS. On the collection of human remains from the battlefield, see James J. Broomall, "Sullivan Ballou's Body: Battlefield Relic Hunting and the Fate of Soldiers' Remains," *CommonPlace*, November 2021, https://commonplace.online/article/sullivan-ballous-body; Cashin, "Trophies of War," 339–67.

13. For a concise overview of the Shenandoah Valley's military and logistical significance to the Confederacy, see the introduction in Gallagher, *Shenandoah Valley Campaign*; and Cozzens, *Shenandoah 1862*, 37–38.

14. Rafuse, *From the Mountains to the Bay*, 84–88.

15. Cozzens, *Shenandoah 1862*, 207–8.

16. RGS to SBS, March 28, 1862, *BECF*, 185.

17. Comey, *Legacy of Valor*, 44.

18. RGS to SBS, April 19, 1862, *BECF*, 195.

19. Noyalas, *Slavery and Freedom in the Shenandoah Valley*, 63.

20. "A new Article of War forbids the military to return escaped slaves to their former owners," House Divided: The Civil War Research Engine at Dickinson College, accessed October 21, 2024, https://hd.housedivided.dickinson.edu/node/38949.

21. Noyalas, *Slavery and Freedom in the Shenandoah Valley*, 70.

22. Burchard, *One Gallant Rush*, 55.

23. Noyalas, *Slavery and Freedom in the Shenandoah Valley*, 67.

24. Dwight, *Life and Letters of Wilder Dwight*, 209.

25. Charles Morse to Father, April 22, 1862, Charles F. Morse Papers, MHS.

26. Alonzo H. Quint, *Congregationalist*, April 5, 1862.

27. RGS to SBS, April 11, 1862, *BECF*, 190; RGS to FS, May 13, 1862, *BECF*, 200.

28. RGS to SBS, March 28, 1862, *BECF*, 186.

29. Shaw's lack of interest in enslaved people encountered on the march stands in contrast with Chandra Manning's contention that soldiers' experience with enslaved people in 1861–62 had a transformative impact on their attitudes about race and slavery and helped build support for emancipation. See Manning, *What This Cruel War Was Over*. For a thorough analysis of the view of Union soldiers regarding slavery and emancipation in 1862, see Hennessy, "Army of Virginia Confronts the 'Moral Spectacle' of Freedom," 15–35.

30. Fry, *Republic in the Ranks*, 37–39.

31. Stewart, *Philanthropic Work*, 24.

32. RGS to SBS, April 19, 1862, *BECF*, 194.

33. RGS to FS, May 13, 1862, *BECF*, 200.

34. Stewart, *Philanthropic Work*, 25.

35. RGS to SBS, May 9, 1862, *BECF*, 197.

36. Quoted in Copeland, *Statement of R. Morris*, 8.

37. RGS to FS, May 19, 1862, *BECF*, 202. Shaw apparently shared Copeland's view, writing to Mary Russell, "Of course you could [find] better soldiers among the Blacks in the North then among the poor contrabands at Port Royal who never had the pluck to run away." See RGS to Mary Russell, June 7, 1862, RGSL-HU.

38. Marvel, *Lincoln's Autocrat*, 226–27.

39. RGS to FS, August 3, 1862, *BECF*, 224.

40. See Taylor, *Fighting for Citizenship*, 39–68.

41. Stewart, *Philanthropic Work*, 27.

42. Quoted in Matsui, *First Republican Army*, 82.

43. RGS to FS, May 27, 1862, *BECF*, 204.

44. Dwight, *Life and Letters of Wilder Dwight*, 219; Morse, *Letters Written During the Civil War*, 62. The fighting at Winchester is covered by Cozzens, *Shenandoah 1862*, 346–77.

45. RGS to SBS, June 13, 1862, *BECF*, 209.

46. Quoted in Richard Duncan, *Beleaguered Winchester*, 99–100.

47. RGS to FS, May 27, 1862, *BECF*, 204–5; and RGS to Mary, June 7, 1862, *BECF*, 208; Comey, *Legacy of Valor*, 50; Charles Morse to Father, June 14, 1862, Charles F. Morse Papers, MHS.

48. RGS to FS, May 27, 1862, *BECF*, 205.

49. Stewart, *Philanthropic Work*, 28.

50. Stewart, *Philanthropic Work*, 28.

51. In his official report for the 2nd Massachusetts, Lieutenant Colonel Andrews listed 7 men killed and 28 wounded. G. Gordon, *History of the Second Massachusetts Regiment of Infantry*, 135–36.

52. RGS to FS, May 27, 1862, *BECF*, 204.

53. Charlie Morse to RGS, June 5, 1862, Charles F. Morse Papers, MHS.

54. RGS to SS, June 6, 1862, *BECF*, 206–7. On the rumors of Confederate civilians executing wounded Union soldiers, see Richard Duncan, *Beleaguered Winchester*, 100–101.

55. RGS to SBS, June 25, 1862, *BECF*, 211.

56. RGS to SBS, June 25, 1862, *BECF*, 212.

57. Sears, *To the Gates of Richmond*, 111–78.

58. Charlie Morse to Ellen, July 4, 1862, Charles F. Morse Papers, MHS.

59. Sears, *To the Gates of Richmond*, 179–336.

60. Stewart, *Philanthropic Work*, 30.

61. RGS to SBS, July 23, 1862, *BECF*, 217–19.

62. SBS to John Elliott Cairnes, July 31, 1862, in Weinberg, *John Elliot Cairnes*, 138; and SBS to John Elliott Cairnes, September 10, 1862, in Weinberg, *John Elliot Cairnes*, 142.

63. RGS to SBS, July 23, 1862, *BECF*; and RGS to SBS, July 28, 1862, *BECF*, 221.

64. Shaw's promotion to captain is dated August 10, 1862. See *Public Documents of Massachusetts*, 196.

65. Quoted in Hennessy, *Return to Bull Run*, 12.

66. RGS to FS, August 3, 1862, *BECF*, 225.

67. Foote, *Rites of Retaliation*, 30–31.

68. On John Pope's orders and its impact, see Matsui, *First Republican Army*, 33–50; Murray and Hsieh, *Savage War*, 190; Blair, *Virginia's Private War*, 79.

69. Pope's outlook on the war in 1862 is explored in Zander, "General Pope Goes to Washington," 105–10. RGS to SBS, July 28, 1862, *BECF*, 221.

70. RGS to SBS, July 28, 1862, *BECF*, 222.

71. Freedmen and Southern Society Project, "The Second Confiscation Act" (July 17, 1862), last updated February 2, 2025, www.freedmen.umd.edu/conact2.htm.

72. SBS to John Elliott Cairnes, July 15, 1862, in Weinberg, *John Elliot Cairnes*, 138.

73. SBS to John Elliott Cairnes, September 10, 1862, in Weinberg, *John Elliot Cairnes*, 143.

74. RGS to FS, August 3, 1862, *BECF*, 225.

75. The movement of armies to Cedar Mountain is covered thoroughly by Krick, *Stonewall Jackson at Cedar Mountain*, 39–67.

76. RGS to SBS, August 12, 1862, *BECF*, 231; Andrew's battle report can be found in F. Moore, *The Rebellion Record*, 318–19.

77. G. Gordon, *History of the Second Massachusetts Regiment of Infantry*, 209; Quint, *Record of the Second Massachusetts Infantry*, 484.

78. RGS to SBS, August 12, 1862, *BECF*, 230.

79. RGS to SBS, August 12, 1862, *BECF*, 231.

80. Stewart, *Philanthropic Work*, 32.

81. RGS to AHS, August 13, 1862, *BECF*, 235.

CHAPTER 6

1. Stewart, *Philanthropic Work*, 31–32.

2. RGS to AHS, August 13, 1862, *BECF*, 234.

3. RGS to SBS, August 19, 1862, *BECF*, 236.

4. Acken, *Through Blood and Fire*, 23.

5. RGS to SBS, August 19, 1862, *BECF*, 236–37.

6. For an overview of these operations, see McPherson, *Battle Cry of Freedom*, 524–28. For a close examination of the movement of armies following the battle of Cedar Mountain, see Hennessy, *Return to Bull Run*, 30–139.

7. Comey, *Legacy of Valor*, 69.

8. RGS to FS, August 29, 1862, *BECF*, 238.

9. On McClellan's return to command of the Army of the Potomac, see Hartwig, *To Antietam Creek*, 46–47.

10. Sears, *Landscape Turned Red*, 75–76.

11. On the significance of Confederate victory at Second Manassas, see Gallagher, "Tide of War," 65–96.

12. Fields, *Slavery and Freedom on the Middle Ground*, 117.

13. On Lee's planning of the Maryland Campaign and the condition of the Army of Northern Virginia, see Harsh, *Taken at the Flood*, 19–65.

14. Hartwig, *To Antietam Creek*, 153.

15. Acken, *Through Blood and Fire*, 37.

16. RGS to FS, September 21, 1862, *BECF*, 240.

17. RGS to FS, September 21, 1862, *BECF*, 240.

18. RGS to FS, September 21, 1862, *BECF*, 240. On the fighting in this sector of the battlefield, see Hartwig, *I Dread the Thought of the Place*, 182–87, 194–98.

19. Charles Morse to Mother, September 21, 1862, Charles F. Morse Papers, MHS.

20. RGS to FS, September 21, 1862, *BECF*, 240.

21. Charles Morse to Mother, September 21, 1862, Charles F. Morse Papers, MHS.

22. "F. to Dear Ones at Home, September 21, 1862," *Massachusetts Spy* (Boston), July 30, 1862.

23. Charles Morse to Mother, September 21 and September 22, 1862, Charles F. Morse Papers, MHS.

24. RGS to FS, September 21, 1862, *BECF*, 241. On the fighting in the West Woods, see Hartwig, *I Dread the Thought of the Place*, 281–92.

25. RGS to FS, September 21, 1862, *BECF*, 240.

26. Wilder Dwight to Elizabeth A. Dwight, September 17, 1862, Theodore F. Dwight Papers, MHS.

27. RGS to SBS, September 25, 1862, *BECF*, 247.

28. Charles Morse to Mother, September 22, 1862, Charles F. Morse Papers, MHS.

29. On Confederate assessment of the Antietam Campaign, see Gary W. Gallagher, "Net Result of the Campaign," 3–43.

30. RGS to SBS, October 14, 1862, *BECF*, 253.

31. According to historian Frank J. Cirillo, abolitionists experienced a "crisis of coherence" over the proclamation's "dispiriting provisions" through to the end of 1862. These concerns, however, were not expressed by the Shaws. See Cirillo, *Abolitionist Civil War*, 151–52.

32. SBS to John Elliot Cairnes, October 16, 1862, in Weinberg, *John Elliot Cairnes*, 147.

33. Stewart, *Philanthropic Work*, 34.

34. RGS to SBS, September 25, 1862, *BECF*, 245.

35. James McPherson argues that Union armies experienced a "backlash" of anti-emancipation sentiment in the summer and fall of 1862. See McPherson, *For Cause and Comrades*, 12–23.

36. RGS to SBS, October 5, 1862, *BECF*, 252.

37. Charles Morse to Father, October 6, 1862, Charles F. Morse Papers, MHS.

38. Quint, *Potomac and the Rapidan*, 48, 170. On reactions to Lincoln's preliminary proclamation in the Army of the Potomac, see Fry, *Republic in the Ranks*, 49–50; Hartwig, *I Dread the Thought of the Place*, 733–38.

39. McPherson, *For Cause and Comrades*, 121. See also Manning, *What This Cruel War Was Over*, 53–80.

40. Military operations during the period after Antietam, through to the end of 1862 is covered in McPherson, *Battle Cry of Freedom*, 568–90; Stoker, *Grand Design*, 191–224; Murray and Hsieh, *Savage War*, 205–49.

41. RGS to SBS, October 14, 1862, *BECF*, 254.

42. RGS to JSL, October 13, 1862, Shaw Family Correspondence, New York Public Library.

43. RGS to JSL, November 21, 1862, *BECF*, 260.

44. Comey, *Legacy of Valor*, 78.

45. Charles Morse to Father, September 26, 1862, Charles F. Morse Papers, MHS.

46. James Kent Stone to Mother, October 9, 1862, copy of letter in possession of the author.

47. Burchard, *One Gallant Rush*, 68.

48. Quint, *Potomac and the Rapidan*, 223.

49. RGS to FS, November 13, 1862, *BECF*, 255. On reactions to McClellan's removal from command in the Army of the Potomac, see Fry, *Republic in the Ranks*, 59–65; Hartwig, *I Dread the Thought of the Place*, 774–78.

50. RGS to SBS, November 17, 1862, *BECF*, 257.

51. RGS to JSL, November 21, 1862, *BECF*, 259.

52. Russell Duncan suggests that a reference to a "private note" by Shaw in a letter written to his mother on November 17, 1862, indicates that he had already proposed to Annie. See *BECF*, 257n5.

53. RGS to SBS, November 21, 1862, *BECF*, 259.

54. RGS to AHS, December 18, 1862, *BECF*, 267.

55. RGS to AHS, November 21, 1862, *BECF*, 261.

56. Waugh, *Unsentimental Reformer*, 61.

57. RGS to SBS, December 1, 1862, *BECF*, 265.

58. RGS to AHS, November 28, 1862, *BECF*, 263.

59. RGS to AHS, November 28, 1862, *BECF*, 264.

60. RGS to AHS, November 28, 1862, *BECF*, 263.

61. Rable, *Fredericksburg! Fredericksburg!*, 132–55.

62. On the fighting at Fredericksburg, see Rable, *Fredericksburg! Fredericksburg!*

63. RGS to FS, December 18, 1862, *BECF*, 266.

64. The fighting of the 20th Massachusetts Infantry Regiment at Fredericksburg is covered in R. Miller, *Harvard's Civil War*, 181–216.

65. RGS to SBS, December 30, 1862, *BECF*, 273. On the skirmish at Whitehall, see Barrett, *Civil War in North Carolina*, 144–46.

66. RGS to AHS, December 18, 18652, *BECF*, 267.

67. RGS to JSL, December 23, 1862, *BECF*, 271–72.

CHAPTER 7

1. Massachusetts Historical Society, "Boston Music Hall: Grand Jubilee Concert, January 1, 1863," accessed December 11, 2023, www.masshist.org/database/viewer.php?item_id=2446; O'Connor, *Civil War Boston*, 127–28.

2. *Liberator* (Boston), June 9, 1863; Mayer, *All on Fire*, 545–47.

3. Douglass, *Life and Times of Frederick Douglass*, 342–46; Blight, *Frederick Douglass*, 382–84; Kantrowitz, *More Than Freedom*, 281–82.

4. Forten, *Journal of Charlotte L. Forten*, 172.

5. Quoted in Meyer, *Colonel of the Black Regiment*, 218–19.

6. Forten, *Journal of Charlotte L. Forten*, 172. On the ceremony, see Fields-Black, *Combee*, 252–52; Wise and Rowland, *Rebellion, Reconstruction, and Redemption*, 165–74.

7. RGS to SBS, January 8, 1863, *BECF*, 275–76.

8. RGS to SBS, January 8, 1863, *BECF*, 274–75.

9. RGS to AHS, January 10, 1863, *BECF*, 276–77.

10. RGS to SBS, January 8, 1863, *BECF*, 275.

11. RGS to AHS, January 10, 1863, *BECF*, 277.

12. Quoted in Burchard, *One Gallant Rush*, 70.

13. RGS to AHS, January 25, 1863, *BECF*, 279.

14. The regiment had been ordered to move toward Fredericksburg to support Burnside's offensive along the Rappahannock River at Fredericksburg.

15. On military operations around Fredericksburg in early 1863, see Rable, *Fredericksburg! Fredericksburg!*, 408–26.

16. Quoted in Nevins, *War for the Union*, 304.

17. On Andrew's wartime views of emancipation and the enlistment of African Americans, see Engle, *In Pursuit of Justice*, 166–67, 182–83.

18. Engle, *In Pursuit of Justice*, 235–37.

19. Egerton, *Thunder at the Gates*, 29–31.

20. Massachusetts Historical Society, "John A. Andrew to Francis Shaw, 30 January 1863," accessed December 15, 2023, www.masshist.org/database/viewer.php?item_id=1785&pid=3.

21. Charles Morse to Robert Morse, January 28, 1863, Charles F. Morse Papers, MHS.

22. This point is emphasized by Russell Duncan, *Where Death and Glory Meet*, 55.

23. John A. Andrew to RGS, January 30, 1863, Massachusetts Governor, Letter Official, 1861–1925, CMA.

24. Quoted in Foote, *Seeking the One Great Remedy*, 107.

25. Trudeau, *Like Men of War*, 12–18. On the Native Guard, see Cade, *Death or Victory*.

26. American Antiquarian Society, "Visions of Freedmen as Soldiers," accessed December 18, 2023, www.americanantiquarian.org/Freedmen/Intros/soldiers.html.

27. Quoted in J. D. Smith, *Lincoln and the U.S. Colored Troops*, 29–30.

28. RGS to AHS, February 4, 1863, *BECF*, 283.

29. Quoted in Burchard, *One Gallant Rush*, 73.

30. Russell Duncan, *Where Death and Glory Meet*, 58.

31. SBS to RGS, February 6, 1863, RGSL-HU.

32. Quoted in Bundy, *Nature of Sacrifice*, 258.

33. RGS to AHS, February 8, 1863, *BECF*, 285.

34. Charles Fessenden Morse to unknown recipient, February 8, 1863, in Morse, *Letters Written During the Civil War*, 119–20.

35. Charles Morse to RGS, February 8, 1863, Charles F. Morse Papers, MHS; RGS to AHS, February 8, 1863, *BECF*, 286–87. On the motivation of white officers to volunteer to command Black soldiers, see Glatthaar, *Forged in Battle*, 39–42. Wongsrichanalai explores the attitudes of young New England college graduates toward commanding Black soldiers in *Northern Character*, 150–54.

36. Higginson, *Four Addresses*, 90.

37. Quoted in *Memorial: RGS*, 6.

38. Charles Morse to RGS, February 8, 1863, Charles F. Morse Papers, MHS.

39. RGS to AHS, February 8, 1863, *BECF*, 286.

40. W. James, *Memories and Studies*, 18.

CHAPTER 8

1. RGS to AHS, February 16, 1863, *BECF*, 287.

2. RGS to FS, February 16, 1863, *BECF*, 288.

3. RGS to AHS, February 16, 1863, *BECF*, 287.

4. Hallowell, *Selected Letters and Papers of N. P. Hallowell*, 73.

5. Appleton's history is covered in Jewell and Van Sickle, *Waging War for Freedom*, 1–19; Russell Duncan, *Where Death and Glory Meet*, 64.

6. Susan Martin, "'As Drowning Men Catch at Straws': William H. Simpkins and the 54th Massachusetts Regiment," *The Beehive*, updated April 9, 2021, www.masshist.org/beehiveblog/2018/10/as-drowning-men-catch-at-straws-william-h-simpkins-and-the-54th-massachusetts-regiment.

7. Bellows, *Two Charlestonians at War*, 102. The Cabot Jackson Russell quote is from Martin, "'As Drowning Men Catch at Straws.'"

8. Quoted in Urwin, "I Want You to Prove Yourselves Men," 44; G. W. James, "Assault on Fort Wagner," 11–12.

9. RGS to John A. Andrew, April 4, 1863, Massachusetts Governor, Letters Official, 1861–1925, CMA.

10. Quoted in Russell Duncan, *Where Death and Glory Meet*, 60.

11. Newspaper clipping, Hallowell Scrapbook, vol. 2, box 2, folder 1, Norwood Penrose Hallowell Papers, MHS.

12. Witt, *Lincoln's Code*, 216; Levin, *Remembering the Battle of the Crater*, 25–27.

13. Quoted in Russell Duncan, *Where Death and Glory Meet*, 61.

14. Newspaper clipping, Hallowell Scrapbook, vol. 2, box 2, folder 1, Norwood Penrose Hallowell Papers, MHS. See Taylor, *Fighting for Citizenship*, 31–34.

15. Newspaper clipping, Hallowell Scrapbook, vol. 2, box 2, folder 1, Norwood Penrose Hallowell Papers, MHS. Rock is quoted in Kantrowitz, *More Than Freedom*, 282–84.

16. Stephen Kantrowitz, "Equality First, Guns Afterward," *New York Times*, March 1, 2013, https://archive.nytimes.com/opinionator.blogs.nytimes.com/2013/03/01/equality-first-guns-afterward/.goo.

17. On the experience of African American families during the antebellum period and how it influenced their view of the war and willingness to serve, see Pinheiro, *Families' Civil War*, 13–52; Mendez, *Great Sacrifice*, 11–28.

18. *Douglass' Monthly*, March 1863, quoted in McPherson, *Negro's Civil War*, 178.

19. Newspaper clipping, Hallowell Scrapbook, vol. 2, box 2, folder 2, Norwood Penrose Hallowell Papers, MHS.

20. Quoted in McPherson, *Negro's Civil War*, 177–78.

21. Emilio, *Brave Black Regiment*, 19.

22. RGS to FS, February 24, 1863, *BECF*, 298.

23. Russell Duncan, *Where Death and Glory Meet,* 70.

24. RGS to Charlie Morse, February 24, 1863, *BECF,* 297.

25. This profile draws heavily from Redkey, "Brave Black Volunteers," 22.

26. Redkey, "Brave Black Volunteers," 24.

27. Redkey, "Brave Black Volunteers," 24.

28. Yacovone, *Voice of Thunder,* 3–19.

29. Adams, *On the Altar of Freedom,* xv–xxxv.

30. Rhea, *Stephen A. Swails,* 1–5.

31. Blight, *Frederick Douglass,* 392; newspaper clipping, Hallowell Scrapbook, vol. 2, box 2, folder 2, Norwood Penrose Hallowell Papers, MHS.

32. Yacovone, *Voice of Thunder,* 33.

33. Russell Duncan, *Where Death and Glory Meet,* 67.

34. See RGS to Charlie Morse, February 21, 1863, *BECF,* 293; RGS to FS, February 25, 1863, *BECF,* 300; RGS to Charlie Morse, March 4, 1863, *BECF,* 305.

35. RGS to Charlie Morse, March 4, 1863, *BECF,* 304.

36. Lydia Maria Child, "A Tribute to Colonel Robert G. Shaw," in *Memorial: RGS,* 121.

37. Quoted in White, *House Built by Slaves,* xvii.

38. RGS to AHS, March 3, 1863, *BECF,* 302.

39. Newspaper clipping, Hallowell Scrapbook, vol. 2, box 2, folder 2, Norwood Penrose Hallowell Papers, MHS.

40. Massachusetts Historical Society, "Letter from Grace Heath to Francis Lee, 15 March 1863," accessed June 24, 2023, www.masshist.org/database/viewer.php?item_id=2450&pid=25.

41. RGS to Charlie Morse, March 4, 1863, *BECF,* 304; O'Connor, *Civil War Boston,* 141.

42. "How a Negro Regiment Looks," n.d., *Springfield (MA) Republican,* newspaper clipping, Hallowell Scrapbook, vol. 2, box 2, folder 5, Norwood Penrose Hallowell Papers, MHS.

43. RGS to Charlie Morse, March 4, 1863, *BECF,* 304.

44. RGS to AHS, March 14, 1863, *BECF,* 308; newspaper clipping, Hallowell Scrapbook, vol. 2, box 2, folder 2, Norwood Penrose Hallowell Papers, MHS.

45. RGS to FS, March 21, 1863, *BECF,* 311.

46. RGS to FS, March 30, 1863, *BECF,* 31–33; James Henry Gooding, *New-Bedford (MA) Mercury,* March 7, 1863; Gooding, *On the Altar of Freedom,* 5.

47. Gooding, *On the Altar of Freedom,* 6.

48. RGS to FS, March 21, 1863, *BECF,* 311; RGS to SBS, March 25, 1863, *BECF,* 313; Higginson, *Army Life in a Black Regiment,* 232.

49. Hallowell, *Negro as a Soldier,* 9; RGS to SBS, March 25, 1863, *BECF,* 313–14, 314n2.

50. RGS to FS, April 24, 1863, *BECF,* 325.

51. Bailey, "One of the Famous 54th Massachusetts," 163; RGS to FS, April 24, 1863, *BECF*; Appleton Scrapbook, 3, John W. Appleton Papers, West Virginia University. On Black deserters, see Glatthaar, *Forged in Battle,* 165.

52. "A Visit to the Camp of the 54th Massachusetts Regiment," *Weekly Anglo-African* (New York), March 28, 1863.

53. "How a Negro Regiment Looks," *Springfield (MA) Republican,* in *Memorial: RGS,* 18.

54. Newspaper clipping, Hallowell Scrapbook, vol. 2, box 2, folder 4, Norwood Penrose Hallowell Papers, MHS.

55. Werstein, *Storming of Fort Wagner*, 47–48.

56. "Speech of Frederick Douglass," *Liberator* (Boston), July 24, 1862.

57. Quoted in Weber, *Copperheads*, 86. On Northern racial attitudes see Escott, *"What Shall We Do with the Negro,"* 53–64.

58. Weber, *Copperheads*, 85; Gac, *Born in Blood*, 185–87.

59. RGS to FS, March 30, 1863, *BECF*, 316; RGS to SBS, April 1, 1863, *BECF*, 317.

60. RGS to SBS, April 1, 1863, *BECF*, 317.

61. RGS to FS, April 3, 1863, *BECF*, 321.

62. RGS to SBS, April 14, 1863, *BECF*; RGS to FS, April 24, 1863, *BECF*, 325.

63. Cecelski, *Fire of Freedom*, 71; Longacre, "Brave Radical Wild," 8–11.

64. Robert Gould Shaw to Governor John Andrew, April 6, 1863, Massachusetts Governor, Letters Official, 1861–1925, CMA.

65. Robert Gould Shaw to Governor John Andrew, April 6, 1863, Massachusetts Governor, Letters Official, 1861–1925, CMA.

66. John A. Andrew to RGS, April 7, 1863, Massachusetts Governor, Letters Official, 1861–1925, CMA.

67. Burchard, *One Gallant Rush*, 89.

68. RGS to Charlie Morse, May 3, 1863, *BECF*, 327.

69. RGS to Charlie Morse, May 3, 1863, *BECF*, 327.

70. The regiment's departure date would eventually take place on May 28, 1863.

71. RGS to FS, May 11, 1863, *BECF*, 329; Emilio, *Brave Black Regiment*, 328.

72. "Presentation of Colors to the Fifty-Fourth Regiment," newspaper clipping, Hallowell Scrapbook, vol 2, box 2, folder 5, Norwood Penrose Hallowell Papers, MHS; Burchard, *One Gallant Rush*, 91; Anna Cabot Lowell Diary, May 9, 1863, Lowell Family Papers, MHS.

73. Burchard, *One Gallant Rush*, 91–92; RGS to SBS, May 18, 1863, *BECF*, 332; newspaper clipping, Hallowell Scrapbook, vol. 2, box, 1, folder 5, Norwood Penrose Hallowell Papers, MHS. Shaw's speech can be found in, Shaw, *Souvenirs of the Massachusetts Fifty-Fourth (Colored) Regiment*, 5–6.

74. Newspaper clipping, Hallowell Scrapbook, vol. 2, box 1, folder 5, Norwood Penrose Hallowell Papers, MHS.

75. Newspaper clipping, Hallowell Scrapbook, vol. 2, box 1, folder 5, Norwood Penrose Hallowell Papers, MHS; Daniel F. Childs Diary, May 28, 1863, MHS. A map of the parade route can be found in Seasholes, *Atlas of Boston History*, 57.

76. Burchard, *One Gallant* Rush, 93; Nell quoted in Minardi, *Making Slavery History*, 166.

77. "The New England Anti-Slavery Convention," newspaper clipping, Hallowell Scrapbook, vol. 2, box 2, folder 7, Norwood Penrose Hallowell Papers, MHS.

78. Kennedy, *John G. Whittier*, 136.

79. Anna Cabot Lowell Diary, May 18, 1863, Lowell Family Papers, MHS.

80. Quoted in McKay, *When the Tide Turned in the Civil War*, 13.

81. Quoted in Burchard, *One Gallant Rush*, 94.

82. Hallowell, *Negro as a Soldier*, 7.

83. Newspaper clipping, Hallowell Scrapbook, vol. 2, box, 2, folder 6, Norwood Penrose Hallowell Papers, MHS.

84. "Departure of the Fifty-Fourth Regiment," newspaper clipping, Hallowell Scrapbook, vol 2, box, 2, folder 5, Norwood Penrose Hallowell Papers, MHS.

85. *National Anti-Slavery Standard* (New York), newspaper clipping, Hallowell Scrapbook, vol. 2, box 2, folder 6, Norwood Penrose Hallowell Papers, MHS.

86. In fact, the concern was so great that a planned march through New York City to encourage the recruitment of Black men was canceled due to concerns of violence.

87. Burchard, *One Gallant Rush*, 93.

88. Quoted in Engle, *In Pursuit of Justice*, 245.

89. Jones, *No Right to an Honest Living*, 251.

90. Digital Commonwealth, "Letter from Sarah Blake Sturgis Shaw, North Shore, to Lydia Maria Child, Sunday, [June 1863?]," accessed November 5, 2023, https://ark.digitalcommonwealth.org/ark:/50959/wm118c43t.

CHAPTER 9

1. RGS to AHS, June 1, 1863, *BECF*, 334–35.

2. Jewell and Van Sickle, *Waging War for Freedom*, 32–33; John Appleton to Wife, Mary, 29, 1863, John W. Appleton Papers, West Virginia University.

3. RGS to AHS, June 1, 1863, *BECF*, 334–35.

4. RGS to AHS, June 1, 1863, *BECF*, 335.

5. Emilio, *Brave Black Regiment*, 35.

6. On David S. Hunter, see E. Miller, *Lincoln's Abolitionist General*.

7. RGS to SBS, June 6, 1863, *BECF*, 340.

8. Jewell and Van Sickle, *Waging War for Freedom*, 36–37.

9. Emilio, *Brave Black Regiment*, 38.

10. Quoted in Wise and Rowland, *Rebellion, Reconstruction, and Redemption*, 29. On the initial occupation of Port Royal and the surrounding area, see Rose, *Rehearsal for Reconstruction*, 3–104; Foner, *Reconstruction*, 50–54; Fields-Black, *Combee*, 155–202.

11. On the early history of the Port Royal Experiment, see Rose, *Rehearsal for Reconstruction*, 3–63; O. V. Burton, *Penn Center*, 9–27; Cimprich, *Navigating Liberty*, 8–12; Wise, *Rebellion, Reconstruction, and Redemption*, 60–82.

12. O. V. Burton, Penn Center, 12–15.

13. Towne, *Letters and Diary of Laura M. Towne*, 8–9.

14. On the wide range of views held by reformers who traveled to Port Royal, see Cimprich, *Navigating Liberty*, 8–12.

15. Quoted in Emilio, *Brave Black Regiment*, 36–37.

16. Rose, *Rehearsal for Reconstruction*, 152–54.

17. Higginson's life is ably covered in Egerton, *Man on Fire*; Rose, *Rehearsal for Reconstruction*, 193–95.

18. Higginson, *Cheerful Yesterdays*, 257.

19. Wilson, "In the Shadow of John Brown," 310–11.

20. On the relationship between Brown and Montgomery in Kansas, see Mildfelt and Schafer, *Abolitionist of the Most Dangerous Kind*, 4 (Montgomery quote), 73–90.

21. Foote, *Rites of Retaliation*, 58.

22. On Montgomery's activities in Kansas, see Dirck, "By the Hand of God," 105–7. On Montgomery's views of African Americans, see Foote, *Rites of Retaliation*, 58–59; Mildfelt and Schafer, *Abolitionist of the Most Dangerous Kind*, 236–37.

23. Cornish, *Sable Arm*, 140.

24. See Foote, *Rites of Retaliation*, 65. On Montgomery's raids, see Conner, *James Montgomery*, 71–79; Mildfelt and Schafer, *Abolitionist of a Most Dangerous Kind*, 155–76.

25. Fields-Black, *Combee*, 218–19.

26. The Combahee River Raid is given exhaustive coverage in Fields-Black, *Combee*, 283–400. See also Mildfelt and Schafer, *Abolitionist of the Most Dangerous Kind*, 177–209.

27. "Colonel Montgomery's Official Report," *Rebellion Record: a Diary of American Events: Documents and Narratives*, vol. 7, ed. Frank Moore, accessed April 14, 2022, www.perseus.tufts.edu/hopper/text?doc=Perseus%3Atext%3A2001.05.0042.

28. Daniel Foster, "In Statu Quo," *Liberator* (Boston), June 19, 1863.

29. Quoted in Looby, *Complete Civil War Journal . . . of Thomas Wentworth Higginson*, 154.

30. RGS to FS, June 5, 1863, *BECF*, 339; RGS to SBS, June 6, 1863, *BECF*, 339.

31. RGS to FS, June 5, 1863, *BECF*, 339.

32. RGS to AHS, June 9, 1863, *BECF*, 341.

33. Jewell and Van Sickle, *Waging War for Freedom*, 47. Construction and maintenance of rice fields is given extensive coverage in Mart Stewart, *"What Nature Suffers to Groe,"* 98–150.

34. Buddy Sullivan, "Cotton Port on the Altamaha: A Historical and Archaeological Perspective of the Darien, Georgia Waterfront," folder 26, and "On the Georgia Tidewater: Loading Sea Island Cotton at Darien c. 1862," folder 27, both in Buddy Sullivan Papers, GHS; Spencer B. King, *Darien*, 66–67.

35. Lewis, *They Called Their Town Darien*, 52.

36. RGS to AHS, June 9, 1863, *BECF*, 342.

37. Emilio, *Brave Black Regiment*, 41.

38. RGS to AHS, June 9, 1862, *BECF*, 342.

39. Description of the looting of Darien can be found in RGS to AHS, June 9, 1863, *BECF*, 342; quoted in Emilio, *Brave Black Regiment*, 40–43.

40. Burchard, *One Gallant Rush*,109.

41. Burchard, *One Gallant Rush*, 108; Fields-Black, *Combee*, 406; Mildfelt and Schafer, *Abolitionist of the Most Dangerous Kind*, 215.

42. RGS to AHS, June 9, 1863, *BECF*, 343.

43. Emilio, *Brave Black Regiment*, 43.

44. John W. M. Appleton Diary, June 12, 1863, p. 23, box 3, John W. Appleton Papers, West Virginia University; Jewell and Van Sickle, *Waging War for Freedom*, 47–48.

45. Quoted in Burchard, *One Gallant Rush*, 110–11.

46. RGS to AHS, June 9, 1863, *BECF*, 343.

47. RGS to AHS, June 9, 1863, *BECF*, 343.

48. *OR*, Ser. I, vol. 14, 466–67.

49. Conner, *James Montgomery*, 99.

50. RGS to AHS, June 9, 1863, *BECF*, 345.

51. Quoted in *Hartford (CT) Weekly Intelligencer*, July 3, 1863; *New York Daily Tribune*, June 24, 1863.

52. RGS to AHS, June 9, 1863, *BECF*, 343.

53. Florida History Online, "Montgomery's Raids in Florida, Georgia, and South Carolina," accessed June 4, 2022, https://history.domains.unf.edu/floridahistoryonline/projects-proj-b-p-html/montgomery-index-html.

54. Quoted in Foote, *Rites of Retaliation*, 75; John W. Appleton Diary, June 12, 1863, pp. 25–25, box 3, John W. Appleton Papers, West Virginia University.

55. Adams, *On the Altar of Freedom*, 29–31.

56. Yacovone, *Voice of Thunder*, 241–42.

57. Quoted in Fields-Black, *Combee*, 403–4.

58. Frederick Douglass, letter-to-the-editor, *The Press*, typescript copy, Hallowell Scrapbook, vol. 2, box 2, folder 10, Norwood Penrose Hallowell Papers, MHS.

59. Foote draws similar conclusions about the men under Montgomery's command in the 2nd South Carolina Regiment. See Foote, *Rites of Retaliation*, 76–77.

60. RGS to AHS, June 9, 1863, *BECF*, 345.

CHAPTER 10

1. RGS to George C. Strong, July 6, 1863, in *Memorial: RGS*, 35.

2. King's time on St. Simons Island is detailed in her memoir, Taylor, *Black Woman's Civil War Memoirs*, 52; D. Williams, *Georgia's Civil War*, 141–45.

3. RGS to AHS, June 15, 1863, *BECF*, 349.

4. RGS to AHS, June 9, 1863, *BECF*, 344.

5. Bailey, *Weeping Time*, 3–20.

6. RGS to AHS, June 9, 1863, *BECF*, 344.

7. On slave rebellions at Hampton Plantation, see Mart Stewart, "*What Nature Suffers to Groe*," 175–76.

8. RGS to Clemence Haggerty, June 17, 1863, *BECF*, 350–51. Lincoln replaced Hunter on June 12, 1863, with Brig. Gen. Quincy Adams Gillmore.

9. RGS to SBS, June 18, 1863, *BECF*, 354.

10. RGS to Charles Morse, June 20, 1863, *BECF*, 356.

11. RGS to Charles Morse, June 20, 1863, *BECF*, 355.

12. RGS to Charles Russell Lowell, June 20, 1863, *BECF*, 356.

13. RGS to FS, June 22, 1863, *BECF*, 357.

14. RGS to SBS, June 28, 1863, *BECF*, 363.

15. Mildfelt and Schafer, *Abolitionist of the Most Dangerous Kind*, 217.

16. RGS to FS, June 24, 1863, *BECF*, 358.

17. Jewell and Van Sickle, *Waging War for Freedom*, 52–53.

18. Wise, *Gate of Hell*, 42–43.

19. O. V. Burton, *Penn Center*, 21.

20. RGS to SBS, July 3, 1863, *BECF*, 373.

21. RGS to AHS, June 26, 1863, *BECF*, 359–60.

22. Mann, "The 'Contact of Living Souls,'" 287.

23. Such a distinction is a reminder of J. Morris Copeland's plan in 1862 to raise a regiment made up of free Northern Blacks, as opposed to one composed of former slaves.

24. Shaw's observations of African Americans were shared by many in the army, including fellow Bostonian Charles Francis Adams Jr., who served as an officer in the First Massachusetts Cavalry. See Lang, *In the Wake of War*, 72–74.

25. Quoted in Emilio, *Brave Black Regiment*, 48. On the pay crisis, see Donald Yacovone, "The Fifty-Fourth Massachusetts Regiment, the Pay Crisis, and the 'Lincoln Despotism,'" in Blatt et al., *Hope and Glory*, 35–51.

26. Quoted in Emilio, *Brave Black Regiment*, 48; Jewell and Van Sickle, *Waging War for Freedom*, 55.

27. Aptheker, *Documentary History of the Negro People*, 482–84.

28. Yacovone, "The Fifty-Fourth Massachusetts Regiment," 50; Mendez, *Great Sacrifice*, 44–80; Pinheiro, *Families' Civil War*, 47–51.

29. O. V. Burton, *Penn Center*, 16–17; Charlotte Forten Grimké, "Life on the Sea Islands (Part I)," *Atlantic Monthly*, May 1864, www.theatlantic.com/magazine/archive/1864/05/life-on-the-sea-islands/308758.

30. RGS to SBS, July 3, 1863, *BECF*, 372.

31. Forten, *Journal of Charlotte L. Forten*, 211–12.

32. RGS to SBS, July 3, 1863, *BECF*, 373; Towne, *Letters and Diary of Laura M. Towne*, 115.

33. Quoted in Morris, *Yes, Lord, I Know the Road*, 111.

34. Forten, *Journal of Charlotte L. Forten*, 214.

35. Forten, *Journal of Charlotte L. Forten*, 214.

36. RGS to SBS, July 3, 1863, *BECF*, 372.

37. Quoted in Burchard, *One Gallant Rush*. 118.

38. RGS to AHS, July 9, 1863, *BECF*, 380.

39. *OR*, Ser. I, vol. 28, pt. I (Reports), 4.

40. Description of the islands and its defenses comes from Burchard, *One Gallant Rush*, 119; Wise, *Gate of Hell*, 6–32.

41. RGS to AHS, July 9, 1863, *BECF*, 380.

42. RGS to AHS, July 13, 1863, *BECF*, 383.

43. On the draft riots, see McPherson, *Battle Cry of Freedom*, 608–11.

44. Grover, *To Heal The Wounded Nation's Life*; Pinheiro, *Families' Civil War*, 13–33.

45. The fighting on James Island on July 16, 1863, is covered in Wise, *Gate of Hell*, 88–93; Trudeau, *Like Men of War*, 74–76.

46. Adams, *On the Altar of Freedom*, 37.

47. Russell Simmons to Mother, July 18, 1863, in *Memorial: RGS*, 45–46.

48. Quoted in Glatthaar, *Forged in Battle*, 136.

49. J. W. M Appleton, "That Night at Fort Wagner," *Putnam's Magazine* 19 (July 1869), 9–11.

50. Cabot Jackson Russell to Father, July 17, 1863, in *Memorial: RGS*, 45.

51. Adams, *On the Altar of Freedom*, 38.

52. *New York Herald*, August 1, 1863, newspaper clipping, Hallowell Scrapbook, vol 2, box 2, folder 11, Norwood Penrose Hallowell Papers, MHS.

53. *OR*, Ser. I, vol. 28, pt. I (Reports), 755.

54. RGS to AHS, July 15, 1863, *BECF*, 385.

CHAPTER 11

1. RGS to AHS, July 15, 1863, *BECF*, 385.

2. RGS to AHS, July 17, 1863, *BECF*, 386.

3. RGS to AHS, July 17, 1863, *BECF*, 386.

4. This story has been cited by numerous authors to add drama to Shaw's final day, but it is important to remember that while he anticipated some sort of military action on Morris Island, he had yet to receive any specific orders that would place his regiment in an assault that day. The story comes from a letter penned by Ned Hallowell that was published in the memorial volume dedicated to Shaw. Though Hallowell may have added his own dramatic touch to the story, there is little reason to deny its veracity. See *Memorial: RGS*, 165–66; Burchard, *One Gallant Rush*, 130–31.

5. The letter did not survive, but it is referenced in Caroline Wells Healey Dall's journal, August 6, 1863, Caroline Wells Healey Dall Papers, MHS.

6. "Characteristic physical features of Morris Island," in *OR*, Ser. I, vol. 28, pt. I (Reports), 14–15.

7. An eighty-man detail was also left on Morris Island at Lighthouse Inlet when the regiment first arrived. See Emilio, *Assault on Fort Wagner*, 8–9; Emilio, *Brave Black Regiment*, 392.

8. John W. Appleton, "Letter written at home, while wounded, after the battle of Fort Wagner, July 18th 1863," box 3, folder 13, 7–8, Caroline Wells Healey Dall Papers, MHS.

9. Special Order No. 9 of 17 July 1863 Morris Island, in *OR*, Ser. I, vol. 28, pt. II, 20; Gillmore, *Engineer and Artillery Operations*, 170–71.

10. Hess, *Field Armies and Fortifications in the Civil War*, 253; *OR*, Ser. I, vol. 28, pt. I (Reports), 12–15; Twiggs, *Defence of Battery Wagner*, 12–13; Wise, *Gate of Hell*, 95–96.

11. E. M. Burton, *Siege of Charleston*, 162. Confederate Brigadier General Taliaferro estimated that roughly nine thousand rounds were fired against the fort on July 18, 1863. See Gen. Beauregard's report of 1863 operations, *OR*, Ser. I, vol. 28, pt. I (Reports), 76.

12. Quincy A. Gillmore, "Report," in *Professional Papers of the Corps of Engineers*, 70–71; Dahlgren, *Memoir of John A. Dahlgren*, 403; Nathaniel Page, "Attack on Fort Wagner," *New York Daily Tribune*, August 1, 1863.

13. Emilio, *Assault on Fort Wagner*, 5–6; Eldridge, *Third New Hampshire*, 320.

14. Nathaniel Paige, "Testimony by a Special Correspondent of the New York Tribune before the American Freedmen's Inquiry Commission, [February?] 1864," in Berlin, Reidy, and Rowland, *Freedom's Soldiers*, 536.

15. Wise, *Gate of Hell*, 100.

16. Emilio, *Brave Black Regiment*, 75. We will never know Strong's side of the story since he died shortly after the assault on Fort Wagner.

17. RGS to AHS, July 17, 1863, *BECF*, 386.

18. "Extract from Letter of Adjutant James," in *Memorial: RGS*, 167.

19. *OR*, Ser. 1, vol. 28, pt. I (Reports), 13.

20. Emilio, *Brave Black Regiment*, 78. The lack of preparation on July 18 stands in sharp contrast with the plan prepared by General Terry for the third assault on Fort Wagner, in *OR*, Ser. I, vol. 28, pt. I (Reports), 208–9.

21. Twiggs, *Defence of Battery Wagner*, 11, 16–18; Hess, *Field Armies and Fortifications*, 253; Wise, *Gate of Hell*, 100.

22. Emilio, *Brave Black Regiment*, 73–78; Appleton, "That Night at Fort Wagner," 13.

23. Decades after the war, Harriet Tubman claimed to have served Shaw his final meal, just before the assault. It is unclear when during his time on Morris Island he would have had time for such a meal. See Larson, *Bound for the Promised Land*, 220, 386n102.

24. Emilio, *Brave Black Regiment*, 77–78.

25. John W. Appleton narrative "Letter," 166, typescript copy in Edwin Gittleman Research Materials, MHS.

26. Quoted in Burchard, *One Gallant Rush*, 136.

27. "Extract from Letter of Lieutenant-Colonel Hallowell," in *Memorial: RGS*, 166.

28. Adams, *On the Altar of Freedom*, 49–50.

29. Emilio, *Brave Black Regiment*, 78.

30. Emilio *Brave Black Regiment*, 79.

31. Wise, *Gate of Hell*, 102–3.

32. G. W. James, "Assault on Fort Wagner," 21–23.

33. "The Late Colonel Shaw," *Harper's Weekly*, August 15, 1863.

34. "Pope's Record," in Luis F. Emilio Papers I, MHS.

35. "Extract from Letter of Lieutenant-Colonel Hallowell," in *Memorial: RGS*, 166.

36. Wise, *Gate of Hell*, 103.

37. House Divided: The Civil War Research Engine at Dickinson College, "Edward L. Pierce to John A. Andrew, July 22, 1863," accessed March 4, 2022, https://hd.housedivided.dickinson.edu/node/40676.

38. *The Press*, August 21, 1863, newspaper clipping, Hallowell Scrapbook, vol. 2, box 2, folder 15, Norwood Penrose Hallowell Papers, MHS.

39. *Colored American* (Washington, DC), June 2, 1900.

40. *Boston Daily Journal*, July 29, 1863; Garth W. James letter, extract, in *Memorial: RGS*, 167; Iredell Jones, Fort Sumter letter, July 20, 1863, *Southern Historical Society Papers* 12 (January–December 1884), 138, https://hdl.handle.net/2027/coo.31924092916604?urlappend=%3Bseq=152%3Bownerid=13510798902296054-172. In his letter in the *Salem (MA) Register*, July 21, 1863, Emilio says only that "The Colonel was seen to fall inside the fort." Louis F. Emilio Papers IV, MHS.

41. Rhea, *Stephen A. Swails*, 40.

42. "When Col. Shaw Was Killed Attacking Battery Wagner," *Index-Journal* (Greenwood, SC), June 23, 1927. In addition, see correspondence between Hassell A. Simpson and Edwin Gittleman as well as Hassell Simpson, "Who Killed Colonel Shaw?" (unpublished manuscript), all in Edwin Gittleman Research Materials, MHS.

43. Captain John W. Appleton narrative of Fort Wagner, typescript copy in Edwin Gittleman Research Materials, MHS; Wise, *Gate of Hell*, 104–5.

44. Though his words vary, accounts of Carney's words can be found in his letter to Luis F. Emilio, reprinted in the *New York Globe*, June 7, 1884. In addition, see *National Tribune* (Washington, DC), January 5, 1893; and *Boston Herald*, January 10, 1898, both clippings in Luis F. Emilio Papers, IV, MHS.

45. Emilio, *Brave Black Regiment*, 87–88; Eldridge, *Third New Hampshire*, 316.

46. Quoted in Quarles, *Negro in the Civil War*, 17.

47. Wise, *Gate of Hell*, 112.

48. "Return of Casualties in the Union Forces," *OR*, Ser. I, vol. 28, pt. I (Reports), 210.

49. Wise, *Gate of Hell*, 114.

50. *Charleston (SC) Daily Courier*, July 21, 1863, quoted in Andrews, *South Reports the Civil War*, 323–25.

51. Newspaper clipping, Hallowell Scrapbook, vol. 2, box 2, folder 11, Norwood Penrose Hallowell Papers, MHS.

52. Teamoh, *Sketch of the Life and Death*, 42–43.

53. Egerton, *Thunder at the Gates*, 135; Faust, *This Republic of Suffering*, 79; Neff, *Honoring the Civil War Dead*, 62.

54. Egerton, *Thunder at the Gates*, 135.

55. Neff, *Honoring the Civil War Dead*, 63.

56. Quoted in McFeely, *Frederick Douglass*, 226.

57. Adams, *On the Altar of Freedom*, 41, 42.

58. Stephens quoted in Richards, *Battle Lines*, 108.

59. Quoted in Russell Duncan, *Where Death and Glory Meet*, 114.

60. Thanks to NPS historian Christopher Barr for pointing this out to me during a walking tour of Beaufort.

61. "The Attack on Fort Wagner," *Liberator* (Boston), August 7, 1863.

62. Forten, *Journal of Charlotte Forten*, 216.

CHAPTER 12

1. SBS to John Elliot Cairnes, November 2, 1863, in Weinberg, *John Elliot Cairnes*, 167.

2. Observations of the family come from Caroline Wells Healey Dall's journal, August 8, 1863, Caroline Wells Healey Dall Papers, MHS.

3. "The Wounded Officers of the Mass. 54th," *Boston Traveler*, July 28, 1863, 2; "The Report of Col. Shaw's Death," *Boston Daily Advertiser*, July 27, 1863, 2.

4. Charles Sumner to FS and SBS, July 29, 1863; Charles A. Dana to Francis and SBS, July 30, 1863; and Alexander Agassiz to FS, August 9, 1863, all in Shaw Family Letters, Boston Athenaeum.

5. Charlotte Forten to SBS, August 16, 1863, quoted in *Memorial: RGS*, 145–46.

6. Fredrickson, *Inner Civil War*, 152–53.

7. Newspaper clipping, *National Anti-Slavery Standard* (New York), Hallowell Scrapbook, vol. 2, box 1, folder 14; Newspaper clipping, *Boston Courier*, Hallowell Scrapbook, vol. 2, box 1, folder 12; and newspaper clipping, *The Press*, August 5, 1863, Hallowell Scrapbook, vol. 2, box 1, folder 12, all in Norwood Penrose Hallowell Papers, MHS.

8. Foote, *Seeking the One Great Remedy*, 119–20.

9. Frank Shaw quoted in Sinclair, *Aftermath of Slavery*, 27.

10. Weinberg, *John Elliot Cairnes*, 167.

11. G. W. James, "Assault on Fort Wagner," 27–28.

12. Quoted in Wixson, *Echoes from the Boys of Company "H,"* 216.

13. Scott, *Fallen Leaves*, 198–99.

14. Brasher, "Debating Black Manhood," 34.

15. Quoted in Brasher, "Debating Black Manhood," 35–36.

16. Foote, *Seeking the One Great Remedy*, 122.

17. *Memorial: RGS*, 78.

18. *Memorial: RGS*, 178.

19. Grover, *To Heal the Wounded Nation's Life*, 162–63. On the donations to the Shaw monument, see the newspaper clipping in Norwood Penrose Hallowell Scrapbooks, vol. 2, box 2, folder 36, Norwood Penrose Hallowell Papers, MHS.

20. Adams, *On the Altar of Freedom*, 66–67.

21. Grover, *To Heal the Wounded Nation's Life*, 127; Unfortunately, until 1920, the Shaw school was staffed almost exclusively by white teachers who imparted the Lost Cause narrative to their Black students. Kytle and Roberts, *Denmark Vesey's Garden*, 156.

22. Sarah Blake Shaw, "Robert Gould Shaw," in Higginson, *Harvard Memorial Biographies*, 183, 203–5 (references to Black soldiers), 209–11 (Shaw's burial).

23. Foote, *Seeking the One Great Remedy*, 121–22; *Memorial: RGS*, 195. On private attempts to memorialize fallen soldiers, see Clarke, *War Stories*, 28–50; SBS to John Elliot Cairnes, December 27, 1864, in Weinberg, *John Elliot Cairnes*, 172.

24. SBS to John Elliot Cairnes, January 30, 1864, in Weinberg, *John Elliott Cairnes*, 170.

25. Lydia Maria Child to SBS, January 17, 1864, Edwin Gittleman Research Materials, MHS; Moland, *Lydia Maria Child*, 420–21; Grover, *To Heal the Wounded Nation's Life*, 114–16.

26. Emerson, *Life and Letters of Charles Russell Lowell*, 286–87; Waugh, *Unsentimental Reformer*, 62–69; Bundy, *Nature of Sacrifice*, 262–80.

27. Waugh, *Unsentimental Reformer*, 78–82; Bundy, *Nature of Sacrifice*, 423–33. Quoted in Foote, *Seeking the One Great Remedy*, 133.

28. Cirillo, *Abolitionist Cause*, 250–52.

29. Emilio, *Brave Black Regiment*, 314.

30. Grover, *To Heal the Wounded Nation's Life*, 124–25.

31. Newspaper clipping, *Boston Evening Transcript*, Hallowell Scrapbook, vol. 2, box 3, folder 3, Norwood Penrose Hallowell Papers, MHS.

32. "The Fifty-Fourth Massachusetts," *New York Daily Tribune*, September 5, 1865; *Boston Daily Advertiser*, September 4, 1865; *Boston Commonwealth*, September 9, 1865.

33. "Monument to Colonel Shaw," *Boston Daily Advertiser*, October 2, 1865, 2.

34. O'Connor, *Civil War Boston*, 48.

35. "Speech of Joshua B. Smith before the Legislature of Massachusetts," *Boston Journal*, March 11, 1875, 1. The speech can also be found in Teamoh, *Sketch of the Life and Death*, 11.

36. See Kantrowitz, *More Than Freedom*, 316–28.

37. SBS to Charles Sumner, October 21, 1865, quoted in Grover, *To Heal the Wounded Nation's Life*, 178n58.

38. Lydia Maria Child to John B. Wight, December 12, 1874, Lydia Maria Child Collection, Wayland (MA) Historical Society. Daniel Tobias Hinchen, "A Treasure Rediscovered: The Civil War Sword of Robert Gould Shaw, 54th Regiment," *Massachusetts Historical Society* (blog), accessed February 4, 2024, www.masshist.org/beehiveblog/2017/07/a-treasure-rediscovered-the-civil-war-sword-of-robert-gould-shaw-54th-regiment. Shaw's sword was removed from his body after his death. It was later retrieved near Goldsboro, NC, by US Colored Troops under the command of Gen. Charles Jackson Paine and was returned to the Shaw family in 1865 by Capt. Solon A. Carter. The sword was later rediscovered by descendants of Shaw's sister Susannah and donated to the Massachusetts Historical Society, where it is currently on display.

39. Carmichael, "Trophies of Victory," 198–221.

40. Sarah's letter-to-the-editor appeared in *Harper's Weekly* on October 1, 1870; SBS to Reverend Robert F. Clute, August 29, 1870, typescript copy in Buddy Sullivan Papers, GHS.

41. SBS to Reverend Robert F. Clute, September 24, 1870; Sarah Blake Shaw to Reverend Robert F. Clute, November 25, 1870, typescript copies in Buddy Sullivan Papers, GHS; King, *Darien*, 93–96.

42. On the history of Reconstruction in Darien, Georgia, see Russell Duncan, *Freedom's Shore*.

43. Francis George Shaw to John Elliot Cairnes, July 10, 1865, in Weinberg, *John Elliot Cairnes*, 106.

44. See K. Williams, *I Saw Death Coming*; L. Williams, *Great South Carolina Ku Klux Klan Trials*.

45. Quoted in Grover, *To Heal the Wounded Nation's Life*, 110.

46. James M. Trotter, "An Original Poem. Fifty-Fourth at Wagner," *Boston Commonwealth*, December 8, 1883.

47. Greenidge, *Black Radical*, 17–29.

48. Halloran, *Thomas Nast*, 99.

49. Holzer and Neely, *Mine Eyes Have Seen the Glory*, 252–53. On Carney's postwar popularity, see Clavin, *Symbols of Freedom*, 203–8.

50. "Another Offer," *Richmond Planet*, June 8, 1895. See also Kachun, *Festivals of Freedom*, 166.

51. See Blight, *Race and Reunion*, 264–71; Cox, *No Common Ground*, 62–66.

52. In addition to the GAR posts, seven Woman's Relief Corps auxiliaries took Shaw's name as well. Grover, *To Heal the Wounded Nation's Life*, 128–29. On the history of the GAR, see Gannon, *Won Cause*.

53. Grover, *To Heal the Wounded Nation's Life*, 139.

54. Grover, *To Heal the Wounded Nation's Life*, 129–30; Hallowell quoted in *Daily Spy* (Worcester, MA), May 29, 1886.

55. See Kantrowitz, *More Than Freedom*, 407–13; Bergeson-Lockwood, *Race Over Party*, 135–44.

56. *Boston Herald*, August 2, 1887; *Boston Journal*, August 2, 1887.

57. Quoted in Grover, *To Heal the Wounded Nation's Life*, 132–33.

58. Faust, *This Republic of Suffering*, 217–18.

59. According to Grover, Edward Atkinson's list of donors does not include a single Black individual. See Grover, *To Heal the Wounded Nation's Life*, 178; Savage, *Standing Soldiers, Kneeling Slaves*, 197.

60. Saint-Gaudens, *Reminiscences of Augustus Saint-Gaudens*, 332.

61. See Augustus Saint-Gaudens to Josephine Shaw Lowell, October 26, 1883, Shaw Family Letters, Boston Athenaeum.

62. Saint-Gaudens, *Reminiscences of Augustus Saint-Gaudens*, 334–35. It is possible that Josephine returned to review the sculptor's progress more than once. On the sculpting of the Black soldiers, see Grover, *To Heal the Wounded Nation's Life*, 217–24.

63. Quoted in Kathryn Greenthal, "Augustus Saint-Gaudens and the Shaw Memorial," in Blatt et al., *Hope and Glory*, 127. In the end, only the names of the five white officers killed in the assault on Fort Wagner were included on the memorial. The names of the enlisted men killed were not added until the 1980s.

64. Saint-Gaudens, *Reminiscences of Augustus Saint-Gaudens*, 343.

65. Quoted in Grover, *To Heal the Wounded Nation's Life*, 228–29.

66. See Janney, *Remembering the Civil* War, 134–36; Blight, *Race and Reunion*, 77; Foster, *Ghosts of the Confederacy*, 36–46; Cox, *No Common Ground*, 41–45.

67. On depictions of the "faithful slave" on Confederate monuments, see Levin, *Searching for Black Confederates*, 97–99; McElya, *Clinging to Mammy*, 127–33; Janney, *Remembering the Civil War*, 261–65.

68. Savage, *Standing Soldiers, Kneeling Slaves*, 162–85; Cox, *Dixie's Daughters*, 60–72, 146–47. Statistics come from Cox, *No Common Ground*, 51.

69. Quoted in Grover, *To Heal the Wounded Nation's Life*, 231.

70. Quoted in Grover, *To Heal the Wounded Nation's Life*, 235.

71. Quoted in Grover, *To Heal the Wounded Nation's Life*, 237. On Washington's Atlanta speech, see Norrell, *Up from History*, 121–28.

72. Bergeson-Lockwood, *Race Over Party*, 182–86.

73. "Shaw's Memory Honored," *Boston Herald*, May 31, 1897; "They Shared Col. Shaw's Glory," *Boston Herald*, May 31, 1897.

74. Gerard S. Moser to Mrs. Dhalle, May 8, 1991, Edwin Gittleman Research Materials, MHS.

75. Saint-Gaudens, *Reminiscences of Augustus Saint-Gaudens*, 83.

76. "The Procession," *Boston Herald*, June 1, 1897.

77. Quoted in Grover, *To Heal the Wounded Nation's Life*, 271.

78. William James's address can be found in *Exercises at the Dedication of the Monument*, 39–56, 42 (quote).

79. Booker T. Washington's address can be found in *Exercises at the Dedication of the Monument*, 57–64.

80. *Exercises at the Dedication of the Monument*, 91–95.

81. "Freedom's Hero Honored," *Springfield (MA) Republican*, May 30, 1897.

82. Quoted in Grover, *To Heal the Wounded Nation's Life*, 301–2.

1. Green, *Unforgettable Sacrifice*, 3–7.

2. On race relations in Boston in the early twentieth century, see Schneider, *Boston Confronts Jim Crow*; Brown and Tager, *Massachusetts*, 243–52.

3. "Shaw's Nurse at Memorial," *Boston Herald*, May 31, 1905.

4. "At Shaw Monument," *Boston Herald*, June 1, 1909.

5. "Along the Route with the Marching Veterans," *Boston Globe*, August 22, 1917.

6. The most thorough study of Dixon's film's debut in Boston and the protests that ensued can be found in Lehr, *Birth of a Nation*.

7. "Elliot Says Play Falsifies History," *Boston Post*, May 3, 1915, 1, 2; Greenidge, *Black Radical*, 214; Lehr, *Birth of a Nation*, 228–33.

8. On Hine's life and career, see Sampsell-Willmann, *Lewis Hine as Social Critic*.

9. The statistics of terror were overwhelming: Between 1880 and 1930, white mobs lynched over 450 African Americans in Georgia alone. These were public executions designed to terrorize entire communities into accepting racial subordination. Atlanta itself had witnessed this systematic violence firsthand. On September 22, 1906, newspaper reports of four alleged assaults on white women by Black men triggered days of white mob violence that killed dozens of Black Atlantans, wounded scores more, and destroyed extensive property throughout the city's African American neighborhoods. On the Atlanta Race Massacre, see Link, *Atlanta*, 181–89.

10. "'Black American' Asks Passage of Anti-Bias Bill," *Boston Globe*, March 20, 1945, 1, 19.

11. "Negro Voter Drive at Evers Rites," *Boston Globe*, June 26, 1963, 8.

12. "We'll 'Catch Hell' Integrating Schools," *Boston Herald*, August 21, 1963; "Peabody Unit Urges School 'Rights' Study," *Boston Record American*, August 21, 1963; "500 in Fraternity March on Hub School Hqs.," *Boston Traveler*, August 20, 1963.

13. "Sargent, White Fail to Meet Bus Protesters," *Boston Herald*, April 4, 1973; "History of Abuse repeated," *Boston Herald*, October 20, 1979.

BIBLIOGRAPHY

PRIMARY SOURCES

Manuscript and Archival Collections

Boston, MA
- Boston Athenaeum
  - Shaw Family Letters
- Commonwealth of Massachusetts Archives
  - Massachusetts Governor, Letters Official, 1861–1925
- Massachusetts Historical Society
  - Caroline Wells Healey Dall Papers
  - Charles F. Morse Papers
    - Anna Cabot Lowell Diary
  - Charles Sedgwick Papers
  - Daniel F. Childs Diary
  - Edwin Gittleman Research Materials
  - Francis Lee Papers
  - James Russell Lowell Papers
  - John A. Andrew Papers
  - John Murray Forbes Papers
  - Lowell Family Papers
  - Luis F. Emilio Papers
  - Norwood Penrose Hallowell Papers
  - Records of the 54h Massachusetts Volunteer Infantry Regiment
  - Theodore F. Dwight Papers

Cambridge, MA
Houghton Library, Harvard University
Frank Vizetelly, Sketches
Index to University Records, 1636–1870 and Sibley's Private Journal, 1847–82
Louisa Jay Barlow, "Notes for a Biography of Rob Gould Shaw"
Robert Gould Shaw Letters
Sarah Blake Sturgis Shaw Papers
Morgantown, WV
West Virginia University
John W. Appleton Papers
New York, NY
New York Public Library
Shaw Family Correspondence
Savannah, GA
Georgia Historical Society
Buddy Sullivan Papers
Wayland, MA
Wayland Free Public Library
Lydia Maria Child Collection

Newspapers and Periodicals

Boston Commonwealth
Boston Daily Advertiser
Boston Daily Journal
Boston Herald
Boston Journal
Cape Ann Light and Gloucester (MA) Telegraph
Charleston (SC) Daily Courier
Colored American (Washington, DC)
The Congregationalist
Daily Spy (Worcester, MA)
Douglass' Monthly
Harper's Weekly
Hartford (CT) Weekly Intelligencer
The Index-Journal (Greenwood, SC)
The Liberator (Boston)
Massachusetts Spy (Boston)
National Anti-Slavery Standard (New York)
National Tribune (Washington, DC)
New-Bedford (MA) Mercury
New York Daily Tribune
New York Globe
New York Herald
New York Times
Post and Courier (Charleston, SC)
Salem (MA) Register
Southern Historical Society Papers
Springfield (MA) Republican
Weekly Anglo-African (New York)

Acken, J. Gregory, ed. *Through Blood and Fire: The Civil War Letters of Major Charles J. Mills, 1862–1865*. Kent: Kent State University Press, 2023.

Adams, Virginia M., ed. *On the Altar of Freedom: A Black Soldier's Civil War Letters from the Front, Corporal James Henry Gooding*. Amherst: University of Massachusetts Press, 1991.

Appleton, J. W. M. "That Night at Fort Wagner." *Putnam's Magazine* 19 (July 1869): 9–16.

Barber, Samuel ed., *A View of Boston Common: A Diary of Notable Events, Incidents, and Neighboring Occurrences*. Mount Pleasant, SC: Arcadia, 2017.

Bayles, Richard M., ed. *History of Richmond County (Staten Island) New York from Its Discovery to the Present Time*. New York: L. E. Preston, 1887.

Bowen, James L. *Massachusetts in the Civil War. 1861–1865*. Springfield, MA: Bryan, 1889.

Clark, Emmons. *History of the Seventh Regiment of New York, 1806–1889*. 2 vols. New York: Published by the author, 1890.

Comey, Richard Lyman, ed. *A Legacy of Valor: The Memoirs and Letters of Captain Henry Newton Comey, 2nd Massachusetts Infantry*. Knoxville: University of Tennessee Press, 2004.

Copeland, R. Morris. *Statement of R. Morris Copeland*. Boston: Prentiss and Deland, 1864.

Dahlgren, Madeleine Vinton. *Memoir of John A. Dahlgren, Rear-Admiral United States Navy*. Boston: James R. Osgood, 1882.

Donovan, Charles F. *Joseph Coolidge Shaw: Boston Yankee, Jesuit, Early Boston College Patron*. Boston: Boston College, 1990.

Douglass, Frederick. *Life and Times of Frederick Douglass*. Hartford, CT: Park, 1882.

Dwight, Elizabeth, ed. *Life and Letters of Wilder Dwight, Lieut.-Col. Second Mass. Inf. Vols.* Boston: Ticknor and Fields, 1868.

Eldridge, D. *The Third New Hampshire and All About It*. Boston: E. B. Stilling, 1893.

Emerson, Edward Waldo, ed. *Life and Letters of Charles Russell Lowell*. 1907. Reprint, Columbia: University of South Carolina Press, 2005.

Emilio, Luis F. *The Assault on Fort Wagner*. Boston: Rand Avery, 1887.

Emilio, Luis F. *A Brave Black Regiment: The History of the 54th Massachusetts, 1863–1865*. 1894. Reprint, New York: Da Capo Press, 1995.

Exercises at the Dedication of the Monument to Colonel Robert Gould Shaw. Boston: Municipal Printing Office, 1897.

Forten, Charlotte L. *The Journal of Charlotte L. Forten*. Edited by Ray Allen Billington. New York: W. W. Norton, 1981.

Frost, Jennett Blakeslee. *The Rebellion of the United States*. New York: Degen Estes and Priest, 1862.

Garrison, Wendell Phillips, and William Lloyd Garrison. *William Lloyd Garrison, 1805–1879: The Story of His Life Told by His Children*. Vol. 3, *1841–1860*. New York: Century Co., 1885.

Gillmore, Quincy Adams. *Engineer and Artillery Operations Against the Defences of Charleston Harbor in 1863*. New York: D. Van Nostrand, 1865.

Gordon, George Henry. *Brook Farm to Cedar Mountain*. New York: Houghton, Mifflin, 1885.

Gordon, George Henry. *History of the Second Massachusetts Regiment of Infantry*. Boston: Alfred Mudge & Sons, 1875.
Hallowell, Norwood P. *The Negro as a Soldier in the War of the Rebellion*. Boston: Little Brown, 1897.
Hallowell, Norwood P. *Selected Letters and Papers of N. P. Hallowell*. Peterborough, NH: Richard R. Smith, 1963.
Harvard College. *Report of the Class of 1860*. Cambridge, MA: John Wilson and Son, 1895.
Higginson, Thomas Wentworth. *Army Life in a Black Regiment*. Boston: Houghton, Mifflin, 1900.
Higginson, Thomas Wentworth. *Cheerful Yesterdays*. Boston: Houghton, Mifflin, 1898.
Higginson, Thomas Wentworth. *Four Addresses*. Boston: Merrymount, 1902.
Higginson, Thomas Wentworth. *Harvard Memorial Biographies*. Cambridge, MA: Sever and Francis, 1866.
James, Garth W. "The Assault upon Fort Wagner." In *War Papers Read Before the Commandery of the State of Wisconsin, Military Order of the Loyal Legion of the U.S.* Milwaukee: Burdick, Armitage and Allen, 1891.
James, William. *Memories and Studies*. New York: Longmans, Green, 1911.
Jewell, James Robbins, and Eugene S. Van Sickle, eds. *Waging War for Freedom with the 54th Massachusetts: The Civil War Memoir of John W. M. Appleton*. Lincoln: Potomac Books, 2025.
Karcher, Carolyn K., ed. *Lydia Maria Child Reader*. Durham, NC: Duke University Press, 1997.
Kemble, Frances, Ann. *Records of Later Life*. New York: Henry Holt and Company, 1883.
Looby, Christopher, ed. *The Complete Civil War Journal and Selected Letters of Thomas Wentworth Higginson*. Chicago: University of Chicago Press, 2000.
Memorial: RGS. Cambridge, MA: Harvard University Press, 1864.
The Monument to Robert Gould Shaw: Its Conception, Completion and Unveiling, 1865–1897. Boston: Houghton, Mifflin and Company, 1897.
Moore, Frank ed. *The Rebellion Record: A Diary of American Events*. Vol. 5. New York: G. P. Putnam, 1864.
Morris, J. Brent, ed. *Yes, Lord, I Know the Road: A Documentary History of African Americans in South Carolina, 1526–2008*. Columbia: University of South Carolina Press, 2017.
Morse, Charles F. *Letters Written During the Civil War, 1861–1865*. Boston: Privately printed, 1898.
Professional Papers of the Corps of Engineers of the United States Army. Washington, DC: Government Printing Office, 1872.
Public Documents of Massachusetts: Being the Annual Reports of Various Public Officers and Institutions. Boston: Wright and Potter, 1864.
Quincy, Josiah ed. *The Journals of Major Samuel Shaw*. Boston: W. M. Crosby and H. P. Nichols, 1847.
Quint, Alonzo Hall. *The Potomac and the Rapidan: Army Notes, from the Failure at Winchester to the Reenforcements of Rosecrans, 1861–3*. Boston: Crosby and Nichols, 1864.

Quint, Alonzo Hall. *The Record of the Second Massachusetts Infantry, 1861–65*. Boston: James P. Walker, 1867.

Russell, William Howell. *My Diary North and South*. 1863. Reprint, Baton Rouge: Louisiana State University Press, 1988.

Saint-Gaudens, Homer, ed. *The Reminiscences of Augustus Saint-Gaudens*. 2 vols. New York: Century, 1913.

Samito, Christian G, ed. *"Fear Was Not in Him": The Civil War Letters of Major General Francis C. Barlow, U.S.A.* New York: Fordham University Press, 2004.

Scott, Robert Garth, ed. *Fallen Leaves: The Civil War Letters of Major Henry Livermore Abbott*. Kent: Kent State University Press, 1991.

Shaw, Francis. *A Biographical Sketch of Robert Gould Shaw*. Boston: New-England Historic Genealogical Society, 1880.

Shaw, Robert Gould. *Blue-Eyed Child of Fortune: The Civil War Letters of Colonel Robert Gould Shaw*. Edited by Russell Duncan. Athens: University of Georgia Press, 1992.

Shaw, Robert Gould. *Letters: RGS*. New York: Collins and Brothers, 1876.

Shaw, Robert Gould. *Souvenirs of the Massachusetts Fifty-Fourth (Colored) Regiment*. Boston: 1863.

Stewart, William R. *The Philanthropic Work of Josephine Shaw Lowell*. New York: Macmillan, 1911.

Swinton, William. *History of the Seventh Regiment National Guard, State of New York, During the War of the Rebellion*. New York: Dillingham, 1886.

Taylor, Susie King. *A Black Woman's Civil War Memoirs: Reminiscences of My Life in Camp with the 33rd U.S. Colored Troops, Late 1st South Carolina Volunteers*. Edited by Patricia W. Romero and Willie Lee Rose. Princeton: Markus Wiener Publishers, 1997.

Teamoh, Robert T. *Sketch of the Life and Death of Colonel Robert Gould Shaw*. Boston: Boston Globe, 1904.

Towne, Laura M. *Letters and Diary of Laura M. Towne*. Edited by Holland, Rupert Sargent. 1912. Reprint, North Charleston: Palmetto, 2019.

Twiggs, Hansford D. D. *Defence of Battery Wagner, July 18, 1863*. Augusta, GA: Chronicle, 1892.

US War Department. *The War of the Rebellion: A Compilation of the Official Records of the Union and Confederate Armies*. 128 vols. Washington, DC: US Government Printing Office, 1880–1901.

Walker, David. *An Appeal to the Colored Citizen of the World*. Boston: 1830. Reprint: New York: Hill & Wang, 1995.

Weinberg, Adelaide. *John Elliot Cairnes and the American Civil War: A Study in Anglo-American Relations*. London: Kingswood Press, 1969.

White, Jonathan W., and Lydia L. Davis, eds. *My Work Among the Freedmen: The Civil War and Reconstruction Letters of Harriet M. Buss*. Charlottesville: University of Virginia Press, 2021.

Wixon, Neal E. ed. *Echoes from the Boys of Company H*. Bloomington, IN: iUniverse, 2008.

Yacovone, Donald, ed. *A Voice of Thunder: The Civil War Letters of George E. Stephens*. Urbana: University of Illinois Press, 1997.

SECONDARY SOURCES

Books

Amory, Cleveland. *The Proper Bostonians*. Madison: E. P. Dutton, 1957.

Andrews, J. Cutler. *The South Reports the Civil War*. Princeton, NJ: Princeton University Press, 1970.

Aptheker, Herbert. *A Documentary History of the Negro People in the United States: From Colonial Times Through the Civil War*. New York: Citadel Press, 1962.

Asch, Chris Myers, and George Derek Musgrove. *Chocolate City: A History of Race and Democracy in the Nation's Capital*. Chapel Hill: University of North Carolina Press, 2017.

Bailey, Anne C. *The Weeping Time: Memory and the Largest Slave Auction in American History*. Cambridge: Cambridge University Press, 2017.

Barrett, John G. *The Civil War in North Carolina*. Chapel Hill: University of North Carolina Press, 1963.

Bellows, Barbara L. *Two Charlestonians at War: The Civil War Odysseys of a Lowcountry Aristocrat and a Black Abolitionist*. Baton Rouge: Louisiana State University Press, 2018.

Bennett, Chet. *Resolute Rebel: General Roswell S. Ripley, Charleston's Gallant Defender*. Columbia: University of South Carolina Press, 2017.

Bergeson-Lockwood, Millington W. *Race Over Party: Black Politics and Partisanship in Late Nineteenth-Century Boston*. Chapel Hill: University of North Carolina Press, 2018.

Berlin, Ira, Joseph P. Reidy, and Leslie S. Rowland, eds. *Freedom's Soldiers: The Black Military Experience in the Civil War Era*. Cambridge: Cambridge University Press, 1998.

Bever, Megan L., Lesley Gordon, and Laura Mammina, eds. *American Discord: The Republic and Its People in the Civil War Era*. Baton Rouge: Louisiana State University Press, 2020.

Blair, William. *Virginia's Private War: Feeding Body and Soul in the Confederacy, 1861–1865*. New York: Oxford University Press, 1998.

Blatt, Martin H., Thomas J. Brown, and Donald Yacovone, eds. *Hope and Glory: Essays on the Legacy of the 54th Massachusetts Regiment*. Amherst: University of Massachusetts Press, 2001.

Bledsoe, Andrew S. *Citizen-Officers: The Union and Confederate Volunteer Junior Officer Corps in the American Civil War*. Baton Rouge: Louisiana State University Press, 2015.

Blight, David W. *Frederick Douglass: Prophet of Freedom*. New York: Simon and Schuster, 2018.

Blight, David W. *Race and Reunion: The Civil War in American Memory*. Cambridge, MA: Harvard University Press, 2001.

Boatner, Mark M., III. *The Civil War Dictionary*. New York: Random House. 1959.

Boles, John B. *Jefferson: Architect of American Liberty*. New York: Basic Books, 2017.

Brasher, Glenn David. *The Peninsula Campaign and the Necessity of Emancipation: African Americans and the Fight for Freedom*. Chapel Hill: University of North Carolina Press, 2012.

Brooke, John L. *"There Is a North": Fugitive Slaves, Political Crisis, and Cultural Transformation in the Coming of the Civil War*. Amherst: University of Massachusetts Press, 2019.

Brown, Richard D. and Jack Tager. *Massachusetts: A Concise History.* Amherst: University of Massachusetts Press 2000.

Bundy, Carol. *The Nature of Sacrifice: A Biography of Charles Russell Lowell, Jr., 1835–64.* New York: Farrar, Straus and Giroux, 2005.

Burchard, Peter. *One Gallant Rush.* New York: St. Martin's Press, 1965.

Burton, E. Milby. *The Siege of Charleston, 1861–1865.* Columbia: University of South Carolina Press, 1970.

Burton, Orville Vernon. *Penn Center: A History Preserved.* Athens: University of Georgia Press, 2014.

Cade, A. J. *Death or Victory: The Louisiana Native Guards and The Black Military's Significance in the Civil War.* Baton Rouge: Louisiana State University Press, 2026.

Carmichael, Peter S. *The War for the Common Soldier: How Men Thought, Fought, and Survived in Civil War Armies.* Chapel Hill: University of North Carolina Press, 2018.

Cecelski, David S. *The Fire of Freedom: Abraham Galloway and the Slaves' Civil War.* Chapel Hill: University of North Carolina Press, 2012.

Cimprich, John. *Navigating Liberty: Black Refugees and Antislavery Reformers in the Civil War South.* Baton Rouge: Louisiana State University Press, 2023.

Cirillo, Frank J. *The Abolitionist Civil War: Immediatists and the Struggle to Transform the Union.* Baton Rouge: Louisiana State University Press, 2023.

Clark, Justin T. *City of Second Sight: Nineteenth-Century Boston and the Making of American Visual Cultures.* Chapel Hill: University of North Carolina Press, 2018.

Clarke, Frances M. *War Stories: Suffering and Sacrifice in the Civil War North.* Chicago: University of Chicago Press, 2011.

Clavin, Matthew J. *Symbols of Freedom: Slavery and Resistance Before the Civil War.* New York: New York University Press, 2023.

Clinton, Catherine. *Fanny Kemble's Civil War: The Story of America's Most Unlikely Abolitionist.* New York: Simon and Schuster, 2000.

Conner, Robert C. *James Montgomery: Abolitionist Warrior.* Philadelphia: Casemate, 2022.

Cornish, Dudley T. *The Sable Arm.* New York: Longmans Green & Co., 1956.

Cox, Karen L. *Dixie's Daughters: The United Daughters of the Confederacy and the Preservation of Confederate Culture.* Gainesville: University Press of Florida, 2003.

Cox, Karen L. *No Common Ground: Confederate Monuments and the Ongoing Fight for Racial Justice.* Chapel Hill: University of North Carolina Press, 2021.

Cozzens, Peter. *Shenandoah 1862: Stonewall Jackson's Valley Campaign.* Chapel Hill: University of North Carolina Press, 2008.

Crawford, Mary Caroline. *Famous Families of Massachusetts.* Boston: Little Brown, 1930.

Crawford, Mary Caroline. *Romantic Days in Old Boston: The Story of the City and of Its People During the Nineteenth Century.* New York: Little Brown, 1910.

Delano, Sterling F. *Brook Farm: The Dark Side of Utopia.* Cambridge, MA: Harvard University Press, 2004.

Dickens, Charles. *American Notes for General Circulation and Pictures from Italy.* London: Chapman and Hall, 1913.

Duncan, Richard R. *Beleaguered Winchester: A Virginia Community at War, 1861–1865.* Baton Rouge: Louisiana State University Press, 2007.

Duncan, Russell. *Freedom's Shore: Tunis Campbell and the Georgia Freedmen*. Athens: University of Georgia Press, 1986.

Duncan, Russell. *Where Death and Glory Meet: Colonel Robert Gould Shaw and the 54th Massachusetts Infantry*. Athens: University of Georgia Press, 1999.

Dyer, Frederick H. *A Compendium of the War of the Rebellion*. Des Moines: Dyer, 1908.

Egerton, Douglas R. *A Man on Fire: The Worlds of Thomas Wentworth Higginson*. New York: Oxford University Press, 2024.

Egerton, Douglas R. *Thunder at the Gates: The Black Civil War Regiments That Redeemed America*. New York: Basic Books, 2016.

Engle, Stephen D. *In Pursuit of Justice: The Life of John Albion Andrew*. Amherst: University of Massachusetts Press, 2023.

Escott, Paul D. *"What Shall We Do with the Negro": Lincoln, White Racism, and Civil War America*. Charlottesville: University of Virginia Press, 2009.

Faust, Drew G. *This Republic of Suffering: Death and the American Civil War*. New York: Knopf, 2008.

Fields, Barbara Jeanne. *Slavery and Freedom on the Middle Ground: Maryland During the Nineteenth Century*. New Haven, CT: Yale University Press, 1985.

Fields-Black, Edda L. *Combee: Harriet Tubman, the Combahee River Raid, and Black Freedom During the Civil War*. New York: Oxford University Press, 2024.

Foner, Eric. *Reconstruction: America's Unfinished Revolution, 1863–1877*. New York: Harper and Row, 1988.

Foote, Lorien. *The Gentlemen and the Roughs: Violence, Honor, and Manhood in the Union Army*. New York: New York University Press, 2010.

Foote, Lorien. *Rites of Retaliation: Civilization, Soldiers, and Campaigns in the American Civil War*. Chapel Hill: University of North Carolina Press, 2021.

Foote, Lorien. *Seeking the One Great Remedy: Francis George Shaw and Nineteenth-Century Reform*. Athens: Ohio University Press, 2003.

Foster, Gaines M. *Ghosts of the Confederacy: Defeat, the Lost Cause, and the Emergence of the New South*. New York: Oxford University Press, 1987.

Fox, Richard Whitman. *Lincoln's Body: A Cultural History*. New York: Norton, 2015.

Fredrickson, George M. *The Inner Civil War: Northern Intellectuals and the Crisis of the Union*. New York: Harper and Row, 1965.

Fry, Zachary A. *A Republic in the Ranks: Loyalty and Dissent in the Army of the Potomac*. Chapel Hill: University of North Carolina Press, 2020.

Gac, Scott. *Born in Blood: Violence and the Making of America*. Cambridge: Cambridge University Press, 2024.

Gallagher, Gary W. *Causes Won, Lost, and Forgotten: How Hollywood and Popular Art Shape What We Know About the Civil War*. Chapel Hill: University of North Carolina Press, 2008.

Gallagher, Gary W., ed. *The Shenandoah Valley Campaign of 1862*. Chapel Hill: University of North Carolina Press, 2003.

Gallagher, Gary W. *The Union War*. Cambridge, MA: Harvard University Press, 2011.

Gannon, Barbara A. *Americans Remember Their Civil War*. Santa Barbara: Praeger, 2017.

Gannon, Barbara A. *The Won Cause: Black and White Comradeship in the Grand Army of the Republic*. Chapel Hill: University of North Carolina Press, 2011.

Glatthaar, Joseph T. *Forged in Battle: The Civil War Alliance of Black Soldiers and White Officers*. New York: Meridian, 1991.

Goodheart, Adam. *1861: The Civil War Awakening*. New York: Knopf, 2011.

Green, Hilary N. *Unforgettable Sacrifice: How Black Communities Remembered the Civil War*. New York: Fordham University Press, 2025.

Greenhough, Sarah, and Nancy K. Anderson. *Tell It with Pride: The 54th Massachusetts Regiment and Augustus Saint-Gaudens' Shaw Memorial*. New Haven: Yale University Press, 2013.

Greenidge, Kerri K. *Black Radical: The Life and Times of William Monroe Trotter*. New York: Liveright, 2020.

Grimsley, Mark. *The Hard Hand of War: Union Military Policy Toward Southern Civilians, 1861–1865*. Cambridge: Cambridge University Press, 1995.

Groeling, Meg. *First Fallen: The Life of Colonel Elmer Ellsworth, the North's First Civil War Hero*. El Dorado Hills, CA: Savas Beatie, 2021.

Gross, Robert A. *The Transcendentalists and Their World*. New York: Farrar, Straus and Giroux, 2021.

Grover, Kathryn. *To Heal the Wounded Nation's Life: African Americans and the Robert Gould Shaw/54th Regiment Memorial*. Cornish, NH: Saint-Gaudens National Historical Park, 2021. https://npshistory.com/publications/saga/shs-shaw-54th-reg-mem.pdf.

Guelzo, Allen C. *Lincoln and Douglas: The Debates That Defined America*. New York: Simon and Schuster, 2008.

Gugliotta, Guy. *Freedom's Cap: The United States Capitol and the Coming of the Civil War*. New York: Hill and Wang, 2012.

Halloran Fiona Dean. *Thomas Nast: The Father of Modern Political Cartoons*. Chapel Hill: University of North Carolina Press, 2012.

Hardesty, Jared Ross. *Black Lives, Native Lands, White Worlds: A History of Slavery in New England*. Amherst, MA: Brightleaf, 2019.

Harsh, Joseph L. *Taken at the Flood: Robert E. Lee and Confederate Strategy in the Maryland Campaign*. Kent, OH: Kent State University Press, 1999.

Hartwig, D. Scott. *I Dread the Thought of the Place: The Battle of Antietam and the End of the Maryland Campaign*. Baltimore, MD: Johns Hopkins University Press, 2023.

Hartwig, D. Scott. *To Antietam Creek: the Maryland Campaign of September 1862*. Baltimore, MD: Johns Hopkins University Press, 2012.

Harvard University Presidential Committee on Harvard and the Legacy of Slavery. *Legacy of Slavery at Harvard: Report and Recommendations of the Presidential Committee*. Cambridge, MA: Harvard University Press, 2022.

Hennessy, John J. *Return to Bull Run: The Campaign and Battle of Second Manassas*. New York: Simon and Schuster, 1993.

Hess, Earl J. *Field Armies and Fortifications in the Civil War*. Chapel Hill: University of North Carolina Press, 2005.

Hirota, Hidetaka. *Expelling the Poor: Atlantic Seaboard States and the 19th-Century Origins of American Immigration Policy*. New York: Oxford University Press, 2017.

Holzer, Harold, and Mark E. Neely. *Mine Eyes Have Seen the Glory: The Civil War in Art*. New York: Orion Books, 1993.

Janney, Caroline E. *Remembering the Civil War: Reunion and the Limits of Reconciliation.* Chapel Hill: University of North Carolina Press, 2013.

Janney, Caroline E., and Kathryn J. Shively, eds. *The Second Manassas Campaign.* Chapel Hill: University of North Carolina Press, 2025.

Jones, Jacqueline. *No Right to an Honest Living: The Struggles of Boston's Black Workers in the Civil War Era.* New York: Basic Books, 2023.

Kachun, Mitch. *Festivals of Freedom: Memory and Meaning in African American Emancipation Celebrations, 1808–1915.* Amherst: University of Massachusetts Press, 2003.

Kantrowitz, Stephen. *More Than Freedom: Fighting for Black Citizenship in a White Republic, 1829–1889.* New York: Penguin Press, 2012.

Kennedy, William Sloane. *John G. Whittier: The Poet of Freedom.* New York: Funk & Wagnalls, 1892.

Kilbride, Daniel. *Being American in Europe, 1750–1860.* Baltimore, MD: Johns Hopkins University Press, 2013.

King, Spencer Bidwell. *Darien: The Death and Rebirth of a Southern Town.* Macon, GA: Mercer University Press, 1981.

Krick, Robert K. *Stonewall Jackson at Cedar Mountain.* Chapel Hill: University of North Carolina Press, 1990.

Kytle, Ethan J., and Blain Roberts. *Denmark Vesey's Garden: Slavery and Memory in the Cradle of the Confederacy.* New York: New Press, 2018.

Lader, Lawrence. *The Bold Brahmins: New England's War Against Slavery (1861–1863).* New York: E. P. Dutton, 1961.

Lang, Andrew F. *In the Wake of War: Military Occupation, Emancipation, and Civil War America.* Baton Rouge: Louisiana State University Press, 2017.

Larson, Kate Clifford. *Bound for the Promised Land.* New York: One World, 2004.

Lehr, Dick. *The Birth of a Nation: How a Legendary Filmmaker and a Crusading Editor Reignited America's Civil War.* New York: Public Affairs, 2014.

Leng, Charles W., and William T. Davis. *Staten Island and Its People: A History 1609–1929.* 2 vols. New York: Lewis, 1929–30.

Leonard, Elizabeth D. *Benjamin Franklin Butler: A Noisy, Fearless Life.* Chapel Hill: University of North Carolina Press, 2022.

Levin, Kevin M., ed. *Interpreting the Civil War at Museums and Historic Sites.* Lanham: Rowman and Littlefield, 2017.

Levin, Kevin M. *Remembering the Battle of the Crater: War as Murder.* Lexington: University Press of Kentucky, 2012.

Levin, Kevin M. *Searching for Black Confederates: The Civil War's Most Persistent Myth.* Chapel Hill: University of North Carolina Press, 2019.

Levine, Bruce. *The Spirit of 48: German Immigrants, Labor Conflict, and the Coming of the Civil War.* Champaign: University of Illinois Press, 1992.

Levinson, David, and Emilie Piper. *On the Other Side of Glory: The Berkshire Men of the 54th Massachusetts Infantry Regiment.* Salisbury, CT: Upper Housatonic Valley National Heritage Area, 2011.

Lewis, Bessie. *They Called Their Own Town Darien.* 1975. Reprint, Darien, GA: Lower Altamaha Historical Society, 2002.

Link, William A. *Atlanta: Cradle of the New South*. Chapel Hill: University of North Carolina Press, 2013.

Long, E. B. *The Civil War Day by Day: An Almanac, 1861–1865*. 1971. Reprint, Cambridge, MA: Da Capo Press, 2008.

Luke, Bob, and John David Smith. *Soldiering for Freedom: How the Union Army Recruited, Trained, and Deployed the U.S. Colored Troops*. Baltimore, MD: Johns Hopkins University Press, 2014.

Manning, Chandra. *What This Cruel War Was Over: Soldiers, Slavery, and the Civil War*. New York: Knopf, 2007.

Martin, Waldo E., Jr. *The Mind of Frederick Douglass*. Chapel Hill: University of North Carolina Press, 1984.

Marvel, William. *Lincoln's Autocrat: The Life of Edwin Stanton*. Chapel Hill: University of North Carolina Press, 2015.

Masur, Kate. *Until Justice Be Done: America's First Civil Rights Movement, From the Revolution to Reconstruction*. New York: W. W. Norton, 2021.

Matsui, John H. *The First Republican Army: The Army of Virginia and the Radicalization of the Civil War*. Charlottesville: University of Virginia Press, 2016.

Mayer, Henry. *All On Fire: William Lloyd Garrison and the Abolition of Slavery*. New York: St. Martin's Press, 1998.

McElya, Micki. *Clinging to Mammy: The Faithful Slave in Twentieth-Century America*. Cambridge, MA: Harvard University Press, 2007.

McFeely, William S. *Frederick Douglass*. New York: W. W. Norton, 1991.

McKay, Martha N. *When the Tide Turned in the Civil War*. Indianapolis: Hollenbeck Press, 1929.

McPherson, James M. *Battle Cry of Freedom: The Civil War Era*. New York: Oxford University Press, 1988.

McPherson, James M. *For Cause and Comrades: Why Men Fought in the Civil War*. New York: Oxford University Press, 1997.

McPherson, James M. *The Negro's Civil War: How American Blacks Felt and Acted During the War for the Union*. New York: Random House, 1965.

Meier, Kathryn Shively. *Nature's Civil War: Common Soldiers and the Environment in 1862 Virginia*. Chapel Hill: University of North Carolina Press, 2013.

Mendez, James G. *A Great Sacrifice: Northern Black Soldiers, Their Families, and the Experience of Civil War*. New York: Fordham University Press, 2019.

Meyer, Howard N. *Colonel of the Black Regiment: The Life of Thomas Wentworth Higginson*. New York: W. W. Norton, 1967.

Mildfelt, Todd, and David D. Schafer. *Abolitionist of the Most Dangerous Kind: James Montgomery and His War on Slavery*. Norman: University of Oklahoma Press, 2023.

Miller, Edward A. *Gullah Statesman: Robert Small from Slavery to Congress, 1839–1915*. Columbia: University of South Carolina Press, 1995.

Miller, Edward A. *Lincoln's Abolitionist General: The Biography of David Hunter*. Columbia: University of South Carolina Press, 1997.

Miller, Richard F. *Harvard's Civil War: A History of the Twentieth Massachusetts Volunteer Infantry*. Hanover: University Press of New England, 2005.

Minardi, Margot. *Making Slavery History: Abolitionism and the Politics of Memory in Massachusetts*. New York: Oxford University Press, 2010.

Mitchell, Charles W., and Jean H. Baker, eds. *The Civil War in Maryland Reconsidered*. Baton Rouge: Louisiana State University Press, 2021.

Mitchell, Reid. *Civil War Soldiers*. New York: Viking, 1998.

Moland, Lydia. *Lydia Maria Child: A Radical American Life*. Chicago: University of Chicago Press, 2022.

Morgan, III, James A. *A Little Short of Boats: The Battles of Ball's Bluff and Edwards Ferry, October 21–22, 1861*. London: Grub Street, 2011.

Murray, Williamson, and Wei-Siang Hsieh. *A Savage War: A Military History of the Civil War*. Princeton, NJ: Princeton University Press, 2016.

Neely Mark E., and Harold Holzer. *The Union Image: Popular Prints of the Civil War North*. Chapel Hill: University of North Carolina Press, 2000.

Neff, John R. *Honoring the Civil War Dead: Commemoration and the Problem of Reconciliation*. Lawrence: University Press of Kansas, 2005.

Nelson, Megan Kate. *Ruin Nation: Destruction and the American Civil War*. Athens: University of Georgia Press, 2012.

Nevins, Alan, *The War for the Union: The Improvised War, 1861–1862*. New York: Charles Scribner's Sons, 1958.

Norrell, Robert J. *Up from Slavery: The Life of Booker T. Washington*. Cambridge, MA: Harvard University Press, 2009.

Noyalas, Jonathan A. *Slavery and Freedom in the Shenandoah Valley During the Civil War Era*. Gainesville: University Press of Florida, 2021.

O'Connor, Thomas H. *Civil War Boston: Home Front and Battlefield*. Boston: Northeastern University Press, 1997.

Peterson, Mark. *The City-State of Boston: The Rise and Fall of an Atlantic Power, 1630–1865*. Princeton, NJ: Princeton University Press, 2019.

Phillips, Ulrich Bonnell. *American Negro Slavery: A Survey of the Supply, Employment and Control of Negro Labor as Determined by the Plantation Régime*. New York: D. Appleton, 1929.

Pinheiro, Holly A., Jr. *The Families' Civil War: Black Soldiers and the Fight for Justice*. Athens: University Press of Georgia, 2022.

Potter, David M. *The Impending Crisis: 1848–1861*. New York: Harper & Row, Publishers, 1976.

Purcell, Sarah J. *Spectacle of Grief: Public Funerals and Memory in the Civil War Era*. Chapel Hill: University of North Carolina Press, 2022.

Quarles, Benjamin. *The Negro in the Civil War*. Boston: Little, Brown, 1953. Reprint, New York: Da Capo, 1989.

Quinn, Edythe Ann. *Freedom Journey: Black Civil War Soldiers and the Hills Community, Westchester County, New York*. Albany: State University of New York Press, 2015.

Rable, George C. *Conflict of Command: George McClellan, Abraham Lincoln, and the Politics of War*. Baton Rouge: Louisiana State University Press, 2023.

Rable, George C. *Fredericksburg! Fredericksburg!* Chapel Hill: University of North Carolina Press, 2002.

Rafuse, Ethan S. *From the Mountains to the Bay: The War in Virginia, January–May 1862*. Lawrence: University Press of Kansas, 2023.

Rawson, Michael. *Eden on the Charles: The Making of Boston*. Cambridge, MA: Harvard University Press, 2010.

Reynolds, David S. *Abe: Abraham Lincoln in His Times*. New York: Penguin Books, 2020.

Rhea, Gordon C. *Stephen A. Swails: Black Freedom Fighter in the Civil War and Reconstruction*. Baton Rouge: Louisiana State University Press, 2021.

Richards, Eliza. *Battle Lines: Poetry and Mass Media in the U.S. Civil War*. Philadelphia: University of Pennsylvania Press, 2019.

Roberts, Cokie. *Capital Dames: The Civil War and the Women of Washington, 1848–1868*. New York: Harper, 2015.

Rose, Willie Lee. *Rehearsal for Reconstruction: The Port Royal Experiment*. Athens: University of Georgia Press, 1964.

Sampsell-Willmann, Kate. *Lewis Hine as Social Critic*. Jackson: University Press of Mississippi, 2009.

Savage, Kirk. *Standing Soldiers, Kneeling Slaves: Race, War, and Monument in Nineteenth-Century America*. Princeton, NJ: Princeton University Press, 1997.

Schneider, Mark R. *Boston Confronts Jim Crow, 1890–1920*. Boston: Northeastern University Press, 1997.

Sears, Stephen W. *Landscape Turned Red: The Battle of Antietam*. Boston: Houghton Mifflin, 1993.

Sears, Stephen W. *To the Gates of Richmond: The Peninsula Campaign*. New York: Ticknor and Fields, 1992.

Seasholes, Nancy S, ed. *The Atlas of Boston History*. Chicago: University of Chicago Press, 2019.

Sheehan-Dean, Aaron. *The Calculus of Violence: How Americans Fought the Civil War*. Cambridge, MA: Harvard University Press, 2018.

Sinclair, William Albert. *The Aftermath of Slavery: A Study of the Condition and Environment of the American Negro*. Boston: Small, Maynard, 1905.

Sinha, Manisha. *The Slave's Cause: A History of Abolition*. New Haven: Yale University Press, 2016.

Smith, John David., ed. *Black Soldiers in Blue: African American Troops in the Civil War Era*. Chapel Hill: University of North Carolina Press, 2002.

Smith, John David. *Lincoln and the U.S. Colored Troops*. Carbondale: Southern Illinois University Press, 2013.

Smith, Joshua M. *Making Maine: Statehood and the War of 1812*. Amherst: University of Massachusetts Press, 2022.

Smith, Marion Whitney. *Beacon Hill's Colonel Robert Gould Shaw*. New York: Carlton Press, Inc., 1986.

Starobin, Paul. *Madness Rules the Hour: Charleston, 1860 and the Mania for War*. New York: Public Affairs, 2017.

Stauffer, John, and Zoe Trodd, eds. *The Tribunal: Responses to John Brown and the Harpers Ferry Raid*. Cambridge, MA: Harvard University Press, 2012.

Stewart, Mart A. *"What Nature Suffers to Groe": Life, Labor, and Landscape on the Georgia Coast, 1680–1920*. Athens: University of Georgia Press, 1996.

Stewart, Matthew. *An Emancipation of the Mind: Radical Philosophy, the War over Slavery, and the Refounding of America*. New York: Norton, 2024.

Stoker, Donald J. *The Grand Design: Strategy and the U.S. Civil War*. New York: Oxford University Press, 2010.

Swift, Lindsay. *Brook Farm: Its Members, Scholars, and Visitors*. New York: Macmillan, 1900.

Taylor, Brian. *Fighting for Citizenship: Black Northerners and the Debate over Military Service in the Civil War*. Chapel Hill: University of North Carolina Press, 2020.

Trudeau, Noah A. *Like Men of War: Black Troops in the Civil War, 1862–1865*. Boston: Little Brown, 1998.

Varon, Elizabeth R. *Armies of Deliverance: A New History of the Civil War*. New York: Oxford University Press, 2019.

Von Frank, Albert J. *The Trial of Anthony Burns: Freedom and Slavery in Emerson's Boston*. Cambridge, MA: Harvard University Press, 1998.

Wallace, Frederic A. *Framingham's Civil War Hero: The Life of General George H. Gordon*. Charleston, SC: History Press, 2011.

Wallenstein, Peter. *Cradle of America: Four Centuries of Virginia History*. Lawrence: University Press of Kansas, 2007.

Warren, Wendy. *New England Bound: Slavery and Colonization in Early America*. New York: Liveright, 2016.

Waugh, Joan. *Unsentimental Reformer: The Life of Josephine Shaw Lowell*. Cambridge, MA: Harvard University Press, 1997.

Weber, Jennifer L. *Copperheads: The Rise and Fall of Lincoln's Opponents in the North*. New York: Oxford University Press, 2006.

Welch, Richard F. *The Boy General: The Life of Francis Channing Barlow*. Kent: Kent State University Press, 2003.

Wells, Jonathan Daniel. *The Kidnapping Club: Wall Street, Slavery, and Resistance on the Eve of the Civil War*. New York: Bold Type Books, 2020.

Werstein, Irving. *The Storming of Fort Wagner: Black Valor in the Civil War*. New York: Scholastic Books, 1970.

White, Jonathan W. *A House Built by Slaves: African American Visitors to the Lincoln White House*. Lanham, MD: Rowman and Littlefield, 2022.

Wilder, Craig Steven. *Ebony and Ivory: Race, Slavery, and the Troubled History of America's Universities*. New York: Bloomsbury, 2013.

Williams, David. *Georgia's Civil War: Conflict On the Home Front*. Macon: Mercer University Press, 2017.

Williams, Kidada E. *I Saw Death Coming: A History of Terror and Survival in the War against Reconstruction*. New York: Bloomsbury, 2023.

Williams, Lou Falkner, *The Great South Ku Klux Klan Trials, 1871–1872*. Athens: University of Georgia Press, 1996.

Wills, Deborah. *The Black Civil War Soldier: A Visual History of Conflict and Citizenship*. New York: New York University Press, 2021.

Winkle, Kenneth J. *Lincoln's Citadel: The Civil War in Washington, DC*. New York: Norton, 2013.

Wise, Stephen R. *Gate of Hell: Campaign for Charleston Harbor, 1863*. Columbia: University of South Carolina Press, 1994.

Wise, Stephen R., and Lawrence S. Rowland. *Rebellion, Reconstruction, and Redemption, 1861–1893*. Vol. 2 of *The History of Beaufort County, South Carolina*. Columbia: University of South Carolina Press, 2015.
Witt, John Fabian. *Lincoln's Code: The Laws of War in American History*. New York: Free Press, 2013.
Wongsrichanalai, Kanisorn. *Northern Character: College-Educated New Englanders, Honor, Nationalism, and Leadership in the Civil War Era*. New York: Fordham University Press, 2016.
Woo, Ilyon. *Master Slave Husband Wife: An Epic Journey from Slavery to Freedom*. New York: Simon and Schuster, 2023.
Woodard, Colin. *Union: The Struggle to Forge the Story of United States Nationhood*. New York: Viking, 2020.
Zabin, Serena A. *The Boston Massacre: A Family History*. Boston: Houghton Mifflin Harcourt 2020.
Zwick, Ed. *Hits, Flops, and Other Illusions: My Fortysomething Years in Hollywood*. New York: Gallery Books, 2024.

Articles, Essays, and Papers

Bailey, Kenneth R. "One of the Famous 54th Massachusetts: A Short Biography of General John W. M. Appleton." *West Virginia History* (1970): 161–79.
Bosco, Carla. "Harvard University and the Fugitive Slave Act." *New England Quarterly* 79, no. 2 (2006): 227–47.
Brasher, Glenn David. "Debating Black Manhood: The Northern Press Reports on the 54th Massachusetts at Fort Wagner." In *American Discord: The Republic and Its People in the Civil War Era*, edited by Megan L. Bever, Lesley J. Gordon, and Laura Mammina, 22–44. Baton Rouge: Louisiana State University Press, 2020.
Carmichael, Peter S. "The Trophies of Victory and the Relics of Defeat: Returning Home in the Spring of 1865." In *War Matters: Material Culture in the Civil War Era*, edited by Joan E. Cashin, 198–221. Chapel Hill: University of North Carolina Press, 2018.
Cashin, Joan E. "Trophies of War: Material Culture in the Civil War Era." *Journal of the Civil War Era* 1, no. 13 (2011): 339–67.
Coulter, E. Merton. "Robert Gould Shaw and the Burning of Darien, Georgia." *Civil War History* 5 (Fall 1959) 363–73.
Dabney, Emmanuel, Beth Parnicza, and Kevin M. Levin. "Interpreting Race, Slavery, and United States Colored Troops at Civil War Battlefields." *Civil War History* 62, no. 2 (2016): 131–48.
Dirck, Brian. "By the Hand of God: James Montgomery and Redemptive Violence." *Kansas History: A Journal of the Central Plains* 27, no. 1–2 (2004): 100–115.
Gallagher, Gary W. "The Net Result of the Campaign Was in Our Favor: Confederate Reaction to the Maryland Campaign." In *The Antietam Campaign*, edited by Gary W. Gallagher, 3–43. Chapel Hill: University of North Carolina Press, 1999.
Gallagher, Gary W. "The Tide of War Has Been Rolled Back: Second Manassas in Confederate Perspective." In *The Second Manassas Campaign*, edited by Caroline E. Janney and Kathryn J. Shively, 65–96. Chapel Hill: University of North Carolina Press, 2025.

Gordon, Lesley J. "'Novices in Warfare': Elmer E. Ellsworth and Militia Reform on the Eve of the Civil War." *Journal of the Civil War Era* 11, no. 2 (2021): 194–233.

Hennessy, John J. "The Army of Virginia Confronts the 'Moral Spectacle' of Freedom." In *The Second Manassas Campaign*, edited by Caroline E. Janney and Kathryn J. Shively, 36–64. Chapel Hill: University of North Carolina Press, 2025.

Holzer, Harold. "Housekeeping on Its Own Terms: Abraham Lincoln in New York." In *State of the Union: New York and the Civil War*, edited by Harold Holzer, 1–16. New York: Fordham University Press, 2002.

Leamon, James S. "The Search for Security in Maine after Penobscot." *Maine History* 21, no. 3 (1982): 119–54.

Longacre, Edward. "Brave Radical Wild: The Contentious Career of Brigadier Edward A. Wild." *Civil War Times Illustrated* 19 (June 1980): 8–11.

Mann, Robert G. "The 'Contact of Living Souls': Shepard Gilbert's Civics Education in Reconstruction South Carolina." *New England Quarterly* 88, no. 2 (2015): 286–315.

Redkey, Edwin S. "Brave Black Volunteers: A Profile of the Fifty-Fourth Massachusetts Regiment." In *Hope and Glory: Essays on the Legacy of the 54th Massachusetts Regiment*, edited by Martin H. Blat, Thomas J. Brown and Donald Yacovone, 21–34. Amherst: University of Massachusetts Press, 2001.

Rudy, John M. "From Tokenism to True Partnership: The National Park Service's Shifting Interpretation at the Civil War's Sesquicentennial." In *Interpreting the Civil War at Museums and Historic Sites*, edited by Kevin M. Levin, 61–76. Lanham, MD: Rowman and Littlefield, 2017.

Sternhell, Yael A. "Revisionism Reinvented? The Antiwar Turn in Civil War Scholarship." *Journal of the Civil War Era* 3, no. 2 (2013): 239–56.

Urwin, Gregory J. W. "I Want You to Prove Yourselves Men." *Civil War Times Illustrated* (November–December 1989): 42–51.

Waugh, Joan. "Francis Channing Barlow's Civil War." In *Cold Harbor to the Crater: The End of the Overland Campaign*, edited by Gary W. Gallagher and Caroline E. Janney, 138–75. Chapel Hill: University of North Carolina Press, 2015.

Waugh, Joan. "'It Was a Sacrifice We Owed': The Shaw Family and the Fifty-Fourth Massachusetts Regiment." In *Hope and Glory: Essays on the Legacy of the 54th Massachusetts Regiment*, edited by Martin H. Blat, Thomas J. Brown and Donald Yacovone, 52–78. Amherst: University of Massachusetts Press, 2001.

Wilson, Keith. "In the Shadow of John Brown: The Military Service of Colonels Thomas Higginson, James Montgomery, and Robert Shaw in the Department of the South." In *Black Soldiers in Blue: African American Troops in the Civil War Era*, edited by John David Smith, 306–35. Chapel Hill: University of North Carolina Press, 2002.

Zander, Cecily, "General Pope Goes to Washington: Radical Republicans and the Failed Hope of the Second Bull Run Campaign." In *The Second Manassas Campaign*, edited by Caroline E. Janney and Kathryn J. Shively, 97–123. Chapel Hill: University of North Carolina Press, 2025.

INDEX

The initials RGS refer to Robert Gould Shaw.